The Dry Gardening Handbook

PLANTS AND PRACTICES FOR A CHANGING CLIMATE

The Dry Gardening Handbook

PLANTS AND PRACTICES FOR A CHANGING CLIMATE

Olivier Filippi

with over 400 colour illustrations

Thames & Hudson

Acknowledgments

I would like to thank a number of people who read the manuscript of this book and who made very valuable comments and suggestions: Aïté Bresson, Jean Burger, Jean-Pierre Demoly, Caroline Harbouri, Pierre Michelot, Patrick Mills and, of course, Clara, who was not only the first to read many of the sections of this book, but above all who shared the work of research and the botanical voyages that inspired it. Katherine Greenberg kindly provided suggestions for American nurseries and titles for further reading for this edition.

All photographs and drawings are by the author.

Endpapers: The bark of Arbutus × thuretiana.
Page 3: Flowers of Erodium trifolium.
Left: Asphodeline lutea.

First published in the United Kingdom in 2008 by
Thames & Hudson Ltd, 181A High Holborn,
London WC1V 7QX

www.thamesandhudson.com

First published in 2008 in hardcover in the United States of America by
Thames & Hudson Inc., 500 Fifth Avenue, New York, New York 10110

thamesandhudsonusa.com

Translated from the French *Pour un jardin sans arrosage* by Caroline Harbouri

British Library Cataloguing-in-Publication Data
A catalogue record for this book is available from the British Library

Library of Congress Catalog Card Number 2007910156

ISBN: 978-0-500-51407-8

Printed and bound in France

Contents

Foreword

For countless gardeners drought is a major preoccupation. Hosepipe restrictions and the realization that water is a precious resource have put gardening into a new perspective.

Making a garden that doesn't need watering is not only possible but also extremely satisfying. By working with – rather than against – drought, we can make remarkable gardens that are both beautiful and original. The main difficulty is the scarcity of information available: it is not so much drought itself that is the problem as a lack of knowledge of the plants and techniques adapted to it. To help gardeners develop a new way of gardening, my wife Clara and I have for years been studying plants that tolerate drought. In this book I want to give you some practical help by sharing the experience we've acquired in more than twenty years of working daily with plants for dry gardens.

This book is divided into three parts. The first examines the behaviour of plants that face drought in their natural habitat. What is drought and how do plants manage to survive when little water is available? The strategies they have developed to adapt to drought give plants a particular beauty, which we can easily enjoy if we respect the natural conditions of our gardens. The second part is concerned with gardening techniques in a dry climate. How do you prepare the soil, when do you plant, how do you maintain a dry garden? Here you will find detailed answers to all these basic questions. The third and longest part describes in detail a wide range of plants adapted to a garden that is not watered. The list of plants is far from exhaustive: there are hundreds, indeed thousands, of other species that could have been described. I have chosen to limit myself to those perennials and shrubs (and therefore on the whole not including annuals, bulbs and larger trees) that are most useful for creating the initial structure of a dry garden.

First and foremost this book is addressed to gardeners in areas with a mediterranean climate ('mediterranean' with a lower case 'm' is used for areas experiencing this type of climate, while Mediterranean with a capital 'M' is used specifically for the geographical region of the Mediterranean Basin). It may also be of interest to gardeners in other regions where drought looks as if it might become a recurrent problem. It is not rare nowadays to hear people speaking of drought in southeast England, in the Paris area or on the Atlantic coast of France. Gardeners in these zones should interpret the plant descriptions in the light of their own climate and soil conditions. Wherever you live, I hope to encourage you to embark on the adventure of making a garden that doesn't need watering. By setting out to make a dry garden you are becoming a gardening pioneer, and your researches, trials and errors will pave the way for the gardeners of the future.

Plants and Drought

An undiscovered diversity

Drought has always been considered as a limitation for gardens. We have all been influenced by the temperate-climate garden model, in which thriving shrubs and lush perennials surround a perfect lawn. Every month, gardening magazines make us dream of superb gardens, generally in northern Europe. Beautiful photographs in gardening books promote an image of rustic scenes, where roses and clematis grow intertwined. Yet in areas with a mediterranean climate these ideal conditions are a dream that can never be fulfilled. Instead of gentle light we have brutal sunshine; instead of rich soil we have the stony garrigue. The drier the climate, the harder it seems to make a garden. It is as if we are engaged in a ceaseless battle against a hostile environment.

Nevertheless, dry climates offer extraordinary gardening possibilities. Paradoxically, thanks to a long tradition of a passion for gardening and botanical research, it is in England that the largest collections of drought-resistant plants have been amassed. These plants are jealously cared for as if they were precious rarities, grown in raised rock gardens to ensure perfect drainage and sometimes cultivated under glass to protect them from an excess of winter wet. Garden-lovers flock to the Royal Horticultural Society's famous garden at Wisley, south of London, to admire a sophisticated rock garden re-created under glass. Its treasures include plants that often no one bothers even to glance at on Mediterranean roadsides – *Rhodanthemum* from Morocco, *Erodium* from Greece or *Sideritis* from Turkey. While English plantsmen pride themselves on their collections of plants for dry conditions, gardeners further south are desperately watering their lawns, but achieve nothing more than a mediocre imitation of an English garden.

Rather than drought, it is often the misguided use of irrigation that limits the range of plants in mediterranean gardens. Many dry-climate plants are in fact easy to grow if we respect the conditions of their native habitat, but become extremely capricious as soon as we try to water them in summer. The cistuses of the garrigue, the ceanothuses that cover the

PAGE 8 Yuccas are native to the deserts of North America. Their magnificent flowers make a splendid sight in the arid environment of their natural habitat.

ABOVE Drought offers extraordinary gardening possibilities if we use plants that are adapted to it. *Epilobium canum* 'Catalina' and *Leucophyllum langmaniae* create a glowing scene in the gentle autumn light.

RIGHT The caper plant often grows in old stone walls alongside paths, as it needs perfectly drained dry soil.

hillsides of California or the capers that billow down Sicilian cliffs quite simply cannot tolerate the combination of heat and moisture. Irrigation during our blazing summers generally proves fatal to them.

If you water your garden in hot weather you will never be able to grow the full range of plants adapted to the mediterranean climate. The beautiful *Salvia candelabrum* will be nothing more than a fantasy, the magnificent *Fremontodendron* covered in golden flowers won't stand a chance. Don't bother even to dream of the vibrant blue of *Lithodora fruticosa* or of the soft, silky pink flowers of *Ebenus cretica*: irrigation will kill them as surely as a powerful dose of herbicide. Automatic watering systems are one of the worst inventions of the modern mediterranean gardener.

ABOVE June flowering in a dry garden. Santolinas and lavenders are very prone to fungal infection if watered in summer.

LEFT Rather than drought, it is often the misguided use of irrigation that limits the range of plants which can be used in Mediterranean gardens.

You may think you are making life easier, while in fact all you're doing is limiting the range of plants that can survive in your garden. Without realizing it, you are helping to reduce the plant palette to uniformity. In region after region, gardens end up all looking much the same, having lost the individual identity that is linked to their particular climate and soil conditions.

What will happen if you stop watering? Well, yes, the plants that need water will die, one after another. So what will be left? Everyone dreads the idea of a miserable-looking garden, where dusty borders contain only a few spiny plants, and wretched shrubs eke out a meagre existence. We feel instinctively that water brings luxuriance and variety, and that dryness restricts our gardening possibilities. Yet exactly the opposite is true. Most gardeners are unaware that the natural flora of mediterranean-climate regions is a lot richer than that of temperate regions.

A few figures will help us to put this diversity into perspective. In France, for example, more than 60%

ABOVE LEFT *Erodium foetidum* growing on the La Clape mountain near Narbonne. In France, more than 60% of plant species are concentrated in the Mediterranean zone, which represents only 19% of the total area of the country.

ABOVE RIGHT *Ebenus cretica* grows on stony screes and mountain cliffs in Crete. The extraordinary diversity of dry-climate plants provides an inexhaustible source of material for the garden.

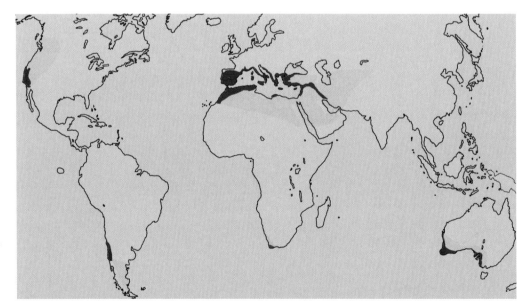

Mediterranean climate regions throughout the world

Most gardeners do not realize that the flora of mediterranean-climate regions is a lot richer than that of temperate zones. Botanists inform us that about 75,000 plant species are subject to a period of summer drought in their natural habitat. These plants come from the mediterranean-climate regions (marked in red on the map), as well as from adjacent zones including mountains, dry steppes and desert fringes (in yellow on the map). (From *The Isoclimatic Mediterranean Biomes*, Le Houérou, 2005.)

of plant species are concentrated in the Mediterranean zone, although it represents only a very small part of the country. In the whole of non-Mediterranean Europe no more than 6,000 species are found, while in the South of France, in the Hérault Department alone, there are more than 2,000 species. The flora of the Mediterranean Basin is one of the richest in the world: 25,000 plant species grow here, which amounts to almost 10% of the world's flora. On the global scale, botanists reckon that about 75,000 plant species undergo a regime of summer drought in the different regions of the world with a mediterranean climate, plus adjacent areas. A good indication of this diversity is the fact that it is often in dry regions that we find the greatest number of endemic species, i.e. plants that grow nowhere else. The Cape Province of South Africa, for example, which enjoys a mediterranean-type climate, has an amazing 5,800 endemic plant

species – compare this to Great Britain where, in an area three times larger and with a damp climate, there are only 24 endemic species.

In order to survive in a difficult environment, dry-climate plants have had to specialize over the course of their evolution. As they adapted to widely varying conditions of soil, exposure, latitude and altitude, they became extremely diversified. Far from limiting the flora, dryness has on the contrary favoured plant diversity in mediterranean-climate regions for thousands of years. This diversity provides an inexhaustible source of plants for our gardens. Do you know how many species you need to create a garden? The answer is somewhere between 100 and 200, perhaps slightly more if you have a large garden or if you are a passionate plantsman. Compared to the extraordinary richness of dry-climate plants, the number of species you need is negligible. So don't be afraid! Pluck up your courage and switch off the programmer, get rid of the dreadful snaking tubes of the drip system and remove the sprinklers. Let nature take care of your garden. If a plant dies, too bad. It obviously wasn't adapted to your conditions and its disappearance has made room for another, more resistant plant.

Plants for the dry garden mostly come from the various regions of the world with a mediterranean climate, defined as one with hot, dry summers and wet winters – which may be mild or cold. Such regions are found in Chile, California, South Africa, Australia and around the Mediterranean Basin itself. However, there are also some very interesting plants for the dry garden that come from the transitional zones between mediterranean-climate regions and neighbouring areas: mountains, dry steppes, desert fringes. The diversity of these environments and the richness of the flora and the beauty of the landscapes in the dry regions of the world are largely unknown to gardeners. Yet if you are to assess a plant's ability to adapt to your garden, it is extremely useful to be familiar with its geographical origin and natural habitat. The following pages invite you to travel to the landscapes of the world's five mediterranean-climate regions, as well as to some of their mountainous or desert transitional zones.

Bupleurum spinosum at the Tizi n Test pass in the Atlas mountains, Morocco. Many plants of interest for the dry garden come from transitional zones between regions with a mediterranean climate and colder mountain regions.

CHILE

Isolated by the ocean, the desert and the high, mountainous barrier of the Andes, Chile is home to numerous endemic species.

The Andes, with their chain of high plateaux and volcanoes with altitudes varying between 5,000 and 6,500 metres, lie less than 100 km from the coast. Extremes of dryness and cold make conditions particularly difficult for plants. Here paja brava, the 'brave grass' (Festuca orthophylla), colours the landscape very near the border with Argentina.

Between Copiapó and Arica lies the Atacama, the driest desert in the world. It almost never rains and yet on the coastal fringes several cactus species survive thanks to the nocturnal fog rolling in from the Pacific. These amazing cylindrical cacti, Copiapoa columna-alba, are crowned with long white hairs, enabling them to trap moisture from the fog.

At the foot of the Andes near Santiago the imposing Chilean palm, Jubaea chilensis, emerges from the matorral. Having long been felled for its palm milk, Jubaea now only survives in a few protected sites.

A narrow strip of land between the Andes and the Pacific Ocean, Chile extends for more than 4,000 kilometres from its southern tip to the border with Peru in the north. Although its average width is only 160 kilometres, the altitude varies from west to east from sea level to summits exceeding 6,000 m. This unique configuration means that all types of climate can be experienced in Chile. In the south there are glaciers and snow-covered volcanoes, and a coast drenched in rain and fog. In the central part of the country the climate is of the mediterranean type, with dry summers and wet winters. As one moves north, the climate becomes inexorably drier, ending in the Atacama, the most arid desert in the world: no rain has been recorded here since records began. If you leave the only road that crosses the Atacama, the legendary Pan-American Highway, and enter a valley climbing up into the Andes, in a matter of hours you pass from a desert to an alpine climate, through amazing transitional landscapes that range from absolute dryness to extreme cold.

For the mediterranean gardener, the zone of most interest lies between Concepción in the south and La Serena in the north. Near Concepción the summer drought lasts no more than one or two months and the annual rainfall is high. The soil is generally acid and shrubs such as *Fabiana imbricata*, *Escallonia rubra* and *Buddleja globosa* can be found, while in the foothills of the Andes remnants of the ancient *Araucaria* forests survive.

Valparaiso and Santiago mark the centre of Chile's mediterranean-climate zone, with four to five months of summer drought. The north-facing slopes (the sunnier orientation in the southern hemisphere) are covered with a type of low-growing vegetation, the matorral, where *Puya*, cacti and evergreen shrubs such as *Sophora macrophylla* grow together. The cooler south-facing slopes are covered in forests of small evergreen trees, fairly similar to our evergreen oak forests, and include *Peumus boldus*, *Escallonia illinita* and *Luma chequen*.

Moving up towards La Serena, the dryness becomes intense, with cacti and spiny *Acacia* predominating in a sparse matorral. On the coast, by contrast, numerous shrubs profit from the fog caused by the cold ocean currents – *Berberis*, *Senna* and *Cestrum parqui* for example, or the curious *Fuchsia lycioides* with minute flowers, often covered with a thick coat of lichen.

OPPOSITE *Buddleja globosa* grows between Santiago and Concepción in a region where the drought does not last for more than two to three months.

BELOW *Puya berteroniana* and *Echinopsis chilensis* in the Las Campanas National Park, near Santiago. The sunnier north-facing slope is covered in a low-growing matorral, while the cooler valley bottom is home to palms and evergreen trees.

The coastal mountains north of San Francisco are home to fine evergreen oak forests. Among the oaks grow Arbutus menziesii, a tall arbutus with red bark, and Aesculus californica, the California chestnut, whose bare silhouette is very surprising in summer: just as it is covered in fruit it loses all its leaves in order to withstand drought.

San Francisco

San Luis Obispo

Los Angeles

On the coast between Los Angeles and San Francisco, the fog coming from the Pacific helps plants survive the long months of drought. In the dense chaparral Artemisia californica grows together with Baccharis pilularis and numerous Salvia species with remarkably aromatic foliage. In spring, the ceanothuses form cascades of blue flowers descending towards the ocean.

Yucca brevifolia, the Joshua Tree, displays its massive vertical shape in the landscape of the Mojave Desert, bathed in sunlight. It can form magnificent trees more than 10 metres tall.

CALIFORNIA

Cool evenings in San Francisco Bay, snowy summits in the Sierra Nevada and burning desert in Death Valley: in California the climate changes dramatically within very short distances, making it possible for a great diversity of plants to exist.

Like Chile, the coast of California benefits from the Pacific fogs. The forest of *Sequoia sempervirens*, the tallest tree in the world, survives in a narrow coastal belt to the north of San Francisco thanks to this fog: countless droplets of moisture form on the branches and then fall to the ground, where the surface roots can take it up, supplying the tree with water during the driest months. Moving inland, the influence of the fog is no longer felt and the landscape changes rapidly to one of forests of evergreen trees, including oaks, arbutuses and *Umbellularia californica*, the California laurel.

Between San Francisco and San Luis Obispo the coast is covered with chaparral, a low-growing and dense type of vegetation that flowers profusely in spring and is regularly regenerated by fire. On the coastal mountains numerous evergreen shrubs grow, such as *Heteromeles arbutifolia*, covered in red berries in winter, *Prunus ilicifolia*, with pale green young shoots, different species of *Arctostaphylos*, whose bark peels in spring, and the spectacular *Fremontodendron californicum* with its brilliant yellow flowers.

Moving further south towards Los Angeles, the dryness increases and the coastal chaparral is enriched with numerous sages, such as the white-leaved *Salvia apiana*, as well as *Salvia mellifera*, with dark green leaves, and the silvery-leaved *Salvia leucophylla*. At the end of spring *Yucca whipplei* stands out on the hillsides with its large candles of white flowers.

As soon as you cross the coastal mountains, the transition to the desert is abrupt and harsh. To the south lies the Sonora Desert, stretching towards Arizona and Mexico. To the east is the Mojave Desert, where fine populations of *Yucca brevifolia* can be seen. Climbing towards the Sierra Nevada, Death Valley is reached, famous for its record temperatures in summer and spectacular landscapes.

OPPOSITE *Salvia* 'Allen Chickering' is a hybrid between two Californian sages, *Salvia clevelandii* and *Salvia leucophylla*. It combines the qualities of its two parents, inheriting its magnificent violet-blue flowers from the former and the silver foliage of the latter. Its aromatic leaves scent the garden throughout the summer.

LEFT In spite of the intense drought and heat, *Atriplex canescens* thrives in the dunes of Death Valley. It is a shrub that is easy to grow in the garden since it withstands cold well and tolerates a variety of soil conditions. With its fine foliage and gracefully arched inflorescences, it is without doubt the most ornamental of all *Atriplex* species.

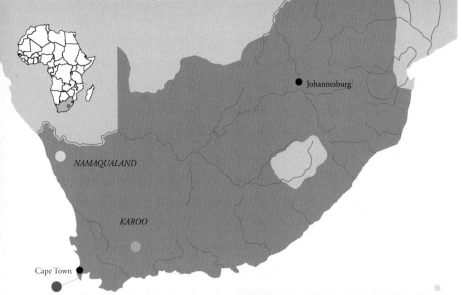

SOUTH AFRICA

Recognized as one of the six greatest floral kingdoms of the world, the Cape region at the southern tip of Africa has a flora of exceptional richness.

The predominant vegetation in the Cape region of South Africa is the fynbos. It is characterized by three large plant families: the Proteaceae, often with spectacular flowers; the heathers, which take unexpected forms and colours; and the curious Restionaceae, whose species variously call to mind rushes, bamboos or grasses. Frequent natural fires are part of the ecological cycle of the fynbos – the resulting open spaces favour the appearance of a remarkable diversity of bulbous plants. Many of the plants common in mediterranean gardens come from

Marking the place where the Atlantic and Indian Oceans meet, the Cape of Good Hope is covered by low-growing vegetation hugging the ground because of the tempestuous winds. The brilliant flowers of Senecio elegans enliven the succulent stems of Euphorbia caput-medusae, which sprawls in cushions of tentacles.

The spectacular silhouette of Aloe dichotoma stands out in the arid plains of Namaqualand. If there has been sufficient rain, the landscape is transformed for a few days in spring into a multicoloured carpet of annual flowering plants, stretching as far as the eye can see.

The powerful clumps of Melianthus major are anchored in a dry watercourse at the foot of the arid plateaux of the Great Karoo. The surrounding hills are home to a great variety of succulent plants, perfectly adapted to the long periods of drought.

the Cape: *Gazania, Euryops, Myrsine, Leonotis, Coleonema* and numerous species of *Pelargonium*.

Further north, in the vast arid expanses of the Karoo, the fynbos gives way to a rich flora of succulent plants: *Malephora, Lampranthus* and *Ruschia* grow with bulbinellas and aloes, creating a landscape which may look stark for most of the year, but which suddenly explodes into brilliantly coloured flowers. Concentrated along ravines in order to make the most of the little extra moisture found there, the generous foliage of *Melianthus* and the coral-red

flowers of *Lessertia* break the monotony of the landscape.

A visit to Namaqualand in the flowering period is a unique experience that every year attracts tourists from all over the world. Yet it is always somewhat chancy, since in this extremely dry region the flowers only appear if the winter rainfall has been sufficient. When this is the case, the entire landscape becomes a meadow of yellow, white, blue and orange flowers. These annual plants have a very short life cycle, so the scene may last for just a few weeks or even only a few days. But Namaqualand has many other species to offer too, succulent plants, bulbs, euphorbias and pelargoniums, all of them highly ornamental and perfectly adapted to drought.

SOUTHWEST AUSTRALIA

Like an island surrounded by deserts and the ocean, southwest Australia is home to a unique flora with a remarkable number of endemic plants.

Two regions in Australia enjoy a mediterranean climate: a small area on the south coast, near Adelaide, and a large crescent in the southwest around Perth. The latter is the richer of the two, with more than 6,000 species, most of which are found nowhere else on earth. The soils here – among the most ancient on

Beneath the twisted shapes of eucalyptuses, Senna artemisoides displays its light mass of yellow flowers. In order to limit water loss, the eucalyptuses hold their leaves vertically, which reduces the surface area exposed to the rays of the sun. Light thus easily penetrates through the Eucalyptus foliage, allowing many plants to flourish underneath.

Between Albany and Esperance the sandy coastal heaths are covered by kwongwan, a rich type of vegetation in which evergreen subshrubs predominate. The similarities between the kwongwan and the fynbos of South Africa are a memory of the time when these two regions were joined together in the ancient southern supercontinent of Gondwana.

Acacia rostellifera is a perfectly round shrub unbothered by the salt-laden wind from the Indian Ocean. Its roots thrust down into the poor soil composed of pure sand, which crunches curiously under foot like snow. Acacias are able to survive in very poor soil thanks to nodules on their roots which fix nitrogen from the atmosphere.

our planet – are extremely poor; their dryness and lack of nutrients have led to remarkable specializations, each species adopting its own strategies to survive in such difficult conditions. The dominant plant families are the Myrtaceae, the Fabaceae and the Proteaceae. *Callistemon, Banksia* and *Grevillea* grow together,

their spectacular flowers giving the landscape a highly exotic appearance to the European visitor. A great many of these plants are often strongly bound up with their native habitat and so unfortunately are difficult to acclimatize in gardens around the Mediterranean.

The southwest point near Cape Leeuwin has the highest rainfall in southwest Australia. Here giant *Eucalyptus* form majestic forests, with a multicoloured carpet of climbing plants beneath them: blue *Sollya*, red *Kennedia* and white clematis. Moving northeast, the annual precipitation steadily decreases, and the *Eucalyptus* growing in the coppices, with their twisted trunks and magnificent bark, are shorter. The understorey of the woodlands near Perth features numerous shrubs and perennials, including an extraordinary variety of terrestrial orchids which attract orchid-lovers from all over the world each spring. Further north, towards Kalbarri, the eucalyptuses give way to acacias in the arid plains, which, after the rainy season, are briefly covered in brightly coloured annuals. Travelling east, beyond Esperance, the dense vegetation of the kwongwan is replaced by the vast, dusty plains of the Nullarbor Desert, whose name means literally 'No Tree'.

Holm oaks climb the limestone mountains of Sardinia. Such mixed forests of oaks, pistachios, Rhamnus and Phillyrea are found everywhere around the Mediterranean. Under repeated assault from grazing or fire, the forests have often given way to lower-growing types of vegetation, known as garrigue, matorral or phrygana in different areas, which are home to a remarkably diverse flora.

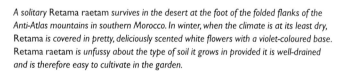

A solitary Retama raetam survives in the desert at the foot of the folded flanks of the Anti-Atlas mountains in southern Morocco. In winter, when the climate is at its least dry, Retama is covered in pretty, deliciously scented white flowers with a violet-coloured base. Retama raetam is unfussy about the type of soil it grows in provided it is well-drained and is therefore easy to cultivate in the garden.

The jagged coast of southeast Turkey is constantly subjected to salt spray. Wind and salt sculpt the thick masses of carob trees, myrtles and wild olives into folds of vegetation.

High mountains, indented coastlines, tiny islands or vast steppe-like plateaux: the lands surrounding the Mediterranean are a true mosaic of soils and microclimates and are host to a unique diversity of ecosystems. In the mediterranean climate plants have evolved in a particular way as they gradually adapted to drought. This evolution, together with the profound influence of human activity dating back almost to the end of the last Ice Age, has resulted in the exceptional richness of the flora of the Mediterranean Basin. In this geographical treasure house there exists a fabulous reservoir of plants for our

gardens, and the first step for any mediterranean gardener should be to get to know and learn to love these plants. For too long neglected, burned or uprooted, the time has come for the status of the wild plants of the garrigue to change – from the gardener's point of view, they have one invaluable quality: they are all drought-resistant.

ABOVE LEFT In spring *Ferula communis* lights up the bare mountains of Crete with its bright yellow umbels. In Greek mythology, it was in the hollow stem of this giant fennel that Prometheus brought fire to mankind, having surreptitiously stolen it from the forge of Hephaistos, the smith of the gods. Fire has always been an integral part of Mediterranean landscapes.

LEFT Nature seems to want to reclaim the ruins of the ancient theatre of Termessos, in the heart of the Taurus mountains in Turkey. For thousands of years, the history of the landscapes around the Mediterranean Sea has been so closely bound up with that of humans that it is often difficult to determine exactly what a 'natural' Mediterranean landscape is.

Survival strategies

In the course of their evolution, the plants of mediterranean-climate regions have developed a range of remarkable strategies to cope with dry conditions. Gardeners can learn a lot from studying these strategies, thereby gaining a better understanding of how to plant and look after dry-climate plants, as well as how to make the most of their various survival techniques in creating natural, beautiful and original mediterranean gardens.

DYING IN SUMMER: ANNUAL PLANTS

The simplest way to escape dry conditions is to disappear when the going gets tough. Annual plants germinate, grow, flower and set seed within a short period. When the heat and drought of summer arrive, annuals are not in the least bothered because they are already dead. However, they have already dispersed their plentiful seeds, thus ensuring the survival of the species, and the cycle is ready to begin all over again. With the first rains at the end of summer these seeds will germinate, and the seedlings will then develop during the damp conditions of autumn. After a brief pause in winter if the cold is severe, the plants will grow rapidly in February or March and burst into flower in spring. Nature is generous with annual plants, endowing them with attractive and brightly coloured flowers, for the plant can't afford to waste time: it needs to attract pollinators as fast as possible before the summer heat sets in and death approaches.

In some desert regions the cycle is even shorter. Often it may only rain once each year; the plant germinates on the same day that it rains, flowers immediately and dies within a few days, scattering a profusion of seeds which will remain hidden in the desert until the rains return the following year. It is a short life but an intense one. These annuals are very brightly coloured and their flowers may briefly carpet vast expanses of land. In Namaqualand in South Africa or on the edge of the Atacama Desert in Chile, landscapes suddenly clothed with flowers are a great attraction. In the southwest of the United States there is an entire network of enthusiasts who keep each other informed in real time on the internet of the day-by-day flowering in the Mojave and Sonora deserts.

Annuals can be a godsend in gardens, and you don't have to go to the ends of the earth to find them. Conscientious gardeners weed their perennial borders meticulously in spring, faces shining with sweat and backs aching, making sure the garden is 'clean'. Yet why get rid of all these annuals? It is easy to weed selectively, leaving wild annuals with attractive flowers. At the end of the season they will produce their seeds and self-seed naturally the following year, adding colour and filling any gaps in recently planted borders. Or the seeds can be harvested in early summer and sown in autumn in other parts of the garden, creating interesting combinations with existing perennials. In our own garden we have fun experimenting, mixing perennials, annuals and biennials: this year we have poppies with *Eschscholzia californica* and *Geranium sanguineum*, next year we plan to try the pretty blue of *Nigella damascena* (love-

in-a-mist) with the luminous yellow of mulleins. I'd also like to copy a combination I saw by the side of the path during a walk in Andalucia: blue viper's bugloss growing with pale pink valerian. Each region has its own annuals, and instead exhausting yourself trying to get rid of them, it is better to get to know them and gently guide them, thus creating cheerful and ephemeral sights. And a corner of the garden set aside for wild annual plants provides a wonderful reservoir of pollinators and beneficial fauna: the greater the diversity, the better the natural balance and the fewer the diseases in the rest of the garden.

HIDING BELOW GROUND: GEOPHYTES

Geophytes are what we generally call bulbous plants. Specialists make a distinction between true bulbs, resembling an onion (tulips, narcissi), corms, which are a swollen basal stem (*Crocus, Sternbergia*), tuberous rhizomes, which are fleshy horizontal stems (asphodels, many irises), and tubers, which are shorter and thicker than rhizomes (Jerusalem artichokes). The strategy used by these plants to cope with drought is similar to that of annual plants: they disappear in order to survive. In this case, however, they don't die. During their growth period they store nutrients and water in their subterranean organs; when the hot weather comes the plants wither and seem to disappear, but below ground the bulb remains alive, stocked up with reserves and ready to start the growth cycle once more with the autumn rains.

The ease with which bulbous plants can be multiplied by simple division during their dormant period makes them valuable allies of the mediterranean gardener. Their flowering is often fairly short-lived but very attractive. Bulbous plants mark the seasonal rhythm of the garden: the amazing blooms of the saffron crocus immediately after the end of summer; multicoloured carpets of cyclamens in autumn; *Iris unguicularis* to help us through the winter; narcissi to herald the spring; glorious *Scilla peruviana* in April; then the alliums just before the summer heat sets in, and *Agapanthus* to soften the brilliant sunlight of July. The Mediterranean Basin, where fire plays an important role in opening up clearings, is very rich in bulbs. But the region with the most extraordinary diversity of bulbous plants is without any doubt the Western Cape of South Africa. After a fire, the fynbos is transformed into a veritable bulb garden, flowering as far as the eye can see.

By planting a mixture of perennials and annuals, it is easy to create colourful pictures. Here cornfield poppies have self-seeded freely amongst *Eschscholzia californica*, *Tanacetum pyrethrum* and *Geranium sanguineum*.

A DOUBLE ROOT SYSTEM

Many dry-climate trees and shrubs develop a double root system in order to cope better with a shortage of water. For instance, imagine a cistus seed germinating in the garrigue in autumn. After a few weeks the first tiny leaves appear. Over the winter the seedling doesn't seem to grow more than a few centimetres – but in fact its most important growth isn't visible since it's taking place out of sight below ground. The cistus is rapidly sending out a long taproot deep into the soil, forcing its way down between the stones. Immediately after germination a countdown begins as the roots try as fast as possible to reach a depth where the seedling can find enough moisture to survive its first summer. While this is happening, the development of the aerial part of the plant is slow: the cistus is producing a limited number of leaves to restrict water loss, but numerous roots to absorb as much moisture as possible from the ground.

If the plant manages to survive its first summer, in addition to its deep root system the cistus will then also develop a branched network of surface roots. These make the most of any water from even the slightest rainfall, as well as absorbing the nutrients that are more plentiful at the soil surface. A number of mediterranean plants adapted to degraded and often very poor soils have developed a symbiotic relationship between their surface roots and mycorrhizal fungi which help the plant exploit the small amount of decomposing organic matter on the surface of the soil. These roots can be very long and extend much further around the base of the plant than might be imagined. Most dry-climate plants have roots five to ten times longer than their aerial stems. The drier the environment, the further the surface roots extend, considerably increasing the total area from which the plant can absorb the water necessary for its survival. Where the soil allows it, roots may reach a great depth. In the Atacama Desert of Chile, the roots of *Atriplex* manage to reach the water table at a depth of more than 10 metres. In France, at the foot of Mont Sainte-Victoire in Provence, small oaks only a few metres tall are anchored in the limestone soil that is deeply fractured with many crevices, cliffs and caves. Speleologists exploring these caves sometimes come across oak roots seeking moisture at a depth of more than 30 metres in underground galleries. *Zizyphus lotus*, seen on roadsides in southern Morocco, often with black

plastic bags snagged on its thorns like flags, has roots which may go down as much as 60 metres to reach the water table.

The root system of mediterranean plants essentially develops in autumn, winter and early spring, when the conditions of soil humidity are favourable. This explains why it is important to start planting in a dry garden as early in autumn as possible: the plants are then at the beginning of their root growth cycle and will establish their root system under good conditions. By the following summer they will be almost independent.

REDUCING TRANSPIRATION: SCLEROPHYLLOUS PLANTS

Photosynthesis harnesses the energy of the sun to manufacture the sugars that plants use for growth. During photosynthesis carbon dioxide is taken from the air and oxygen is released back into the atmosphere. This gaseous exchange takes place in the stomata, situated on the surface of the leaves of the plant. The stomata are like small chambers with an opening (the ostiole) of varying size that communicates with the air outside. The plant also transpires during photosynthesis, and this is what interests us here: as the gaseous exchange of carbon dioxide and oxygen takes place, a significant amount of water vapour is lost through the open stomata.

In order to limit transpiration, sclerophyllous plants have developed thick, leathery, evergreen leaves with an upper surface covered with a glossy and impermeable cuticle (the word 'sclerophyllous' comes from the Greek *sklēros*, 'hard' and *phyllon*, 'leaf'). All the stomata are on the underside of the leaves, the side most protected from the sun. In summer, the openings of the stomata are reduced to a minimum to reduce water loss. In some plants, such as the oleander, the stomata are even hidden in 'stomatic crypts', deep holes furnished with hairs which make it possible to slow water loss even further. The garrigue and maquis around the Mediterranean contain many sclerophyllous plants: holm oak, arbutus, phillyrea, bupleurum, buckthorn, lentisk, myrtle. Their handsome evergreen foliage and dark silhouettes make these plants an excellent backbone for the dry garden.

This method of reducing transpiration is very effective, but it has one important consequence for the growth cycle of sclerophyllous plants. Transpiration is necessary for growth, since it powers the 'pump' which causes nutrient-carrying sap to rise from the roots to the aerial parts of the plant. For a plant trying to withstand drought, reducing water loss by closing the stomata is all very well – but it also reduces gaseous exchange and hence photosynthesis and growth.

Sclerophyllous plants, which are particularly well adapted to a dry environment, generally have a period of summer dormancy. This is the opposite of the cycle familiar in temperate-climate plants, which enter a dormant period in winter after losing their leaves. Thanks to their evergreen foliage, sclerophyllous plants grow in autumn, winter and spring and then become dormant in summer, the 'off-season' for mediterranean plants. So this is another good reason

for planting in autumn rather than spring: if you plant it in autumn, the sclerophyllous plant is at the beginning of its growth phase, while the later in spring you plant it, the closer it is to entering its dormant phase as the summer heat sets in. It can thus only hang on to life as best it can while awaiting autumn, when at last it can become established and begin to grow.

SUMMER DORMANCY: PLANTS THAT LOSE THEIR LEAVES IN SUMMER

While sclerophyllous plants opt for a period of summer dormancy, some dry-climate plants have taken this strategy to extremes: they lose their leaves entirely during the dry season. No leaves means no photosynthesis, hence no water loss. All that remains is the plant's skeleton, ready to put forth leaves again as soon as the autumn rains arrive. In gardens in the South of France, *Sarcopoterium spinosum* loses its leaves only in conditions of exceptional drought. In contrast, in the eastern Mediterranean where the plant originates, the climate is much drier, and in summer *Sarcopoterium* is reduced to a spiny skeleton. This loss of leaves can be ornamental: a leafless *Sarcopoterium* looks striking and original, while the spiny euphorbia, *Euphorbia acanthothamnos*, is absolutely spectacular in its bare summer state.

The more arid the environment, the more plants tend to accumulate different strategies of adapting to drought. *Argania spinosa*, the tree emblematic of southern Morocco, possesses not only sclerophyllous leaves but also a remarkably extensive root system, which explains the widely spaced trees typical of the landscapes of the Sous valley. *Argania* is also able to enter into a state of total dormancy by losing its leaves in a dry season. If the summer is not too hot and dry, *Argania* keeps its leaves – to the delight of the goats that climb high into the trees to browse on the young branches. If, however, the summer is extremely dry, *Argania* adapts by losing all its leaves and waiting for better times. It even possesses the unusual faculty of being able to prolong this state of dormancy for several years if need be, which gives it an excellent

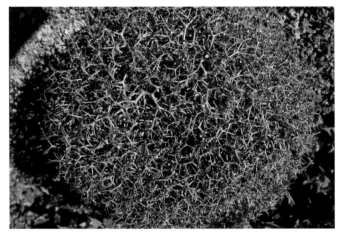

ability to survive cycles of intense drought. When at last the rains return, *Argania* puts out leaves once more, starts to flower again and produces its fruit, the argan nut, from which a delicious oil is extracted.

REDUCING EXPOSED SURFACES

In addition to transpiration, leaves also naturally lose water through simple evaporation from the epidermis, the outer protective layer of cells. The term evapotranspiration is used to cover the combined water losses from a plant's leaves. One of the strategies adopted by dry-climate plants to limit evaporation is to reduce the surface area of leaves exposed to the sun. At first glance, a rosemary leaf might simply seem to be a narrow, almost linear leaf, but a magnifying glass reveals a completely different picture. Under high magnification, it is possible to see that the edges of the leaf are folded over towards the underside. If you

could unroll them, you'd see that the rosemary leaf is in fact much broader than it first appears. The rosemary maintains a large leaf surface to carry out photosynthesis, but folds the leaf edges over in order to reduce the surface directly exposed to the sun, and hence minimize water loss through evaporation.

Another way of reducing the amount of leaf surface exposed to the sun is to shrink the size of the leaves. Many dry-climate plants seem to be vying with each other to see which can achieve the smallest leaf: there are linear leaves (*Dianthus pyrenaeus*), needle-like leaves (*Genista hispanica*), minute leaves (*Teucrium subspinosum*) and leaves reduced to simple overlapping scales (*Juniperus phoenicea*). Cacti go one better and have reduced their leaves to the point where they have disappeared altogether, being transformed instead into spines, which also serve to protect the plant against predators. In their case, it is the stem that carries out photosynthesis. Obviously,

reducing the surfaces able to capture the energy of the sunlight also means a decrease in photosynthesis; this explains the slow growth rate of many plant species with very small leaves.

There is an additional way of reducing the area of leaf surface exposed to the sun: instead of spreading their leaves horizontally to receive the sun at right angles, some plants turn their leaves vertically or align them to the axis of the sun's rays. The leaves of *Stipa gigantea*, like many other grasses, start out as sheathed culms, and then unfurl and stand upright, giving them a rush-like appearance. *Yucca aloifolia* is highly dangerous precisely because of its leaves, which are as sharply pointed as bayonets and grow upwards; this is not only a defence against predators but also an adaptation to dry conditions.

Phlomis lycia is a fine example of what is known as seasonal dimorphism: its leaves change according to the season in order to adapt to climatic conditions.

Argania spinosa is able to enter a state of total dormancy: during a prolonged drought it loses all its leaves and may wait several years until favourable conditions return before sprouting again. It is seen here growing with the cactiform euphorbia, *Euphorbia echinus* subsp. *echinus*, near the Sous valley in southern Morocco.

Until May its leaves are broad and green, and spread wide to catch the sun and ensure photosynthesis during the plant's growing season. At the end of spring, however, the plant loses these broad leaves and the new growth that appears is very different in appearance. The summer leaves of *Phlomis lycia* are narrow, covered with an amazing golden wool, and are held almost perfectly vertically. Incidentally, in the clever way that nature often arranges things, the fallen spring leaves create a litter which as it decomposes releases organic compounds with anti-germination properties: in this way the phlomis protects itself against the germination of other species which could compete for water in the same living space.

SHELTERING FROM THE HEAT: HAIRY PLANTS AND GREY FOLIAGE

If you walk in your garden in the early afternoon on a really hot day, instinctively you will turn towards the first patch of shade available beneath a tree or pergola in order to seek shelter from the heat. Plants with grey foliage have developed a simple and effective way of 'getting into the shade': they are covered with white hairs that reflect the sunlight. Beneath these hairs the leaves are green, because photosynthesis can only take place through the action of sunlight on the green pigment in leaves. This is clearly visible when the leaves are wet: after a heavy thunderstorm the leaves

ABOVE LEFT Native to the Balearic Islands, *Teucrium subspinosum* has minute leaves: the reduction of the leaf surface enables the plant to limit the amount of water lost by evaporation.

ABOVE RIGHT *Phlomis lycia* has two types of leaf: after aiding the plant's springtime growth, its broad green leaves are replaced at the beginning of summer by narrow leaves, which are held vertically to avoid the sun's rays and are covered with an amazing golden wool.

RIGHT The leaves of *Salvia argentea* appear silver because they are covered with a dense network of white hairs. At the same time as reflecting the sun's rays to reduce the heat of the leaves, these hairs also serve as a filtering windbreak that limits water loss by creating a microclimate around the stomata.

OPPOSITE In a dry garden, the silvery foliage of *Tanacetum densum* subsp. *amanii* sets off flowering sages, the pale pink *Salvia* 'Mrs Beard' and blue *Salvia chamaedryoides*.

of *Stachys byzantina*, for example, become almost green as the sodden hairs cling to them, the whole plant taking on the miserable look of a wet dog.

The protection offered by hairs on leaves in fact forms a double strategy of resistance to both heat and drought. On the one hand, the dense web of hairs reflects the sunlight and reduces the heat on the leaf surface, thus directly reducing evaporation. On the other, the hairs serve as a 'windbreak', creating a microclimate over the ostioles of the stomata and conserving some of the water vapour produced during the gaseous exchange of photosynthesis. A brief examination under a magnifying glass will reveal the great range of types of hair on grey-leaved plants: silky down, thick wool, long supple hairs or a shaggy mass, branching or umbrella-shaped hairs. This diversity offers gardeners a magnificent variety of shades of grey, white or silver foliage and allows us to create plantings where the soft appearance of the grey foliage not only serves as the perfect foil for flowering plants, but is in itself beautiful throughout the year. Grey-leaved plants are at their very best in the dry garden: the thirstier the plant is, the more it reinforces its defences against drought and the more beautiful it becomes.

CAPTURING MOISTURE FROM THE AIR

Some plants have an extra specialization in order to make use of the moisture present in the air. In addition to their role in protecting the plant from the rays of the sun, the hairs on the leaves are also very

efficient at trapping moisture. At the end of summer, in the early morning after a still night, dew is visible everywhere, covering all the plants in the garden. The amount of droplets trapped by the hairs on grey-leaved plants is significantly greater than that simply deposited on ordinary leaves. Furthermore, the droplets trapped by the hairs take longer to evaporate, maintaining coolness and humidity around the plant's surface for several hours. In arid climates with almost no rain, some plants even manage to survive by absorbing through their stomata the small amount of water from nocturnal humidity that is trapped by the hairs on their leaves.

On the coast of Chile north of La Serena, large, fine-meshed nets were until recently spread on the hillsides to capture the *camanchaca*, the nocturnal fog rolling in from the Pacific Ocean. By this simple and ingenious method, the moisture recovered supplied drinking water to the coastal villages. Today these installations have been replaced by the usual urban water supply systems, but the daily fog caused by the cold Humboldt Current still enables rich vegetation to survive along Chile's desert coast. The curious *Copiapoa columna-alba*, a thick cactus that grows in the form of pleated columns, has long white hairs at its tip, the better to capture the *camanchaca* (see photo on page 14). As well as northern Chile, other dry regions of the world where the vegetation depends on

coastal fog include the Atlantic coasts of southern Portugal and Morocco, California and the western coasts of South Africa and Namibia.

When the hot air from the Namib Desert meets the cold air produced by the Benguela Current flowing north from Antarctica, a nocturnal fog is formed that regularly bathes the coastal zone of Namibia. In the vast plains of sand and dust where annual precipitation is extremely low – in the region of 20 mm per year – a strange plant manages to survive thanks to this fog. In spite of its extraordinary longevity – some specimens are almost 2,000 years old – *Welwitschia mirabilis* only produces two leaves during its entire lifetime. These spread out on either side of the rootstock and are split into tangled, tentacle-like ribbons, making it look more like some sea monster stranded on the beach than a normal plant. To resist drought, *Welwitschia* has developed several remarkable strategies. To begin with, it has the classic double root system – a strong taproot capable of pushing several metres down into the sand to access deep-level water and to anchor the plant against the violent desert winds, as well as a network of branching secondary roots to profit from the moisture deposited every night by the fog. Instead of concealing a small number of stomata on the undersides of the leaves as most dry-climate plants do, *Welwitschia* has instead an extraordinary density of stomata all over its leaves, on both the upper surfaces and undersides: these stomata are capable of directly 'drinking' the fog at night. In order to avoid losing too much water through these stomata during the daytime, *Welwitschia* has adopted a modified photosynthesis cycle, similar to that of succulent plants: its stomata open during the night and close during the day. Lastly, the particular way its leaves are arranged, like sloping gutters all round the rootstock, means that the water that condenses on the leaves is channelled to the ground, the droplets flowing gently to just where the plant's surface roots are waiting for them. A true 'natural watering can', *Welwitschia* succeeds in watering itself thanks to the nocturnal fog.

IN A BUBBLE OF SCENT

A walk in the garrigue in the evening after a very hot day is an amazing olfactory experience. There is the thick and sticky smell of *Cistus monspeliensis*, the delicate scent of the aspic lavender (*Lavandula latifolia*), the whiff of tar from *Bituminaria bituminosa* and the acid freshness of *Calamintha nepeta* growing along the sides of the path. The mediterranean flora possesses a unique range of aromatic plants. In Crete the powerful scent of *Salvia fruticosa* mingles with the more peppery fragrance of *Satureja thymbra*, the pretty pink-flowered savory; in Turkey *Teucrium* species and rare oreganos abound, including *Origanum dubium* with a scent at once piquant and powdery; in Cyprus the scent of *Salvia dominica* can be so strong at midday that it is almost suffocating. And when you arrive at Corsica by ship, even before you land you can catch on the wind the bouquet of scents from the maquis: the sharp, fruity tang of the myrtles and the spicy fragrance of the everlasting flowers that give colour to the coastal cliffs.

The production of essential oils is an interesting strategy by which aromatic plants adapt to the difficult conditions of the mediterranean climate. Aromatic plants are of course found not only around the Mediterranean Sea, but in all the mediterranean-

ABOVE Marabout near Telouet, in the High Atlas of Morocco. Deforestation and over-grazing have left the mountain bare, resulting in serious erosion. In the foreground only the sparse clumps of *Artemisia herba-alba* have been spared by the sheep because of their strong smell.

LEFT The leaves and flower spikes of *Salvia indica* are covered with glandular hairs which release a highly volatile essential oil. In periods of great heat, the evaporation of these oils cools the air in the immediate vicinity of the plant, protecting it in an air-conditioned bubble of scent.

climate regions of the world. Among the best-known examples are the eucalyptuses of Australia, the scented pelargoniums from South Africa, the Chilean myrtles, such as *Luma chequen*, whose leaves are raspberry-scented, and the many sages of California. The primary role of essential oils is to protect the plant against predators, either herbivores or insects. In some degraded landscapes of southern Morocco, for example, the pressure from grazing flocks is so great that only a very small number of species survive, such as rue and artemisia, which the sheep leave untouched because of their strong smell. A second, more complex, role of essential oils is to combat competition from other species: the litter of decomposing leaves formed beneath cistus or thyme plants, for instance, releases substances that inhibit the germination of competing plants.

Although scientific studies are still under way, it is suggested that essential oils may also help the plant withstand dry conditions and strong solar radiation. Essential oils are produced by special organs, the glandular hairs. Even more effectively than the simple hairs on grey-leaved plants, the dense web formed by these glandular hairs traps a small film of air on the leaf surface which serves as a barrier against the air outside, thus limiting water loss from the stomata. The evaporation of essential oils also has a cooling effect on the environment immediately around the plant, protecting its leaves from burning due to an excessive rise in temperature in the epidermis. In periods of extreme heat, the evaporation of essential oils may be very significant, hence the unique scent of mediterranean vegetation in summer. In California, in the hills around Hollywood, *Salvia apiana* gives off such a quantity of essential oils that it is visible as a mist floating above the chaparral. The stronger the plant's scent, the more it is protecting itself against heat and sun. Their essential oils enable aromatic plants to shelter within an air-conditioned bubble – a small private atmosphere created around each plant.

CONSERVING WATER: SUCCULENT PLANTS

The tissues of succulent plants have particularly large cells, creating a sponge-like structure which can act as a water reservoir, enabling the plant to get through long periods of drought. This is the first, most obvious adaptation of succulents to drought; many also show an interesting physiological adaptation in stem structure and leaf arrangement. For instance, the stems of the succulent euphorbias have large vertical ribs, giving them their characteristic canalized cross-section. The shade projected by these vertical ribs means that a significant area of the stem can benefit from relative coolness during part of the day. In *Sedum ochroleucum* and *S. sediforme*, commonly found in the stony expanses of the garrigue of Montpellier in southern France, the leaves are arranged in vertical spires along the length of the stem; the lower leaves are thus shaded by those above

Cape Pertusato in southern Corsica. To withstand salt and drought, plants hug the ground, taking on cushion- or ball-like shapes. The dense clumps of *Helichrysum microphyllum* seem to flow down towards the sea, while above are the first cascades of prostrate rosemary.

them, and these in turn by those above them, as the position of the sun changes throughout the day.

However, the most remarkable adaptation in succulent plants has to do with a modification of the photosynthesis cycle. Storing water is all very well, but it is useless if it is lost as vapour through the stomata during photosynthesis. The stomata of a normal plant open during the day and close at night. Photosynthesis requires the energy of the sunlight, and so carbon dioxide is extracted from the air in full daylight for immediate use. In succulent plants, however, the stomata close during the day when it is very hot and open at night, when transpiration is less. Carbon dioxide is absorbed through the stomata during the night and fixed by means of a special chemical reaction, then used during the day to permit photosynthesis to take place without opening the stomata – in other words, without water loss through transpiration.

SALT, WIND, COLD AND DROUGHT: BALLS AND CUSHIONS

In coastal areas the salt carried by the wind from the sea is a major limiting factor for vegetation, since only a restricted range of highly specialized plants can tolerate the extreme conditions created by salt spray. Salt acts on leaves like a regular and intense drought. Because of the difference in osmotic pressure (the difference in pressure on either side of the cell membrane), salt literally draws water out of the plant's tissues. To protect themselves, plants hug the ground, hiding behind each other; salt spray thus 'sculpts' the vegetation into the characteristic sheet-like effect so often seen on mediterranean coasts.

The glossy leaves of sclerophyllous plants, perfect for reducing evapotranspiration, are also useful in combating salt, since their impermeable cuticle protects the cells very effectively. However, in some coastal areas there has been a noticeable reduction in the number of sclerophyllous plants, linked to maritime pollution: spray containing hydrocarbons, lifted from the surface of the sea by the wind, is attacking the glossy cuticle and at the same time destroying the fragile mechanism by which these plants resist salt.

Wind plays a significant role in dehydrating the cells of the epidermis, and since most dry-climate regions are also subject to strong prevailing winds, this makes conditions even more difficult for plants. In the South of France, the mistral and the tramontane sweep the coastal plains, bringing icy cold in winter and burning heat in summer. When the mistral reaches the coasts of Corsica, it whips the sea into waves and sends salt spray far inland, increasing the pressure on the vegetation. Battered by strong winds, the cork oaks of central Sardinia grow in the curious flag-shape much photographed for tourist postcards.

In North Africa, the dry and burning wind from the Sahara blows towards the Mediterranean, depositing fine grains of red soil sometimes even as far afield as France. In South Africa, in the Cape Province, the prevailing wind called the 'Cape Doctor' sometimes seems to come straight from the South Pole. Occasionally it is so strong that to cross certain roads in Cape Town pedestrians have to hold on to

These *Ononis* growing in the dunes south of Essaouira, Morocco, resemble rocks placed in the sand. Battered by the wind, salt spray and the abrasive action of the sand, the plant huddles into itself so that it exposes only the smallest possible surface.

ropes temporarily strung between the traffic lights. In southern California, the Coachella Valley is covered with thousands of wind turbines, exploiting the hot wind that continuously blows from the deserts of Arizona towards Los Angeles. Thus wind is an integral part of the mediterranean climate, and compounds the water stress suffered by plants.

So how do plants cope with wind? Tough, leathery sclerophyllous leaves, leaves enveloped in a thick coat of hairs, leaves that are tiny or folded over – all these adaptations to drought also serve to protect the plant against wind. However, the most effective way for the plant to withstand wind is to grow in a dense ball-shape. As the wind, the abrasive action of sand and – near the sea – the salt spray batter it, the plant closes in on itself to expose the smallest possible surface. It becomes rounder and flatter, as dense and compact as a cushion. East of Figuig, in one of the most arid regions of Morocco, *Fredolia aretioides* develops into a perfectly hemispherical cushion. *Fredolia* grows very slowly, only a few millimetres each season, incorporating into its mass wind-blown grains of sand

and becoming over the years as hard as rock. The tougher the conditions, the more the plant becomes hard and compact. Woe betide anyone who aims a kick at *Fredolia aretioides*: the plant won't flinch, it's the person's toe that will be broken!

Many plants growing at higher altitudes in arid mountains must withstand not only wind, summer heat and maximum solar radiation, but also extreme cold in winter, and the same adaptations to wind and drought can also serve to protect the plant against cold. Spiny xerophytes (the word 'xerophyte' comes from the Greek, *xeros*, 'dry' and *phyton*, 'plant') are small, dense, ball-shaped plants that have transformed the tips of their branches into sharp points. Thanks to their compact growth habit and small number of leaves, they expose only a limited surface to wind or drought, and their spines also protect them from grazing by sheep, goats and other herbivores.

These curious-looking plants can be spectacular, for instance *Erinacea anthyllis*, a spiny ball-shaped broom covered in magnificent blue flowers in spring,

To resist cold and drought at an altitude of over 4,000 metres in the Andes, *Azorella lycopodioides* grows only a few millimetres each year. After several centuries the plant becomes enormous – a monumental mass of convoluted protuberances on which the tiny flowers create an amazing yellow glow. On the left is Clara, giving an indication of the scale of the plant. For almost 20 years, Clara and I have devoted ourselves passionately to studying plants' strategies for resisting drought in their natural habitat.

which is found on the exposed mountain ridges of Spain and Morocco. Another plant emblematic of extreme conditions is *Azorella lycopodioides*, which grows at an altitude of between 4,000 and 5,000 metres in the Andes, near the borders between Chile and Bolivia. This strange plant grows extremely slowly – after several decades it forms a tiny bright green cushion that is truly charming. Perfectly adapted to the conditions of drought and extreme cold in the Andes, it can live for an extremely long time – even centuries. *Azorella* then becomes enormous, a monumental mass of juxtaposed excrescences that sometimes resembles a comfy armchair on which the hiker, tired from the lack of oxygen, might long to sit and rest to get his or her breath back. However, although the plant may look soft, touching it brings a

big surprise: it is even harder than *Fredolia* – a real rock of a plant!

But of course you don't have to go as far as to plant only rock-hard plants in your borders. Cushion- and ball-shaped plants are valuable for providing structure in the mediterranean garden. There are the undisputed classics, such as lavenders, santolinas and prostrate rosemaries. There are also other lesser-known plants with a perfect rounded shape that are very useful for structuring space or as groundcover. The 'Cretan' scabious, *Scabiosa cretica*, is naturally completely round and its evergreen, slightly silky foliage remains handsome throughout the year. It has a long flowering period each year, producing a profusion of lavender-blue flowers. The Balearic St John's Wort, *Hypericum balearicum*, forms a compact and dark rounded mass with fine, slightly curly leaves, that are lit up by its large yellow flowers throughout late spring.

Thanks to their extraordinary diversity, plants that are adapted to dryness can provide an inexhaustible source of material for the garden. The concept of a natural mediterranean garden is based above all on this wealth of shape, leaf colour, texture and scent which we can use to create structure in the garden that will remain interesting throughout the whole year, not just in the flowering season. It is the plants' mechanisms of adaptation to drought that give the mediterranean garden its charm, its profound identity and its unique character, for it is only in an unwatered garden that the beauty of dry-climate plants can truly be seen. If we use plants that are adapted to dry conditions, then the drier the garden, the more beautiful it becomes.

The concept of a natural mediterranean garden is based above all on the wealth of shapes, colours and scents which are used to create a structure that will remain interesting throughout the whole year, even outside the flowering seasons.

A scale of drought resistance

In horticulture, the word 'drought' is in fact poorly defined. The diversity of conditions in the mosaic of climates and soils that surround the Mediterranean has given rise to a real communications problem among gardeners. Is a common lilac, a *Salvia officinalis* or a *Cistus monspeliensis* able to withstand drought? We all have an immediate, more or less instinctive, answer to such questions, yet each gardener may well reply differently. Drought is a relative concept, and the absence of any instrument by which to define it more exactly has for a long time limited the creation of unwatered gardens. How indeed is it possible to know whether a plant will resist drought if there is no common reference point that would allow gardeners to exchange experiences?

TEMPERATURE AND PRECIPITATION

Agronomists speak of 'physiological drought' when a plant suffers hydric deficit – that is, it loses more water by evapotranspiration than it can absorb through its roots. In temperate-climate plants hydric

deficit causes the leaves to wither, followed by a progressive 'burning' of the young shoots and ultimately a total loss of foliage and possibly, if the drought is prolonged, even the death of the plant. If, by contrast, during the thousands of years of its genetic evolution the plant has managed to acquire special strategies for adapting to drought (see pp. 24–39), it will be able to get through the period of water shortage without difficulty.

Annual precipitation is not in itself a parameter that can be used to define drought. Montpellier in the South of France and Cambridge in eastern England have the same average annual rainfall, yet the plants and landscape of these two places are completely different. Although there are a number of secondary factors that come into play, what principally determines hydric deficit is the relation between temperature and precipitation: an increase in temperature causes greater evapotranspiration, while a decrease in precipitation makes water less available to the roots.

Physiological drought was studied in depth during the last century by plant geographers such as Henri Gaussen and Louis Emberger. They defined the climatic conditions in which plants start to suffer hydric deficit: a month is considered dry if its average temperature (in degrees Celsius) is greater than half its precipitation (in millimetres). For example, if the total precipitation in a particular month amounts to 40 millimetres and the average temperature is higher than 20 °C, plants will suffer from hydric deficit. This definition of drought, which might seem too technical and difficult to apply to the specific conditions in your garden, becomes easier to understand if we look at a climatic diagram.

A TOOL FOR INDICATING DROUGHT

The climatic or 'ombrothermic' diagram (from *ombros*, 'rain' in Greek) shows the changing temperature and precipitation levels in a given place from January to December. To avoid errors in interpretation arising from year-by-year variations, which can be quite significant in the mediterranean climate, the diagram is based on data over 30 years. Designed by Gaussen, this diagram has been used by

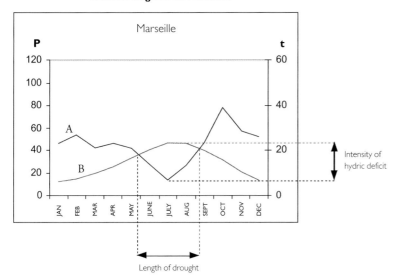

Climatic diagram for Marseille

The blue curve represents the average monthly precipitation from January to December (**P** expressed in millimetres on the left-hand scale).

The red curve represents the average monthly temperature from January to December (**t** expressed in °C on the right-hand scale).

Plants experience drought when the red curve passes above the blue precipitation curve.

most scientists researching into drought. For instance UNESCO uses it in order to define the dry zones throughout the world. It is a simple tool that allows us to visualize the duration and intensity of hydric deficit for plants in a given region: there is a drought when the red temperature curve rises above the blue precipitation curve. Thanks to the above climatic diagram, we can see that drought, in other words hydric deficit, lasts on average for three months in the Marseille region: June, July and August. The use of climatic diagrams has made it possible to draw drought maps, useful to the gardener because they help to indicate the conditions of drought to which plants are subjected in their native habitat.

Map of drought around the Mediterranean

Plants have widely varying capacities to resist drought depending on their geographical place of origin. These data should be modified according to local microclimates: there may be pockets of dryness in a humid region – for example the Ile d'Oléron on the Atlantic coast of France, where many naturally occurring cistuses are found – and pockets of humidity in dry regions – such as the west-facing side of the Sierra de Ronda in southern Spain, where the Spanish fir *Abies pinsapo* grows. With global warming, the dry zones may extend further north than their current distribution.

(Map redrawn after Dallmann, 1998, Emberger, Gaussen, Kassas, de Philippe, 1962, Demoly, personal communication, 2006.)

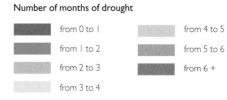

Number of months of drought

from 0 to 1	from 4 to 5
from 1 to 2	from 5 to 6
from 2 to 3	from 6 +
from 3 to 4	

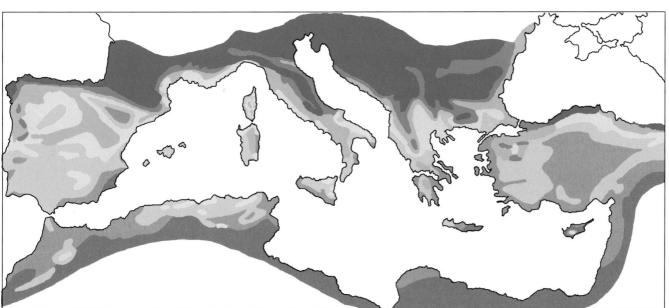

FROM LONDON TO OUARZAZATE, PROGRESSIVE DRYNESS

DAMP CLIMATE, NO DROUGHT

In the climatic diagram for London, the lengthening of the days is accompanied by a regular increase in temperature, favouring photosynthesis. It rains throughout the year: there is no period of hydric deficit and the growth of temperate-climate plants is steady even in full summer. We are in the kingdom of the lush green lawn.

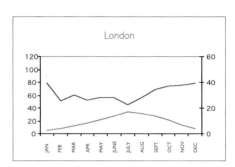

NOT MORE THAN ONE MONTH OF DROUGHT

In Toulouse, after the abundant rainfall of spring, there is a gap in the precipitation in July, when temperatures are at their maximum: hydric deficit makes its first small appearance. Forests are dense but a different shade of green; the landscape of mixed deciduous and evergreen trees has taken on a mediterranean colour.

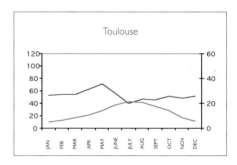

TWO TO THREE MONTHS OF DROUGHT

At Montélimar, the rainfall cycle has the characteristics of a mediterranean climate: a summer gap followed by abundant rain in autumn. However, the high annual precipitation does not reflect what the plants experience: there is a hydric deficit for two months in summer, but the torrential rain in autumn often falls in too brief a time to be retained by the soil.

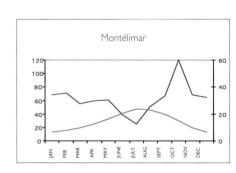

THREE TO FOUR MONTHS OF DROUGHT

Marseille represents the typical climate of the northern seaboard of the Mediterranean, with three long months of drought in summer and the classic peak in rainfall in autumn. These particular climatic conditions, in combination with almost 5,000 years of human pressure on nature, have shaped a unique landscape of great botanical richness: the garrigue.

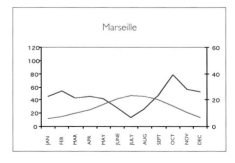

FOUR TO FIVE MONTHS OF DROUGHT

At Granada in southern Spain, the drought lasts more than four months and the intensity of the hydric deficit becomes significant. Along the spectacular Suspiro del Moro route, *Cistus clusii*, *Phlomis purpurea* and *Lavandula lanata* form the basis of a low-growing garrigue that clings to the limestone mountains.

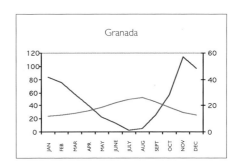

FIVE TO SIX MONTHS OF DROUGHT

With five to six months of hydric deficit, Athens has a climate typical of the eastern Mediterranean – very dry in summer although still wet in winter. The conditions are tough yet the landscape displays a remarkably diverse flora. The flowers of *Salvia fruticosa* light up the stony hillsides, along with *Ballota*, origanos and euphorbias.

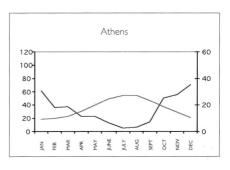

SIX TO SEVEN MONTHS OF DROUGHT

More than six months of drought and a hydric deficit of great intensity: at Marrakech drought is a major constraint for plants, which need to be highly specialized to withstand it. The blue palm, *Chamaerops humilis* var. *cerifera*, survives, together with *Lavandula dentata*, in the valleys of the foothills of the Atlas mountains.

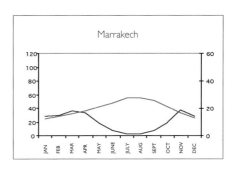

DESERT CLIMATE, CONTINUAL DROUGHT

Ouarzazate, the beginning of the desert: rainfall is extremely low and the hydric deficit permanent. The rare plants adapted to these conditions face intense drought throughout the whole year. Thanks to its extensive root system, *Acacia erhembergiana* survives in the Hamada, the stony desert stretching south of the Anti-Atlas towards Mauritania.

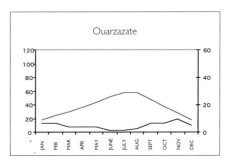

YOUR OWN CLIMATIC DIAGRAM

Do you want to have a climatic diagram for your own region? Get in touch with your nearest meteorological service and they will give you the necessary data. You need to ask for the monthly averages for temperature and precipitation for the past 30 years. With this information, you can draw your own climatic diagram. The scale on the vertical axis should be worked out so that the precipitation value corresponds to twice the temperature value, because this is how physiological drought for plants is defined (see p. 41).

Numerous internet sites also provide climatic diagrams for the main cities throughout the world. You could try the following:

- http://www.globalbioclimatics.org/ plot/diagram.htm
  2,284 climatic diagrams for the whole world are listed A–Z by country.

- http://www.klimadiagramme.de
  Choose a country and then a city to see its climatic diagram (in German).

- http://fr.weather.com/
  Select a town and then click on 'Climatologie'. You will get the monthly temperature and precipitation averages, enabling you to draw your own climatic diagram.

If you are not confident of being able to set up your diagram correctly – so that the precipitation value is twice the temperature value – you can find a ready-made table on

- http://www.geofri.ch/Textes/didactique/ methodologie/diagramme_climatique.xls
  – *the diagram will download (in Excel) and you can fill in your own data.*

EVERYONE'S DROUGHT IS DIFFERENT

Although it is fun to see the climatic diagram for your region, it should be remembered that there are

numerous other factors that can determine the actual drought conditions experienced by plants in any particular garden. The nature and depth of the soil, the amount of shade, competition from tree roots, as well as wind and salt can all have a significant effect on the way plants react.

According to their texture and depth, different types of soil have different abilities to retain water. The stony soil of the garrigue, the clay of the plains, the alluvial silt of ancient river beds, the leaf mould under woodlands and the sand of coastal areas vary widely in the amount of water that they can hold and make available to roots. A clay soil retains moisture well, so that roots can find damp even when a drought has set in. A sandy soil, on the contrary, is very free-draining. Even in regions where the climatic curve

TOP RIGHT *Rhamnus alaternus* at the foot of a south-facing wall. The nature and depth of the soil, the amount of shade, wind and salt, and competition from tree roots can all perceptibly affect the behaviour of a plant subjected to drought.

RIGHT *Calystegia soldanella*, frequently seen on the shores of the Mediterranean, also grows in the dunes of the Ile de Ré in western France. Gardeners outside mediterranean zones may find themselves confronting drought problems because the particular conditions in their garden may create significant dryness.

reveals no summer drought, the slightest shortage of rain can create a temporary hydric deficit for plants growing in a very well-drained soil. This is the case in some areas on the Atlantic coast of France, for example the Ile de Ré, where the use of plants from the Mediterranean can compensate for the drought caused by the sandy soil.

Orientation and aspect play an important part in evapotranspiration. This is very clear in mountainous parts of the Mediterranean, where, in the same valley, the vegetation can change completely from the side facing the sun to the side with a shady exposure. In the eastern Pyrenees, for example, one slope may be covered with holm oaks while on the opposite slope beeches predominate. In France, the Sainte-Baume offers a striking contrast. The north flank of this mountain is home to a famous forest, where huge beeches and lime trees provide light shade for centuries-old hollies and yews. Higher up, the forest suddenly ends and gives way to a baking limestone ridge, swept by the mistral. From this ridge the view to the sea is largely open, for on the stony south-facing slopes only cushion-shaped plants clinging to the ground can survive, such as *Santolina chamaecyparissus*, *Teucrium aureum* and *Genista lobelii*. The dryness in a garden with south-facing terraces will be different from that in a garden on a cool north-facing slope, even if they are only a few hundred metres apart.

Competition from tree roots is another cause of drought frequently seen in gardens, regardless of their climatic zone. Large trees act as pumps, drying out the soil as their incredibly dense network of roots takes up all available water. Even in a relatively damp climate, drought becomes a problem for shrubs and perennials growing near trees. Hydric stress in summer can thus be greater beneath an old lime tree in Toulouse than it is on open ground in Perpignan. And the range of plants adapted to such conditions is markedly reduced, since they must be able to withstand both drought and shade.

The cliffs of Gibraltar lie between sea and ocean – on the Mediterranean side *Asteriscus maritimus* and *Antirrhinum* cling to the vertical rockface, while on the Atlantic side acanthuses thrive in rich undergrowth on gentle slopes. Only a few hundred metres apart, the level of dryness is completely different, depending on sun and orientation.

Stipa pennata in June on the Albion plateau in Provence. The great increase in evapotranspiration due to wind is one of the factors that most accentuate drought.

Wind accentuates the difficult conditions plants are subject to: winter cold, summer drought, salt in coastal areas and sometimes the abrasive effect of sand. The great increase in evapotranspiration from leaves caused by wind is the factor that most accentuates drought, whether in a mediterranean or an oceanic climate, or on mountain passes and exposed ridges.

Carried by the sea spray, the salt deposited on coastal plants has a brutal effect on their leaves. Most plants cannot tolerate the direct action of salt – their leaves rapidly become burned by the powerful dehydration brought about by contact with salt spray, as the salt sucks water out through the cell walls. In our own experimental garden which is occasionally affected by salt spray, we have been able to observe an interesting correlation between a plant's adaptation to drought and its adaptation to salt, the mechanisms often being the same.

In all seaside gardens the drought resistance code must be modified according to the proximity to the sea and the frequency of salt spray. Only plants that are truly halophile (i.e., that tolerate salt, from the Greek *halos*, 'salt' and *philos*, 'friend') can be planted as first-line protection directly in front of the sea.

A DROUGHT RESISTANCE CODE

From the sea creeks (*calanques*) of Marseille to the mountains of Turkey, and from the meadows of Larzac to the sands of the Sahara, drought varies throughout the regions of the Mediterranean. Thus, depending on their place of origin, plants are adapted to drought to a greater or lesser degree. The *Cistus populifolius* that grows on the slopes of the Cévennes, the *Cistus albidus* of the Montpellier garrigue and the *Cistus parviflorus* found on the Akamas peninsula of Cyprus experience different conditions in their natural habitat, and it is obvious in the garden that they don't all have the same drought resistance. Similarly, an *Olearia* from New Zealand, a *Yucca* from California, a *Buddleja* from China and an *Aloe* from South Africa have widely varying abilities to resist drought. To express such differences in behaviour we can list plants on a scale, classifying them according to their degree of drought resistance when grown under the same conditions in a particular garden. Thanks to this scale, gardeners anywhere will find it easier to create a garden that doesn't require watering, for they will be in a better position to select plants that are adapted to their own climatic conditions.

Each plant in the A–Z section of this book is given a drought resistance code ranging from 1 to 6. Number 1 denotes the plants that are least resistant (being able to cope with about one month of drought with a low degree of hydric deficit), while 6 denotes those with the greatest resistance (six to seven months of drought and intense hydric deficit). In theory it is possible go even higher than 6 in the scale, but, practically speaking, with more than seven months of drought we are in desert conditions, which are beyond the scope of the present book.

The purpose of the drought resistance scale is to help gardeners choose the right plant for the right place. It does not provide an absolute definition of drought, but is a relative scale, allowing a plant to be compared to others whose behaviour is already known in the specific conditions of your garden. You must thus calibrate your garden, taking as reference points plants whose behaviour you already know. If *Buddleja officinalis* and *Elaeagnus × ebbingei* (both of which are 2.5 on the scale) succeed without watering in your garden, you could try any plant coded 2.5 or higher. If, however, the leaves of *Buddleja officinalis* hang down miserably all summer and if *Elaeagnus × ebbingei* already looks sad by July and has scorched leaves in August, then it would be sensible to choose only plants with a higher code.

These codes have been established by observing the behaviour of plants in many gardens around the Mediterranean, as well as by studying plant communities (plants that live together under the same conditions in the natural environment) in the mediterranean-climate regions of the world. I have deliberately kept the scale simple so that it can be used by the greatest number of gardeners; each gradation corresponds to an additional month of drought. For some plants it seemed useful to refine the scale by giving them intermediate codes, such as 2.5 or 3.5. Because of the many other parameters that affect drought, a more precise scale would not fit the extreme diversity of conditions characteristic of mediterranean gardens.

However, in the unique conditions of your own garden you may be able to make a more finely tuned personal drought resistance scale: you could grade a plant 2.8 to differentiate it from another plant that you might have graded 2.4 or 2.6. Everyone's drought varies and everyone can refine his or her own scale. The aim of the scale is to provide a tool for all gardeners to gain a better knowledge of the plants adapted to their unwatered gardens.

ABOVE LEFT *Stipa tenacissima* rises above *Phlomis lychnitis* in Andalucia. To help all gardeners choose plants adapted to the conditions of their garden, the plants in this book are classified on a scale according to their degree of drought resistance.

ABOVE RIGHT *Eryngium giganteum* in front of *Asphodeline liburnica* in June, before the great heat sets in. The drought resistance scale is a relative scale that enables new plants to be compared with ones whose behaviour is already known in individual gardens.

Drought and the Garden

Choosing drought-adapted plants

Installing an automatic watering system seems to have become something of a reflex for the dry-climate gardener. People think that in order to give plants a better start, it's a good idea to improve growing conditions in their gardens. So when they want to acquire new plants, it's simply a matter of making a trip to the local garden centre and buying roses, hydrangeas, clematises or *Prunus laurocerasus* according to the impulse of the moment. They may not necessarily know the requirements of all these plants, but no matter: with water and a bit of peat and potting compost everything seems possible. Yet in the mediterranean climate you can do a great deal better than this. Instead of struggling against the climate and soil, it would be more worthwhile spending your energy discovering plants that are adapted to the local environment. Rather than changing the growing conditions, what you need to change is the range of plants you grow.

PAGE 48 At the end of spring the garden is almost foundering under the weight of its flowers. The graceful spikes of *Perovskia abrotanoides* emerge from *Achillea coarctata*, whose beautiful yellow flowers appear in succession for several months

RIGHT *Asphodelus cerasiferus* resists drought, cold, alkaline soils, fire, and even grazing by sheep. In a mediterranean garden, we need to make a radical shift in perspective – instead of improving growing conditions, we should search for species adapted to the local environment.

And don't be in a hurry: before beginning to make your garden, it's a good idea to pause for a moment. If you plant too hastily, there's a good chance that you'll select unsuitable species and thus risk a great many setbacks. It's worth taking a few weeks to choose the right plants rather than subsequently spending years struggling to keep alive poorly adapted plants, which will in any case end up dying in a heat wave or a prolonged drought. In the garden, the battle against drought is lost right from the word go.

So what should you plant? If you garden in a mediterranean climate, the simplest thing is to begin by studying what is around you. Take a fresh look at natural habitats such as the garrigue: here lies an inexhaustible reservoir of plants for the garden. They are necessarily adapted to local conditions since they have lived here for time out of mind. Plant asphodels and euphorbias, myrtles and rosemaries. Try the delicately fragrant Etruscan honeysuckle or let yourself be tempted by the strong scent of the lentisk. Discover the incredible diversity of *Teucrium* and *Phlomis* species. Get to know the artemisias, with their finely cut leaves, or the countless cistuses whose petals are crumpled like old silk. In the mediterranean climate, the very best gardening school of all is the garrigue.

It's also a good idea to examine nearby gardens to learn more about other plants adapted to your environment. If you concentrate on gardens that receive little maintenance or have been abandoned you will find out which plants can survive without any outside help. You'll discover the Algerian iris that spreads naturally, the acanthuses and periwinkles that cover the ground beneath trees, and hundred-year-old Banksia roses climbing into trees. Local wild plants and 'abandoned' plants in old gardens make up the best list for your first plantings.

Finally, if you're planning to plant untried species from among the profusion available at nurseries and plant fairs or through mail-order catalogues, you'll need to take the time to learn about their cultural requirements. Before trying a new plant you should always ask yourself three basic questions: is it adapted to my type of soil? Does it tolerate cold? Will it withstand drought? In this book the soil

requirements, hardiness (tolerance of cold) and drought resistance code denoting its ability to withstand drought (see pp. 40–47) are given for each plant. Don't let yourself be led astray by the colour of the flowers or by an attractive photograph: first of all check the essentials. Be sensible – if a plant obviously doesn't suit your conditions, strike it off your list!

ALKALINE SOILS

If your soil is alkaline, as most soils around the Mediterranean are, it's not worth trying to grow calcifuge (lime-hating) species. The alkalinity will prevent their roots from absorbing iron from the soil, which affects their metabolism and they will rapidly show signs of chlorosis: yellowing leaves, an arrest of growth and finally death. You can, for example, grow many species of lavender in alkaline soil, such as *Lavandula angustifolia*, *Lavandula latifolia*, *Lavandula lanata* and a host of others. But there's one lavender you'll never be able to grow, *Lavandula stoechas*, which is only happy in acid soils. Similarly, among many mediterranean plants such as the ceanothuses, the cistuses or the callistemons, there are some species that like alkaline conditions and others that can't tolerate them. You thus need to be particularly careful when choosing plants: checking their tolerance of alkaline soils is of prime importance.

In the less likely case that your soil is acid, the range of plants you can grow will be much greater. Most wild mediterranean-climate plants can in fact adapt without problem to acid soil, even when their natural habitat is limestone rocks. *Cistus albidus*, for instance, is happy in the alkaline soils of the Montpellier garrigue in the South of France, yet grows equally well in acid soil. Close to the Abbaye de Fontfroide near Narbonne, on a famous site studied by botanists for several centuries, *Cistus albidus* grows among many acid-loving cistuses, such as the pretty *Cistus crispus*. The natural hybrid of these two species is also very abundant there: *Cistus* × *pulverulentus*, an amazingly floriferous plant that is one of the best cistuses for groundcover in gardens.

Chlorosis is a complex matter, since it depends on the pH value, the level of active alkalinity, plus the type of soil – either more or less 'asphyxiating'. Drainage thus plays an important role: plants become chlorotic much more quickly in compact clay soils that remain saturated with water in winter. Hence it is often difficult to know to what extent alkalinity is going to be a problem for plants, especially since the soil may vary significantly from one part of the garden to another. To avoid making mistakes over which plants are adapted to your conditions, I suggest you make a few experimental plantings which will subsequently serve as a guide. You can easily test an area of your garden by planting close together several cistuses which have different tolerances of alkalinity:

Cistus albidus (well adapted to alkaline soils), *Cistus salviifolius* (which prefers neutral soils) and *Cistus ladanifer* (which only grows on acid soils). After a few months, according to the behaviour of these indicator plants you will discover which type of plant is adapted to your soil.

COLD

Cold is a major limiting factor for garden plants. People often associate the mediterranean climate with mildness, and indeed many gardeners succumb to the temptation of planting subtropical plants. However, apart from a few protected coastal zones, minimum temperatures can sometimes fall very low, mediterranean winters being highly variable. At the end of February 1956 a great wave of cold killed vines and olive trees in the hinterland of Montpellier. The winter of 1789 is often cited as one of the coldest the South of France has ever experienced – the port of Marseille was blocked by ice. More recently, the succession of hard winters in 1985, 1986 and 1987 made a clean sweep of gardens in the South of France, killing all plants that were not fully hardy.

And even if the prospect of global warming suggests the possibility of recurrent periods of prolonged drought and heat waves, there is still the chance that winters may sometimes be extremely cold. Summer 2003 is remembered for its exceptional heat wave in southern Europe, but in February 2005 a great

cold wave hit the countries around the Mediterranean, with temperatures of about –10°C in Andalucia causing great damage in gardens. Clara and I were on a plant-hunting trip at the time and were cut off by snow at Tafraoute, a stone's throw from the desert of southern Morocco, in a region where it had not snowed in living memory.

The hardiness of a plant depends on many factors. Mediterranean gardeners often take pride in announcing the number of degrees below zero that their thermometers registered in the early morning. But the duration of frost is at least as important as degree. A drop in temperature to –10°C for a few hours just before dawn is not at all the same thing as when the thermometer remains at –10°C for several weeks at a time. In the Mediterranean region, the temperature usually rises during the day, thanks to the bountiful sunshine, and it is rare for the soil to freeze to any great depth. Depending on the suddenness of the frost, the degree to which plants have been grown hard (i.e., in tough conditions) also influences their sensitivity.

The humidity of the soil is another important factor. Many mediterranean plants can tolerate dry cold, but will die under the combined effects of cold and damp. This is why using straw or dry leaves to protect mediterranean plants against cold can often be fatal, because this material retains moisture and can

ABOVE RIGHT Hoar frost on foliage. The hardiness of a plant depends on many factors, including the minimum temperature, the duration of the cold, the degree to which the plant has been 'grown hard' and the humidity of the soil.

RIGHT February 2005: a cactiform euphorbia under snow, near the Tizi n Tarakatine pass in southern Morocco. People often associate the mediterranean climate with mildness, but mediterranean winters can sometimes be very cold indeed.

cause the plant to rot. What is needed is perfect drainage around the base of the plant to help it survive the winter.

The age of a plant also affects its resistance to cold. A well-established plant can put out fresh growth from the rootstock after a harsh winter, while a young plant, still weakly rooted in the soil, won't have the strength to send out new shoots in spring. Finally, we should note that an individual species may have different 'ecotypes': during the course of its evolution, the species gradually adapts to particular conditions, such as cold, in a given site. Selecting such ecotypes sometimes makes it possible for us to grow species in a cold area that are generally considered to be tender. We have, for instance, long been passionately involved in a search for hardy ecotypes of the oleander, examining the highest sites where oleanders grow in the wadis of the Moroccan High Atlas mountains. And we are now looking for hardy ecotypes of *Lavandula dentata*: a dream that promises the pleasure of travels to come.

It is thus not possible to make any absolute pronouncements on whether a plant can resist cold. But a very useful approximation can be given to gardeners by indicating a margin of temperatures below which the plant risks being seriously damaged in a given region. For example, we can state that in the Montpellier region in the South of France, *Salvia africana-lutea* is hardy to about −4 to −6°C. In northern France, where the cold is prolonged and conditions are wetter, the same *Salvia africana-lutea* might not be able to withstand temperatures below 0 to −2°C. The indications of hardiness that I give for each plant in this book refer to the type of cold seen around the Mediterranean Basin, which normally doesn't last very long. They will therefore need to be adjusted according to the type of cold experienced in your region, depending on how prolonged and how wet it is.

SMALL, TOUGH AND STOCKY: A NEW CRITERION OF QUALITY

If you have carefully chosen a species by checking its cultural requirements with respect to soil, cold and drought, it has every chance of being well adapted to your conditions. But to make sure it gets off to a really good start you also need to know how to choose the individual plant that you're about to put in your garden.

The harsher the climate conditions, the more we need to plant small plants which have been grown hard. If you choose a plant that is already large, bear in mind that for it to have grown so fast it will have been raised in the nursery under much too favourable conditions. It has become accustomed to generous doses of fertilizer and to water on demand. And while it may look as if it's in perfect health, in reality it is extremely fragile, having lost the necessity to adapt to tough conditions. The leaves are over-large, their stomata are open to the maximum, the density of the hairs on the leaf surfaces is sparse. The plant has forgotten what drought is. When it leaves the nursery for your garden, a plant that is too big will experience a brutal shock. Suddenly the daily watering stops and the plant finds itself on its own in a hostile environment without the resources to cope. It will

ABOVE LEFT This young oleander from the High Atlas mountains in Morocco is growing at high altitude in a wadi which in winter turns into a cascade of ice. The selection of hardy ecotypes makes it possible to grow oleanders in cold areas where the classic varieties do not survive.

ABOVE RIGHT *Salvia africana-lutea* grows in well-drained soil on the Atlantic coast of the Cape Province of South Africa. It can produce new growth from the rootstock after temperatures of about −4 to −6°C in the Montpellier area because the soil does not freeze deeply, thanks to the rise in daytime temperatures.

suffer severe stress and attempt urgently to develop the adaptation mechanisms it lacks, with progressive closure of the stomata, followed by yellowing then partial fall of the leaves; it will then enter into a dormant phase. It may take several months, or even more than a year, for the plant to recover from the stress of being planted out. The result is the opposite of what had been intended: instead of having a large plant that creates an immediate effect, the gardener is left with a miserable-looking plant shedding its leaves and whose growth is checked.

So what is the optimum size for planting out? When you choose your plant, the key word is balance. The volume of the foliage above ground must be balanced to the volume of the root system. It's easy to assess this balance: if the height of the pot is 15 to 20 centimetres, a good quality plant for the dry garden will also be about 15 to 20 centimetres tall. There's no need to become an obsessive wielder of tape measures and slide rules – this concept of balance can be assessed at a glance. A year-old plant grown in a 2-litre pot whose foliage is dense and compact will get off to a remarkably good start. Whenever you can, always choose plants that are small, stocky and many-branched: they will survive the transition between the pampered growing conditions in the nursery and the conditions in your garden without suffering damage.

ROOT QUALITY

When we buy a plant, we instinctively check the quality of its foliage, but tend to forget to think about its roots. Yet whether the plant gets off to a good start depends above all on the quality of its roots. Root quality is a taboo subject in the horticultural world. Everyone knows there's a problem, but no one wants to discuss it. So what's it all about? A plant grown in a pot initially puts out roots that grow normally in all directions. Then, suddenly, the roots are blocked by the wall of the pot. Since they have to continue growing in order to nourish the plant, they first follow the wall of the pot and then turn inwards. The more the plant grows, the more the roots twist: if the plant remains too long in the pot, the roots go on twisting until they have formed a tight knot. This is sometimes known as 'root girdling' or 'root circling'.

What happens when this plant is transplanted into the ground? It seems reluctant to send out new roots downwards, as if it still somehow retained a memory of the root deformation imposed by the walls of its pot. Only small secondary roots will start to grow beyond the knot of roots and the plant will have trouble anchoring itself properly in the soil. It will grow, but its roots will never manage to develop properly. In the case of woody plants – trees, shrubs

or sub-shrubs – there is an even more serious consequence: if the plant finally does manage to become established, the base of the trunk will slowly grow wider until one day, after five or ten years depending on the species, the collar of the plant will be strangled by the circular knot of roots formed in the pot. This is one of the main causes of the premature death – often wrongly attributed – of woody plants in the garden.

In mediterranean gardens the problem of root girdling is even more serious than in temperate climates. Because the root knot markedly slows the development of main roots down towards the deeper levels of the soil which are always damper, it makes the plant more susceptible to drought. After a few years, the imbalance between the amount of foliage above ground and the poorly developed root system can create severe hydric stress. Thus a plant which, given the climate of its place of origin, ought to have done better, can sometimes display a surprising lack of drought resistance. On pulling up this plant, there's a strong chance you'll find a major root knot problem, with very few roots having managed to grow deep into the soil to extract the moisture needed by the plant.

The problem of the root knot is less serious for herbaceous perennials since they regenerate by suckers, layering or rhizomes. In a few years the plant

thus escapes by itself from the twisted knot of its original pot-grown rootstock. But for all woody plants – trees, shrubs and sub-shrubs – the root knot is a major defect, prejudicial to the plant's ability to grow on, to its drought resistance, to its behaviour in wind, and, in the long term, to its lifespan.

Various models of 'intelligent' pots already exist which are designed to combat the formation of root knots. However, since they are expensive, not widely known and difficult to use in large-scale production, they are unfortunately ignored by nurserymen. Only regular demand from customers who care about quality may lead to a change in nursery practices in the future. Pots made out of biodegradable material, such as coconut fibre or peat (though in general the use of peat should be avoided), allow roots to grow through their sides, thus producing a sort of natural 'root pruning' effect, as if the tip of each root is being pinched off as soon as it emerges from the pot. Hence, instead of twisting around in the pot, roots branch out regularly in all directions. But precisely because they are biodegradable, these pots disintegrate quickly and become difficult to handle, which explains why they haven't met with much success in nurseries. Nevertheless, they may be suitable for the private individual who wants to produce good quality plants on a small scale.

Effect of pot cultivation on the root system

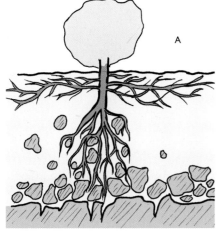
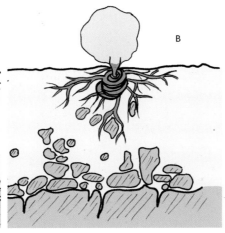

FAR LEFT The effect of pot cultivation on the root system.

A The optimal root system of a mediterranean shrub: some of the plant's roots grow straight down in order to find moisture during periods of great drought, while there is also a dense network of surface roots to absorb even slight rainfall.

B Grown for too long in a round pot, the plant is strangling itself with its knotted ball of roots. After a few years, the atrophied root system will be inadequate to meet the plant's needs and it risks dying of thirst in a prolonged drought.

LEFT Cultivated in a forestry-type pot, this plant has roots which grow downwards, ready to attain depth rapidly, enabling it to resist drought better.

Directly inspired by the containers used in the production of forestry plants, horticultural pots do exist which have strong vertical ridges on the interior that guide roots downwards, thus preventing them from twisting. The bottom of these pots consists of an open grid to ensure a natural pruning of the roots that grow from the bottom of the rootball. In a dry climate, this type of pot has one great advantage: its tall, narrow shape allows the root system to have reached a good depth by the time the plant is planted out, so that the roots can start developing fast in the dampest level of the soil.

What do you do if the only plants you can find in your area are grown in traditional pots? The first rule is to try to buy a young plant, grown in its pot for only six months, or at most a year. The older the plant, the more likely it is to suffer from root girdling and the more serious the problem. If the roots are not too badly twisted, you can try to unwind them when you transplant the plant into the ground and spread them out in the planting hole. This is a fairly delicate operation, but it's better to break a few roots than to leave the knot as it is.

You can also copy a technique sometimes used in nurseries when a plant is being repotted into a larger pot. Using a sharp blade, make two vertical incisions in the rootball to cut any roots that are twisting. But beware: this dramatic technique should only be tried in autumn or winter when the plant is not water-stressed. It also requires a reduction of the aerial parts of the plant: by cutting its roots you drastically reduce their capacity to absorb water, so you must also reduce evapotranspiration by lessening the surface area of the foliage.

THE RIGHT PLANT IN THE RIGHT PLACE

In spite of all the care you have taken selecting species and checking the quality of the plants, you must still be prepared for some trial and error in the garden. So many factors affect the way plants grow that it is not possible to be absolutely sure of the result. A dry garden is always something of an experimental garden. Plants are living beings: some will do well, others will die. It's usually not the plant's fault, but the gardener's. Is a plant barely surviving in its corner? Maybe it's in the wrong place. You've tried a *Geranium macrorrhizum* for its scented foliage, but you forgot that it should be planted in shade. Your caper plant died after a few months? You didn't know that it should be planted on a small mound of stones.

In a natural mediterranean garden there's only one motto: the right plant in the right place. If a plant isn't happy where you've put it, it's not too serious, just replace it with something else. The pleasure of gardening lies not so much in the final result as in the endless discoveries to be made about the behaviour of plants and the way they evolve in the garden.

Geranium macrorrhizum is a good groundcover plant for the dry garden, provided it is planted in shade in fairly deep soil. In our garden we have only one motto: the right plant in the right place. Don't hesitate to make at least three trials, in different conditions, before deciding that a plant isn't suitable.

Successful planting

SOIL PREPARATION

To understand how best to prepare the soil in a dry garden, all you need to do is observe mediterranean plants in their natural environment. Fires, grazing and drastic felling have over the millennia led to a degraded landscape which has suffered from severe erosion. Take a walk in the garrigue and look at the ground beneath your feet: all the good soil has disappeared, washed away by heavy rains. Only the stones remain and often the bedrock is exposed. Yet this mineral environment supports a remarkable diversity of plants, which make the most of the smallest fissures to send their roots down as deep as possible below the stones. In the course of their evolution, dry-climate plants have adapted to soil conditions which may seem harsh, but which suit them perfectly: not good, deep, moist soil, but rather a soil that is stony, poor and well-drained.

Above all, dry-climate plants need good drainage. Drought doesn't scare them – it's what they're designed for. What they can't cope with is asphyxiation in heavy, compacted soil in gardens where during the rainy season the water forms puddles that hang around for a long time. If your soil is light and permeable, or if your garden consists of a series of descending terraces with old stone retaining walls, you are lucky, because your soil will be naturally

well drained and you don't need to do anything. But if your garden remains waterlogged for weeks after rain, with a clay soil that is rock-hard in summer and heavy and sticky in winter, then don't plant a single thing: you absolutely must begin by dealing with drainage.

The simplest way to drain the soil is to raise your beds. A gravelled path below these beds will be adequate to drain water from them. If the area is particularly damp, a drain can be buried under such paths. There is no need for your raised beds to be miniature mountains. Adding soil to a height of 20–30 centimetres above the original ground level is quite adequate. You can use the soil excavated when paths or drainage trenches are constructed, or the topsoil set aside when a new house is built. If the soil is really clayey, it is best to mix it with river, or sharp, sand at a ratio of up to 30–50% sand. In this way, you

Ensuring good drainage for successful planting

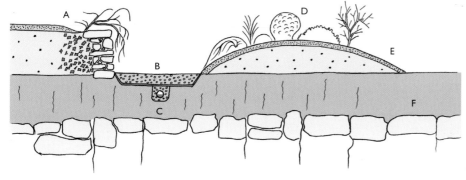

ABOVE LEFT In a mediterranean garden the ideal time for planting is just before the rainy season. The earlier a plant goes in, the longer it has to become established during autumn and winter, which will help it to get through its first summer without difficulty.

ABOVE RIGHT New planting: neither potting compost nor fertilizer should be added, nor should any other artificial means be used to force growth. What is wanted during the first year is a well-established plant whose foliage is limited in volume to reduce evapotranspiration and whose root system is as well developed as possible.

can create raised beds with excellent drainage that are perfectly suited to dry-climate plants.

It is in fact useful always to keep a heap of sand tucked away in a corner of the garden, ready to add to improve the drainage for any future small-scale plantings. But take care that you have the right kind of sand: sharp or river sand has grains that are rounded, and improves drainage, while quarry sand, produced when rock is crushed, has pointed grains that make clay set as hard as concrete.

There are of course other techniques and materials that can be used to improve drainage – pebbles, rounded gravel, pozzolano, drystone walls – but creating raised beds with a mixture of soil and sand is often the easiest solution. One advantage is that it allows you to model the site at the same time, before you start planting: a flat and uninteresting piece of land can be transformed into the beginnings of a real landscape, while the arrangement of paths between the beds gives a mediterranean feel to the garden, resembling the paths that wind through the garrigue.

If you have just created a raised bed, the soil will be worked to perfection and all that remains for you to do is to start planting. However, if you are planting directly into the original soil, which may not have been cultivated (i.e. dug) for a long time, you will need to decompact it to a depth of at least 30 to 40 centimetres. The more the soil is aerated, the faster the roots will be able to penetrate deep, enabling plants to get through their first summer better. It's worth spending two days with the garden fork rather than the whole summer with a hosepipe. Although

tempting, a brief session with a power-driven cultivator on the surface of the soil is not enough: the result may look good, but in reality the rotation of the blades can create a hard pan below the surface which will check root growth. For large areas, subsoiling with a tractor equipped with decompaction claws is a good idea, because it aerates the soil to some depth while at the same time preserving its original strata – biological activity being most significant in the topsoil. But for small gardens you'll need to summon up your courage: your choice is between a pickaxe and a garden fork, and you'll be able proudly to show off your blisters as proof of the serious work that is going into the preparation of your soil.

WHEN TO PLANT

In a mediterranean garden, autumn is the ideal time for planting, just before the beginning of the rainy season. This takes the best advantage of the natural growth cycle of the plant, which then has plenty of time to become established under the most favourable conditions. Drought-adapted plants have a growth cycle which is the opposite of that of temperate-climate plants: they grow in autumn, winter and spring, followed by a marked dormant period in summer when the heat sets in. From the moment the first rains fall in autumn their roots begin to grow, making the most of the moist and still warm soil. During its first months, the plant may not appear to grow much – but this doesn't matter since its important growth is taking place below ground.

The root system is developing and branching, trying to make its way down into the earth as fast as possible. This period just after planting is like a countdown before the heat and drought return. The earlier a plant goes into the ground, the more time it has to establish itself in autumn and winter so that it will be able to get through its first summer without difficulty.

Rapid growth is not what is wanted during the plant's first year. No potting compost or fertilizer should be added, nor any other artificial means used to force growth. During the first year all we want is a well-established plant whose foliage is limited in volume in order to reduce evapotranspiration and whose root system is as well developed as possible. It is only during the second year that the plant will increase visibly in size, often in a spectacular manner, as if to make up for lost time. The root system is by now strong enough to support vigorous growth, and it is surprising how, in a few years, the plants are already large enough to give structure to the garden. In the dry garden plants grow a lot faster than might be imagined, provided of course that the initial rules have been respected: choosing drought-adapted species, preparation of the soil and autumn planting.

THE PLANTING HOLE AND WATERING BASIN

If you've already carefully decompacted the soil, then the planting hole is not much more than a formality – a few strokes with a mattock and that's it. However, where decompaction of the whole soil surface could not be carried out, for example on steep slopes where there is a danger of erosion, particular care should be taken with the planting hole. A young shrub grown in a 1- or 2-litre pot requires a hole at least 30 centimetres wide and 40 centimetres deep, which is equivalent to the average volume of its roots after the first year. Don't add peat, don't add compost, don't add manure! The bottom of the hole should simply be filled with the original soil mixed with sand or gravel to form a light mixture which will allow the water you then give it to penetrate below the plant's rootball in a few minutes, in order to encourage the roots to grow downwards by creating a moist zone at depth.

If the plant's roots are twisted into a knot, now is the time to try to disentangle them gently, spreading the roots out in the planting hole. Then fill in the hole with the same permeable mixture of the original soil and sand or gravel, so that water can penetrate it without problem. Tread the plant in firmly but carefully to make sure that the soil is in contact with the entire rootball and that there are no air pockets which might allow the roots to dry out. If at all possible, avoid plants raised in a medium that is too rich in peat: as soon as the rootball dries it will shrink like an old sponge, so that instead of remaining in contact with the soil in the planting hole the roots will suddenly find themselves in an air bubble.

Now for the watering basin – perhaps the most important thing of all. Novice gardeners always tend to make the watering basin too small, which is more or less useless. The watering basin has to retain the water that we provide for the plant and prevent it from escaping in all directions over the surface of the soil. Water that flows over the surface is water lost, because it evaporates. Only the water that penetrates the soil deeply will be of use to the plant.

The size of the basin depends on the nature of the ground – how permeable it is – but in general a good basin should be at least 60 centimetres in diameter and 20 centimetres deep, in order to hold 20 to 30 litres of water at a time. When planting is too dense to permit an individual basin for each plant, the basin can be wider and surround several plants. Care should be taken that its edges are perfectly level so that the water doesn't overflow on one side when it is filled.

A first watering is given immediately after planting, filling the basin to the brim even if the plant doesn't look thirsty. The purpose of this is to finish settling the soil around the rootball and to provide the plant with a significant reserve of water deep in the ground; with this, it will be able to survive until the arrival of the autumn rains.

Novice gardeners always make the watering basin too small: a good basin should be at least 60 centimetres in diameter and 20 centimetres deep in order to hold 20 to 30 litres of water at a time.

Best water-management practices

For plants that have been established for several years, drought is not a problem. If they are drought-adapted, they will behave exactly like plants in the wild in dry climates, having the strategies necessary to protect themselves against heat and drought. But for plants less than a year old, the first summer is going to be difficult. Their roots are not yet deep enough for the plant to be independent. So the summer following planting is a transitional period and the vigilant gardener must take care to provide water, even for species that are naturally drought-resistant.

WHEN AND HOW TO WATER

The best way to get a young plant accustomed to drought is to water as infrequently as possible, but copiously each time – the water must form a patch of moisture deep in the ground, well below the level of the rootball, in order to 'draw' the roots downwards. Roots always grow towards the zones with most moisture. With infrequent but copious watering, the

ABOVE The first summer after planting is a transitional period and the gardener must take care to provide water, even for species that are naturally drought-resistant.

RIGHT A traditional watering technique in fields of barley in the Atlas mountains in Morocco. Practised all around the Mediterranean for centuries, 'furrow' irrigation allows the water to penetrate slowly deep into the earth, thus creating a patch of moisture which draws the roots downwards.

roots will grow down towards the lowest levels of soil, where moisture lasts longest without evaporating. The plant thus keeps its roots damp and will be able to manage for two or three weeks without hardship, even if up above the wind, sun and heat are drying out the soil surface. On the contrary, 'sprinklings', such as a giving a plant a small quantity of water every evening, artificially makes it more sensitive to drought. Repeated superficial watering makes the plant produce a thin carpet of roots just below the surface, exactly where evaporation is greatest. In this way the plant will not develop independence: if you forget to water it you will immediately see it suffering, with its tongue hanging out, and then, a few days later, it will look as if it's on the verge of dying of thirst.

Every time we water, some of the water is wasted, in effect being given directly to the sun without being used by the plant. In summer in the South of France the direct evaporation from the soil after watering can amount to 5 litres per square metre in 24 hours. So what is the best way to water in order to limit this loss by evaporation? For borders planted with shrubs and perennials, watering by sprinkler is in fact the very worst method. Instead of watering deeply, the entire surface is watered; moreover the umbrella effect of the plant foliage, as well as direct evaporation from the soil, mean that only a small part of the water provided can be used by the plants. Sprinkler irrigation favours the development of surface roots to the detriment of

deep ones. It also encourages the germination of countless weeds which, by taking water from the soil, compete with the new planting. What is more, sprinkler irrigation favours the appearance of many diseases such as rust, *Oidium*, *Aescochyta* and *Phytophthora*.

Watering into a basin around the base of the plant is far more efficient. Instead of pointlessly wetting the entire surface of the border, the water held in the basin can gradually sink by gravity to a depth of 30 or 40 centimetres. This is why the size of the watering basin is so important: it needs to hold enough water at each watering. Having created the basin when the plant is first planted, it should be remade at the beginning of the summer since it may have been damaged during winter and spring by wind, rain and weeding. I can never repeat it often enough: a good watering basin should have a minimum diameter of 60 centimetres and a depth of 20 centimetres in order to hold 20 to 30 litres of water each time. If the basin is too small, the water simply flows away over the surface of the ground instead of penetrating deep into the soil: the water rapidly evaporates and the plant is permanently thirsty.

The timing of the watering will vary according to the nature of the soil and the climatic conditions. Very sandy soils hold little water, so a slightly smaller quantity of water should be given more frequently. Clay soils retain moisture for a long time, so waterings

FAR LEFT Cracks forming in clay soil. Each time we water, part of the water is wasted, evaporating directly in the sun without being used by the plants. In the blazing heat of summer, the rate of evaporation may be very significant, in the region of 5 litres per square metre in 24 hours.

LEFT The watering basin is of prime importance: it allows the water to penetrate to a good depth rather than flowing away over the surface of the soil.

may be more widely spaced. In rocky soils, wonderful damp pockets remain even longer beneath large stones – a real delight for roots.

In order to estimate as accurately as possible the quantity of water needed at each watering for your particular soil, try the trench test system. In early summer, when the drought has already set in, fill the watering basin around a plant to the brim, measuring the amount of water you are using with a bucket or watering can. Wait 48 hours until the surface has dried out. Then, not too near the base of the plant so as not to damage its roots, use a mattock to open a narrow, deep trench so that you can check the moisture in a cross-section of the soil. A few days after watering the soil should still be quite damp at a depth of 30 to 40 centimetres – below the rootball of the plant – the zone where moisture is of most use to the roots. If the soil is dry at this depth, next time you water double the quantity and check again by opening up another trench near another plant. It is worth making the effort to check like this in the first year, for this fine-tuning of your watering is of prime importance and will be useful to you not just in the first year of your new planting, but also for all your planting in subsequent years.

As an example, here is the watering rhythm we use in our garden for new plants less than one year old. Our soil is clayey, we are near Montpellier in a hot and windy region, but the atmospheric humidity in summer is often higher than average because of our proximity to the sea. In a normal summer, without significant rainfall between mid-May and early September, we give 20 litres of water approximately once every three weeks to plants put in during the previous autumn. These 20 litres allow the young plants to get through a fortnight without problem – but we try to delay watering for another week at least. During this last week, water stress becomes apparent to a greater or lesser degree depending on the species: some plants seem on the point of withering, some leaves turn yellow and fall. This brief period of stress is in fact extremely useful in encouraging plants to fight against drought; it is now that they devote all their energy, all their determination to survive, to sending out deeper roots. This watering rhythm is of course only feasible for plants planted out at the beginning lof the autumn, so that they have had time to develop good roots during the winter. If, in spite of all our principles, we carry out some supplementary planting in spring, we need to water these newer plants a lot more frequently in their first summer, giving about 10 to 15 litres once a week.

Hoeing the surface of the watering basin a few days after watering limits water loss through evaporation. Due to the capillary action of the soil, water always has a tendency to move upwards towards the surface, where it evaporates – this is particularly true of clay soils, in which capillary action is more marked than in soils that drain well. By aerating the top few centimetres, surface hoeing disrupts the capillary continuity of the soil, thus promoting better retention of water deeper down. In subsequent years mulching (see pp. 67–69) can be used to conserve humidity in the soil, but in the first year we avoid mulching around the bases of our new plants since good aeration here is of prime importance. This reduces the risk of cryptogamic diseases (fungal diseases that reproduce by spores), linked to artificial humidity

Types of watering.

A A short daily sprinkling creates a moist zone near the surface. Roots then develop where evaporation is greatest: the plant will withstand drought very poorly in future years.

B Drip irrigation programmed to run |three times a week for half an hour. Roots are concentrated in a restricted damp zone. Weakened by irrigation, the plant will not be independent in future years.

C Copious watering at widely spaced intervals (20 to 30 litres every two weeks). By drawing roots downwards, deep watering makes the plant more resistant to drought. Hoeing the watering basin after watering prevents loss of water by evaporation.

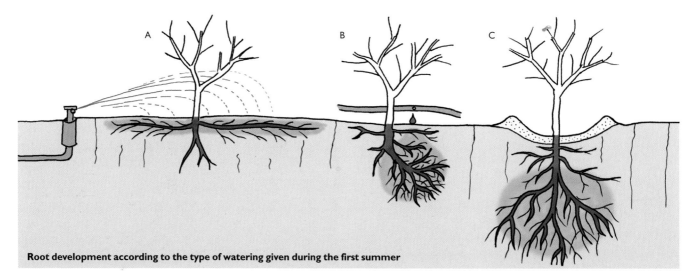

Root development according to the type of watering given during the first summer

during the hot period of the year, and allows the soil round the base of the plant to dry out rapidly after each watering.

Drip irrigation can be equally effective, but is often badly used in gardens. A small amount of water given several times a week creates a limited zone of moisture in which roots become concentrated, thus weakening the plant instead of accustoming it to drought. If you use drip irrigation, you should programme it to provide a deep watcring at widely spaced intervals, as in watering basins. In our garden we consider that it's not worth installing black tubing everywhere, when it would only be used four or five times in the first summer. However, drip irrigation comes into its own for the regular watering of vegetable gardens and plants grown in pots on the patio.

Does a young plant always look thirsty in spite of all your efforts? If so, it means there's a problem. To identify what is wrong, run rapidly through the list of planting rules that must be adhered to in dry climates. Is the species adapted to the degree of drought in your area? Was the plant small and sturdy, with the volume of its aerial parts balanced in relation to the size of its root system? And how about the roots? Were they in good condition, without a twisted knot at the bottom of the pot? Was it planted out in autumn, just before the first rains? Is your watering sufficiently copious each time, checked by means of a trench? If you think about these questions carefully, you will easily identify the cause of the problem.

Don't be stubborn: there's no point battling against your garden. If in the course of the first year some plants don't do well, simply give up on them without getting upset. Either the species is not adapted to your conditions or there's some problem like a root knot or poor planting conditions which will jeopardize the plant's future. In a mediterranean garden every failure is positive – by understanding our mistakes we'll be able to start again the following autumn under better conditions.

FOR THOSE WHO INSIST, A QUESTION OF ZONES

A well thought-out choice of species, good planting conditions and proper watering will allow your plants to be entirely independent after their first year. No more watering! No more hoses dragging through the garden, no more programmers and electronic valves that break down just when you're on holiday. You will quite simply have succeeded in creating a 'natural' garden with plants that are adapted to your soil and climate.

But are you perhaps not satisfied with the idea of an entirely dry garden? The motives that inspire gardeners to make a garden which doesn't need watering are many: a landscaping interest in mediterranean plants, an ecological decision not to waste a precious resource, or the simple desire to reduce water bills. I am hoping to encourage you to make a garden that doesn't need watering by using only plants that are perfectly drought-resistant. But depending on your own motivations, you may choose to adopt a progressive approach to creating a dry garden. Do you want at all costs to keep a few mandarin trees growing against the wall of the house? Are you a plantsman who collects arums and hostas and other water-demanding species? Everyone has his or her own reasons, everyone has his or her own way of gardening, and likes dryness to a greater or lesser degree.

If you are going to water some of the plants in your garden there is one error you should avoid: mixing

Beschorneria yuccoides in a pot. While a watering basin is best for perennials and shrubs growing in the open ground, drip irrigation is ideal for the vegetable garden and for plants growing in pots on the patio.

ABOVE LEFT Water has always played an important part in Mediterranean gardens, as the history of Roman or Andalusian gardens shows. But you don't have to water your garden to enjoy its presence. A shady bench and a simple fountain providing the sound of running water are enough to create a cool and peaceful corner.

ABOVE RIGHT From its pond the green toad (*Bufo viridis*) contemplates the frenzied activity of gardeners who water their borders every evening. The motives for creating a garden that doesn't need watering are various and complementary: a landscaping interest in mediterranean plants; laziness when faced with the huge task of watering; or the desire not to waste a precious resource.

species without taking into account their water requirements, then irrigating them all in the same way. Your water-demanding plants will always be thirsty, while your garrigue plants will rapidly die from too much water. In a garden that is partially watered it is very much in your interest to create separate zones or sectors in which you group plants according to their water requirements. If you plant all your 'thirsty' plants in the same area, you make life simpler for yourself: no more need to drag around long lengths of hosepipe that keep getting twisted simply in order to water two or three plants at the far end of the garden. And by keeping a zone entirely unwatered you'll be able to enjoy the whole range of mediterranean plants that hate being watered in summer, such as the lavenders, rosemaries, cistuses, ceanothuses, santolinas, *Choisya* or the various Californian sages.

Your garden can thus be visualized as a series of concentric circles spreading outwards from the house. The further from the house you get, the drier the garden, while close to the house, in a zone that is easily accessible for watering, you can group those plants which have higher water requirements. The zones that will be watered most will of course include the vegetable garden, pot plants and the 'nursery area' where you raise cuttings and seeds in order to have new treasures ready to be planted out the following autumn. Only these zones are worth watering by automatic irrigation if you go away on holiday during the hot season.

A zone with intermediate watering needs could include lawn alternatives. You don't have to be a visionary to see that the traditional lawn is an absurdity in mediterranean climates. If you nurture a deeply rooted feeling that you can't be happy without a vast, lush lawn, then perhaps you ought to consider going to live in Cornwall. To replace smaller areas of lawn you could, however, choose from a range of groundcover plants adapted to the mediterranean climate which will tolerate a moderate amount of being walked on, equivalent to normal family demands. Some of these plants withstand drought relatively well (*Phyla nodiflora*, *Achillea crithmifolia*, *Cynodon* 'Santa Ana'), while others will need a weekly watering in summer (*Zoysia tenuifolia*, *Frankenia laevis*, *Thymus ciliatus*).

It is only for such lawn alternatives that watering by sprinkler can be justified. Most of these plants spread by means of creeping stems which form roots along their length as they come into contact with the soil. Thus, when they need water, their whole surface must be watered. Whatever the species used, areas of lawn alternatives should still be kept to an absolute minimum. People often imagine that they need a huge expanse of lawn, but all too often the only person who walks over a traditional lawn in its entirety is the unfortunate individual who has to mow it every Sunday. Limiting the area of lawn alternatives to a few tens of square metres means that both water consumption and the need for weeding are reduced, and such a 'lawn' can more easily be integrated into the spirit of a mediterranean garden.

The idea of distinct watering zones enables us to create different ambiences – a mini-oasis near the house and a scented garrigue garden further off.

Nevertheless, there is a risk involved in having an irrigated zone near the house. If there is a severe drought and your local authorities institute a hosepipe ban, it is this zone, right under your nose, that will look miserable, while the rest of the garden will sail through the summer, tranquil and unaffected. Bit by bit you may find yourself reducing the watered parts of the garden, won over by the pleasures of dry gardening. As you become more familiar with dryness you will find yourself accepting it, until one day, like us, you may realize that you can't do without it, since it is a marvellous way of making an original garden that is adapted to the local environment. In a mediterranean climate, loving your garden means learning to love drought.

In the Botanic Garden of Cagliari in Sardinia a disused noria (waterwheel) acts as a support for a drought-resistant climbing plant. As we become familiar with drought we come to accept it, since it is the best way of making an original mediterranean garden, using plants that are adapted to the local environment.

DYING OF THIRST IN WINTER

In cold areas, a particular kind of winter drought can affect recent plantings with evergreen foliage.

After only a few months in the ground, the young plant does not yet have deep roots. Following a period of intense cold, the soil may freeze, sometimes to a depth of as much as 20 centimetres. Such deep frost means that water is totally unavailable to the plant, the frozen soil becoming worse than a desert. Luckily, during the cold time of year the plant's water requirements are virtually zero. However, at the end of a cold spell there is often a wide variation between daytime and night-time temperatures.

When the temperature rises during the day, a plant in full sun rapidly begins to transpire and therefore has an immediate need for water. But the roots cannot draw any moisture from the soil that has not yet had time to thaw out. In this situation the plant experiences a water deficit as brutal as if it had been sliced through with secateurs. It may suffer badly or even die within the space of a few hours.

Very often plant deaths that are due to frost-induced drought are confused with the direct damage caused by frost to the above-ground parts of the plant; we may thus wrongly conclude that a perfectly hardy plant is sensitive to frost. To avoid this problem, we can water a few most precious plants with tepid water in order to thaw the ground around the rootball.

In cold areas it is also possible to mulch around the base of young evergreen plants in advance of cold weather to reduce the risk of deep frost, although mulching too close to the base of the plant during its first year may cause other damage (see the remarks on mulching, pp. 67–69).

FAR LEFT Since antiquity, Istanbul has suffered from a lack of water. In order to maintain a water supply, vast underground cisterns were built during the Byzantine period, as magnificent as cathedrals. In areas where water shortages are frequent, the construction of a cistern ensures enough water in summer for reasonable watering of the vegetable garden and a few pots on the patio.

CENTRE After determined mobilization by local associations, the level of Mono Lake, one of the sources of water for Los Angeles, has risen slightly in recent years. In spite of the drought and the heat, immense lawns are watered copiously every night in the residential neighbourhoods of Los Angeles. And in the South of France it is almost impossible to count the number of lawn-covered roundabouts outside villages – a sad reflection of the lack of common sense among mediterranean gardeners.

ABOVE RIGHT In a partially irrigated garden, separate zones can be created, grouping plants according to their water requirements. A lawn alternative, *Frankenia laevis*, covers a small area near the house and can easily be given the weekly watering that it needs.

Maintaining the dry garden

FROM WEEDING TO MULCHING

New plantings need to be weeded regularly. In autumn and spring the mild temperatures and damp soil favour the germination of countless spontaneous plants – we call them 'weeds' since they grow at the wrong time and in the wrong place. Taking advantage of our well-prepared soil, these weeds grow fast during their first year and may compete with our plants, both via their roots, which take up water and nutrients from the soil, and through their leaves, which can hide the light from and suffocate young plants.

Do you enjoy weeding? For us, weeding is a relaxation. At the end of the day, when work in our nursery is over, Clara and I attack a small section of the garden together. We gently disengage the young

plants, one after the other, like so many small marvels. Often they are new species which we have collected in the past couple of years, and as we weed them we take

ABOVE A garden full of phlomis. What is the best way to reduce the weed problem? The simplest approach is to fill the entire space with plants, covering the surface of the ground completely so that weeds cannot germinate.

RIGHT It is possible to create natural-looking scenes in the spirit of the garrigue, though using a much wider plant palette.

the time to observe them closely and study their behaviour. There's the golden *Teucrium* we found in Gibraltar, and over here, look, this one's the grey, silky *Stachys* that was growing in the ruins of the ancient stadium at Delphi… In small doses, weeding is one of the best moments in gardening – but the pleasure can soon turn into a punishing chore. After a few hours your knees and back hurt. If the area is too big, weeding turns into real forced labour. So it's a good idea to be sensible at the planning stage of creating your garden: rather than planting the entire garden in a single season, it's worth doing it bit by bit in successive years, so that the maintenance of your new plantings during their first year is easier.

How can the weed problem be kept to a minimum in subsequent years? As you progressively plant your garden, the areas to be maintained grow larger. Each year in autumn and spring weeds burst into life, and it is hard to know where to begin. The simplest solution is to fill all the space by completely covering the soil. Wherever bare earth is visible, weeds will sprout, but if you fill every bit of free space with shrubs or perennial groundcover, the weeds will no longer be able to grow. To combat weeds use evergreen plants with a height of at least 10 to 20 centimetres. The thicker the foliage, the less light will penetrate through it to the soil and the less easy it becomes for weeds to germinate. The entire garden can thus be thought of as a 'groundcover garden', which is structured with carpeting plants of various heights

whose successive layers create interesting perspectives. The perennials, grasses and upright shrubs emerging from this mass of groundcover create a natural look, closely resembling the appearance of the garrigue.

Another way of limiting weeds is to mulch the soil. Our own garden is really too large for it to be practical to hand-weed all of it. We thus systematically mulch all our borders from the second year after planting. The result has exceeded our expectations; not only has the number of weeds steadily decreased, but the plants in the mulched areas have become more and more beautiful. We still prefer to wait a year before mulching, and to begin with we maintain our new plantings by hand-weeding.

It is better to leave the watering basin fully exposed during the first year, both so that the amount of water given to the plant each time can be controlled, and so that the surface of the basin can be hoed when necessary. Moreover, a thick mulch piled closely around young plants can actually retain too much moisture round the base of the plant and lead to the appearance of fungal diseases. In our own garden we thus work in two stages: we weed by hand during the first year, then cover the soil with a thick layer of mulch from the following autumn. If the planting density is right, after a few years the plants themselves will grow to cover the soil, over the mulch. Weeds are now nothing more than a bad memory.

We use two types of mulch. Between large-growing plants we spread a thick layer of organic mulch. Pine

FAR LEFT To reduce maintenance, the whole garden can be treated as a 'groundcover garden'. Paved or gravel paths add a contrast in texture and facilitate movement around the garden.

CENTRE Mulching the soil not only shows off the foliage of plants to best effect – here *Sempervivum calcareum* – but also suppresses the germination of weeds and limits water loss by evaporation.

LEFT Nothing is more painful than weeding between spiny cactuses. In this cactus garden intelligent use has been made of a pebble mulch: there are no more weeds and the plants have the perfect drainage that they need.

bark, cocoa bean shells and linen or hemp waste are
available commercially, but we prefer to use prunings
from our own garden passed through a shredder. For
the mulch to be effective, you need to spread a layer
at least 20 centimetres thick, since these mulches
settle in a few months and their volume is reduced
by almost half. Once settled, the layer should still be
at least 10 centimetres thick if it is successfully to
prevent weed germination.

Mulch has the further advantage of keeping the soil
damp by preventing direct evaporation by the sun.
This is of particular importance for us since we stop
watering our plantings from their second year. The
plants' surface roots can then develop just below the
mulch, where the biological activity in the soil is
greatest, while their deep roots benefit from moist soil
for a longer period. An excellent alternative to

chemical herbicides, mulching enables the
mediterranean gardener to grow plants that are more
beautiful and more drought-resistant. In order to
combat perennial weeds such as dandelion, bindweed
and aristolochia, we temporarily lay a sheet of plastic
beneath the mulch, which we then remove after a few
years.

Between smaller plants we prefer to use a mineral
mulch. Indeed, low-growing mediterranean plants
very often come from areas with poor, extremely well-
drained soil and they cannot tolerate the addition of a
large amount of organic matter around them. Gravel
prevents the germination of weeds and at the same
time makes the surface drainage perfect: it is
particularly suitable for santolinas, lavenders,
Helichrysum and the numerous grey-leaved rock
plants. As it settles less than organic mulches, the

layer of gravel can be spread thinner – only about 10 to 12 centimetres thick. Hence it is very useful for mulching carpet-forming plants such as *Achillea umbellata*, *Teucrium ackermanii* or *Dianthus corsicus*, which would be buried under the thickness of an organic mulch.

The numerous different colours and grain sizes of gravel available make it possible to set off foliage to its best advantage. In our garden we use mainly calcareous gravels, with a grain size of 10 to 30 millimetres: the absence of fine particles makes it harder for weeds to germinate. However, certain plants in the garden are so happy in the gravel that they seed themselves freely. We frequently discover seedlings of *Iris unguicularis*, *Limonium*, cistuses, santolinas and asphodels. If there is not enough space for them to develop properly we remove them. But

often we leave them to grow where they appear: they may fill in a gap naturally or form an unexpected and pleasing combination with the plants around them.

Weeding is thus not simply a negative process of removing weeds, but can instead be an excitingly creative job, through which we give a gentle nudge to the natural evolution of the garden.

THE DRY MEADOW

The lizard orchid, *Himantoglossum hircinum*, appeared spontaneously in our garden. If you keep areas of your garden as 'dry meadow', you will promote the appearance of decorative wild flowers.

If you still have uncultivated areas in your garden, don't do battle with the weeds! On the contrary, just leave any plant that wants to grow there. With an occasional scything, you will then have a 'dry meadow' in your garden, which will be green from autumn to spring and then turn yellow in summer.

In large gardens it is well worth leaving an area as a dry meadow. In this way you maintain reserves of beneficial fauna which will mean you can worry less about plant diseases in the cultivated areas. By scything at the end of spring you can favour the production of seed from the most ornamental wild species, either annual or perennial.

Our garden is almost entirely cultivated, but we always keep a long strip, running the length of an old hawthorn hedge, as a dry meadow. Here we have the pleasure each year of watching the progression of the wild orchids that magically appeared by themselves: first *Barlia robertiana*, then a little later the elegant lizard orchid, *Himantoglossum hircinum*.

ABOVE LEFT A shredder is one of the best investments for large gardens. Prunings can be recycled to be used as a mulch which will both suppress weeds and conserve moisture in the soil.

BELOW LEFT *Gaura lindheimeri* self-seeds very easily, slipping itself into gaps between perennials and shrubs. Here, we left a few plants of *Gaura lindheimeri* as we weeded, to brighten the dark mass of *Lavandula* x *intermedia* 'Grosso'.

PRUNING

Many mediterranean plants actually like being pruned every year. Lavenders, santolinas, rosemaries and cistuses can all be lightly sheared in autumn in order to maintain their compact ball shape. If left unclipped, these plants have a tendency to form old wood and become leggy, which shortens their life. Clipping the tips of the stems encourages them to branch, and maintaining a dense habit will mean the plant will live longer. In the wild, santolinas, lavenders and rosemaries live in stony ground that has almost no soil. They are naturally dwarfed by the harsh conditions of their environment and live for many years without problem. By contrast, in the garden the plant grows too fast; it reaches maturity in just a few years, thus shortening its lifespan. If constricted rootballs are the most common cause of premature plant deaths, the second most frequent cause is certainly the fact that conditions in the garden are in fact too favourable for a great many native mediterranean species.

No watering and no weeding: with time, the amount of maintenance required in a mediterranean garden is so reduced that there is almost nothing for you to do. So for the sheer pleasure of it you can set about shaping the plants to make the most of their natural forms and to accentuate the contrasts between those that grow in rounded ball shapes and those that have a graceful, upright habit.

Take a walk through your garden in autumn, and, as the inspiration strikes you, lightly sculpt a *Teucrium fruticans*, or the dense thorny mass of a *Sarcopoterium*, or the shaggy fleece of a *Ballota acetabulosa*. Maybe an old specimen of *Arbutus* could do with having its lower branches removed, to show off its twisted branches and brilliantly coloured bark. If one year you don't have enough time, well, that doesn't matter, you just won't prune anything. Are a few upright rosemaries getting bare and leggy at the base, and

perhaps rapidly approaching the end of their lives? No matter, they were probably not well-adapted to your heavy soil. Once they're dead, you can replace them with a longer-living plant, such as a lentisk or a phillyrea.

PESTS AND DISEASES

To avoid diseases in an ornamental garden, I recommend two simple principles, which we apply in our own garden: first, increase diversity and secondly use as few chemical remedies as possible. In the old days, it was common practice to surround the garden by a square-clipped hedge consisting of a single species, usually cypress or *Prunus laurocerasus*. Apart from their depressingly wall-like appearance, these monocultural hedges were a breeding ground for diseases. Since most hedging plants are propagated by cuttings that are all of the same clone, there is no genetic diversity to restrict the spread of a disease. It thus only needs one plant to be affected for the entire hedge to become diseased. This is why we sometimes see hedges of *Euonymus japonicus* covered with scale insect from one end to the other, or rows of cypress looking as if they were scorched by the fungus *Coryneum cardinale*, or hedges of *Prunus laurocerasus* riddled with perforating *Oidium*. Avoid monoculture in hedges, perennial and shrub borders, and groundcover. The more plant diversity you have, the less risk of disease there is.

If, in spite of diversity in your garden, a plant is suddenly attacked by a pest, chemical pesticides are not the most effective solution. A pesticide may kill a few aphids immediately, but it will only increase the aphid problem in the long term. For without knowing it, you are also killing ladybird larvae just as they are getting ready to feast on the nice fat aphids now appearing on tender new shoots. The result is therefore the opposite of what you intended: by disrupting the balance between the pest and its

ABOVE LEFT Following individual personal inspiration, the gardener can lightly sculpt the plants in the borders to show off their natural forms and accentuate the contrast between ball-shaped plants and taller, more vertical shapes. The silver ball on the right is *Teucrium fruticans*.

ABOVE RIGHT To reduce the risk of diseases in the ornamental garden, the simplest solution is to increase diversity. This small bed, where valerian, sages, centaureas and euphorbias self-seed, requires no special care or treatment, and forms a small, natural scene in the garden requiring very little maintenance.

natural predator, you are encouraging the development of whole colonies of aphids – only now instead of having a few score of them you will have thousands. And if you insist on continuing to use a pesticide, things will only get worse: in a few generations the aphids will have developed a strain resistant to the active component of the product you've been using – quite simply you will no longer be able to kill them.

Rather than combating them, pesticides generally encourage pests in the long term, whereas with just a tiny bit of patience your pest problem will resolve itself within a few weeks. For both diseases and pests it is much better to begin by taking preventative steps, in other words by asking yourself whether or not it might be poor gardening practices that have led to the appearance of the disease or the harmful insect. If you water *Choisya ternata* by drip irrigation, a fungus will develop around the collar of the plant: the solution is not to use a chemical treatment against *Phytophthora* but to get rid of the drip irrigation. If you put an oleander right in the middle of a lawn that is watered by sprinklers, don't be surprised if you see its branches affected by bacterial oleander canker: this systematically develops if you wet the oleander's leaves regularly. Start by moving the oleander or, better still, by getting rid of the lawn. If you give fertilizer to a *Cistus salviifolius*, its tender and swollen wood will be irresistible to all the mealybugs in the neighbourhood. Instead of spraying with a particularly toxic product, remove the mealybugs with a soapy sponge and stop fertilizing the plant.

Before reaching for the spray gun it is better to take the time to understand the cause of the problem and to try to prevent it rather than cure it. In a mediterranean garden most problems are usually connected to the artificial weakening of a plant by excessive irrigation or fertilizing. Begin by eliminating irrigation and feeding, and many diseases will disappear of their own accord. In an orchard or olive grove where rows of identical plants are grown, pests and diseases may be a real problem and chemical treatment or biological alternatives may be necessary. But where ornamental gardens are concerned, there is nothing easier than having a garden that is never sprayed at all.

In the garrigue, the santolinas are never affected by *Phytophthora*, the lavenders never suffer from die-back and the cistuses don't die prematurely. All you need do in your garden is to copy nature – in other words do nothing at all. If in spite of everything a plant is always diseased, don't insist, let it die without regrets. Rather than struggle to save one particular plant, try another: tell yourself that there are thousands of other species, equally beautiful and easier to grow, just waiting to be planted in your garden, as can be found in the following section of this book.

FAR LEFT A ladybird clambers over the flowers of *Lithodora fruticosa* – ladybird larvae are voracious consumers of aphids. Before rushing to use a pesticide, which often has the effect of disrupting the balance between pests and their natural predators, always consider whether poor gardening practices might not have artificially fostered diseases and harmful insects.

ABOVE RIGHT The innocent indecency of this germinating almond invites the gardener to transplant it carefully. Reducing the maintenance needed in the garden sets you free to spend more time on other more interesting jobs. You can, for example, try propagating your own plants. The simple processes of sowing seeds or taking cuttings are accessible to everyone, and are some of the greatest delights in gardening. To help you get started, specific advice on propagation is given for each species listed in the following section of this book.

LEFT *Epilobium canum* 'Western Hills'. If a plant isn't happy in your garden, try something else. Tell yourself that there are thousands of other species, just as beautiful and easier to grow, waiting to be planted in your garden.

An A to Z of Plants for the Dry Garden

The descriptions of plants include the following information:

The botanical name (genus, species, variety or subspecies, cultivar), as well as the common English name, where one exists.

Technical information on the plant, consisting of: its geographical place of origin; its height and spread; what sort of position it prefers; its hardiness; and its drought resistance code (see pp. 46–47). Take the time to read this information – it's of great importance if you are to choose the right plant for the right place.

Detailed descriptions of the foliage and flowers, with suggestions about possible combinations with other plants, and advice on cultivation. The plant's soil requirements are noted at the end of each description.

Specific advice on propagation by simple techniques that the plant-lover can easily use in his or her garden.

For each genus the principal species are given, followed by an additional list of species and varieties described more briefly, marked in the text by the symbol •

Each year in spring, *Asphodelus cerasiferus* is adorned with shining, satin-textured flowers.

Acanthus mollis
(Acanthaceae) Bear's Breeches

ORIGIN NORTHERN GREECE, ALBANIA, CROATIA
HEIGHT OF FOLIAGE 50 CM
HEIGHT IN FLOWER 1.25 M
SPREAD 80 CM TO 1 M
POSITION SUN OR SHADE
HARDINESS −12 TO −15 °C (THE FOLIAGE MAY BE
PARTIALLY SCORCHED BY THE COLD BELOW −8 °C)
DROUGHT RESISTANCE CODE 4

The plant's name comes from the Greek *akantha*, 'thorn', and the Latin *mollis*, 'soft'. It thus instantly evokes all the ambivalence of the acanthus: it is soft yet thorny, and it is evergreen in winter yet unexpectedly loses its leaves in summer. The acanthus is a plant which rarely leaves gardeners indifferent. Some love it, others seem to hate it. However, in a dry garden it is at any rate a perennial that is robust and easy to grow, happy in sun or shade – I belong to the camp of those who love it.

The large, dark-green, highly decorative lobed leaves are evergreen in winter. The plant spreads by means of its thick fleshy roots which are able to store water and food reserves, allowing the plant to get through the dry period in summer when it is dormant. In June the vigorous flower spikes give the plant a spectacular silhouette. The white flowers, partially enclosed in broad purple sepals, are furnished with thorny bracts: there's no way you can collect the seeds if you're not wearing gloves! After flowering the foliage dries out, then disappears completely, and the plant is dormant until autumn.

The white flowers of *Acanthus mollis* are enclosed in spectacular purple sepals and furnished with thorny bracts.

From north to south in the Mediterranean, the different species of *Acanthus* become progressively more spiny. In the north of Greece is found *Acanthus mollis*, with its large dark green leaves; in the Peloponnese it is replaced by *Acanthus spinosus*; and beneath the burning sun of Crete it is *Acanthus spinosissimus* that colonizes wastelands by the sea, as seen here.

To cover the gaps it leaves in our garden in summer we like to grow acanthus together with plants whose cycle is the opposite, deciduous in winter and flowering in summer: *Caryopteris incana*, *Ceratostigma griffithii* and *Perovskia* 'Blue Spire' for shades of blue, or *Lobelia laxiflora*, *Dicliptera suberecta* and *Epilobium canum* for warm hues. The acanthus tolerates alkaline conditions well and adapts easily to all soil types. It has a predilection for stony ground beneath ruins, to which it adds an antique charm. It can cope with competition from the roots of mature trees: in fact it is one of the best perennials for planting under oaks or pines. In old gardens it may become naturalized beneath trees and form sizeable colonies, which can prove hard to get rid of.

Propagation is by division at the end of summer or by seed in spring.

• ***Acanthus spinosus*** has finely cut leaves which are markedly thorny. It was in fact *Acanthus spinosus* rather than *Acanthus mollis* that originally inspired the acanthus-leaf motif seen in the Corinthian capitals of ancient architecture. According to historians, the first person to use this motif was Callimachus, a sculptor of the 5th century BC, who carved it on the capital of a column in Corinth, copying a wild plant that grew near his workshop – and it is *Acanthus spinosus* that grows wild in Corinth. **ORIGIN** SOUTHERN GREECE AND TURKEY **HARDINESS** −12 TO −15 °C **DROUGHT RESISTANCE CODE** 5

Acer monspessulanum
(Aceraceae) Montpellier Maple

ORIGIN MEDITERRANEAN BASIN
HEIGHT 5 M OR MORE (BUT IT TAKES YEARS!)
SPREAD 3 M OR MORE
POSITION SUN
HARDINESS −15 °C AND BELOW
DROUGHT RESISTANCE CODE 4

The Montpellier Maple is a charming small tree, frequently seen on inland hills around the Mediterranean. Since it grows slowly, it is usually planted in gardens as a shrub, often as a hedge in combination with other native species such as *Rhamnus alaternus*, *Phillyrea angustifolia* or *Pistacia lentiscus*. Its small, leathery, three-lobed leaves are a brilliant green and take on wonderful hues in November – yellow, orange or sometimes red – before falling at the end of autumn. The discreet, yellowy-green flowers appear in April and are followed by numerous winged red seedpods that remain decorative throughout autumn. The Montpellier Maple tolerates alkaline conditions well and likes poor and stony soils.

Propagate by seed. To overcome seed dormancy, the seeds must undergo a long period of low temperatures: in cold areas they can be sown outdoors in September and left outside all winter, after which germination will take place from March. Otherwise the seeds must be stratified by soaking them for 48 hours and then keeping them in the refrigerator for 3 or 4 months in a bag of moist vermiculite, at a temperature of about 4ºC, after which they should be sown in spring.

The orange flames of *Acer monspessulanum* light up the autumn landscape in southern Spain.

Achillea millefolium
(Asteraceae) Milfoil, Yarrow

ORIGIN EUROPE, ASIA MINOR
HEIGHT OF FOLIAGE 10 TO 15 CM
HEIGHT IN FLOWER 60 CM
SPREAD 50 CM OR MORE
POSITION SUN OR SEMI-SHADE
HARDINESS −15 °C AND BELOW
DROUGHT RESISTANCE CODE 2.5

The genus *Achillea* is named for the Greek hero Achilles. In the *Iliad* Achilles heals the warriors' wounds by applying dressings containing *Achillea millefolium*, having learnt the virtues of this plant while studying herbs with his teacher, the centaur Chiron. We find references to the antiseptic and wound-healing properties of *Achillea millefolium* in the different names by which it has been known over the centuries. In Roman times it was called *herba militaris*, and sanguinary and yarrow in England during the Middle Ages, since it was used to help the formation of scar tissue on arrow wounds. It is a perennial with dark-green evergreen leaves finely cut into very many leaflets, hence its other common name, milfoil (=a thousand leaves). The stock spreads by rhizomes and forms a dense groundcover which can be used as a lawn alternative for areas that are not walked on too much. The flowers, white or sometimes pinkish, are borne in long spikes in June–July. *Achillea millefolium* tolerates alkaline conditions well and adapts easily to all types of soil, even clay. It can cope with competition from tree roots, which makes it a good groundcover near trees. If used as a lawn alternative, it should be mown two or three times in spring and early summer to keep it as a carpet close to the ground.

Propagation is by seed at the beginning of summer or in spring. It can be sown in situ or in pots for pricking out later.

• ***Achillea clypeolata*** has long silver leaves which become almost white in summer. The luminous yellow flowers, borne on strong flowering spikes from May to July, spread in broad convex corymbs, or plates (the name *clypeolata* comes from the Latin *clypeus*, the name of a round shield used by

A dry garden in early summer. In the foreground *Achillea clypeolata* shows off its flat plates of yellow flowers in front of a row of *Lavandula* × *intermedia* 'Grosso'.

the Romans). **ORIGIN** BALKANS **HARDINESS** −15 °C AND BELOW **DROUGHT RESISTANCE CODE** 3.5

• *Achillea coarctata* grows rapidly into a spreading groundcover thanks to its strong rhizomes. The finely cut silver-grey leaves are closely crowded together (the name *coarctata* comes from the Latin *coarto*, 'gather' or 'compress'). The bright yellow flowers are abundant in May–June and recur in autumn. **ORIGIN** BALKANS **HARDINESS** −15 °C AND BELOW **DROUGHT RESISTANCE CODE** 3

• *Achillea crithmifolia* has pretty grey-green evergreen leaves that are finely cut. It forms an excellent groundcover which can be used as a lawn alternative for areas that are not walked on too much. The creamy-white flowers are not very abundant, and this allows the plant to stay low and dense even when it is not mowed. We like to combine it with *Phyla nodiflora* for a lawn that looks good all year round: the *Phyla* predominates when the *Achillea* is partially dormant in summer, while the handsome winter foliage of the *Achillea crithmifolia* hides the bare stems of the *Phyla* when it loses its leaves in winter. **ORIGIN** MOUNTAINOUS REGIONS IN THE BALKANS **HARDINESS** −15 °C AND BELOW **DROUGHT RESISTANCE CODE** 2.5

• *Achillea nobilis* spreads rapidly thanks to its long rhizomes, and forms a vigorous groundcover with a tendency to become invasive. In our garden, the little pot we originally planted has spread the length of a path that is more than 10 m long. The soft creamy-yellow flowers are remarkably abundant in May–June, after which the plant becomes partially dormant during the summer period. It can be used to colonize wild spaces at the end of the garden or can be planted on slopes to combat erosion. **ORIGIN** SOUTHERN EUROPE **HARDINESS** −15 °C AND BELOW **DROUGHT RESISTANCE CODE** 3

• *Achillea umbellata* has small, finely cut silver leaves. The plant forms a carpeting cushion that is very decorative in rock gardens, as edging or between paving stones. The abundant umbels of pure white flowers are borne on short flowering spikes

in April–May. **ORIGIN** MOUNTAINS OF CENTRAL AND SOUTHERN GREECE **HARDINESS** −15 °C AND BELOW **DROUGHT RESISTANCE CODE** 4

Agapanthus praecox
(Alliaceae)

ORIGIN SOUTH AFRICA (THE EASTERN CAPE PROVINCE)
HEIGHT OF FOLIAGE 30 TO 40 CM
HEIGHT IN FLOWER 60 TO 80 CM
SPREAD 30 TO 40 CM
POSITION SUN OR SEMI-SHADE
HARDINESS THE FOLIAGE IS SCORCHED BY TEMPERATURES LOWER THAN −6 °C BUT THE ROOTSTOCK RESPROUTS AFTER SHORT PERIODS OF −10 OR −12 °C
DROUGHT RESISTANCE CODE 3.5

This plant's name comes from the Greek *agapein*, 'to love', and *anthos*, 'flower'. Why was it named Love Flower? Could it be from the ancient Xhosa tradition in South Africa, according to which young brides wore long necklaces made of agapanthus roots to ensure the health of their future children? *Agapanthus praecox* is a fleshy-rooted perennial that forms clumps which spread slowly by means of rhizomes. Its long strap-shaped green leaves are thick and evergreen. Its blue flowers, arranged in very decorative spherical umbels, are borne on long stems in July. The agapanthus tolerates alkaline conditions well. It prefers a deep, friable, well-drained soil. There is much confusion in the horticultural world surrounding the nomenclature of agapanthuses, so that even botanists often have different views on the number of species that exist in South Africa. According to the most recent publication (Snoeijer 2004), the classic garden agapanthuses,

usually called *Agapanthus africanus* or *Agapanthus umbellatus*, are in fact all cultivars of *Agapanthus praecox* – *Agapanthus africanus* being a distinct, small-growing species that is not cultivated in gardens because it flowers very little there: its flowering in the fynbos is triggered by fire.

Propagation is by division in late summer or by fresh seed: seed collected in gardens in the northern hemisphere should be sown in autumn, while fresh seed received directly from South Africa should be sown in spring. Natural hybrids occur if seed is collected from a garden where several different agapanthuses are growing.

• *Agapanthus praecox* 'Albidus' has white flowers.

• *Agapanthus campanulatus* is a deciduous species with large blue flowers. It prefers shade or semi-shade. **HEIGHT IN FLOWER** 1 M **HARDINESS** −12 TO −15 °C FOR SHORT PERIODS **DROUGHT RESISTANCE CODE** 2

• *Agapanthus caulescens* subsp. *angustifolius* has deciduous leaves and beautiful dark-blue flowers. **HEIGHT IN FLOWER** 1 M **HARDINESS** −12 TO −15 °C FOR SHORT PERIODS **DROUGHT RESISTANCE CODE** 2

• *Agapanthus* 'Purple Cloud' is a hybrid, probably of *Agapanthus praecox* and *Agapanthus inapertus*. The leaves are evergreen and the remarkable dark violet-blue large flowers are borne on long stems. **HEIGHT IN FLOWER** 1 M TO 1.5 M **HARDINESS** −12 TO −15 °C FOR SHORT PERIODS **DROUGHT RESISTANCE CODE** 3

Agave americana
(Agavaceae) Century Plant

ORIGIN MEXICO
HEIGHT OF FOLIAGE 1.5 M
HEIGHT OF FLOWER SPIKE 5 TO 10 M
SPREAD 1.5 M, BUT IT SPREADS BY OFFSETS IN ALL DIRECTIONS
POSITION SUN
HARDINESS ABOUT −10 °C
DROUGHT RESISTANCE CODE 6

The brilliant yellow flowers of *Achillea coarctata* are wonderfully set off by the softness of its silver foliage.

Achillea nobilis forms a carpet beneath *Genista aetnensis*, with supple branches weighed down by scented flowers.

In July graceful umbels of *Agapanthus praecox* 'Albidus' rise above the green foliage.

The agave's name may come from the Greek *agauos*, 'glorious' or 'noble', because of the plant's beauty. According to another interpretation, it derives from Agave, an aunt of Dionysos, who performed the orgiastic rites of the maenads in the hills above Thebes and, as described in the *Bacchae* of Euripides, killed her own son in a frenzy – an allusion perhaps to the effects of the alcoholic drinks obtained from mescal, the fermented juice of the agave.

Agave americana has an imposing silhouette, with its great rosettes of grey-blue leaves. The sharp points at the tips of these leaves are dangerous: avoid planting agaves where people pass and in gardens where there are children. The majestic floral spike appears after 15 to 20 years and signals the death of the mother plant, but the abundant offsets that the plant has produced all round it grow rapidly in its place. *Agave americana* tolerates alkaline conditions well and prefers poor, well-drained soils. In the hot regions around the Mediterranean the agave can naturalize and become invasive.

Propagation is by offsets at the end of winter.

Ajania pacifica
(Asteraceae)

ORIGIN CENTRAL AND EAST ASIA
HEIGHT 30 CM
SPREAD 50 CM
POSITION SUN
HARDINESS −15 °C AND BELOW
DROUGHT RESISTANCE CODE 2.5

This perennial has been happy for several years in one of the least hospitable areas of

The flowers of *Ajania pacifica* are very welcome at the beginning of November, since not much else is flowering.

our garden. The plant spreads slowly by stolons to form a pretty, regular-shaped cushion. Its semi-evergreen velvety grey leaves have a narrow silver border. The fairly discreet yellow flowers open into a profusion of little cushions in October to November, a season when most flowering in the garden is over. *Ajania pacifica* tolerates alkaline conditions well. It is a plant that is easy to grow, undemanding as to soil type and long-lived. As the stems have a woody base that is bare in winter, they can be cut to the ground in February or thereabouts to encourage new growth, so you can enjoy the elegance of the fresh foliage in spring.

Propagation is by division in autumn or by softwood cuttings in spring.

Akebia quinata
(Lardizabalaceae) Chocolate Vine

ORIGIN CHINA, JAPAN, KOREA
HEIGHT AND SPREAD 10 M
POSITION SUN OR SEMI-SHADE
HARDINESS −12 TO −15 °C
DROUGHT RESISTANCE CODE 3

A climbing plant with twining stems and attractive tough leaves, divided into five leaflets, that are deciduous or semi-evergreen. The bunches of small, brownish-violet-coloured flowers appear in April–May and are pleasantly scented (with a hint of white chocolate); they include separate male and female flowers. The curious and edible egg-shaped fruits are only produced if the female flowers are pollinated by male flowers of another variety of *Akebia*, for example *Akebia quinata* 'Alba'. These fruits have many uses in Chinese medicine and are supposed to have the interesting property of being able to calm hypochondriacs. *Akebia* is an easily grown and very vigorous climber that can be used to cover large pergolas. It tolerates alkaline conditions well and prefers deep, friable soils.

Propagation is by softwood cuttings in spring.

• *Akebia quinata* **'Alba'** is a form with pale pink or cream flowers, which can be used to pollinate *Akebia quinata* for fruit production.

Alcea rosea
(Malvaceae) Hollyhock

ORIGIN ASIA MINOR
HEIGHT IN FLOWER 1.5 TO 2 M
SPREAD 40 TO 50 CM
POSITION SUN
HARDINESS −15 °C AND BELOW
DROUGHT RESISTANCE CODE 3

The hollyhock evokes all the charm of old gardens. It self-seeds abundantly in warm

Alcea rosea, the hollyhock, self-seeds freely in poor soils at the foot of stone walls.

sunny positions, often at the foot of old walls, as it likes poor and stony soils. Though often considered to be a biennial, in the South of France it usually behaves as a perennial. In winter its large round leaves form a rosette close to the ground. In spring the plant grows rapidly taller, all its energy being devoted to the production of the strong flower spike which in good conditions may reach a height of 2 metres. The large, veined, cup-shaped flowers range in colour from white to pink, mauve or yellow according to the variety. The hollyhock tolerates alkaline conditions well. At the end of the season the leaves become spotted with rust, but at this point you can cut the plant down, remembering to save seed to scatter elsewhere in the garden.

Propagate by seed, sown in situ *in autumn or in pots in spring. Varieties of hollyhock interbreed easily and different colours may grow from seed.*

Aloe striatula
(Aloaceae)

ORIGIN SOUTH AFRICA (KAROO) AND THE MOUNTAINS OF LESOTHO, TO AN ALTITUDE OF 2,000 M
HEIGHT 1.5 M
SPREAD 2 M OR MORE
POSITION SUN
HARDNESS −10 TO −12 °C
DROUGHT RESISTANCE CODE 5

This is the shrubby aloe that is most resistant to cold. It forms a large shrub with a floppy growth habit, its thick branches

Aloe striatula is the hardiest of the shrubby aloes. Its thick waxy leaves limit water loss, so the plant has an excellent resistance to drought.

sprawling over the ground to a greater or lesser extent. The long, fleshy, evergreen leaves are striated with fine parallel marks, hence the name *striatula*. The orange-yellow flowers on long spikes appear in May–June. *Aloe striatula* tolerates alkaline conditions well; it prefers light, well-drained soils. If pruned every year at the end of winter it has a regular dome shape, which is very decorative when the plant is covered in flowers.

Propagation is by stem section cuttings in autumn or spring. The cuttings can be dried out for a few days to allow them to scar over before being planted in pots or directly in the ground.

There are a great many other *Aloe* species that are of interest for dry gardens in mild climates. To discover more about this genus, I recommend the recently reissued and excellent guide, *Aloes of South Africa* (see Further Reading). Brigitte and Jo Issa have a fine collection of aloes in their nursery specializing in plants from the southern hemisphere (see appendix Useful Addresses).

Aloysia virgata
(Verbenaceae)

ORIGIN ARGENTINA
HEIGHT 4 TO 5 M
SPREAD 2 M
POSITION SUN
HARDNESS −8 TO −10 °C
DROUGHT RESISTANCE CODE 4

Sometimes one has pleasant surprises. We came across *Aloysia virgata* in Lindsay Blyth's garden in Andalucia and she kindly gave us a few cuttings. As so often when gardeners discover a new plant which seems too good to be true, we told ourselves that it probably wouldn't do well in our garden. Yet it has adapted extremely well to our cold and dry conditions. It is an upright shrub with deciduous or semi-evergreen leaves, whose flexible young branches have a slightly weeping habit. The strongly scented white flowers form spikes at the tips of the branches from April to July. Their delicious almond fragrance can perfume an entire area of the garden on warm evenings. *Aloysia virgata* tolerates alkaline conditions well. It prefers fairly deep and well-drained friable soils. It can be reshaped every year at the end of winter to maintain a dense habit.

Propagation is by softwood cuttings in spring.

• *Aloysia triphylla* is lemon verbena, rather greedy for water, but worth a place in all vegetable gardens. The leaves should be harvested before the first frosts to make pleasant tisanes all winter long. **ORIGIN** CHILE,

To resist drought better, Anagyris foetida operates a reverse-season rhythm. It starts into green in autumn, its flowers open in the middle of winter and it loses its leaves at the end of spring as the plant becomes dormant to get through the summer heat.

ARGENTINA **HARDINESS** −8 TO −10 °C (THE FOLIAGE IS BURNT BY THE COLD AT TEMPERATURES BELOW −2 TO −4 °C BUT THE PLANT GROWS AGAIN FROM THE ROOTSTOCK IN SPRING) **DROUGHT RESISTANCE CODE** 2

Anagyris foetida
(Fabaceae) Stinking Bean Trefoil

ORIGIN MEDITERRANEAN BASIN
HEIGHT 2 M
SPREAD 1 M
POSITION SUN
HARDNESS −10 TO −12 °C
DROUGHT RESISTANCE CODE 5

Anagyris is often described as stinking because it gives off a strong smell if you scratch the bark or break off a branch – but don't be put off, if you leave the plant in peace it has no odour. It is a large shrub with light-green leaves and illustrates one of the best drought-resisting strategies of mediterranean plants: it keeps its leaves in autumn, winter and spring when it needs them for photosynthesis, then loses them entirely in summer and becomes dormant, so that it is indifferent to the drought. In summer this shrub has a surprising bareness: it is as entirely deciduous as a tree would be in winter in a temperate climate. Its pretty greenish-yellow flowers appear in the middle of winter, forming tight clusters in the leaf axils from January to April. In our garden we have copied an interesting natural plant association that we saw in the Atlas mountains on the road to Tizi n Test – *Anagyris foetida* growing side by side with a dark violet-blue flowered *Teucrium fruticans*: the two plants flower at the same time of year and make a handsome contrast. *Anagyris foetida* tolerates alkaline conditions well and adapts easily to all soil types. It is a robust plant, easily grown.

Propagation is by seed in autumn. The seeds should be prepared before sowing by boiling them for 10 to 15 seconds then leaving them to swell in the water for 24 hours. The seeds are poisonous.

Anisodontea malvastroides
(Malvaceae)

ORIGIN SOUTH AFRICA, CAPE PROVINCE
HEIGHT 2 M
SPREAD 2 M
POSITION SUN
HARDINESS −8 TO −10 °C
DROUGHT RESISTANCE CODE 3

A fast-growing shrub with a sprawling habit, its small evergreen leaves are irregularly toothed and lobed and resemble a miniature fig leaf (the name *Anisodontea* comes from the Greek *anisos*, 'unequal', and *odous,* genitive *odontos,* 'tooth'). It flowers very abundantly throughout its growth period, with a flower in each leaf axil. In a mild climate it grows and flowers all year, but in our garden it flowers most in spring with a repeat show in the autumn: it is partially dormant in summer because of drought and in winter because of cold. The delicate flowers are shaped like a flared cup, and the base of each pale pink petal is marked with attractive dark veining. *Anisodontea malvastroides* tolerates alkaline conditions well and is unfussy about soil type. You can prune it annually at the end of winter, shortening the stems by about one third, in order to prevent the plant from becoming leggy as it ages.

Propagation is by softwood cuttings in autumn or spring.

The glowing veins of *Anisodontea malvastroides* guide pollinating insects towards the base of the petals, where they can find beads of nectar.

• *Anisodontea capensis* is the classic garden *Anisodontea* since it is suitable for growing in pots to decorate patios and terraces. The abundant flowers, like little pink cups, are produced throughout the year in mild climates. ORIGIN SOUTH AFRICA HARDINESS −4 TO −6 °C DROUGHT RESISTANCE CODE 2

Anthyllis cytisoides
(Fabaceae)

ORIGIN SPAIN
HEIGHT 60 CM
SPREAD 60 CM
POSITION SUN
HARDINESS −10 TO −12 °C
DROUGHT RESISTANCE CODE 5

A sub-shrub with evergreen grey leaves and striking silvery-white stems. From April to June the plant is covered in small pale yellow flowers. At the new botanic garden in Barcelona *Anthyllis cytisoides* is planted in the middle of large masses of *Lavandula*

Anthyllis cytisoides and Lavandula dentata self-seed freely in a large, wild border in the new Barcelona botanic garden.

dentata, forming a very attractive combination. In spring their pale yellow and pale mauve colours marry to perfection. *Anthyllis cytisoides* tolerates alkaline conditions well. It prefers dry, stony, well-drained soils. The plant self-seeds easily in poor soils: it can be seen colonizing roadsides, slopes and wasteland throughout southern Spain.

Propagation is by seed in autumn after treating the seeds with hot water: place the seeds in boiling water and leave them overnight to swell.

Antirrhinum barrelieri
(Scrophulariaceae) Snapdragon

ORIGIN SPAIN, SOUTHERN PORTUGAL
HEIGHT OF FOLIAGE 20 TO 30 CM
HEIGHT IN FLOWER 1 M TO 1.2 M
SPREAD 60 CM
POSITION SUN
HARDINESS −10 TO −12 °C
DROUGHT RESISTANCE CODE 5

Near Ronda in southern Spain, *Antirrhinum barrelieri* colonizes the ground at the base of the cliffs.

An upright perennial with narrow evergreen leaves that take on attractive red tints in winter. The large pale pink flower spikes are produced continuously from March to July. If you squeeze the sides of the flower it snaps open like a mouth – hence the common name 'snapdragon' – a perfect way to amuse children in the garden. (The name *Antirrhinum* comes from the Greek *anti*, 'opposite', 'instead of', and *rhis*, genitive *rhinos*, 'nose' or 'snout', referring to the shape of the flower.) *Antirrhinum barrelieri* tolerates alkaline conditions well and is particularly happy in poor, stony soils where it self-seeds freely. If the faded flowers are removed, the plant will flower again abundantly in autumn.

Propagation is by seed or by softwood cuttings in spring.

• *Antirrhinum glutinosum* forms a downy, silvery, carpeting cushion. In May–June the large white flowers, delicately veined in pink, hide the leaves completely. This very decorative little rock garden plant grows

The gentle face of *Antirrhinum glutinosum* is transformed into a snapping dragon when the flower is pinched between two fingers.

In the Corbières massif, not far from the Cathar castles, *Antirrhinum majus* grows on a rock ridge, keeping watch over the landscape like a sentinel.

slowly. It requires a light soil with perfect drainage, otherwise its crown may rot with the autumn and winter rains. **ORIGIN** SPAIN **HARDINESS** −8 TO −10 °C **DROUGHT RESISTANCE CODE** 3.5

• *Antirrhinum majus* is the snapdragon with pinkish-mauve flowers that is common in the South of France. It can be grown in association with *Centranthus angustifolius* to colonize stony parts of the garden. **ORIGIN** SOUTH OF FRANCE, IBERIAN PENINSULA **HARDINESS** −12 TO −15 °C **DROUGHT RESISTANCE CODE** 4

• *Antirrhinum hispanicum* is a small, easily grown perennial, covered in pale pink flowers with a yellow throat in April–May. **ORIGIN** SOUTHERN SPAIN (IT HAS COLONIZED THE SCREES ALL ROUND GRANADA) **HARDINESS** −10 TO −12 °C **DROUGHT RESISTANCE CODE** 5

Arbutus unedo

(Ericaceae) Arbutus, Strawberry Tree

ORIGIN SOUTHERN EUROPE
HEIGHT 5 M OR MORE
SPREAD 2 TO 3 M
POSITION SUN OR SEMI-SHADE
HARDINESS −12 TO −15 °C
DROUGHT RESISTANCE CODE 4

The arbutus is a small, slow-growing tree, often used in gardens as a shrub. It can be planted as a single specimen or mixed with other shrubs to create an evergreen background in tall, free-growing hedges. Its dark green, evergreen leaves are leathery and

Every year in spring the red bark of *Arbutus* × *thuretiana* peels off to make way for new bark that is a bright pistachio-green and as soft and smooth as new skin.

glossy. It makes a particularly attractive sight in autumn, when it is covered in small, white, bell-shaped flowers at the same time that its red fruits are ripening, a year after flowering. The fruits are edible, although their rough texture is not very pleasant: generally, in spite of their tempting colour, which is reminiscent of ripe strawberries, people rarely eat more than one (the name *unedo* comes from the Latin *unum edo*, 'I eat just one'). Although *Arbutus unedo* grows wild in neutral or acid soils, it acclimatizes well to the garden even if the soil is alkaline, provided that it has perfect drainage.

Propagate the species by fresh seed. The cultivars of Arbutus unedo *and the various hybrids are propagated by semi-ripe cuttings in autumn, but rooting can be slow. Air layering also produces good results.*

• *Arbutus unedo* var. *rubra* has pretty pink flowers and a dense growth habit: in our garden it is one of the best autumn-flowering shrubs. The flowers are slightly darker in shade.

• *Arbutus andrachne* is a tree with fine, smooth, orange-red bark. The young shoots take on a bronze colour in winter. In nature it grows in alkaline soils, unlike *Arbutus unedo*. **ORIGIN** EASTERN MEDITERRANEAN **HARDINESS** −10 TO −12 °C **DROUGHT RESISTANCE CODE** 5

Propagation is by fresh seed collected in the wild (seed of Arbutus andrachne *collected in gardens usually results in hybrids).*

• *Arbutus* × *andrachnoides* is the hybrid of *Arbutus unedo* and *Arbutus andrachne*. When young it has the dark bark of *Arbutus unedo*, but as it ages its bark peels to reveal the fine orange-red bark of *Arbutus andrachne*. There are many clones of *Arbutus* × *andrachnoides* which resemble more or less closely one or other of the parents.

• *Arbutus* × *thuretiana* is the hybrid of *Arbutus canariensis* and *Arbutus andrachne*. Its remarkable red bark, as smooth as skin, cracks at the end of spring and then peels off, revealing new bark of an amazing pistachio-green colour which gradually darkens until it is red again: a wonderful effect much sought after by gardeners. **HARDINESS** −10 TO −12 °C **DROUGHT RESISTANCE CODE** 4

Artemisia

(Asteraceae) Wormwood

The genus *Artemisia* is named after Artemis, the goddess of hunting, nature and fertility in Greek mythology. Having seen her mother Leto suffer as she gave birth to

The silky hairs that cover the finely cut leaves of *Artemisia arborescens* enable it to trap the night dew.

Apollo (Artemis and Apollo were twins), Artemis then assisted women in difficult childbirths, giving them wormwood, a plant with many medicinal properties. Artemis was also the goddess of the moon, and one of her functions was to refresh plants with nocturnal dew in summer when Zeus slept too long on Mount Olympus and forgot to send his beneficial storms: the silver hairs which make the foliage of artemisias so beautiful are perfect for trapping dew at night.

Artemisia alba

ORIGIN MOUNTAINS OF SOUTHERN EUROPE
HEIGHT 50 CM
SPREAD 80 CM
POSITION SUN
HARDINESS −15 °C AND BELOW
DROUGHT RESISTANCE CODE 3.5

A woody perennial with pretty, semi-evergreen and finely cut grey-green leaves which give off an agreeable smell of camphor. Its numerous small greyish-yellow flowers form a light mass that smothers the plant in summer. It can be lightly clipped in autumn to accentuate its natural growth habit – a large, ground-covering cushion. *Artemisia alba* tolerates alkaline conditions well and adapts easily to all soil types, even clay. It is a robust plant, easy to grow and long-lived, and of proven value in the mediterranean garden.

Propagation is by softwood cuttings in spring.

Artemisia arborescens

ORIGIN MEDITERRANEAN BASIN
HEIGHT 1.25 TO 1.5 M
SPREAD 1 TO 1.25 M
POSITION SUN
HARDINESS −6 TO −8 °C
DROUGHT RESISTANCE CODE 4

A shrub with evergreen, silvery, finely cut leaves that are very aromatic. The plant grows fast and forms a large rounded mass. It is not very long-lived – after about ten years it is probably time to replace it – but as it is easily propagated and grows fast we can forgive it for its short lifespan. Regular pruning every year in autumn helps to maintain a more compact shape and prolongs its life. It grows well from the base if it has to be cut down to the ground for any reason: in our garden this often happens when the aerial parts of the plant suffer from frost in a hard winter. *Artemisia arborescens* tolerates alkaline conditions well. It prefers poor stony soils with perfect drainage.

Propagation is by softwood cuttings in autumn or spring.

• *Artemisia arborescens* **'Carcassonne'** is useful because of its better resistance to cold. Plants sometimes have strange origins: this cultivar appeared from seed in the old open-air rubbish dump of the town of Carcassonne. It survived the extremely cold winter of 1985, which is why we selected it. Of rounded and compact habit, it does not exceed 1 m in height, and is one of the best silver-leaved shrubs in our garden.
HARDINESS −10 TO −12 °C

• *Artemisia arborescens* **'Porquerolles'** is a dwarf cultivar that forms a small, very regular ball shape about 60 cm across. Unfortunately it is less drought-resistant and in our garden always suffers in summer. In an oceanic climate it forms remarkable silver topiary, unique of its kind. **DROUGHT RESISTANCE CODE** 2.5

Artemisia canariensis

ORIGIN CANARY ISLANDS
HEIGHT 80 CM
SPREAD 80 CM
POSITION SUN
HARDINESS −8 TO −10 °C
DROUGHT RESISTANCE CODE 4

A shrub with handsome, divided, evergreen leaves that are highly aromatic. Silver in winter, they become almost white in summer. The plant grows fast and forms a very decorative regular ball-shape. Because of the great luminosity of its silver foliage, it is one of the best plants to use in the garden to create a contrast with dark-leaved sclerophyllous shrubs. The numerous small pale yellow flowers appear from April to July. Although it originates from volcanic soils, *Artemisia canariensis* tolerates alkaline conditions well. It adapts to the garden easily, no matter what the type of soil. Another pleasant surprise is that, in spite of its Canary Island origin, this plant is fairly hardy. If desired, a light pruning in autumn can be carried out to accentuate its natural ball shape.

Propagation is by softwood cuttings in spring.

Artemisia lanata

ORIGIN MOUNTAINS OF SOUTHERN EUROPE
HEIGHT OF FOLIAGE 5 CM
HEIGHT IN FLOWER 15 TO 20 CM
SPREAD 30 TO 40 CM
SITUATION SUN
HARDINESS −15 °C AND BELOW
DROUGHT RESISTANCE CODE 3

This plant has several different names, depending on the author consulted: *Artemisia assoana, Artemisia campestris* subsp. *borealis, Artemisia caucasica, Artemisia nana, Artemisia pedemontana* or *Artemisia lanata*. I'm not certain that *Artemisia lanata* is the correct name, but it describes the soft look of this plant very well. It is a pretty, carpeting perennial with silky, finely cut silver foliage. The stems put down roots wherever they come in contact with the soil, which enables the plant to spread progressively wider until it forms a dense groundcover. It can be used in various ways in the garden – as a silver edging along a path, in the cracks between paving stones, as a carpet through which bulbs and small perennials may emerge, or even as an original lawn alternative for small areas that are rarely walked on. The flowers are attractive, which is not always the case with artemisias: a multitude of tiny silver heads on short flowering spikes catch the light in May–June. If the spent flowers are removed, the foliage will remain denser in summer.

Propagation is by division in autumn or by softwood cuttings in spring, just before flowering.

Artemisia ludoviciana 'Silver Queen'

ORIGIN NORTH AMERICA
HEIGHT IN FLOWER 50 CM (OR MORE IF THE SOIL IS COOL)
SPREAD 80 CM AND MORE
POSITION SUN
HARDINESS −15 °C AND BELOW
DROUGHT RESISTANCE CODE 3

A perennial with handsome, long, narrow, deciduous, silver foliage (the cultivar 'Valerie Finnis', which closely resembles it, can be distinguished by its irregularly toothed leaves). With its vigorous rhizomes, the plant develops into a wide-spreading groundcover. It is especially beautiful in spring when the buds pierce through the soil and form a carpet of silvery young shoots that are extremely luminous. The stems grow taller in summer and bear long spikes of yellowish-grey flowers, which are not themselves of major interest. *Artemisia ludoviciana* tolerates alkaline conditions well. It is unfussy about soil type and is an easily grown, long-lived plant. It is often used beneath spring-flowering shrubs, which it sets off with its fine foliage. In autumn the plant can be cut back to ground level.

Propagation is by division at the end of winter or by softwood cuttings in spring, before flowering.

The luminous young shoots of *Artemisia ludoviciana* 'Silver Queen' spread beneath the opulent mass of *Euphorbia cyparissias* 'Tall Boy'.

The fine heads of *Artemisia lanata* catch the light. In winter the silky foliage of this artemisia makes a magnificent silver carpet.

There are many other species of artemisia, interesting for the diversity of their silver foliage. Often gardeners only know 'Powis Castle', which, however, is one of the least well adapted since it is very short-lived in mediterranean conditions. Here is a selection of further species that do well in our garden:

• *Artemisia absinthum:* this is absinthe, with a strong bitter smell, that inspired painters and poets in the 19th century. It's a useful plant in a natural garden as it attracts aphids very early in the season, which in turn attract natural predators, thus contributing to the protection of other plants. We place it not far from the vegetable garden so that it can benefit from the irrigation this receives in summer – drought resistance is not its strong point. **ORIGINS** MOUNTAINS OF EUROPE, NORTH AFRICA AND ASIA **HARDINESS** −15 °C AND BELOW **DROUGHT RESISTANCE CODE** 2

• *Artemisia caerulescens* subsp. *gallica* is a small rhizomatous perennial which appears spontaneously on the coast very near our garden. We allow it to colonize the edges of the paths in our nursery freely. Its grey, semi-evergreen, finely cut leaves have a surprising smell, like a mixture of camphor and ripe bananas. **ORIGIN** SOUTH OF FRANCE **HARDINESS** −10 TO −12 °C **DROUGHT RESISTANCE CODE** 4

• *Artemisia cana* is a shrub with a very powerful, almost violent, scent for those who enjoy extreme experiences. **ORIGIN** WESTERN UNITED STATES **HARDINESS** −12 TO −15 °C **DROUGHT RESISTANCE CODE** 4

• *Artemisia* 'Canescens' forms an attractive low-growing groundcover. The silver foliage, with a curly appearance, takes on an amazing violet hue in winter. Botanists are not in agreement as to the origins of this plant. **HARDINESS** −15 °C AND BELOW **DROUGHT RESISTANCE CODE** 3

• *Artemisia cretacea* has a strong scent, reminiscent of olive oil. The deciduous silver-grey leaves disappear beneath a mass of yellowish-grey flowers in summer. **ORIGIN** MOUNTAINS OF ITALY **HARDINESS** −15 °C AND BELOW **DROUGHT RESISTANCE CODE** 4

• *Artemisia dracunculus* var. *sativa* is tarragon, with deliciously aromatic leaves. I enjoy cooking as much as I enjoy gardening and if I were allowed to have just one herb for the kitchen in our garden, I think it would be this! **ORIGIN** WIDE DISTRIBUTION IN THE NORTHERN HEMISPHERE **HARDINESS** −15 °C AND BELOW **DROUGHT RESISTANCE CODE** 2.5

• *Artemisia herba-alba*, with its extraordinary scent, is well known to all those who love North Africa. In spite of

Artemisia pontica makes a good groundcover, threading its way down through stones by means of its rhizomes.

intensive grazing, it survives in the semi-desert zones of the Atlas and Anti-Atlas mountains. When no mint is available, this is one of the plants used to flavour tea and is also among the herbs that flavour the famous snail broth, possessed of innumerable medicinal virtues, eaten at nightfall on Jemaa-el-Fna Square in Marrakech. This artemisia is sometimes classed in the genus *Seriphidium*. **ORIGIN** STEPPE PLAINS OF THE MAGHREB **HARDINESS** −12 TO −15 °C **DROUGHT RESISTANCE CODE** 6

• *Artemisia maritima* is a rhizomatous perennial with white and very aromatic semi-evergreen leaves finely cut into narrow ribbons. Santonina, an extract with vermifuge and anti-parasite properties, derives its name from semen-contra, i.e. 'seed against [worms]', imported from Asia. In fact these are not seeds, but the tiny flower buds of various artemisias including *Artemisia maritima*. **ORIGIN** SALINE STEPPES OF ASIA **HARDINESS** −15 °C AND BELOW **DROUGHT RESISTANCE CODE** 4

• *Artemisia pontica*, the little absinthe, is a rhizomatous perennial which grows into an attractive carpeting groundcover. The grey, finely cut, deciduous leaves are aromatic. Pliny the Elder praised it in his *Natural History* for its numerous medicinal properties. **ORIGIN** MOUNTAINS OF SOUTHERN EUROPE **HARDINESS** −15 °C AND BELOW **DROUGHT RESISTANCE CODE** 2.5

• *Artemisia tridentata* covers wide steppe-like spaces in New Mexico, colouring the plateaux surrounding the deep cleft of the Rio Grande an amazing shade of grey-blue. *Artemisia tridentata* is a strongly scented evergreen shrub whose leaves were traditionally used by Native Americans as an antiseptic. **ORIGIN** HIGH ALTITUDE DESERTS IN THE SOUTHWESTERN UNITED STATES **HARDINESS** −15 °C AND BELOW **DROUGHT RESISTANCE CODE** 6

• *Artemisia vallesiaca* forms a mist of semi-evergreen, aromatic, silver leaves as finely cut as lace. This rhizomatous perennial is well suited to covering the ground beneath deciduous shrubs. **ORIGIN** SOUTHERN ALPS

Asphodeline lutea likes poor, well-drained soil. Together with *Euphorbia acanthothamnos* it seeds itself in the screes below one of the last remaining natural cypress forests in Crete.

HARDINESS −15 °C AND BELOW **DROUGHT RESISTANCE CODE** 3

Asphodeline lutea
(Asphodelaceae) Jacob's Rod

ORIGIN MEDITERRANEAN BASIN
HEIGHT OF FOLIAGE 20 CM
HEIGHT IN FLOWER 60 CM OR MORE
SPREAD 30 CM
POSITION SUN
HARDINESS −12 TO −15 °C
DROUGHT RESISTANCE CODE 5

A perennial with tuberous rhizomes and numerous thin, linear leaves which form a regular rosette. The leaves are evergreen in winter and deciduous in summer, after the plant has finished flowering. The beautiful

The ephemeral flowers of *Asphodeline lutea* open in the morning and wither in the evening, but numerous other buds are lined up along the flowering stem, patiently waiting their turn.

bright yellow flowers appear on a stiff spike in May–June. This asphodel is common in the mountains of southwest Crete, where it can be seen growing with *Ballota pseudodictamnus*, *Sarcopoterium spinosum* and *Thymus capitatus* in a beautiful landscape like a natural garden. *Asphodeline lutea* tolerates alkaline conditions well, and likes poor, well-drained soil.

Propagation is by seed in spring.

• ***Asphodeline liburnica*** self-seeds freely in the driest parts of the garden. It flowers later (June–July) and we like to associate it with *Salvia chamaedryoides*, *Perovskia atriplicifolia* or *Lavandula* × *intermedia* to create beautiful patches of yellow and blue in early summer. **ORIGIN** GREECE **HARDINESS** −12 TO −15 °C **DROUGHT RESISTANCE CODE** 5

Asphodelus microcarpus
(Asphodelaceae) Asphodel

ORIGIN MEDITERRANEAN BASIN
HEIGHT OF FOLIAGE 30 CM
HEIGHT IN FLOWER 80 CM TO 1 M
SPREAD 50 CM
POSITION SUN
HARDINESS −12 TO −15 °C
DROUGHT RESISTANCE CODE 5

Asphodels have long been associated with death: according to popular belief, they served as food for the dead, who gnawed at their fleshy roots from below. In the

Asphodelus microcarpus colonizes areas that have been degraded by the repeated assaults of fire and over-grazing. The asphodel's fleshy roots store water and nutrients, thus enabling it to survive in summer when it becomes dormant to withstand drought.

Asphodelus fistulosus is a pioneer plant which colonizes uncultivated land and roadsides.

Odyssey, when Odysseus descends into the underworld to collect the prophecy of Tiresias, he sees the shades of the dead slowly wandering through a field of asphodels. Vast expanses covered with asphodels are a common sight around the Mediterranean, in landscapes degraded by the repeated grazing of sheep and goats. Asphodels are indeed able to resist all assaults on them and they colonize any free space, replacing species that have been wiped out by over-grazing or fire. *Asphodelus microcarpus*, one of the most decorative species of the genus, is a robust perennial with tuberous roots. Its large, grey-blue leaves are evergreen in winter and deciduous in summer, after flowering, when the plant becomes dormant to withstand drought. The pretty white flowers are star-shaped, their petals delicately veined with green. They are borne on strong branching spikes, which give the plant a striking architectural silhouette during its flowering season, from April to June. *Asphodelus microcarpus* tolerates alkaline conditions well and withstands salt spray. It likes poor, well-drained soil.

Propagation is by seed, preferably in autumn. Seed sown in spring germinates well, but the seedlings can rot when they rapidly lose their first leaves at the beginning of summer.

• ***Asphodelus albus*** is a vigorous perennial with thick, unbranched flowering spikes tightly covered in white flowers. It likes rocky places. **ORIGIN** EUROPE, NORTH AFRICA

(AROUND THE MEDITERRANEAN IT IS MORE OF A MOUNTAIN SPECIES) **HARDINESS** −15 °C AND BELOW **DROUGHT RESISTANCE CODE** 4

• ***Asphodelus cerasiferus*** is common in the South of France, where its handsome spikes stand out in the landscape of the garrigue after fires. It is easily recognizable by its large fruits (*cerasiferus* means 'cherry-bearing', in contrast with *microcarpus* which means 'having small fruit'). **ORIGIN** WESTERN MEDITERRANEAN BASIN **HARDINESS** −15 °C AND BELOW **DROUGHT RESISTANCE CODE** 5

• ***Asphodelus fistulosus*** looks very different, with its clump of linear, cylindrical, hollow leaves (*fistulosus* is from the Latin, *fistula*, 'pipe'). Its abundant small white flowers cover the plant from the end of winter and continue to be produced until June. It colonizes waste ground and roadsides and self-seeds easily in gardens. **ORIGIN** MEDITERRANEAN BASIN **HARDINESS** −12 TO −15 °C **DROUGHT RESISTANCE CODE** 5

Atriplex canescens
(Chenopodiaceae) Salt Bush

ORIGIN SOUTHWESTERN UNITED STATES
HEIGHT 1.25 TO 1.5 M
SPREAD 1.5 M
POSITION SUN
HARDINESS −12 TO −15 °C
DROUGHT RESISTANCE CODE 6

A shrub with evergreen leaves that are golden-grey, becoming silver in summer (*canescens* means 'whitening' in Latin). When it flowers in summer, the pliable tips

In a dry garden, contrasting foliage allows a permanent structure to be created that is attractive throughout the year. On the left, the silver foliage of *Centaurea pulcherrima* catches the eye, on the right the slightly soft mass of *Atriplex nummularia* dominates, and lower down the velvety leaves of *Phlomis grandiflora* emerge from the dark glossy foliage of *Ceanothus griseus var. horizontalis* 'Yankee Point'.

POSITION SUN
HARDINESS −12 TO −15 °C
DROUGHT RESISTANCE CODE 6

A shrub with thick, grey, evergreen leaves, which are edible: they have a pleasant salty taste and may be used in salads. In summer the plant is covered with insignificant greyish flowers. *Atriplex halimus* tolerates alkaline conditions well and has an excellent resistance to salt spray. It is also one of the ornamental shrubs whose roots are best able to withstand high concentrations of salt. A few years ago, passing through the Negev Desert on our way to Kibbutz Ein Gedi, we saw *Atriplex halimus* growing in extreme conditions beside mountains of salt extracted from the Dead Sea. *Atriplex halimus* can take clipping and is often used to make first-line hedges in coastal areas in order to protect gardens from the salt spray. In fact it looks better when clipped, otherwise the dry flower spikes remain on the tips of the branches for a long time and can make the plant look a bit sparse.

Propagate by softwood cuttings in spring.

• *Atriplex lentiformis*, similar to *Atriplex canescens*, has a stiffer, more upright habit. The margins of its linear leaves are turned upwards, resembling narrow gutters, thus

of its branches bend horizontally, giving the plant a striking appearance (the flowers themselves are barely visible). Female plants are subsequently covered with curious and decorative winged fruits, whose weight makes the branches bow down in cascades. These fruits were traditionally ground by Native Americans to produce a flour which served as the basis for making desert bread. *Atriplex canescens* tolerates alkaline conditions well. Although it grows in the desert dunes of southwestern America, it adapts easily to many different garden conditions, even clay soils. As with all *Atriplex* species, its root system is very deep, making it remarkably resistant to drought.

In order to propagate the more decorative female plants, we avoid using seed: propagation is by softwood cuttings in May.

Atriplex halimus
Tree Purslane, Shrubby Orache

ORIGIN EUROPE AND MEDITERRANEAN BASIN, ON COASTS
HEIGHT 1.5 TO 2 M
SPREAD 1.5 TO 2 M

The dark silhouette of an oak stands out in a rocky expanse covered in *Ballota acetabulosa*. This Greek landscape could provide the inspiration for a 'natural' garden requiring minimal maintenance; a few touches of colour could be added with sages, *Perovskia* or bupleurums.

ABOVE The pretty grey leaves of *Ballota pseudodictamnus* naturally form a rounded mass which can be accentuated by clipping in autumn. RIGHT *Ballota pseudodictamnus* near Patara in Turkey.

reducing the area of leaf surface exposed to the sun. ORIGIN SOUTHWESTERN UNITED STATES, NORTHERN MEXICO HARDINESS −10 TO −12 °C DROUGHT RESISTANCE CODE 6

• *Atriplex nummularia* has large, rounded, grey-blue leaves that are slightly soft and have undulating margins. It is a small shrub, cultivated for fodder in some of the arid regions of the world. ORIGIN AUSTRALIA HARDINESS −8 TO −10 °C DROUGHT RESISTANCE CODE 6

• *Atriplex spinifera* has small, grey-blue, lanceolate leaves. If the plant suffers extreme water stress the leaves become deciduous in summer. As they grow woody, the tips of the branches become slightly spiny. The plant is extremely resistant to salt spray and salty soils. ORIGIN SOUTHWESTERN UNITED STATES HARDINESS −10 TO −12 °C DROUGHT RESISTANCE CODE 6

Ballota acetabulosa
(Lamiaceae)

ORIGIN GREECE, TURKEY
HEIGHT 40 TO 50 CM
SPREAD 60 CM
POSITION SUN
HARDINESS −10 TO −12 °C
DROUGHT RESISTANCE CODE 5

A woody perennial, all parts of which – stems, leaves and inflorescences – are entirely covered in woolly hairs. The round evergreen leaves are tightly packed on the stems and the plant grows naturally into a large and very decorative silver-grey cushion. The pink flowers appear from April to July and are rather inconspicuous, as if the foliage makes the plant sufficiently handsome already. After flowering, the large cup-shaped bracts (the name *acetabulosa* comes from the Latin *acetabulum*, 'a vinegar beaker') remain on the stems all summer. In the past, these woolly bracts were used as wicks for oil lamps. You can try it for yourself: float the bract upside down in olive oil and light the tip, which will then burn gently. *Ballota acetabulosa* tolerates

alkaline conditions well and is resistant to salt spray, but it hates winter wet and so requires well-drained soil. It can be pruned in autumn to remove the faded flowers and to sculpt the dense foliage to emphasize its ball or cushion shape.

Propagation is by seed in autumn or by softwood cuttings in spring.

• *Ballota hirsuta* has pretty grey-green downy evergreen leaves. The spikes of pinkish-white flowers appear in June–July. ORIGIN SPAIN, PORTUGAL HARDINESS −10 TO −12 °C DROUGHT RESISTANCE CODE 5

• *Ballota pseudodictamnus*, False Dittany, closely resembles *Ballota acetabulosa*, though the round leaves are larger and the plant grows bigger: with age, it forms magnificent cushions. ORIGIN GREECE HARDINESS −12 TO −15 °C DROUGHT RESISTANCE CODE 5

Beschorneria yuccoides
(Agavaceae)

ORIGIN MEXICO
HEIGHT OF FOLIAGE 60 TO 80 CM
HEIGHT IN FLOWER 1.5 TO 2 M

SPREAD 60 CM
POSITION SUN OR SEMI-SHADE
HARDINESS −8 TO −10 °C
DROUGHT RESISTANCE CODE 4

A rhizomatous perennial that forms a large rosette of narrow, blue-green, evergreen leaves. The leaf tips are often gracefully bent outwards, giving the plant a fountain-like habit. From June to August, the spectacular inflorescences appear, the heavy red flower spikes leaning sideways, as if they were about to collapse under the weight of the flowers. The hanging tubular flowers, an amazing bright green, are enclosed in highly decorative red bracts. These flowers are rich in nectar: in their natural biotope they are visited by hummingbirds which ensure pollination. *Beschorneria yuccoides* is happy in acid, neutral or slightly alkaline soils, but it does require perfect drainage since it hates winter wet. It can be planted at the margins of woodland, where it can cope with competition from the roots of mature trees; in Mexico it often grows among widely spaced oaks. It can also be grown in a pot, where its highly decorative architectural form can be admired. Unlike other members of the Agavaceae family, *Beschorneria* does not die after flowering.

Propagate by seed in spring.

Bignonia capreolata
(Bignoniaceae) Crossvine

ORIGIN SOUTHEAST UNITED STATES
HEIGHT AND SPREAD UP TO 10 M
POSITION SUN OR SEMI-SHADE
HARDINESS −10 TO −12 °C
DROUGHT RESISTANCE CODE 4

The name 'bignonia' is applied to several climbing plants of interest for dry gardens, including *Campsis*, *Macfadyena*, *Podranea* and *Tecomaria*. *Bignonia capreolata* is a fast-

The flowers of *Bignonia capreolata* open into trumpets and give off a sweet scent of coffee and chocolate.

growing climber with stems equipped with branching tendrils that are highly efficient at attaching the plant to its support (*capreolata* means 'furnished with tendrils'). These tendrils end in small discs which act like suckers and can stick to the smoothest surfaces. The dark-green, leathery, evergreen leaves take on violet hues in winter. The flowers, which appear from April to July, open into long red trumpets with petals tipped with yellow. While not in the least spectacular, their scent is unique: they give off a sweet fragrance of coffee mixed with chocolate. *Bignonia capreolata* tolerates alkaline conditions well and is unfussy about soil type.

Propagation is by softwood cuttings in spring.

Brachyglottis monroi
(Asteraceae)

ORIGIN NEW ZEALAND
HEIGHT 60 TO 80 CM
SPREAD 80 CM TO 1 M
POSITION SUN
HARDINESS −10 TO −12 °C
DROUGHT RESISTANCE CODE 3

A shrub with attractive, thick, evergreen leaves, the upper surface of which is grey-green, while the undersides are covered in a white felt that serves to limit water loss. The wavy leaf margins are emphasized by an attractive narrow white border. The plant has a regular growth habit and forms a plump cushion. Its yellow flowers appear in June–July; they are not very abundant, but since the main attraction of the plant is its foliage, this doesn't matter. *Brachyglottis monroi* tolerates alkaline conditions well and is resistant to salt spray. It prefers friable, well-drained soils. It is not necessary to prune it in autumn as its natural habit is perfect; it is a long-lived and easy plant that does not require any particular care.

Propagation is by softwood cuttings in autumn or spring.

• *Brachyglottis* 'Sunshine' is a shrub with silver-grey foliage which forms a ball measuring 1 metre in height and spread. In June it is covered in yellow daisies. **ORIGIN** NEW ZEALAND **HARDINESS** −10 TO −12 °C **DROUGHT RESISTANCE CODE** 2.5

Buddleja alternifolia
(Buddlejaceae) Butterfly Bush

ORIGIN NORTHWEST CHINA
HEIGHT 2 TO 3 M
SPREAD 2 TO 3 M
POSITION SUN
HARDINESS −15 °C AND BELOW
DROUGHT RESISTANCE CODE 3.5

A shrub with narrow deciduous leaves. Its long branches have a slightly weeping habit.

The scented flowers of *Buddleja* 'Lochinch' go well with its light-coloured foliage. The spring flowering may be repeated in autumn if the summer has not been too dry.

The flowers, lilac-coloured and scented, appear in May–June, arranged in small round bunches along the whole length of the branches, giving the plant a most unusual appearance. They attract a host of butterflies – a delightful sight. *Buddleja alternifolia* tolerates alkaline conditions well and is unfussy about soil type. This is a robust plant that is easy to grow and long-lived. As it flowers on the previous year's growth it should be pruned, if required, just after flowering in order not to reduce the following year's flowering – but in our garden we prefer not to prune it at all, for its tangled, tumbling habit is part of its charm.

Propagation is by hardwood cuttings in winter.

• *Buddleja alternifolia* 'Argentea' has grey foliage which contrasts softly with its flowers. The branches have a more upright habit than those of the type.

Buddleja 'Lochinch'

ORIGIN OF PARENTS CHINA
HEIGHT 1.5 TO 2 M
SPREAD 1 M
POSITION SUN
HARDINESS −12 TO −15 °C
DROUGHT RESISTANCE CODE 2

A dense and branching shrub with semi-evergreen leaves. It is a hybrid of *Buddleja davidii*, whose abundant flowering it has inherited, and *Buddleja fallowiana*, whose compact habit and attractive foliage it possesses: the leaves are grey above and downy silver on the undersides. The scented pale violet flowers go perfectly with the foliage. They appear in May–June and attract a multitude of butterflies. If the summer has not been too dry, it may flower again, slightly less abundantly, in autumn. *Buddleja* 'Lochinch' tolerates alkaline conditions well and is unfussy about soil type. It is an easily grown plant in gardens that are not too dry.

Propagation is by softwood cuttings in spring.

Buddleja marrubiifolia

ORIGIN TEXAS AND MEXICO, IN THE CHIHUAHUA DESERT
HEIGHT 1 TO 1.25 M
SPREAD 1 M
POSITION SUN
HARDINESS −6 TO −8 °C, OR PERHAPS SLIGHTLY COLDER IF THE SOIL IS VERY DRY
DROUGHT RESISTANCE CODE 5

A shrub with small, downy, evergreen leaves that become almost white in summer. The lightly scented flowers are perfectly round and resemble bright orange balls. They appear more or less throughout the year, with a peak flowering period in spring, when they are visited by many butterflies. *Buddleja marrubiifolia* tolerates alkaline conditions well. It requires a dry, poor soil with perfect drainage. We discovered this fairly rare plant when we visited a small nursery in Tucson, Arizona; by good luck the few, tiny, dust-like seeds we brought back with us germinated and produced several plants which have acclimatized well in our garden. We like to grow this *Buddleja* with other grey-leaved shrubs such as

Leucophyllum langmaniae, Artemisia canariensis, Centaurea pulcherrima or *Helichrysum orientale*. By playing with textures and volumes we succeed in creating amazing cascades of silver.

Propagation is by seed in autumn or by softwood cuttings in early spring. The cuttings should be grown in a well-drained medium as they rot easily.

Buddleja officinalis

ORIGIN CHINA
HEIGHT 3 M
SPREAD 1.5 M
POSITION SUN
HARDINESS −8 TO −10 °C (FLOWERING IS DELAYED IF THE WINTER IS COLD)
DROUGHT RESISTANCE CODE 2.5

A shrub with evergreen leaves that are green above and downy grey on the undersides. The numerous pale mauve flower spikes appear in the middle of winter. From January to the beginning of April their sweet honey scent perfumes the air for several metres around the plant. In our garden we have planted it next to a path, where we pause for the pleasure of smelling its flowers. *Buddleja officinalis* tolerates alkaline conditions well and is unfussy about soil type. It is fairly fast-growing and requires no maintenance.

Propagation is by seed in autumn or by softwood cuttings in late spring.

Buddleja saligna

ORIGIN SOUTH AFRICA
HEIGHT 3 M OR MORE
SPREAD 2 M
POSITION SUN
HARDINESS −10 TO −12 °C
DROUGHT RESISTANCE CODE 4

A large shrub or small tree with long, slightly leathery, evergreen leaves. Glossy green above and downy silver on the undersides, they resemble the leaves of the olive tree – and in fact this shrub is called 'false olive' in South Africa. The cream-coloured flowers are grouped in short clusters and have a pleasant elder-like scent. They are remarkably abundant – in autumn the plant literally bends under the weight of its flowers. *Buddleja saligna* tolerates alkaline conditions well, is resistant to salt spray and is unfussy about soil type. It grows rapidly and tolerates pruning, making it a good plant for a free-growing hedge, where its autumn flowering is splendid.

Propagation is by seed or softwood cuttings in spring.

Buddleja salviifolia

ORIGIN SOUTH AFRICA
HEIGHT 3 M OR MORE
SPREAD 2 M
POSITION SUN
HARDINESS −10 TO −12 °C
DROUGHT RESISTANCE CODE 3.5

A shrub or small tree with handsome, long, evergreen leaves, green and rough-textured above and white and downy beneath. The numerous spikes of scented flowers, creamy white with an orange throat, appear from February to April. *Buddleja salviifolia* tolerates alkaline conditions well and is resistant to salt spray. It is unfussy about soil type. In our garden we like to grow it in association with other early-flowering shrubs such as *Teucrium fruticans, Medicago arborea* and *Buddleja officinalis* to create cheerful and colourful borders at the end of winter. A magnificent specimen grows in the botanic garden of Kirstenbosch, included in the collection of South African medicinal plants. A small label informs us that a decoction of the roots soothes colic – always useful to know when travelling!

Propagation is by seed in autumn or by softwood cuttings in spring.

• *Buddleja agathosma* has large white woolly leaves. The delicate lilac-pink flowers appear in spring. ORIGIN SOUTH AFRICA HARDINESS −8 TO −10 °C DROUGHT RESISTANCE CODE 3

• *Buddleja crispa* has rounded, white, woolly leaves. Its lilac-pink, scented flowers are grouped in short clusters. It flowers for a long time in spring and then again in autumn, in other words for most of the year in a mild climate. ORIGIN FROM AFGHANISTAN TO SOUTHWEST CHINA HARDINESS −8 TO −10 °C DROUGHT RESISTANCE CODE 3

• *Buddleja globosa* is famous for its amazing orange-yellow spherical inflorescences which appear in spring. If the dry period goes on for too long, this shrub loses its leaves at the end of summer and does not look particularly attractive (some of the blackened leaves remain on the plant). It prefers soils that are not too alkaline. ORIGIN CHILE HARDINESS −10 TO −12 °C DROUGHT RESISTANCE CODE 2

• *Buddleja loricata* has attractive, narrow, grey-green leaves with a rough texture. Both the stems and the undersides of the leaves are covered in silvery or golden hairs. The flowers, creamy white with an orange throat, are scented. This is a dense shrub, easy to integrate in a free-growing hedge. ORIGIN SOUTH AFRICA HARDINESS −10 TO −12 °C DROUGHT RESISTANCE CODE 3.5

• *Buddleja myriantha* has golden-grey downy leaves which make an interesting contrast in spring to its short spikes of violet-blue flowers. It is an easily grown and long-lived compact shrub. ORIGIN TIBET HARDINESS −12 TO −15 °C DROUGHT RESISTANCE CODE 3

There are numerous other species and varieties of *Buddleja*.

Bulbine frutescens
(Asphodelaceae)

ORIGIN SOUTH AFRICA
HEIGHT OF FOLIAGE 30 CM
HEIGHT IN FLOWER 50 TO 60 CM
SPREAD 60 CM OR MORE
POSITION SUN
HARDINESS −4 TO −6 °C
DROUGHT RESISTANCE CODE 5

A perennial with long, cylindrical, succulent evergreen leaves. The woody bases of the stems root wherever they touch the ground

Bulbine frutescens 'Hallmark' flowers almost throughout the year in a pot on our terrace. In winter we move it to a position against the house wall and under the eaves, so that it benefits from the warmth of the house.

Impervious to drought, *Bupleurum fruticosum* flowers from June to August, lighting up the garden with its greenish-yellow umbels when most other plants have long been dormant.

and the plant makes a thick groundcover. Pretty yellow flowers with a protruding boss of stamens open progressively up the delicate arched flower stalks, beginning at the bottom. Flowering can be repeated throughout the year in mild climates, but ceases in winter if it is cold. *Bulbine frutescens* tolerates alkaline conditions well and prefers poor, well-drained soils. As it is too tender to be planted in the open ground in our garden, we grow it in a container on our terrace, where we can enjoy its unusual and decorative flowers for many months. We have combined it with a *Lavandula* 'Goodwin Creek Grey', which has handsome violet-blue spikes.

Propagation: it is easy to remove the stems with bases already sprouting aerial roots – all that is necessary then is to repot them.

• *Bulbine frutescens* '**Hallmark**' is a cultivar with luminous orange flowers.

Bupleurum fruticosum
(Apiaceae) Shrubby Hare's Ear

ORIGIN MEDITERRANEAN BASIN
HEIGHT 1.5 TO 2 M
SPREAD 1 M
POSITION SUN OR SHADE
HARDINESS −12 TO −15 °C
DROUGHT RESISTANCE CODE 5

An evergreen shrub with blue-green leaves that are thick and leathery and are covered with a glossy cuticle, limiting water loss through evaporation. Its flowering is a surprise: the umbels of greenish-yellow flowers appear in full summer, from June to August, as if the plant doesn't care in the least about the drought. The slightly scented flowers give off an unexpected

aroma in the middle of the day, reminiscent of peppers grilled on an open fire. *Bupleurum fruticosum* is tolerant of alkaline soils, is resistant to salt spray and prefers well-drained soils. In our garden it self-seeds naturally and we usually leave young plants to grow wherever they see fit. We like to let our borders evolve naturally, and this often leads to interesting and unexpected plant associations. This is how we discovered one of the best combinations for a dry garden – a vigorous *Bupleurum* had seeded itself into a large bed of *Perovskia* and the happy marriage of their blue and yellow flowers now constitutes one of the most beautiful summer scenes in our garden, lasting on through the long months of drought.

Propagation is by fresh seed in autumn, immediately after harvesting.

Bupleurum spinosum

ORIGIN MOUNTAINS OF SPAIN AND MOROCCO
HEIGHT 30 CM
SPREAD 30 CM
POSITION SUN
HARDINESS −15 °C AND BELOW
DROUGHT RESISTANCE CODE 5

Bupleurum spinosum is a typical example of the plants known as spiny xerophytes: to resist the cold, drought and wind that characterize Mediterranean mountain peaks, the plant huddles into itself and forms a curious spiny cushion. *Bupleurum spinosum* has small linear leaves which are evergreen in winter, but which may fall in summer if there is a serious drought, leaving the plant's branched skeleton exposed to view. The summer flowers are arranged in small

yellowish-green umbels. The pedicels (flower stems) harden after the flowering is finished and turn into branched spines – their amazing bright green colour makes them very decorative. *Bupleurum spinosum* tolerates alkaline conditions well; it prefers poor, stony, very well-drained soils. It is a highly original-looking rock garden plant and is sought after by garden lovers – but its rate of growth is slow, so if you're in a hurry, you'd better forget about it.

Propagation is by fresh seed in autumn.

• *Bupleurum gibraltaricum* has large leathery leaves of a darker green than those of *Bupleurum fruticosum*. It forms a handsome shrub which grows equally well in sun or shade. The greenish-yellow inflorescences appear in summer. **ORIGIN** MOUNTAINS OF SOUTHERN SPAIN AND MOROCCO **HARDINESS** −12 TO −15 °C **DROUGHT RESISTANCE CODE** 5

Buxus sempervirens
(Buxaceae) Box

ORIGIN SOUTHERN EUROPE, ASIA MINOR, NORTH AFRICA
HEIGHT UP TO 6 M (MORE OFTEN 1 TO 2 M IN GARDENS)
SPREAD UP TO 2 M
POSITION SUN OR SHADE
HARDINESS −15 °C AND BELOW
DROUGHT RESISTANCE CODE 4

A shrub or small tree with small, leathery, aromatic, dark-green leaves that are evergreen. The foliage takes on interesting bronze or orangeish shades in autumn and winter, and sometimes at the end of summer in drought years. When we take cuttings in autumn, we like to go up to the Larzac plateau to enjoy the austere landscape coloured by the rusty foliage of the box that clings to rocks sculpted by erosion. The greenish flowers, with their bunches of yellow stamens, appear in April. Box grows very slowly and its wood is remarkably hard (the hardest in the world after ebony); boxwood has an attractive yellow colour and is used to make small objects. *Buxus sempervirens* tolerates alkaline conditions well and is unfussy about soil type. Since it takes well to pruning, box is traditionally used as an edging plant. In our garden, however, we prefer to let it grow naturally and we like to use its dark foliage to provide a contrast in borders of grey-leaved plants.

Propagate by semi-ripe cuttings in autumn or winter. It's no use being in a hurry: box roots very slowly!

• *Buxus balearica* has fine oval leaves, thick and leathery and very dark. Once established, it grows (slightly) faster than *Buxus sempervirens* and can ultimately form

BOTANICAL NAMES OR COMMON NAMES?

Caesalpinia gilliesii is sometimes called Bird of Paradise, a charming and evocative name that might seem easier to remember than the plant's botanical name. But, as so often with common names for plants, Bird of Paradise may lead to confusion. A plant may have several common names and, conversely, different plants may be known by the same common name. Bird of Paradise is thus used to designate both *Strelitzia reginae*, a large perennial from South Africa, and *Caesalpinia gilliesii*, a native of South America, also sometimes called the Little Flame Tree – just like its cousin, *Caesalpinia pulcherrima*, which in contrast comes from India. Yet one mustn't mix up these two Flame Trees with the Hyères Flame Tree (*Sesbania punicea*, which certainly does not come from Hyères), nor of course with the Great Flame Tree, *Delonix regia*, a tropical tree which also belongs to the Caesalpiniaceae family. Feeling confused? To improve communication between gardeners, it's often best to use the botanical names: they aren't in the end so very difficult and lead to fewer errors.

The origins of botanical names are in any case full of stories which can help in remembering them. *Caesalpinia*, for example, is named after Andreas Cesalpini, a botanist from Pisa, who was Pope Clement VIII's doctor. In 1583 Cesalpini published *De Plantis Libri*, one of the first works to base taxonomy on the study of the sexual organs of flowers, at a time when most theologians were denouncing the very idea of sexuality in plants. Every time I look at a *Caesalpinia* shamelessly flaunting its vigorous arched stamens to the sky I imagine the battle launched against Cesalpini by those furious theologians.

The handsome red stamens of *Caesalpinia gilliesii* point skywards. If the seedpods are removed as soon as they form, the plant continues to flower generously throughout the summer.

a small tree with a handsome regular crown. Fine specimens can be seen in old parks in the South of France, for instance in the Jardin des Plantes at Montpellier. **ORIGIN** BALEARIC ISLANDS, SARDINIA, SOUTHERN SPAIN **HARDINESS** −12 TO −15 °C **DROUGHT RESISTANCE CODE** 4

Caesalpinia gilliesii
(Caesalpinaceae) Bird of Paradise

ORIGIN ARGENTINA, URUGUAY
HEIGHT 1.5 TO 2 M
SPREAD 1.5 M
POSITION SUN
HARDINESS −12 TO −15 °C
DROUGHT RESISTANCE CODE 4

A deciduous shrub or small tree with leaves finely cut into numerous leaflets, giving the plant a luxuriant, light look. Spectacular conical inflorescences open on the tips of the stems in June–July, and sometimes even into September. They are composed of soft yellow flowers, from which burst forth gracefully arched red stamens. Although they are beautiful, it isn't a good idea to approach too close to examine them, for they give off a curious and rather unpleasant smell. *Caesalpinia gilliesii* tolerates alkaline conditions well. It prefers friable soils that are fairly deep and well-drained, and is an easy-to-grow and long-lived shrub. With age it develops a small trunk, like a miniature tree, the base of which can be hidden by lower-growing plants placed around it. In our garden we've surrounded it with *Salvia microphylla* 'Royal Bumble', whose generous red-velvet flowers associate well with the warm colour of the *Caesalpinia* flowers.

Propagation is by seed in autumn, after giving the seeds a hot water treatment: pour boiling water over them and then leave them to swell overnight.

Calamintha nepeta
(Lamiaceae) Lesser Calamint

ORIGIN SOUTHERN EUROPE, NORTH AFRICA
HEIGHT IN FLOWER 40 CM
SPREAD 40 CM

POSITION SUN
HARDINESS −12 TO −15 °C
DROUGHT RESISTANCE CODE 4

A rhizomatous perennial with semi-evergreen downy foliage. The plant gives off a powerful scent, something like a mixture of mint and bitumen (the name *Calamintha* comes from the Greek, *kalos*, 'beautiful', and *mintha*, 'mint'). While not spectacular, this plant flowers very prettily, with a mist of small, very pale blue flowers from June to October. *Calamintha nepeta* tolerates alkaline conditions well and prefers poor, stony, well-drained soils. In our garden we like to plant it where people pass by, near either stepping stones or a gravel path, where it self-seeds freely: on hot summer days as the leaves are crushed underfoot, the scent of the *Calamintha* is deliciously refreshing.

Propagation is by seed in autumn or by softwood cuttings in spring.

Callistemon rigidus
(Myrtaceae) Bottlebrush

ORIGIN AUSTRALIA
HEIGHT 3 M OR MORE
SPREAD 1.5 M
POSITION SUN
HARDINESS −10 TO −12 °C
DROUGHT RESISTANCE CODE 5

An evergreen, bushy, stiff-stemmed shrub with dark-green, tapering, leathery leaves. In May the plant is covered in amazing red and gold inflorescences that look just like bottlebrushes (hence the common name

The colourful young shoots of *Callistemon acuminatus* appear just before the purple-red bottlebrush flowers.

Callistemon salignus flowers several times a year, each new growth period generating abundant flowering.

of this plant). What you are in fact looking at are the magnificent light red stamens, each bearing at its tip a small mass of dark yellow pollen (the name *Callistemon* comes from the Greek *kallistos*, 'most beautiful', and *stēmōn*, 'stamen'). Although not very well known, *Callistemon rigidus* is certainly the most adaptable of the many callistemons we have tried in our garden. It tolerates our difficult soil (clayey and alkaline) without problem and has a good resistance to cold. It is also the most drought-resistant of all the callistemons. It grows rapidly and its stiff, slightly gangling, habit is striking. To show it off to its best, it can be planted as a single specimen emerging from among low-growing or carpeting plants.

Propagation is by seed in autumn or by semi-ripe cuttings in autumn or spring.

• *Callistemon acuminatus* has pretty purple-red flowers and pinkish-brown, silky young growth. It is suitable for acid, neutral or slightly alkaline soils. ORIGIN AUSTRALIA HARDINESS −8 TO −10 °C DROUGHT RESISTANCE CODE 3

• *Callistemon viminalis* 'Little John' is a compact plant that forms a regular ball shape. The vermilion flower spikes appear several times throughout the year. It is suitable for acid, neutral or slightly alkaline soils and is easily grown in a pot. ORIGIN AUSTRALIA HARDINESS −6 TO −8 °C DROUGHT RESISTANCE CODE 4

• *Callistemon salignus* has decorative soft and silky young shoots that are tinted with

pink or red. A pleasant surprise is that it flowers three or four times a year, its new growth producing a fresh flush of blooms in spring or autumn. The inflorescences are of a very striking pale greenish-yellow colour, which is soft and almost translucent. It tolerates alkaline conditions well, but does require a light, well-drained soil. ORIGIN AUSTRALIA HARDINESS −8 TO −10 °C DROUGHT RESISTANCE CODE 4

• *Callistemon* 'Violaceus' has narrow leaves and a flaring, fountain-like habit. The flowers are a pretty pale mauve. It is suitable for acid, neutral or slightly alkaline soils. Experts differ as to the correct name of this plant: some consider it to be a species while others believe it to be a cultivar or a hybrid. HARDINESS −10 TO −12 °C DROUGHT RESISTANCE CODE 3.5

There are numerous other species and varieties of *Callistemon*; Chantal and Thierry Railhet have a fine collection in their nursery, for instance (see appendix Useful Addresses).

Campsis grandiflora
(Bignoniaceae)

ORIGIN CHINA
HEIGHT AND SPREAD UP TO 6 M
POSITION SUN
HARDINESS −15 °C AND BELOW
DROUGHT RESISTANCE CODE 3

A climbing plant with vigorous twining stems. Aerial roots growing from these stems enable the plant to cling to a wall like ivy. The deciduous green leaves are divided into large, toothed leaflets. It flowers all summer and its bunches of broad, open trumpets are spectacular. The flowers are bright orange when they open, fading to a delicate soft apricot colour. If you look closely into the yellow, red-striped throat of a flower, you will see quite clearly the large arching stamens from which the plant gets its name (*Campsis* is from the Greek *kampsis*, 'curvature', from the form of the stamens). *Campsis grandiflora* tolerates alkaline conditions well and is unfussy about soil type. It is an easy plant to grow and is long-lived: the fine knotted trunks of specimens over a hundred years old can be seen adorning the pillars of old pergolas. If *Campsis* grows too big, it can be cut back in winter without affecting the following year's flowering,

since the flowers are produced on new wood.

Propagation is by hardwood cuttings in winter or by layering in autumn. It is also possible to propagate by seed in spring, but plants grown from seed take many years to flower.

• *Campsis radicans*, the Trumpet Vine, is a rapidly growing climber with stems which have numerous aerial roots that enable the plant to cling to walls unaided. The orange-red flowers, shaped like narrow trumpets, are produced repeatedly throughout the summer. The plant has a tendency to spread by suckers at the foot of walls and rapidly covers very large areas. A fine example can be seen in the Jardin des Plantes in Montpellier, where an entire wall on the right near the Boulevard Henri IV entrance is covered with an old specimen. ORIGIN SOUTHWESTERN UNITED STATES HARDINESS −15 °C AND BELOW DROUGHT RESISTANCE CODE 3

• *Campsis radicans* 'Flava' has attractive sulphur-yellow flowers.

• *Campsis* × *tagliabuana* 'Madame Galen' is a hybrid of *Campsis grandiflora* and *Campsis radicans*. This is the plant that is often called 'bignonia', although the name may be used for other species or varieties of *Campsis*, as well as the numerous other climbing species belonging to the Bignoniaceae family. It is an excellent climbing plant that flowers profusely in summer, useful for covering walls (it is self-clinging) or large pergolas. HARDINESS −15 °C OR BELOW DROUGHT RESISTANCE CODE 3

Propagation is possible by hardwood cuttings in winter, but plants grown from grafts are preferable since they are more vigorous. A slit graft is made at the end of winter in the fleshy neck of the roots of Campsis radicans.

Capparis spinosa
(Capparaceae) Caper

ORIGIN MEDITERRANEAN BASIN
HEIGHT 50 CM
SPREAD 1.5 M OR MORE
POSITION SUN
HARDINESS −12 TO −15 °C
DROUGHT RESISTANCE CODE 6

A sub-shrub with thick, blueish-green, deciduous leaves. The long branches are furnished with curved thorns and have a spreading or rambling habit. The plant's highly developed root system

The magnificent trumpet flower of *Campsis grandiflora*: the arched stamens, from which the plant derives its name, emerge from the narrow throat.

enables it to resist drought well and allows it the luxury of flowering in full summer, when most mediterranean plants are dormant. The flowers are beautiful, one of the jewels of the dry garden: the large white corolla opens to reveal a magnificent bunch of fine long stamens, white with violet-coloured tips. The flowers are produced repeatedly from June to September, but the plant is best known for its flower buds – these are the capers that are picked in early summer and then pickled. The fruits that ripen in autumn resemble gherkins and can also be eaten. *Capparis spinosa* tolerates alkaline conditions well. It is often said that you need to plant five capers to succeed with just one, yet it is a plant that is easily grown provided you respect its main requirement: it needs to be planted among stones, ideally on top of a drystone wall, and it should not be irrigated in summer.

Propagation is by fresh seed in summer, immediately after harvesting. Propagation is also possible by cuttings of large sections of hard wood in winter, but the success rate is low. According to an old tradition, a cross-shaped cut should be made in the base of the cuttings and a grain of wheat inserted into it: is this because the germination of the wheat releases enzymes that help rooting, or is it simply that the fact of keeping the cut open leads to a concentration of rooting hormones?

• *Capparis spinosa* '**Inermis**' is a thornless variety occasionally found in Crete or on the Cycladic islands. The growth habit and flowering of the plant (and the production of the capers) are identical to those of the type.

Caryopteris incana
(Verbenaceae)

ORIGIN CHINA, JAPAN
HEIGHT 60 CM
SPREAD 60 CM
POSITION SUN
HARDINESS −12 TO −15 °C
DROUGHT RESISTANCE CODE 2.5

A deciduous or semi-evergreen sub-shrub with grey-green, slightly aromatic leaves. The remarkably intense violet-blue flowers appear after the first rains in September or October, and have the additional delightful feature of attracting numerous butterflies whose beautiful wing colours contrast with the darker flowers. In our garden we grow *Caryopteris incana* in association with *Ceratostigma plumbaginoides, Helianthus maximiliani* and *Epilobium canum* 'Catalina', creating a brightly coloured scene in late summer. *Caryopteris incana* tolerates alkaline conditions well; it prefers friable, fairly deep soils. The herbaceous shoots die after flowering and can be cut back to just above the woody base of the foliage.

Propagation is by seed in autumn or by softwood cuttings in spring.

• *Caryopteris mongholica* is a sub-shrub with pale blue flowers appearing in August–September. **ORIGIN** MONGOLIA, NORTHERN CHINA **HARDINESS** −12 TO −15 °C **DROUGHT RESISTANCE CODE** 2

• *Caryopteris* × *clandonensis* '**Kew Blue**' is one of the hybrids of *Caryopteris incana* and *Caryopteris mongholica*. It forms a compact sub-shrub with deciduous grey-green leaves that are very aromatic (they smell of turpentine). The flowers, of a fine luminous violet-blue, appear in August–September.

Ceanothus griseus var. horizontalis 'Yankee Point' grows well in our garden thanks to its tolerance of alkaline soils.

HARDINESS −12 TO −15 °C **DROUGHT RESISTANCE CODE** 2.5

Catananche caerulea
(Asteraceae) Cupid's Dart

ORIGIN MEDITERRANEAN BASIN
HEIGHT OF FOLIAGE 10 CM
HEIGHT IN FLOWER 50 CM
SPREAD 30 CM
POSITION SUN OR SEMI-SHADE
HARDINESS −12 TO −15 °C
DROUGHT RESISTANCE CODE 4

A perennial that forms a rosette of long, grey-green, evergreen leaves. The branching floral spikes bear a multitude of pretty blue flowers in June–July, followed throughout the summer by decorative globular fruits covered by silvery bracts. In Languedoc this plant is often called 'cigalou' because of the cicada-like sound the bracts make as they rub against each other in the wind. *Catananche caerulea* tolerates alkaline conditions well. It prefers light, well-drained soils – in heavy soil it is fairly short-lived.

Propagate by seed in autumn.

Ceanothus 'Concha'
(Rhamnaceae) Californian Lilac

ORIGIN PROBABLE HYBRID OF CEANOTHUS IMPRESSUS AND CEANOTHUS PAPILLOSUS, TWO SPECIES ORIGINATING FROM CALIFORNIA
HEIGHT 3 M
SPREAD 3 M
POSITION SUN
HARDINESS −10 TO −12 °C
DROUGHT RESISTANCE CODE 4

A large evergreen shrub with long, glossy dark-green leaves. In March the plant is covered with decorative mauveish-red buds, followed in April by scented flowers of a magnificent brilliant deep blue. *Ceanothus* 'Concha' tolerates alkaline conditions well. Like most evergreen ceanothuses it has a relatively short lifespan, from twelve to fifteen years at most. It lives longer if the soil is dry and stony, with good drainage. Be careful: ceanothuses are prone to *Phytophthora*, a fungus affecting the collar

In September, as soon as the first rains arrive, the garden emerges from its summer torpor. Many plants flower at this season, including *Caryopteris incana*, with its intense violet-blue flowers.

of the plant when the soil is hot and damp – they should never be watered in summer.

Propagation is by semi-ripe cuttings in autumn.

• *Ceanothus griseus* var. *horizontalis* 'Yankee Point' has spreading, layered branches, making a thick groundcover. In April it produces abundant bright blue flowers that are sweetly honey-scented and attract countless bees. *Ceanothus griseus* var. *horizontalis* 'Yankee Point' tolerates alkaline conditions well and is unfussy as to soil type: it is one of the happiest ceanothuses in our garden, although the foliage is often slightly scorched by the cold. **ORIGIN** CALIFORNIA **HARDINESS** −8 TO −10 °C **DROUGHT RESISTANCE CODE** 4

• *Ceanothus* 'Ray Hartman' has vigorous foliage and grows to resemble a small tree. The flower buds appear in autumn, and if the winter is mild the plant begins to flower very early, and is covered with thousands of scented light blue flowers in spring. It tolerates alkaline soils very well if there is perfect drainage. **ORIGIN** CALIFORNIA **HARDINESS** −8 TO −10 °C **DROUGHT RESISTANCE CODE** 4

• *Ceanothus* 'Skylark' is reputed to be one of the hardiest ceanothuses. Its handsome, glossy, dark green foliage makes a fine contrast with the pale blue flowers in April–May. It tolerates alkaline soils well if there is perfect drainage. The plant is often found under the name *Ceanothus* 'Victoria'. **ORIGIN** CALIFORNIA **HARDINESS** −12 TO −15 °C **DROUGHT RESISTANCE CODE** 4

Those who love ceanothuses should note a fascinating book: *Ceanothus*, by David Fross and Dieter Wilken (see Further Reading).

Centaurea bella
(Asteraceae)

ORIGIN CAUCASUS
HEIGHT OF FOLIAGE 10 TO 15 CM

Centaurea bella forms a low-growing groundcover for edging or rock gardens. Its elegant flowers are produced in succession over several months in spring.

Centaurea ragusina growing among stones on the Adriatic coast of Croatia. This plant is only happy in the poorest and stoniest parts of the garden.

HEIGHT IN FLOWER 20 TO 30 CM
SPREAD 40 CM
POSITION SUN
HARDINESS −15 °C AND BELOW
DROUGHT RESISTANCE CODE 4

The genus *Centaurea* is named after the centaur Chiron, who was a herbalist and doctor (and Achilles' tutor in Greek mythology), because of the medicinal properties of some *Centaurea* species. *Centaurea bella* is a perennial with attractive grey-green evergreen leaves. The stems root wherever they touch the soil, enabling the plant to spread to form a good dense groundcover. The mauve-pink flowers are produced in succession from March to June; borne on short flower spikes, they have an elegant silhouette. The plant lends itself to many uses in the garden: as edging along a path, between paving stones or stepping stones, as a carpet beneath roses or shrubs, or even as a striking lawn alternative where it is not walked on too much. We like to grow it with *Tanacetum densum* subsp. *amanii* and *Artemisia lanata* to create a lawn-like carpet of grey-green, white and silver leaves. *Centaurea bella* tolerates alkaline conditions well and is unfussy about soil type. It is a robust and adaptable plant which requires no maintenance and which is long-lived: quite simply, it is one of the best perennials in our garden!

Propagate by division in autumn or by softwood cuttings in spring.

• *Centaurea pulcherrima* forms a magnificent rounded clump of long, finely cut, silver-grey leaves (the name *pulcherrima* means very beautiful). The pink flowers, not very numerous, appear

Centranthus ruber self-seeds profusely, colonizing wild areas of the garden.

in June–July. *Centaurea pulcherrima* doesn't like good garden soils – it grows too fast and dies after a few years. It lives longer if given tough treatment and if planted in poor, stony, very dry soils. **ORIGIN** CAUCASUS, ASIA MINOR **HARDINESS** −12 TO −15 °C **DROUGHT RESISTANCE CODE** 5

• *Centaurea ragusina* attracts attention because of the remarkable silvery-white colour of its foliage. The large yellow flowers appear in June–July. It likes stony, very dry soils and withstands salt spray. **ORIGIN** DALMATIA (THE NAME RAGUSINA DOESN'T COME FROM RAGUSA IN SICILY, BUT FROM THE OLD NAME FOR DUBROVNIK IN CROATIA, WHICH IS ALSO RAGUSA) **HARDINESS** −12 TO −15 °C **DROUGHT RESISTANCE CODE** 5

In the morning light of June, the flowers of *Centranthus angustifolius* 'Mauve' emerge behind *Stipa tenuissima*.

The soft flowers of *Centranthus angustifolius* contrast with the harsh environment in which the plant thrives.

pioneer plant to colonize poor and rocky slopes, together with *Euphorbia characias* and *Dorycnium hirsutum*.

Propagation is by seed in autumn or by softwood cuttings in early spring.

• ***Centranthus angustifolius*** has narrow blue-green leaves and pale pink flowers. It does well among stones: the less soil there is, the happier the plant. **ORIGIN** SOUTH OF FRANCE, SPAIN, MOROCCO. IN THE HÉRAULT REGION OF FRANCE, THERE ARE FINE COLONIES IN THE LARGE SCREES AT THE FOOT OF THE CLIFFS OF SAINT-GUILHEM-LE-DÉSERT **HARDINESS** −12 TO −15 °C **DROUGHT RESISTANCE CODE** 5

Cerastium tomentosum
(Caryophyllaceae) Snow-in-Summer

ORIGIN ITALY
HEIGHT 10 TO 20 CM
SPREAD 50 CM OR MORE
POSITION SUN
HARDINESS −15 °C AND BELOW
DROUGHT RESISTANCE CODE 2

A perennial with small, downy, silvery-white evergreen leaves. The stems cover the soil and the plant forms an attractive carpet which cascades down rocks and low walls. In May it is covered in a profusion of pure white flowers. *Cerastium tomentosum* tolerates alkaline conditions well and prefers stony well-drained soils – its lifespan is shorter if it is planted in heavy soils. In the Mediterranean region it is happier in gardens at some altitude, since conditions in the plains and coastal areas are often too hot for it in summer.

Centranthus ruber
(Valerianaceae) Valerian

ORIGIN EUROPE, NORTH AFRICA, ASIA MINOR
HEIGHT IN FLOWER 60 CM
SPREAD 50 CM
POSITION SUN OR SEMI-SHADE
HARDINESS −15 °C AND BELOW
DROUGHT RESISTANCE CODE 4

A perennial with semi-evergreen leaves. It produces its pink flowers abundantly from May to July and may flower again lightly in autumn. The flowers are grouped together along the long stems. If you examine an individual (tiny) floret under a magnifying glass, you will see that it has a curious shape, with a long arched spur that serves as a reservoir of nectar for butterflies (*Centranthus* comes from the Greek *kentron*, 'spur', and *anthos*, 'flower'). Different forms exist with white, crimson or mauve flowers, which create handsome masses of colour when planted together. *Centranthus ruber* tolerates alkaline conditions well and is not fussy about soil type, tolerating both stony soil and clay. It self-seeds profusely: we like to leave it to grow as it pleases in our garden, where it fills gaps between perennials or shrubs. It can also be used as a

Cerastium candidissimum is smothered in flowers in May.

At the end of summer the magnificent blue of *Ceratostigma plumbaginoides* heralds the welcome coolness of autumn days.

Propagation is by seed in spring or by softwood cuttings in autumn.

• **Cerastium candidissimum** has dazzling white foliage (*candicum* means 'white' and *candidissimum* 'whiter than white'). We collected this pretty perennial on the path leading up to Mount Parnassus, about a day's walk from the ancient site of Delphi. **ORIGIN** MOUNTAINS OF GREECE **HARDINESS** −12 TO −15 °C **DROUGHT RESISTANCE CODE** 3

Ceratostigma plumbaginoides
(Plumbaginaceae)

ORIGIN WESTERN CHINA
HEIGHT 25 CM
SPREAD 30 TO 40 CM
POSITION SUN OR SEMI-SHADE
HARDINESS −15 °C AND BELOW
DROUGHT RESISTANCE CODE 3.5

A perennial with deciduous leaves which turn bright red in autumn. The plant spreads slowly by means of rhizomes, gradually forming a thick carpet. Its flowers appear from mid-summer onwards and are produced in succession until the first frosts: they are an absolutely remarkable deep ultramarine blue that contrasts attractively with the foliage as it turns red in autumn. *Ceratostigma plumbaginoides* tolerates alkaline conditions well and is unfussy about soil type. It is a robust, easily grown plant that is long-lived: magnificent carpets of it are found in many old parks in the South of France. We like to combine it with the luminous yellow flowers of *Sternbergia lutea*, whose glossy foliage occupies the ground in winter when the *Ceratostigma* is bare, and then disappears in summer when the *Ceratostigma* is in full growth.

Propagation is by division in winter or by softwood cuttings in late spring.

• **Ceratostigma griffithii** is a dense sub-shrub with semi-evergreen leaves that take on mauve hues in autumn and winter. The pretty blue flowers appear from August to October. **ORIGIN** HIMALAYAS **HARDINESS** −12 TO −15 °C **DROUGHT RESISTANCE CODE** 4

• **Ceratostigma wilmottianum** has deciduous leaves that turn red in autumn; its blue flowers appear at the end of summer. It has a more lax habit than *Ceratostigma griffithii*. It is the best known of the shrubby ceratostigmas, but in our garden it is thirsty and often looks unhappy in summer. **ORIGIN** WESTERN CHINA **HARDINESS** −15 °C AND BELOW **DROUGHT RESISTANCE CODE** 2

Cercis siliquastrum
(Caesalpiniaceae) Judas Tree

ORIGIN SOUTHEAST EUROPE, ASIA MINOR
HEIGHT 5 TO 8 M, SOMETIMES MORE

SPREAD 4 M
POSITION SUN
HARDINESS −15 °C AND BELOW
DROUGHT RESISTANCE CODE 5

A deciduous shrub or small tree with heart-shaped leaves that can take on attractive shades of yellow in autumn. The bright pink flowers, arranged in clusters, appear before the leaves in March–April, emerging directly from the dark bark on old branches and on the trunk. They cover the branches, and every year the flowering of the Judas Tree is a moment of pure pleasure in the garden. The flowers are followed by brown seedpods, flattened at both ends, which remain on the plant for a long time (the name *Cercis* comes from the Greek *kerkis*, a weaver's shuttle, referring to the shape of the seedpods). *Cercis siliquastrum* tolerates alkaline conditions well. In nature it grows in stony soil (magnificent specimens can be seen on the rocky slopes of the Taurus mountains, growing with *Acer sempervirens* and *Cedrus libani* subsp. *stenocoma*), but it adapts easily to all garden soils, even heavy clay. It is a robust and easily grown plant.

Propagation is by seed in autumn, after giving the seeds hot water treatment: pour boiling water over them and leave them to swell overnight.

Chamaemelum nobile 'Flore Pleno'
(Asteraceae) Chamomile

ORIGIN EUROPE, NORTH AFRICA
HEIGHT OF FOLIAGE 5 CM
HEIGHT IN FLOWER 15 CM
SPREAD 30 TO 40 CM
POSITION SUN
HARDINESS −15 °C AND BELOW
DROUGHT RESISTANCE CODE 2

A carpeting perennial with small, semi-evergreen, finely cut leaves that are a fresh light green. When crushed, the leaves give off a pleasant scent reminiscent of green apples (the name *Chamaemelum* comes from the Greek *chamai*, 'on the ground', and *mēlon*, 'apple'). Chamomile has been valued since antiquity for its numerous medicinal virtues including antibiotic and wound-healing properties, while it also helps against flatulence. The stems root wherever they touch the soil and chamomile makes an outstanding low-growing groundcover plant. It can be used as a lawn alternative for small areas that are only moderately walked on, creating an apple-scented lawn. The rounded heads of small white flowers on short flower spikes appear in early summer. Chamomile tolerates alkaline conditions well and is resistant to salt spray. It prefers friable soils that are fairly deep and well-drained.

Propagation is by division in autumn or by softwood cuttings in spring.

Deliciously scented, the flowers of *Choisya* 'Aztec Pearl' perfume an entire area of the garden.

Choisya ternata
(Rutaceae) Mexican Orange

ORIGIN MEXICO
HEIGHT 1.5 TO 2 M
SPREAD 2 M
HARDINESS −12 TO −15 °C
DROUGHT RESISTANCE CODE 4

An evergreen shrub with glossy green aromatic leaves. When crushed, the leaves give off a subtle scent of capers and peppers. The plant has a dense habit and naturally forms a ball shape. The attractive pure white flowers open in March–April and appear again in autumn. They are pleasantly scented and attract butterflies. *Choisya ternata* tolerates alkaline conditions well and prefers well-drained soils. It can cope with root competition and thus can be planted beneath widely spaced large trees – it even tolerates dense shade, but in this case its habit is less compact. Be careful, it is very prone to *Phytophthora*, a fungus attacking the collar of the plant which develops when the soil is hot and damp: you must never water this plant in summer.

Propagation is by semi-ripe cuttings at the beginning of winter.

• *Choisya 'Aztec Pearl'*, the hybrid of *Choisya ternata* and *Choisya arizonica*, has elegant leaves, finely cut into dark green leaflets. The leaves are very aromatic and when crushed give off a fresh scent of citrus fruit and green peppers. The pure white flowers are larger than those of *Choisya ternata* and are deliciously scented. We planted one in the shade of a Banksia rose near the house and it perfumes our entire terrace in spring. **HARDINESS** −12 TO −15 °C **DROUGHT RESISTANCE CODE** 5

Cistus
(Cistaceae) Rock-Rose

The name *Cistus* comes from the Greek *kistē*, 'a basket', referring to the shape of the fruits which open to the sky like small

Seedlings of *Cistus salviifolius* colonize space cleared by a fire. *Cistus* is a pioneer plant, associated with fire ecology. Its lifespan is relatively short, about 10 to 15 years.

baskets full of seeds. When conditions are right, these seeds germinate by the thousand, sometimes creating a veritable 'lawn' of seedlings springing up closely together. The cistus is a pioneer species, associated with the ecology of forest fires. In nature it germinates as a result of the brief, intense heat of a fire and over the next few years proceeds to colonize the entire space cleared by burning. Its white or pink flowers, as delicate as crumpled silk, can colour whole hillsides of recently burnt garrigue. Then, as the garrigue regrows and taller shrubs take its light, the cistus gives way to other plants. Its lifespan is relatively short, around ten to fifteen years, though in exceptional cases cistuses may live longer, particularly in non-mediterranean climates: we have heard of a specimen of *Cistus laurifolius* in the Arboretum of Barres, in the Loiret region of France, that is over thirty years old. A light annual pruning of the tips of the stems in early autumn helps maintain a compact and branching shape and may increase the longevity of cistuses.

Cistuses are perhaps the plants that best express the spirit of the garrigue: their flowers may look fragile, yet they are remarkably robust plants. They grow in poor, degraded, stony soils, where centuries of erosion caused by fires and grazing have left the rock bare. So to grow cistuses successfully in the garden we need to replicate their natural conditions as closely as possible. The poorer and better drained the soil, the happier cistuses will be. Conversely, if the ground is too rich or if the soil is heavy and waterlogged in winter, cistuses do badly and are shorter-lived.

It is not only the flowers of cistuses that are beautiful – the diversity of their foliage can create plantings that are attractive throughout the year: *Cistus ladanifer* var. *sulcatus* (top left), *Cistus albidus* (above) and *Cistus laurifolius* (left).

When planted, they require neither potting compost nor fertilizer; in fact a generous addition of pebbles or sand is what they like best.

Be careful, though: different cistus species and cultivars have widely differing tolerance of alkalinity so you need to select them carefully according to your soil. If you are not sure what type of soil you have in your garden, it's worth taking the time to conduct an experiment by planting a few cistuses that have different requirements. You could, for example, plant a *Cistus ladanifer*, which only grows in acid soil, a *Cistus salviifolius*, which tolerates neutral or slightly alkaline soils, and a *Cistus albidus*, which tolerates alkaline soils well. In less than a year you will be able to assess the behaviour of these indicator plants and choose the species that are best adapted to your garden.

Some cistuses, such as *Cistus albidus*, have a good tolerance of alkaline conditions, but tend to become chlorotic

As delicate as crumpled silk, new cistus flowers open in the morning with the first rays of the sun. In the evening, all that remains is a carpet of fallen petals on the ground.

if the soil remains too wet in winter, and it is very easy to confuse problems caused by too heavy a soil with problems caused by alkalinity: before anything else, think of drainage.

Our garden contains a large collection of cistuses, collected during our study trips around the Mediterranean or resulting from exchanges made with other cistus-lovers. Here is a selection of thirty species and varieties from the almost two hundred in our collection. It wasn't easy for me to choose – I love all of them!

Cistus albidus

ORIGIN WESTERN MEDITERRANEAN
HEIGHT 1 M
SPREAD 1 M
POSITION SUN
HARDINESS −10 TO −12 °C
DROUGHT RESISTANCE CODE 4.5

A shrub with evergreen, downy, light-grey leaves (the name *albidus* means 'whitish', referring to the fact that the leaves are covered in thick hairs which reflect the light). In April–May the pink flowers delicately marry with the downy grey foliage to create a delicate picture that contrasts with the tough environment in which the plant lives in the wild. *Cistus albidus* tolerates alkaline conditions well. It requires a poor and stony soil that has perfect drainage – if the soil is too heavy, the roots are asphyxiated and the plant rapidly develops chlorosis in winter, in spite of its tolerance of alkalinity. Its lifespan is about ten years. In conditions of extreme drought this cistus loses some of its leaves, enabling the plant to limit water loss but making it is less ornamental in late summer. As soon as the first rains arrive new leaves sprout and in autumn the plant is bushy and handsome once more. One interesting detail is that as cistus leaves fall to the

The name rock-rose is very apt: stony ground is what cistuses like best. *Cistus albidus* has pretty pink flowers that marry extremely well with its downy grey foliage.

Cistus atriplicifolius, formerly classed as a *Halimium*, is the longest-flowering cistus in our garden. In spite of the heat, its flowering continues into July, and sometimes even for the whole summer.

ground they form a thick litter which, as it decomposes, releases organic compounds that inhibit the germination of competing species. In a massed planting of cistuses you will find almost no weeds.

Propagation is by seed in autumn. The seeds should be collected in the wild from sites containing only this species in order to avoid all risk of hybridization. A much better germination rate is achieved for all cistuses if the seeds are scarified: they should be rubbed briefly between two sheets of sandpaper in order to remove some of the tough skin that surrounds the seed and inhibits germination. Seed dormancy can also be broken by simulating the action of fire by putting the seeds in an oven heated to 150 ºC for 10 minutes.

Cistus atriplicifolius

ORIGIN SOUTHERN SPAIN, MOROCCO
HEIGHT 1 TO 1.25 M
SPREAD 80 CM
POSITION SUN
HARDINESS −10 TO −12 °C
DROUGHT RESISTANCE CODE 5

For a long time classed as a *Halimium*, this plant is now considered to be a cistus, following the revision of the genus recently published by Jean-Pierre Demoly (see Further Reading). *Cistus atriplicifolius* is a shrub with handsome silver-grey, evergreen leaves. The golden yellow flowers, preceded by elegant dark red buds, appear from May to July. Flowering may sometimes continue into September if the summer is not too dry. The leaves, buds and flowers form a striking contrast: this is certainly one of the most beautiful cistuses in our garden. We grow it in association with *Salvia* 'Allen

Chickering' and *Perovskia* 'Blue Spire' to create an attractive scene in early summer, consisting of yellow and blue flowers mingled with different shades of grey foliage. *Cistus atriplicifolius* is happy in acid, neutral or slightly alkaline soils. Its lifespan is about ten years: the poorer, drier and better drained the soil, the longer it lives.

Propagation is by scarified seed in autumn. The seeds should be collected in the wild from sites containing only this species in order to avoid all risk of hybridization. The young seedlings are very susceptible to wilt and rotting: they should be kept in a well-ventilated place and are better sown in widely spaced pots rather than seedboxes in order to limit the spread of cryptogamic diseases.

Cistus creticus
Cretan cistus

ORIGIN MEDITERRANEAN BASIN
HEIGHT 1 M
SPREAD 1 M
POSITION SUN OR SEMI-SHADE
HARDINESS −8 TO −10 °C
DROUGHT RESISTANCE CODE 5

A shrub with grey-green evergreen leaves with irregular undulations. The foliage of *Cistus creticus* can be aromatic, according to the variety. The leaves of the most aromatic variety produce ladanum, a resin that has been used since antiquity in medicine and perfumes. In the villages of Crete, ladanum was traditionally harvested in one of two ways: either by flailing the sticky young shoots with a *ladanisterion*, a sort of broad rake equipped with leather strips, or by combing the beards of the goats that had passed over cistus-covered hillsides. The pretty luminous pink flowers appear in

Cistus creticus and *Salvia pomifera* growing side by side in the White Mountains of Crete.

April–May. *Cistus creticus* has different degrees of resistance to alkalinity depending on its geographical place of origin. We have selected several that tolerate alkaline conditions well, including the cultivar 'Bali' (collected at Bali, Crete, where *Cistus creticus* grows at the foot of a fine stand of *Arbutus andrachne*). *Cistus creticus* has a relatively long lifespan – about twelve to fifteen years – particularly if grown in poor, very dry soil. It withstands salt spray and is often seen growing right by the coast on Mediterranean islands, Corsica, Crete and Cyprus.

Propagation is by semi-ripe cuttings in autumn or by scarified seed in autumn. The seed should be collected in the wild from sites where only this species grows in order to avoid all risk of hybridization.

• *Cistus creticus* f. *albus* is a form with pretty white flowers. The clone that we grow has a compact habit, tolerates alkalinity well and is particularly long-lived.

Cistus ladanifer f. maculatus

ORIGIN SOUTHWEST EUROPE, NORTH AFRICA
HEIGHT 2 M OR MORE
SPREAD 1 TO 1.25 M
POSITION SUN
HARDINESS −10 TO −12 °C
DROUGHT RESISTANCE CODE 5

An upright shrub with long, dark green, evergreen leaves. The leaves and young shoots are sticky and very aromatic in hot weather: this is because they are covered in ladanum, used in Spain for making perfumes. The spectacular large white flowers appear in April–May. At the bases of the petals, around the central bunch of stamens, are dark red blotches, very finely drawn, as if with strokes of a Chinese brush. A form exists in the wild that does not have these blotches. *Cistus ladanifer* often grows in dense colonies, so that whole hillsides can be transformed into a magnificent landscape of white flowers contrasting with the dark foliage. In France, near Saint-Chinian in the Hérault region, there is a famous site where vast expanses of *Cistus ladanifer* may be seen on the Saint-Pons road just outside the village. *Cistus ladanifer* only grows in acid soil. It likes poor, stony soils, and lives for about ten years.

Propagation is by scarified seed in autumn. The seed should be collected in the wild from sites where only this species grows in order to avoid all risk of hybridization.

• *Cistus ladanifer* var. *sulcatus* grows in southern Portugal, near Cape St Vincent in the Algarve. It has a compact habit, not growing more than 1 m tall in the wild. Its

dark leaves are covered in a thick layer of ladanum, making it the most aromatic of all cistuses and as sticky as fly-paper! The large white flowers do not have dark blotches. It can be planted in acid, neutral or slightly alkaline soil that is well drained. Bob Page, the English cistus specialist, collected *Cistus ladanifer* var. *sulcatus* f. *bicolor* in Portugal, rare in the wild, some selections of which have spectacular markings.

Cistus laurifolius

ORIGIN MOUNTAINS OF SOUTHERN EUROPE, NORTH AFRICA AND TURKEY
HEIGHT 2 M OR MORE
SPREAD 1 TO 1.25 M
POSITION SUN OR SEMI-SHADE
HARDINESS AROUND −20 °C
DROUGHT RESISTANCE CODE 5

A vigorous shrub with large, thick, leathery evergreen leaves of a matt green. The tender young shoots are sticky and aromatic, while old leaves are often covered in an attractive silver bloom. This species flowers late: the white flowers opening in May–June, by which time most cistuses are approaching the end of their flowering season. For several weeks before they open, the flowers are preceded by long, bright red buds, which are highly decorative. *Cistus laurifolius* grows in acid, neutral or slightly alkaline soil. Its natural habitat is in the mountains and as a result it is remarkably hardy. It covers entire slopes in the western Pyrenees, where it is buried under snow in winter. Fine expanses of this cistus grow along the little road that winds above the village of Eus, just opposite Canigou in the French Pyrenees. It should be planted in poor, well-drained soil and is fairly long-

lived – from twelve to fifteen years. The base becomes bare as the plant ages, but this allows its twisted trunk, with handsome bark peeling off in strips of a warm reddish-orange colour, to be appreciated.

Propagate by scarified seeds in autumn. The seed should be collected in the wild from sites where only this species grows in order to avoid all risk of hybridization.

• *Cistus laurifolius* subsp. *atlanticus* has a compact habit, forming a dense mass not exceeding 1 metre in height. There are good places to see it in the Middle Atlas, between Azrou and Ifrane, where it often grows in association with *Cytisus battandieri* in clearings in the large cedar forests; the tailless Magot monkey, *Macaca sylvana*, may also occasionally be spotted here.

Cistus salviifolius

ORIGIN MEDITERRANEAN BASIN, CAUCASUS
HEIGHT UP TO 1 M DEPENDING ON THE VARIETY
SPREAD 1 M OR MORE
POSITION SUN OR SEMI-SHADE
HARDINESS −12 TO −15 °C
DROUGHT RESISTANCE CODE 4

A dense, branching shrub with a variable habit: in the wild it may develop into a regular ball shape, or it may cover the ground in a vigorously growing carpet. The rounded, grey-green, evergreen leaves have a rough texture. The pretty cup-shaped flowers open in April–May and are a soft ivory-white. *Cistus salviifolius* is

The magenta blooms of *Cistus* x *argenteus* 'Blushing Peggy Sammons' mingle with the white flowers of *Cistus laurifolius*. These two cistuses are distinguished by their remarkable hardiness, making it possible to plant them outside mediterranean climate zones.

distinguished from other cistus species by its good tolerance of shade: it often colonizes the light undergrowth in forests of oak or pine. It grows in acid, neutral or slightly alkaline soil. It requires good drainage and easily becomes chlorotic in winter if the soil is too heavy: in the wild it always grows in stony or sandy soil. It withstands salt spray, so that it is frequently found growing very near the sea, both around the Mediterranean and on Atlantic coasts. It lives for about ten to twelve years.

Propagation is by semi-ripe cuttings in autumn or by scarified seed in autumn. The seed should be collected in the wild from sites where only this species grows in order to avoid all risk of hybridization.

• *Cistus salviifolius* 'Bonifacio' is a selection with creeping stems that forms an excellent carpeting groundcover. We collected it in Corsica, on the cliffs of Cape Pertusato, where cistuses and rosemaries, for centuries forced to hug the ground by violent winds and salt spray, have evolved genetically a carpeting habit.

Cistus × aguilari

HEIGHT 2 M
SPREAD 1.25 M
POSITION SUN OR SEMI-SHADE
HARDINESS −10 TO −12 °C
DROUGHT RESISTANCE CODE 4

This natural hybrid of *Cistus ladanifer* and *Cistus populifolius* var. *major* was collected in Spain at the beginning of the 20th century by Oscar Warburg. Its official name is *Cistus × aguilari* nvar. *pilosus* nf. *Oscari*, but it is grown today under the name *Cistus × aguilari*. It is a vigorous shrub with upright branches and a pyramidal habit. Its long, dark green, evergreen leaves have broadly undulating margins. It is clear from the stickiness of its young shoots and its strong scent in hot weather that *Cistus ladanifer* is one of its parents. The handsome white flowers, of an impressive size, seem to be arranged on the foliage in successive tiers. *Cistus × aguilari* grows in acid, neutral or slightly alkaline soil and lives for about ten to twelve years.

Propagation is by semi-ripe cuttings in autumn.

• *Cistus × aguilari* 'Maculatus' has spectacular large purple blotches at the base of its petals. A back-cross between *Cistus × aguilari* and *Cistus ladanifer* f. *maculatus*, made in 1920 by Oscar Warburg, its official name is *Cistus × aguilari* nvar. *pilosus* nf. *maculatus*, but it is cultivated as *Cistus × aguilari* 'Maculatus'. It grows only in acid soils. **DROUGHT RESISTANCE CODE** 4

Majestically reaching almost 2 metres in height, *Cistus × aguilari* is transformed into a cascade of white flowers in May.

Large purple blotches stain the spectacular flowers of *Cistus* × *aguilari* 'Maculatus'.

Cistus × *cyprius* has inherited qualities from both its parents: *Cistus ladanifer* has given it its purple blotches and *Cistus laurifolius* its excellent hardiness.

Cistus × argenteus 'Blushing Peggy Sammons'

HEIGHT 1.2 M
SPREAD 1 M
POSITION SUN
HARDINESS AROUND −15 °C
DROUGHT RESISTANCE CODE 4

A shrub with grey-green evergreen foliage and handsome magenta flowers which appear in April–May. In our garden we've created multicoloured plantings by mixing various cistuses with white, pale pink and bright pink flowers: in spring, in the midst of this cascade of colour, *Cistus* × *argenteus* 'Blushing Peggy Sammons' stands out as it has the darkest-coloured flowers. It lives for about twelve to fifteen years. Its parentage is rather complicated (a triple hybrid of *Cistus albidus*, *Cistus creticus* and *Cistus laurifolius*), but all that needs to be remembered is that its hardiness comes from its parent *Cistus laurifolius*. It tolerates alkalinity as long as the soil has perfect drainage. If the soil is too heavy it suffers from root asphyxiation and rapidly becomes chlorotic in winter.

Propagate by semi-ripe cuttings in autumn.

• *Cistus* × *argenteus* '*Peggy Sammons*' has lighter-coloured flowers of an astonishing tender pink with metallic glints.

Cistus × cyprius

HEIGHT 1.5 TO 2 M
SPREAD 1 M
POSITION SUN
HARDINESS AROUND −15 °C
DROUGHT RESISTANCE CODE 5

Cistus × *cyprius* is a natural hybrid of *Cistus ladanifer* and *Cistus laurifolius*: if you look carefully you can find fine specimens growing among its parents at the great cistus site near Saint-Chinian in the Hérault region of France. It forms a vigorous shrub with an upright habit. Its long, thick, leathery evergreen leaves are often covered in a grey bloom that contrasts well with the dark, sticky young shoots that are highly aromatic in the heat. *Cistus* × *cyprius* grows in acid, neutral or slightly alkaline soil. It has inherited good characteristics from both its parents: from *Cistus ladanifer* it gets its large, purple-blotched flowers, while *Cistus laurifolius* has given it its excellent hardiness and greater toleration of alkalinity. Its attractive flowers emerge from red buds in April–May. A fine garden plant, it is both robust and easy to grow and has a good lifespan – in our garden the oldest specimen, aged fifteen years, still flowers faithfully each spring. Unfortunately, it is hard to propagate and so is rarely found in nurseries.

Propagation is by semi-ripe cuttings in autumn. Rooting is slow and the success rate low. The cuttings must be examined regularly so that dead leaves can be removed to avoid providing a breeding ground for grey rot.

• *Cistus* × *cyprius* var. *ellipticus* '**Elma**' is a hybrid of *Cistus ladanifer* var. *sulcatus* and *Cistus laurifolius*. It has a more compact habit and dark green aromatic leaves covered in ladanum. It flowers exceptionally profusely: in April–May the plant is covered in large, soft, ivory-white flowers. In late afternoon the petals fall all at once, creating a superb ephemeral carpet on the ground reminiscent of a Japanese print.

Cistus × florentinus

HEIGHT 1 M
SPREAD 1 M
POSITION SUN OR SEMI-SHADE
HARDINESS AROUND −12 TO −15 °C
DROUGHT RESISTANCE CODE 4

Cistus × *florentinus* is a natural hybrid of *Cistus monspeliensis* and *Cistus salviifolius*, and is often found wherever its two parents grow together in the wild: we know of several specimens in the garrigue a few kilometres from our nursery. It is a compact and branching shrub with an attractive ball-shaped habit. Its long, narrow, evergreen leaves are agreeably scented in the heat. In April–May the plant is covered in a mass of small white flowers which are grouped in scorpioid inflorescences (shaped like the tail of a scorpion), as is the case with all the hybrids of *Cistus monspeliensis*. *Cistus* × *florentinus* tolerates alkaline conditions well. It requires well-drained soil: if the soil is too heavy, it will suffer from root asphyxiation and may become chlorotic in winter, in spite of its good tolerance of alkalinity. It has a lifespan of ten to twelve years. In conditions of extreme drought this cistus may lose some of its leaves, enabling it to limit water loss effectively, but making it less ornamental at the end of summer.

Propagation is by semi-ripe cuttings in autumn.

• *Cistus* × *florentinus* '**Tramontane**' forms a low groundcover, very dense and branching, with dark green foliage contrasting well with its numerous small white flowers. In our garden it is the best of the cistuses with a carpeting habit: an excellent groundcover for dry slopes and rock gardens.

LEFT *Cistus × florentinus* is covered in small flowers as light as butterflies.

ABOVE *Cistus × pauranthus* 'Natacha' is a compact cistus, with an attractive rounded shape.

BELOW In the Corbières, near the Abbey of Fontfroide, *Cistus × hybridus* grows at the edges of holm oak woods. In April–May its foliage disappears beneath a multitude of flowers.

Cistus × hybridus

HEIGHT 80 CM TO 1 M
SPREAD 1 TO 1.5 M
POSITION SUN OR SEMI-SHADE
HARDINESS AROUND −15 °C
DROUGHT RESISTANCE CODE 4

Near the Abbey of Fontfroide, southwest of Narbonne in the Corbières area is a remarkable botanic site, known for centuries, where successive generations of experts have studied numerous cistus species and their natural hybrids. *Cistus × hybridus*, a natural hybrid between *Cistus populifolius* and *Cistus salviifolius*, is common there. It is a shrub with very dense foliage which forms a perfectly regular dome shape. Its dark green, rough-textured evergreen leaves disappear in April–May beneath the multitude of white flowers set off by a large central bunch of yellow stamens. *Cistus × hybridus* grows in acid, neutral or slightly alkaline soil. At Fontfroide it is found growing both in sun and in semi-shade, often beneath holm oaks – it can even tolerate dense shade, although in this situation it flowers noticeably less. Its lifespan is relatively long, about twelve to fifteen years.

Propagation is by semi-ripe cuttings in autumn.

Cistus × pauranthus

HEIGHT 80 CM TO 1 M
SPREAD 80 CM TO 1 M
POSITION SUN
HARDINESS −8 TO −10 °C
DROUGHT RESISTANCE CODE 5

Cistus × pauranthus is a natural hybrid between *Cistus salviifolius* and *Cistus parviflorus* that is occasionally found in

Cyprus or in Crete. It is a well-branched shrub with attractive, grey-green, evergreen leaves which have a rough texture. The numerous cup-shaped pink flowers appear in April to May. It is a highly decorative plant, looking from a distance like a pink-flowered *Cistus salviifolius*. *Cistus × pauranthus* tolerates alkaline conditions well. It requires perfectly drained soil: if the soil is too heavy it suffers from root asphyxiation and may become chlorotic in winter, in spite of its good alkalinity tolerance.

Propagation is by semi-ripe cuttings in autumn.

• *Cistus × pauranthus* 'Natacha' is a cultivar which we selected near Vai, at the eastern tip of Crete, on hillsides overlooking the famous beach where the rare palm tree

Phoenix theophrasti is a protected species. It is a very compact shrub that forms an amazingly perfect regular cushion, as if it had been clipped as topiary. The pastel pink, almost white, flowers are very small but very abundant: they can completely cover the plant in April. In our garden we like to combine *Cistus × pauranthus* 'Natacha' with other Cretan plants, such as *Scabiosa minoana*, *Helichrysum orientale*, *Satureja thymbra*, *Salvia pomifera* or *Hypericum empetrifolium*, so that a stroll in the garden momentarily becomes a delightful invitation to travel. One thing to note is that this cistus is not very hardy: its foliage starts to become burnt at temperatures of −6 to −8 °C (we have noticed, however, that it is much hardier if it is grown in poor, dry, extremely well-drained soil).

Cistus × pulverulentus

HEIGHT 40 TO 60 CM
SPREAD 1.25 TO 2 M, SOMETIMES MORE
POSITION SUN
HARDINESS −10 TO −12 °C
DROUGHT RESISTANCE CODE 4

Cistus × pulverulentus is a hybrid between *Cistus albidus* and *Cistus crispus*. It is a vigorous shrub with a spreading habit that makes an excellent groundcover for poor, dry slopes. In the form usually grown, it is clear from its crinkled grey-green evergreen leaves with undulating margins that *Cistus crispus* is the dominant parent. The vibrant colour of the flowers, an amazing dark pink, is eye-catching. They are produced in succession from May until the beginning of July, making this one of the longest flowering cistuses, despite the onset of the summer heat. In conditions of intense drought it may lose some of its leaves, which enables the plant to limit water loss, but does make it look less ornamental at the end of summer. *Cistus × pulverulentus* tolerates alkaline conditions well and withstands salt spray. It requires soil that is perfectly drained; if the soil is too heavy the plant suffers from root asphyxiation and may become chlorotic in winter, in spite of its tolerance of alkalinity. It has a good lifespan of about twelve to fifteen years and over the course of the years it can grow very large. Our oldest specimen, aged about fifteen years, has a spread of more than 3 metres, forming a magnificent cascade of flowers in late spring.

Propagation is by semi-ripe cuttings in autumn.

Over the centuries successive authors have described *Cistus × pulverulentus* under different names, leading to great confusion as to exactly what it should be called. Linnaeus himself made the first mistake when he studied the plant in the Narbonne region: not realizing it was a hybrid, he gave the plant a species name (*Cistus incanus*).

Unfortunately the name *Cistus incanus* was subsequently used by various botanists to designate other species, resulting in a tangle of erroneous names which only specialists would now dare to attempt to unravel. If the priority rule that governs botanical names were followed, this plant should be called *Cistus × incanus*. However, in order to avoid creating further confusion I prefer for the time being to stick to the name *Cistus × pulverulentus*, which is currently used in horticulture. Whatever its name, it is an exceptional plant.

• *Cistus × pulverulentus* **Gp** *Delilei* is a natural hybrid frequently found near the Abbey of Fontfroide in the Aude region of France. It has the same parents as *Cistus × pulverulentus*, but its handsome downy grey foliage indicates that *Cistus albidus* is the dominant one. It is a vigorous shrub which develops into a large, regular ball shape. We grow a form with soft luminous pink flowers. It is a very adaptable, easy to grow and particularly long-lived plant. If I had room for just one cistus, I think this is the one I'd choose. **HEIGHT** 1 M **SPREAD** 1 TO 1.5 M

Cistus × purpureus

HEIGHT 1.25 M
SPREAD 1.25 M
POSITION SUN
HARDINESS −10 TO −12 °C
DROUGHT RESISTANCE CODE 5

Cistus × purpureus is a hybrid of *Cistus creticus* and *Cistus ladanifer*. It is a dense, branching shrub which forms a large regular ball shape. Its long, dark green, evergreen leaves have an agreeable scent in hot weather. Large flowers – a purplish-pink, set off by fine maroon blotches – appear in April–May. These spectacular bright flowers form an attractive contrast with the dark foliage. *Cistus × purpureus* tolerates alkaline conditions well. It requires dry, perfectly drained soil: if the soil is too heavy it suffers from root asphyxiation and may become chlorotic in winter, in spite of its good tolerance of alkalinity. It lives about ten to twelve years.

Propagate by semi-ripe cuttings in autumn.

Cistus × purpureus is easy to grow, and its luminous flowers and fine dark foliage, aromatic in the heat, make it one of the most prized plants in the dry garden.

Cistus × pulverulentus flowers late, when most cistuses have already finished flowering. Its intense colour glows in the hot June light.

With its vigorous spreading habit, *Cistus × pulverulentus* is one of the best groundcovers for rocky slopes. Here *Eschscholzia californica* mingles its dazzling blooms with the dark pink flowers of the cistus, creating a cheerful and colourful scene that requires very little maintenance.

Cistus × *ralletii* has a fairly short lifespan of only about ten to twelve years, but its flowers are so beautiful that one can easily forgive it.

• *Cistus* × *purpureus* 'Alan Fradd' is a mutation with white flowers with a dark red blotch at the base of the petals. Its foliage and habit are so similar to those of *Cistus* × *purpureus* that it is hard to tell them apart if they are not in flower. It is worth growing them together, for the colours of their flowers set each other off well.

• *Cistus* × *purpureus* f. *holorhodeos* has unusual pretty Indian-pink flowers whose petals have no blotches (in Greek *holorhodeos* means 'entirely pink'). The edges of the petals turn upwards, like a gutter, giving an unusual shape to the flower.

Cistus × ralletii

HEIGHT 1.25 M
SPREAD 1 M
POSITION SUN
HARDINESS −8 TO −10 °C
DROUGHT RESISTANCE CODE 3

Cistus × *ralletii* is a hybrid of *Cistus creticus* and *Cistus symphytifolius* (a cistus from the Canary Islands). It has broad, grey-green, evergreen leaves with slightly undulating edges. Its fine clear pink flowers are exceptionally abundant and are produced in succession from April until the beginning of July, entirely covering the plant: this is one of the most floriferous cistuses in our collection, a true ball of flowers! We have been told that in an oceanic climate it can flower non-stop all summer long. *Cistus* × *ralletii* grows in acid, neutral or slightly alkaline soil. It requires poor, well-drained soil and has a medium lifespan of about ten to twelve years.

Propagation is by semi-ripe cuttings in autumn.

Cistus × skanbergii

HEIGHT 60 CM
SPREAD 80 CM TO 1 M
POSITION SUN
HARDINESS −10 TO −12 °C
DROUGHT RESISTANCE CODE 4

Cistus × *skanbergii* is a natural hybrid of *Cistus monspeliensis* and *Cistus parviflorus*. It is found in Cyprus on the rocky slopes of the Akamas peninsula, where the limestone rocks, white in the heat of the sun, contrast with the dark blue sea. This hybrid sometimes grows so abundantly that it almost seems to dominate the phrygana, as if trying to supplant its parents. It is a dense and branching shrub, which forms a large spreading ball. Its linear evergreen leaves are grey and downy. The flowers, of a pale salmon pink, are grouped in scorpioid inflorescences (shaped like the tail of a scorpion), reminiscent of its parent *Cistus monspeliensis*. They appear in April and are remarkably abundant, compensating for their small size. *Cistus* × *skanbergii* tolerates alkaline conditions well. It requires a dry, perfectly drained soil, without which its lifespan is reduced and it easily becomes chlorotic in winter in spite of its good tolerance of alkalinity. Its lifespan is in the medium range, about ten to twelve years. In conditions of intense drought it may lose some of its leaves, which enables it to limit water loss effectively but makes it less ornamental at the end of summer.

Propagate by semi-ripe cuttings in autumn.

The gentle colour of *Cistus* × *skanbergii* lends it a subtle charm. It can be clipped lightly in winter to accentuate its natural regular ball shape.

Cistus × verguinii 'Paul Pècherat'

HEIGHT 1 M
SPREAD 1.25
POSITION SUN OR SEMI-SHADE
HARDINESS −12 TO −15 °C
DROUGHT RESISTANCE CODE 4.5

Cistus × verguinii is a natural hybrid of *Cistus salviifolius* and *Cistus ladanifer*. It can be seen growing among it parents on Tibidabo, whose beautiful wild slopes overlook the bustle of Barcelona. The cultivar 'Paul Pècherat' appeared spontaneously as a seedling in the Pècherat arboretum in the Charente-Maritime region of France, which has a huge collection of cistuses. Its narrow, evergreen, dark green leaves are agreeably aromatic in hot weather. It is a dense and branching shrub which spreads with age to form an impressive mass. It is worth noting that it regrows well from old wood after severe pruning, something unusual in cistuses. Its white flowers appear in April and are shaped like open cups, with a fine dark purple, almost black, blotch at the base of the petals. The genetic pool sometimes turns up surprises: *Cistus × verguinii* 'Paul Pècherat' is notable for its good tolerance of alkalinity, unexpected in view of its parentage. It lives for at least fifteen years and is an excellent variety, robust and easy to grow. In our garden, of all the white cistuses with a dark marking, it is the one that behaves best.

Propagation is by semi-ripe cuttings in autumn.

Clematis armandii
(Ranunculaceae)

ORIGIN CHINA
HEIGHT AND SPREAD 5 M
POSITION SUN OR SHADE
HARDINESS −12 TO −15 °C
DROUGHT RESISTANCE CODE 3

A climber with long twining stems (*Clematis* comes from the Greek *klēma*, 'vine shoot', 'twining stem') and dark green, evergreen leaves that are thick and leathery. In Feburary to March the plant is covered in a profusion of pretty white flowers that are sweetly scented. *Clematis armandii* tolerates alkaline conditions well. It prefers friable, fairly deep soils. If planted against a wall it will need support as it is not self-clinging. It is often planted at the foot of a small tree so that it can scramble through the branches; it can even be planted beneath a tree in dense shade, where it will have a tendency to climb high among the branches seeking the light and flowering in the sun. Each year in our garden we await its flowering with happy impatience: appearing at the same time as the first almond blossom, the delicate flowers of *Clematis armandii* herald the imminent end of winter.

Propagation is by soft-tip cuttings in spring.

Propagation is delicate: since the nodes are widely spaced along the stem, a section with a single node should be cut and inserted in the potting compost up to leaf level.

Appearing at the same time as the almond blossom, the white cascades of *Clematis armandii* herald the imminent end of winter.

Clematis cirrhosa

ORIGIN MEDITERRANEAN BASIN
HEIGHT AND SPREAD 2 TO 3 M
POSITION SUN OR SEMI-SHADE
HARDINESS −12 TO −15 °C
DROUGHT RESISTANCE CODE 5

A climber with delicate twining stems which coil easily round their supports. (In Latin *cirrhosa* means 'twisting like a tendril'. Don't be confused: this clematis has nothing at all to do with cirrhosis – which derives from the Greek *kirrhos*, 'orange', describing the colour of the diseased liver.) The shiny dark green leaves take on attractive bronze tints in cold weather. They are evergreen in winter, but wither and fall around July, so that the plant can get through the summer without suffering from drought. The creamy-white, bell-shaped flowers are numerous and open very early, appearing in February–March, sometimes earlier if the winter is mild, and occasionally even in autumn. We like to have *Clematis cirrhosa* climbing through large deciduous shrubs such as *Vitex*, *Punica* or *Cotinus*, since their growth cycles are complementary: the clematis decorates the bare branches with cascades of flowers in winter, while its leaves have fallen in summer when the shrubs are in full growth. *Clematis cirrhosa* tolerates alkaline conditions well and withstands salt spray. It is unfussy about soil type and is an attractive, graceful plant that is easy to grow.

Propagation is by softwood cuttings in autumn or spring.

At the beginning of May our cistus garden almost founders beneath the abundance of the flowers. In the foreground the white flowers of *Cistus × verguinii* 'Paul Pècherat' contrast well with its handsome dark foliage.

In February the twining stems of *Clematis cirrhosa* twist around the stems of a pistachio in the Atlas mountains. Its creamy-white, slightly lax flowers stand out against the deep blue winter sky.

• *Clematis flammula* is deciduous. In summer and early autumn it is covered in tiny white flowers, which are extremely sweetly scented, followed by decorative feathery silver seed heads. It can be grown as a climbing plant or used as groundcover on slopes where conditions are difficult. It withstands salt spray. **ORIGIN** GARRIGUE AND COASTAL DUNES AROUND THE MEDITERRANEAN **HARDINESS** −12 TO −15 °C **DROUGHT RESISTANCE CODE** 4

Coleonema album
(Rutaceae)

ORIGIN COASTS AND MOUNTAINS OF THE CAPE PROVINCE, SOUTH AFRICA
HEIGHT 1.5 M
SPREAD 1 M
POSITION SUN
HARDINESS −8 TO −10 °C
DROUGHT RESISTANCE CODE 4

A shrub with very fine foliage resembling that of heather. The evergreen leaves give off a pleasantly sharp scent when crushed, like a mixture of caramel, cinnamon and citrus. An essential oil is extracted from them, used in South Africa to repel mosquitoes and soothe insect bites (you can use it like citronella, simply rubbing the leaves on your skin, which remains scented for a long time). In our garden the plant forms an upright ball, but in its natural environment the wind and salt often cause it to hug the ground, as at the Cape of Good Hope where this species is abundant. It grows here in the front line, just behind the great rocks on the shore, exposed to the tempestuous winds that seem to come straight from the South Pole. The pliable branches are covered in very decorative tiny white flowers from January to April, or even from November in a mild climate. *Coleonema album* tolerates alkaline conditions well. It prefers light, well-drained soils and has a perfect ability to withstand salt spray.

Unperturbed by strong winds, *Coleonema album* grows on the coast near the Cape of Good Hope in South Africa. In our garden it is an elegant shrub with foliage that releases a delicate scent when crushed.

Propagation is by seed in autumn or by softwood cuttings in spring, after flowering.

• *Coleonema pulchrum* has pretty pink star-shaped flowers that open from January to April. **ORIGIN** SOUTH AFRICA **HARDINESS** −6 TO −8 °C **DROUGHT RESISTANCE CODE** 4

Colutea arborescens
(Fabaceae) Bladder Senna

ORIGIN SOUTHERN EUROPE, NORTH AFRICA
HEIGHT 2 M
SPREAD 1 M
POSITION SUN
HARDINESS −15 °C AND BELOW
DROUGHT RESISTANCE CODE 3.5

A shrub with composite deciduous leaves. Its discreet yellow flowers appear in May–June and are followed by curious inflated seedpods that remain ornamental throughout the whole summer. *Colutea* has a branching habit when young, but as it ages the base of the plant becomes bare and forms a small trunk. It has a reputation for not liking pruning: the name *Colutea* comes from the Greek, *kolouō*, 'to cut short' or 'mutilate', since according to ancient writers the plant was in danger of dying if pruned. *Colutea arborescens* tolerates alkaline conditions well. It is unfussy about soil type and is a robust shrub that is easy to grow.

Propagation is by seed in autumn after hot water treatment: pour boiling water on the seeds then leave them overnight to swell.

Convolvulus cneorum
(Convolvulaceae)

ORIGIN CROATIA, ALBANIA, AMONG STONES AND ROCKS NEAR THE SEA
HEIGHT 50 CM
SPREAD 60 TO 80 CM
POSITION SUN
HARDINESS −10 TO −12 °C
DROUGHT RESISTANCE CODE 4

A shrub with beautiful silky, silver evergreen leaves. The plant forms a spreading ball and will cascade downwards if grown on top of a

After flowering, *Colutea arborescens* continues to be ornamental for a long time thanks to its curious inflated seedpods which are translucent.

low stone wall. Flowering begins in April and continues until July. Elegant pink buds appear amidst the silver foliage, which then open into widely flaring white flowers, each petal marked by a delicate pink vein. *Convolvulus cneorum* tolerates alkaline conditions well. It requires a light sandy soil that is very well drained. It does not tolerate humidity in summer since it is prone to fungal diseases which lead to die-back of the branches and the rapid death of the plant. It is a slightly capricious species, but so beautiful that it is definitely worth making the effort to provide the cultivation conditions that suit it. In our garden we have planted it on a small mound (40 centimetres high and 1 metre wide) made of large stones and sand mixed with a little soil, and the plant is perfectly happy. It is easy to grow in a pot on the terrace, provided it is planted in a medium that has good drainage and that consists of a high proportion of pebbles and sand.

Propagation is by softwood cuttings in autumn.

• *Convolvulus sabatius* is a creeping perennial covered in pretty blue flowers from May to July. It can climb a little if it finds some support. A striking blue and white effect is created if it is planted in association with *Cistus × florentinus* 'Tramontane', for the flowers are of exactly the same size and look as if they are growing on the same plant. **ORIGIN** NORTH AFRICA **HARDINESS** THE ROOTSTOCK CAN TOLERATE TEMPERATURES OF −10 TO −12 °C BUT THE FOLIAGE IS DECIDUOUS AT −6 TO −8 °C **DROUGHT RESISTANCE CODE** 3

Coronilla glauca
(Fabaceae)

ORIGIN MEDITERRANEAN BASIN
HEIGHT 1 TO 1.25 M
SPREAD 1 M
POSITION SUN OR SEMI-SHADE
HARDINESS −12 TO −15 °C
DROUGHT RESISTANCE CODE 3.5

A shrub with thick, blue-green, evergreen leaves. The plant naturally forms an attractive dense mound, covered in deliciously scented bright yellow flowers from the end of January to the beginning of April. The flowers are tightly packed together on circular inflorescences (the name *Coronilla* comes from the Latin *corona*, 'crown', referring to the shape of the inflorescences). *Coronilla glauca* self-seeds very freely and can be used as a pioneer plant on slopes or in the wild areas of large gardens. We like to grow it in association with other species that perfume the mild air in early spring, such as *Choisya* 'Aztec Pearl', *Buddleja officinalis* or *Euphorbia characias* subsp. *wulfenii*. *Coronilla glauca* tolerates alkaline conditions well. It prefers poor, stony, well-drained soils. In extreme drought it may lose some of its leaves, enabling it to limit water loss. Like most pioneer species, it has a relatively short lifespan of ten to twelve years.

Propagation is by seed in autumn after hot water treatment: poor boiling water on to the seeds then leave them to swell overnight. It can also be propagated by softwood cuttings at the end of winter, just before the flowers form.

• *Coronilla glauca* '**Citrina**' has beautiful flowers of a superb soft pale yellow. It self-seeds freely, but reverts to the bright yellow of the type: it needs to be replaced frequently, but is easy to propagate by softwood cuttings taken just before flowering.

• *Coronilla emerus* is deciduous in winter. Its springtime flowering is less profuse, but it is a valuable species for colonizing shady parts of the garden: it is happy under pines or oaks. **ORIGIN** SOUTHERN EUROPE **HARDINESS** −15 °C AND BELOW **DROUGHT RESISTANCE CODE** 3

• *Coronilla juncea* only keeps its leaves for a few months in winter. As soon as temperatures rise the plant loses its leaves and its thin cylindrical branches make it look surprisingly like a small rush. It is covered in a profusion of bright yellow flowers from February to April. This is a plant that likes stony soils and withstands salt spray well. It is, for example, commonly found round the sea creeks of the Marseille area: in spring the attractive bright yellow bushes clinging to the rocks make a beautiful contrast with the dark blue sea.

Convolvulus cneorum needs light, perfectly drained soil, otherwise it is short-lived. We like to plant it on top of a stone wall so that its beautiful silver foliage can cascade over the edge.

Detail of an inflorescence of *Coronilla glauca* 'Citrina'. The name *Coronilla* comes from the Latin *corona*, 'crown', referring to the way the flowers are arranged.

Coronilla juncea growing upright on rocky ridges in the Sierra del Cardò, near Tarragona in Spain.

ORIGIN MEDITERRANEAN BASIN **HARDINESS** −12 TO −15 °C **DROUGHT RESISTANCE CODE** 5

• *Coronilla minima* forms a carpet of small, thick, blue-green leaves. It is an easily grown plant for the rock garden, and is covered in yellow flowers in May–June. Good places to see this plant can be found in the Hérault region of France, where it grows among dolomitic rocks in the Mourèze corrie, together with *Helichrysum stoechas* and *Globularia alypum*. **ORIGIN** SOUTHERN EUROPE **HARDINESS** −15 °C AND BELOW **DROUGHT RESISTANCE CODE** 5

• *Coronilla ramosissima* is a little-known species which we collected at an altitude of about 1,500 metres in the Anti-Atlas, where it grows in an arid environment among amazing cactiform euphorbias (*Euphorbia echinus* subsp. *echinus*). It has numerous small evergreen leaves, thick and glaucous, tightly packed on slightly twisted stems, and is covered in small yellow flowers in April–May. **ORIGIN** MOROCCO **HARDINESS** −10 TO −12 °C **DROUGHT RESISTANCE CODE** 6

Very early in spring the coronillas are covered in flowers. The dark silhouette of a cypress is framed by the bright yellow of *Coronilla glauca*, while in the foreground the pale yellow flowers of the form 'Citrina' soften the scene. Other plants here are (from left to right) *Teucrium fruticans*, *Bupleurum fruticosum*, *Atriplex canescens*, *Juniperus oxycedrus* and *Artemisia arborescens*.

Correa alba
(Rutaceae) Australian Fuchsia

ORIGIN AUSTRALIA
HEIGHT 1.5 TO 2 M
SPREAD 1.5 M
POSITION SUN
HARDINESS −8 TO −10 °C
DROUGHT RESISTANCE CODE 4

A branching shrub with evergreen foliage. The grey-green leathery leaves have a downy, silvery underside. They give off a pleasant lemony scent when crushed and are used in Australia to make a tea. The numerous white flowers, like little star-shaped bells, have a waxy look. They appear from January to April, then again in autumn, and sometimes even throughout the year in a mild climate. *Correa alba* tolerates alkaline conditions well. It prefers light, well-drained soils. It withstands salt spray extremely well. A slight annual pruning of the tips of the branches in autumn helps the plant maintain a dense and compact habit.

Propagation is by softwood cuttings in spring.

Cotinus coggygria
(Anacardiaceae) Smoke Bush

ORIGIN SOUTHERN EUROPE, ASIA
HEIGHT 1.5 TO 2 M
SPREAD 1.5 M
POSITION SUN
HARDINESS −8 TO −10 °C
DROUGHT RESISTANCE CODE 4

A deciduous large shrub or bushy tree with green leaves that take on fine orange-red tints in autumn. The small yellow-green flowers appear in May–June and once they are over, the flower stalks become elongated and form long plumes covered with hairs, lending the inflorescences a remarkable and very decorative feathery appearance. They remain on the plant all summer and, like the leaves, take on fine autumn colours. *Cotinus coggygria* tolerates alkaline conditions well. In the wild it grows on rocky hillsides, but it adapts easily to all garden soils, even heavy clay. It is a robust, easily grown plant.

Propagation is by softwood cuttings in late spring or by air layering in autumn.

• *Cotinus coggygria* 'Grace' has large leaves that are a light red and turn a magnificent translucent orange or fiery red in autumn. Its luminous colours are very useful for brightening free-growing hedges or massed plantings of evergreen shrubs.

• *Cotinus coggygria* 'Royal Purple' has dark purple leaves which can be used to create an interesting contrast with plants with light-coloured foliage.

In the wild, *Cotinus coggygria* grows on rocky hillsides, but in the garden it adapts easily to all soil types, even clay.

Crocus sativus
(Iridaceae) Saffron

HEIGHT 20 CM
SPREAD 20 CM
POSITION SUN
HARDINESS −15 °C AND BELOW
DROUGHT RESISTANCE CODE 5

Cultivated since time immemorial, saffron is a plant with uncertain origins. Experts consider it to be a hybrid of two wild *Crocus* species that appeared in Greece or Turkey several thousand years ago. The saffron bulb is a corm (swollen stem base) which is dormant in summer. The fine linear leaves appear in autumn, persist through the winter and disappear when the heat sets in. In October the flowers appear straight out of the soil. They are extremely beautiful, with their violet-veined, soft lilac-coloured corollas acting as a foil for the long bright red stigmas. These stigmas are harvested by hand and dried to produce the saffron used as a spice. It is hardly surprising that saffron is so expensive: a mere 150,000 flowers are required to make one kilo of spice. How about harvesting your own saffron? It is easy to grow: the bulbs are planted around June and can be divided each summer to increase production. Instead of planting them in a row as in a traditional vegetable garden, we like to scatter them all over the garden, in association with carpeting groundcover plants such as *Artemisia lanata* or *Thymus ciliatus*. *Crocus sativus* tolerates alkaline conditions well; it prefers light, well-drained soils.

Propagation is by division of the corms in early summer.

Many other bulbs, such as *Allium christophii*, *Scilla peruviana* and *Sternbergia lutea*, and are worth growing with the

The feathery inflorescences of *Cotinus coggygria* 'Grace' are held above light red foliage.

saffron crocus in dry gardens (see Useful Addresses for possible suppliers).

Cytisus battandieri
(Fabaceae)

ORIGIN MOROCCO, IN THE MIDDLE ATLAS AND THE RIF
HEIGHT 3 TO 4 M
SPREAD 2 TO 3 M
POSITION SUN
HARDINESS −12 TO −5 °C
DROUGHT RESISTANCE CODE 4

An upright, tree-like shrub with deciduous or semi-evergreen grey-green leaves which are covered in a fine silky down, as are the young shoots. The leaves are divided into three leaflets and are edged with a narrow bright silver margin that is highly

decorative. The dense clusters of bright yellow flowers appear in May–June and have a sweet scent of pineapple. *Cytisus battandieri* grows in acid, neutral or slightly alkaline soils which are well-drained. It is a rapidly growing shrub with an open, airy habit. The tips of the branches can be pruned annually in late winter to maintain a compact and branching habit.

Propagation is by seed in autumn after hot water treatment: pour boiling water over the seeds then leave them to swell overnight.

Dasylirion longissimum
(Agavaceae)

ORIGIN MEXICO
HEIGHT OF FOLIAGE 1.5 TO 2 M
HEIGHT IN FLOWER 4 M OR MORE
POSITION SUN
HARDINESS −8 TO −10 °C
DROUGHT RESISTANCE CODE 5

A woody plant with a short stipe (stalk) topped by a crown of linear dark green leaves, leathery and evergreen. The leaves radiate out in all directions from the heart, forming a sphere and giving the plant its marvellous and highly decorative, architectural appearance. In summer the plant sends out a spectacular flowering spike, standing above the foliage like a tall candle (it only begins to flower after it is ten or fifteen years old). The small yellowish flowers are tightly arranged all along the

inflorescence (*Dasylirion* comes from the Greek, *dasys*, 'dense', and *leirion*, 'lily'). The flower spike remains on the plant long after the flowers have withered, often until winter. *Dasylirion longissimum* tolerates alkaline conditions well. It withstands cold better if the soil is very well drained. It is fairly slow-growing, but is easy to grow. To show off its unique silhouette it is often grown as a single specimen plant, for example at the top of a rock garden. It can also be grown in a container to ornament patios or terraces.

Propagation is by seed in spring: patience is required – after a year you will have a plant with three thread-like leaves.

• **Dasylirion acrotrichum** has blue-grey dentate leaves with a curious tuft of fibres at the tips, like a dishevelled paintbrush (*acrotrichum* comes from the Greek *akros*, 'tip', and *trichos*, 'hair'). The plant forms an attractive sphere, more compact than *Dasylirion longissimum*, and after many years develops a small trunk. The flowering spikes may reach a height of 4 metres.
ORIGIN MEXICO HARDINESS −8 TO −10 °C
DROUGHT RESISTANCE CODE 5

Delosperma cooperi
(Aizoaceae)

ORIGIN SOUTH AFRICA
HEIGHT 10 CM

Dasylirion longissimum displays its silhouette at the Domaine du Rayol, not far from St Tropez, where the gardens recreate the landscapes of the different regions of the world with a mediterranean climate.

Like a giant asparagus, the flowering spike of *Dasylirion acrotrichum* grows longer day by day, reaching a height of about 4 metres in a few weeks.

SPREAD 40 CM OR MORE
POSITION SUN
HARDINESS −10 TO −12 °C
DROUGHT RESISTANCE CODE 4

A carpeting perennial with fleshy, cylindrical, evergreen leaves. The leaves are covered in small crystal-like papillae (pimples) that catch the light. Although it is fairly slow-growing, it makes a good groundcover plant thanks to the fact that its stems root wherever they touch the soil, allowing it to spread progressively. It has many uses in the garden: as groundcover in a rock garden or between paving stones, falling over a low wall or cascading from a pot. It can also be planted on green roofs,

In southern Morocco saffron is cultivated in small fields carved out of the flanks of the Anti-Atlas mountains. In the souk of Tafraoute warm scents arise from the open sacks, including those of saffron, henna and za'atar. In the dry garden hundreds of aromatic plants can be grown to delight our eyes and noses.

Delosperma cooperi spreads over pebbles, making an excellent groundcover for rock gardens.

The flowers of Dianthus corsicus are tiny, but their spicy scent is remarkable; in the background Antirrhinum glutinosum is beginning to open.

where it can survive in a thin layer of substrate with only an occasional watering. In summer the plant is covered in brilliant magenta flowers which have narrow petals radiating from white stamens. *Delosperma cooperi* tolerates alkaline conditions well. It prefers stony soils that have perfect drainage.

Propagation is by softwood cuttings in autumn or spring.

Dianthus anatolicus
(Caryophyllaceae) Pink

ORIGIN TURKEY
HEIGHT OF FOLIAGE 10 CM
HEIGHT IN FLOWER 25 CM
SPREAD 40 CM
POSITION SUN
HARDINESS −15 °C AND BELOW
DROUGHT RESISTANCE CODE 3.5

The name *Dianthus* comes from the Greek *Dios*, 'of Zeus', and *anthos*, 'flower': doubtless because of their beauty, pinks were considered to be the flower of the gods. *Dianthus anatolicus* is a little-known species, but is a pretty perennial that forms a spreading cushion of narrow, evergreen, blue-green leaves. The numerous white flowers, faintly washed in pink, appear in May–June. The tips of the petals are delicately cut into fine fringes, creating an impression of lightness. *Dianthus anatolicus* tolerates alkaline conditions well. It is unfussy about soil type and is an easily grown and long-lived plant.

Propagation is by seed in autumn or by softwood cuttings in early spring before flowering.

• *Dianthus corsicus* has tightly packed green leaves and makes a charming dense cushion which looks like turf. In spring the plant is covered in bright pink flowers with a remarkable spicy scent: a few plants are enough to perfume a whole corner of the garden in the evening. **HARDINESS** −10 TO −12 °C **DROUGHT RESISTANCE CODE** 3.5

• *Dianthus pyrenaicus* 'Cap Béar' makes a perfectly round grey-blue cushion with small needle-like leaves that are tightly packed like a little hedgehog. The tiny pale pink flowers appear in June. It is a cultivar of the Pyrenean pink which we collected at Cap Béar (near Banyuls), where all the vegetation looks as if it had been flattened by the violence of the winds and the salt spray. It should be planted in poor soil that

The delicately fringed flowers of Dianthus anatolicus open in May–June. Because of their beauty, pinks were considered in antiquity to be the flower of the gods.

is well drained. **HARDINESS** −15 °C AND BELOW **DROUGHT RESISTANCE CODE** 4

Dicliptera suberecta
(Acanthaceae)

ORIGIN URUGUAY
HEIGHT 40 CM
SPREAD 60 CM
POSITION SUN OR SEMI-SHADE
HARDINESS THE FOLIAGE DIES WITH THE FIRST FROST BUT THE ROOTSTOCK CAN SURVIVE TEMPERATURES OF ABOUT −10 TO −12 °C
DROUGHT RESISTANCE CODE 3.5

Often called *Justicia* or *Jacobinia*, *Dicliptera suberecta* is a perennial with attractive grey-green leaves that have a soft, velvety texture. In frost-free areas the plant is evergreen, but in our garden the foliage is killed by frost every year. However, it puts out vigorous new growth in spring. The young stems – as brittle as glass – grow rapidly, so that by summer the plant has formed a handsome rounded mass. The rootstock spreads slowly, gradually forming a dense groundcover.

From June to September the plant is covered in orange-red tubular flowers, pollinated in their native habitat by hummingbirds that come to drink the nectar contained at the bottom of the corolla. *Dicliptera suberecta* tolerates alkaline conditions well. It likes light, well-drained soils: the rootstock may rot in winter if the soil is waterlogged. It is an excellent perennial providing colour in the garden in summer along with other brightly coloured plants such as *Epilobium canum*, *Salvia darcyi* or *Ceratostigma plumbaginoides*.

Propagation is by softwood cuttings in autumn or spring.

Dicliptera suberecta looks miserable when its leaves wither in winter, but what a delight it is in summer!

Dorycnium pentaphyllum
(Fabaceae)

ORIGIN MEDITERRANEAN BASIN
HEIGHT 60 CM
SPREAD 80 CM
POSITION SUN
HARDINESS −12 TO −15 °C
DROUGHT RESISTANCE CODE 5

A dense, pliable and branching sub-shrub. The small, evergreen, silvery-grey leaves are divided into five leaflets (botanists would say three leaflets surrounded by two stipules that resemble leaflets). In June–July numerous small white flowers, rich in nectar, cover the plant in a light mass. *Dorycnium pentaphyllum* tolerates alkaline conditions well and can withstand salt spray. It prefers poor, well-drained soils, where it will self-seed freely. In soil that is heavy or too rich it tends to grow too fast, greatly reducing its lifespan.

Propagation is by seed in autumn after hot water treatment: pour boiling water over the seeds then leave them to swell overnight.

It can also be propagated easily by softwood cuttings in spring.

• *Dorycnium hirsutum* has attractive downy silvery-grey leaves. It is short-lived, but self-seeds very freely in the garden. It can be used as a pioneer plant to colonize large slopes or wild parts of the garden with, for example, *Cistus albidus*, *Coronilla glauca*, *Euphorbia characias* and *Centranthus ruber*. In May–June it is covered in pretty pinkish-white flowers with silky sepals. **ORIGIN** MEDITERRANEAN BASIN **HARDINESS** −10 TO −12 °C **DROUGHT RESISTANCE CODE** 4

Drosanthemum hispidum
(Aizoaceae)

ORIGIN SOUTH AFRICA (NAMAQUALAND)
HEIGHT 15 TO 20 CM
SPREAD 60 TO 80 CM OR MORE
POSITION SUN
HARDINESS −8 TO −10 °C
DROUGHT RESISTANCE CODE 6

A spreading perennial with creeping stems which grow rapidly and put down roots wherever they touch the soil. The fleshy evergreen leaves are small and cylindrical and closely packed. As with most succulent plants of the Aizoaceae family, the leaves are covered in shiny bumps, or papules, which catch the light – in *Drosanthemum* they are especially visible. These bladder-like papules are composed of special cells capable of swelling to store more than ten thousand times the volume of water contained in normal cells. Arranged in relief on the epidermis, they act both as an external reservoir of water and as a filter to protect the plant from the sun's rays. A brief examination with a magnifying glass clearly reveals these swollen papules that decorate the surface of the leaves, making the plant look as if it was covered in droplets of dew (the name *Drosanthemum* is from the Greek *drosos*, 'dew', and *anthos*, 'flower').

In April–May the plant disappears beneath a mass of bright pink flowers, their colour so intense that one almost has to look away. *Drosanthemum hispidum* tolerates alkaline conditions well and prefers well-drained soils. It makes an excellent groundcover for large rock gardens or can be grown cascading down a wall. It can also be grown on green roofs, where it can live in a shallow substrate. In our experience, it is one of the rare plants (along with *Malephora lutea*) that can survive on green roofs without watering in the climatic conditions of the South of France. In periods of severe water deficit, *Drosanthemum hispidum* may lose a large proportion of its leaves, thus becoming less ornamental until the first rains of autumn arrive.

Propagation is by softwood cuttings in autumn or spring.

Ebenus cretica
(Fabaceae)

ORIGIN CRETE
HEIGHT 60 TO 80 CM, SOMETIMES MORE
SPREAD 60 TO 80 CM
POSITION SUN
HARDINESS −10 TO −12 °C
DROUGHT RESISTANCE CODE 5

A semi-evergreen shrub with silky, silvery leaves. The pretty pink flowers appear in May and are arranged in conical inflorescences covered in long silky hairs. Initially, these inflorescences appear bicoloured since the open lower flowers are

Self-sown *Dorycnium pentaphyllum* among a bed of perennials: its mist of white flowers envelops the yellow inflorescences of *Achillea clypeolata*.

The dazzling flowers of *Drosanthemum hispidum* seem to jostle one another for a place in the sun.

pink while the upper flowers, still in bud, are buried in a thick mass of silver hairs. *Ebenus cretica* tolerates alkaline conditions well. It requires a poor, stony soil with perfect drainage, otherwise it is short-lived. In the wild it is found in the gorges that bisect the mountains of southern Crete, where it can be seen clinging to screes or rocky outcrops. It is a plant of great beauty, much sought after by plant lovers.

Propagation is by seed in autumn. After carefully removing the silky pod, scarify the tiny seeds by rubbing them between two sheets of sandpaper. Then pour boiling water over the seeds and leave them to swell for 12 hours. The germination rate is irregular and usually fairly poor. The young seedlings are very sensitive to too much water.

Echinops ritro
(Asteraceae) Globe Thistle

ORIGIN SOUTHERN EUROPE
HEIGHT IN FLOWER 60 TO 80 CM, SOMETIMES MORE
SPREAD 60 CM
POSITION SUN OR SEMI-SHADE
HARDINESS −15 °C AND BELOW
DROUGHT RESISTANCE CODE 3

A deciduous perennial with grey-green leaves that are deeply cut into spiny lobes, rather like the leaves of a thistle. The undersides of the leaves are covered in dense hairs that form a whitish felt. The attractive metallic-blue flowers appear from May to June and may continue to be produced throughout the summer. They are arranged in striking and highly decorative spherical heads (the name *Echinops* comes from the Greek *echinos*, 'hedgehog', and *opsis*, 'appearance'). *Echinops ritro* tolerates alkaline conditions well and prefers rocky, well-drained soils. It is best to avoid watering it – with irrigation it becomes susceptible to aphids and to *Oidium*, a fungal disease that destroys its foliage in summer.

Propagation is by seed in autumn.

Elaeagnus angustifolia
(Elaeagnaceae) Oleaster

ORIGIN SOUTHERN EUROPE, ASIA
HEIGHT 5 M OR MORE
SPREAD 4 M AND MORE
POSITION SUN
HARDINESS −15 °C AND BELOW
DROUGHT RESISTANCE INDEX 3.5

A shrub or small tree which sometimes produces suckers. Its deciduous leaves are grey on the upper surface and silvery on the underside, and resemble the leaves of the olive (the name *Elaeagnus* comes from the Greek *elaia*, 'olive tree', and *agnos*, 'pure' – as in the name of *Vitex agnus-castus*, another large deciduous shrub). The branches are armed with strong thorns and this shrub is often used to create impenetrable protective hedges, together with *Poncirus trifoliata* and *Hippophae rhamnoides*.

In our garden we grow it not so much for its thorns as for its remarkable fragrance. The small, sweetly scented yellow flowers appear in May. In still weather they can perfume an entire area of the garden with their sweet, sugary, honey-like scent. The flowers are followed in autumn by edible fruit, shaped like small olives – a feast for birds. *Elaeagnus angustifolia* tolerates alkaline conditions well and is perfectly resistant to salt spray. It is unfussy about soil type and is a robust, easily grown shrub. It can be pruned in autumn to keep it compact, but watch out for the thorns on branches that are lying in the ground: there's nothing like them for puncturing wheelbarrow tyres!

Propagation is by seed in autumn or hardwood cuttings in winter.

• *Elaeagnus angustifolia* **var.** *caspica* is a variety with thornless branches. Its broad leaves, silvery on both sides, are very decorative. In our garden this variety suckers more than *Elaeagnus angustifolia* itself.

Elaeagnus × ebbingei

HEIGHT 3 M OR MORE
SPREAD 2 TO 3 M OR MORE
POSITION SUN OR SEMI-SHADE
HARDINESS −15 °C AND BELOW
DROUGHT RESISTANCE CODE 2.5

Elaeagnus × ebbingei is a hybrid between *Elaeagnus macrophylla* and *Elaeagnus pungens*, both native to Japan. Its leathery, evergreen leaves are grey-green above and silvery on the underside. In spring the new shoots grow very rapidly and have a curious rusty colour with silvery highlights. The small white flowers appear from September to November. They are discreet and are hidden in the foliage, but are deliciously scented. *Elaeagnus × ebbingei* tolerates alkaline conditions well. It prefers friable, well-drained soils: in heavy soils it tends to suffer from chlorosis. Watch out, this is a vigorous shrub. It was once popular as a plant for square-clipped hedges, and a whole generation of gardeners spent interminable Sundays trying to keep it within the dimensions originally intended – but the more you prune it, the more it grows! It is better suited to free-growing hedges where it can develop comfortably among other large evergreen shrubs.

Propagate by stem section cuttings, the thickness of a pencil, in autumn, using good well-ripened wood from the previous year's growth.

Epilobium canum 'Western Hills'
(Onagraceae) California Fuchsia

ORIGIN SOUTHWESTERN UNITED STATES
HEIGHT 60 CM
SPREAD 1 M OR MORE
POSITION SUN
HARDINESS −12 TO −15 °C
DROUGHT RESISTANCE CODE 4

A perennial with narrow, grey, downy leaves. In mild climates the leaves are sometimes semi-evergreen, but in our garden they dry out completely in winter,

Ebenus cretica will reveal the charms of its silky flower spikes only in the dry garden – if it is watered in summer it will promptly die.

In August, the bristling heads of *Echinops ritro* fill the dry expanses of the limestone plateau of Larzac, in the southern Massif Central of France.

The flowers of *Elaeagnus angustifolia* var. *caspica* merge discreetly with its magnificent silvery foliage.

giving the plant an unattractive appearance from December onwards. We therefore cut it back to ground level, and at the end of winter the new growth emerging from the soil makes a handsome silvery carpet. Year by year the plant increases in width thanks to its strongly suckering rootstock: it can in fact become fairly invasive. The flowers are remarkably abundant and appear in succession from July to October, at a time when most plants are dormant for the summer. A bright orange-red, they are shaped like flaring tubes with a protruding bunch of long stamens. The small swollen pedicels, or flower stalks, later turn into pods filled with a huge number of tiny seeds (the name *Epilobium* comes from the Greek *epi*, 'above', and *lobion*, 'pod'). *Epilobium canum* 'Western Hills' tolerates alkaline conditions well and prefers light, well-drained soils. With its exuberant summer flowering it is one of the best perennials for the dry garden.

Propagation is by softwood cuttings in spring.

There are many taxa of *Epilobium canum* which differ in their growth habit and flower colour. Most flower at the end of summer, later than the cultivar 'Western Hills'. They are sometimes found under their old name of *Zauschneria californica*. Here are a few which look particularly good in our garden:

• *Epilobium canum* 'Albiflora' has green leaves and pure white flowers. Its flexible stems spread outwards and the plant suckers vigorously, making it a good groundcover. **HEIGHT** 30 CM

• *Epilobium canum* 'Catalina' has handsome silky silvery foliage which sets off its intensely coral-red flowers. **HEIGHT** 60 CM

• *Epilobium canum* subsp. *angustifolia* has small grey leaves and a slender growth habit, the tips of its stems bending over under the weight of its bright orange flowers. It does not sucker much. **HEIGHT** 60 TO 80 CM

• *Epilobium canum* subsp. *garrettii* has green leaves and prostrate stems and makes a good groundcover. **HEIGHT** 20 TO 30 CM

Eragrostis curvula
(Poaceae) Love Grass

ORIGIN SOUTH AFRICA
HEIGHT OF FOLIAGE 60 CM
HEIGHT IN FLOWER 1 M
SPREAD 80 CM TO 1 M
POSITION SUN
HARDINESS −12 TO −15 °C
DROUGHT RESISTANCE CODE 4

A grass with linear green leaves that take on attractive golden tints in winter. It spreads slowly, eventually forming a dense clump, with long, flexible leaves that move in the slightest breeze. The light inflorescences appear in summer, like a mist of fine spikelets arranged in a heart shape (the name *Eragrostis* comes from the Greek *eros*, 'love', and the Latin *agrostis*, 'grass': some people consider this an allusion to the shape of the spikelets, while others see in Love Grass an invitation to lie down on its fine and supple leaves). *Eragrostis curvula* tolerates alkaline conditions well and is an easily grown grass, unfussy about soil type. In windy areas it is very decorative when planted en masse, for as its leaves move in the wind they form ceaselessly undulating waves.

Propagation is by seed in autumn or by division of the clumps in winter.

Erica multiflora
(Ericaceae) Heather

ORIGIN MEDITERRANEAN BASIN
HEIGHT 60 TO 80 CM
SPREAD 60 CM
POSITION SUN OR SEMI-SHADE
HARDINESS −12 TO −15 °C
DROUGHT RESISTANCE CODE 4

A sub-shrub with small, narrow, dark green leaves that are evergreen. Its very branching stems form a dense rounded mass. The flowers, small pink bells tightly held in bunches on the tips of the stems, appear from September to December. As they fade they take on a striking auburn colour and the dry inflorescences remain decorative throughout the winter. *Erica multiflora* differs from most other heathers in its good tolerance of alkalinity. It likes stony, well-drained soils and is resistant to salt spray. Magnificent specimens can be seen in the *calanques* (creeks) of the Marseille area, their pink flowers emerging in autumn from among the pale blue rosemaries in an impressive geological setting where white cliffs plunge into a dark sea.

Propagate by seed in spring or by cuttings in autumn, taken from non-flowering side shoots.

Erigeron karvinskianus
(Asteraceae) Mexican Fleabane

ORIGIN MEXICO
HEIGHT 30 CM
SPREAD 40 CM
POSITION SUN OR SEMI-SHADE
HARDINESS −10 TO −12 °C
DROUGHT RESISTANCE CODE 3

A perennial with supple branching stems that forms a dense mass, more or less spreading. In mild climates the small leaves are evergreen, but they fall as soon as the temperature drops below about −5 °C. In the flowering season, which extends from April to October – usually with a pause in the heat of the summer – the plant is covered in a profusion of small daisy-like flowers which are white or sometimes tinged with pink. The plant self-seeds freely along the edges of paths, between paving stones or in crevices in old stone walls. The seeds are easily dispersed by the wind thanks to their little plume of white silk (the name *Erigeron* comes from the Greek *ēri*, 'early', and *geron*, 'old man', referring to the powder-puff of white silk that appears on the seeds as soon as they start to ripen). In our garden we like to combine *Erigeron karvinskianus* with *Geranium sanguineum*, *Nepeta × faassenii* and *Stipa pennata*, their flowers mingling in a delightful spring scene. *Erigeron karvinskianus* tolerates alkaline conditions well and is unfussy about soil type. It is a generous plant, so easy to grow that it would be a pity for any mediterranean garden to be without it.

Propagation is by seed in autumn or by softwood cuttings in spring.

Erodium trifolium
(Geraniaceae)

ORIGIN ASIA MINOR
HEIGHT 25 CM
SPREAD 30 CM
POSITION SUN OR SEMI-SHADE
HARDINESS −10 TO −12 °C
DROUGHT RESISTANCE CODE 3

A perennial with handsome, downy, grey-green leaves divided into three broadly rounded lobes. The leaves are evergreen in winter and deciduous in summer as the

Erigeron karvinskianus and *Nepeta racemosa* have both self-seeded in this little trough. By leaving plants to propagate themselves freely in the garden, interesting natural plant combinations may be discovered, sometimes more successful than the original plan.

plant becomes dormant to get through the summer drought. It then lives on the reserves that it amassed during the wet season in its fat, fleshy, carrot-shaped roots which penetrate deep into the ground between the stones. Its blooms light up the garden from the end of winter: flowering begins in February and continues until May, when the last flowers disappear together with the leaves before the brutal onset of the heat. The flowers are very beautiful: their white satiny petals are veined with violet and the two upper petals bear large dark red blotches. As the flowers fade they make way for the characteristic seed head of erodiums: a swollen pod tapering into a long beak, reminiscent of the head of a heron (the name *Erodium* comes from the Greek *erōdios*, 'heron'). When the seed is ripe, the beak curls up into a fine spiral, which allows the seed to be carried off by the wind or to become caught in an animal's fur, ensuring its dispersal. The plant self-seeds easily in the garden too, and it's always a pleasure to see its magnificent flowers emerging in an unexpected place. *Erodium trifolium* tolerates alkaline conditions well and is unfussy about soil type. It is an easily grown perennial that is long-lived in our garden.

Propagate by root cuttings at the end of summer or by fresh seed in spring. The seed should be harvested just at the moment when the beak is beginning to curl into a spiral, before it is dispersed by the wind: if you are too late there will be no seed left!

Eryngium amethystinum
(Apiaceae) Sea Holly

ORIGIN SOUTHEAST EUROPE
HEIGHT IN FLOWER 50 CM
SPREAD 40 CM
POSITION SUN
HARDINESS −15 °C AND BELOW
DROUGHT RESISTANCE CODE 4

As soon as winter draws to a close, *Erodium trifolium* lights up the garden, its coloured petals sending out a signal to pollinators.

Unaffected by drought, *Eryngium amethystinum* displays its crowns of metallic violet-blue spiny bracts in full summer.

A perennial with tough, thorny, grey-green leaves divided into segments. The foliage is generally deciduous, but the basal rosette may remain evergreen if the winter is not too cold. The plant comes into flower in July–August, with widely branched inflorescences. The flowers are arranged in globular heads, surrounded at the base by a crown of fine spiny bracts that are highly decorative. The stems, flowers and the crown of bracts are a remarkable metallic violet-blue colour with silver highlights. *Eryngium amethystinum* tolerates alkaline conditions well. It prefers stony, well-drained soils. It is an amazing plant which you can easily make the most of by planting it in the middle of silver carpeting plants such as *Artemisia lanata* or *Tanacetum densum* subsp. *amanii*.

Propagation is by seed in autumn. Watch out, it's prickly, so you need to wear gloves when collecting the seed!

Eschscholzia californica
(Papaveraceae) California Poppy

ORIGIN SOUTHWESTERN UNITED STATES
HEIGHT OF FOLIAGE 15 TO 20 CM
HEIGHT IN FLOWER 40 CM
SPREAD 20 CM
POSITION SUN
HARDINESS −12 TO −15 °C
DROUGHT RESISTANCE CODE 5

Don't be put off by its difficult-looking name: *Eschscholzia* is a perfectly simple perennial, easy to grow. Its blue-green, finely divided foliage may be deciduous or semi-evergreen. The flowers, produced in succession from April to September, are broadly cup-shaped and yellow or bright orange according to the variety. The petals have a brilliance which makes their colour particularly luminous. The flowers are followed by narrow seedpods which open at the end of summer to release huge quantities of small black seeds that germinate easily in light soil. *Eschscholzia* behaves like an annual in colder climates or like a short-lived perennial in milder areas – but it self-seeds so generously that it seems completely perennial. In the semi-desert zones of California it sometimes colonizes vast areas, lighting up the hills with its brilliant blooms: it is the official flower of the State of California. In Native American tradition the plant's thick transparent sap has many uses: it is slightly narcotic (*Eschscholzia* is a cousin of *Papaver somniferum*, the opium poppy) and is also reputed to have sedative and aphrodisiac properties. *Eschscholzia californica* tolerates alkaline conditions well and is resistant to salt spray. It prefers friable soils with perfect drainage. Take care to plant it in a sunny position – the flowers remain closed in the shade.

Propagation is by seed in autumn. It can be sown in pots and pricked out later or sown directly in the ground.

• *Eschscholzia californica* **var. maritima** forms a more compact clump, with handsome silvery-blue foliage and bright yellow flowers. **ORIGIN** CALIFORNIA, COASTAL **HARDINESS** −10 TO −12 °C **DROUGHT RESISTANCE CODE** 5

Euphorbia
(Euphorbiaceae) Spurge

Euphorbias are easy to recognize by their abundant latex, a sort of thick white sap which coagulates when exposed to the air. The best-known latex comes from *Hevea brasiliensis*: this tree euphorbia native to South America is tapped to collect the raw material of natural rubber. After vulcanization, rubber acquires an amazing elasticity, and is used for making things as diverse as aeroplane tyres and condoms.

Fresh euphorbia latex may produce irritation or blistering of the skin, but was for a long time used for its medicinal properties. The name *Euphorbia* was in fact given to the genus in the 1st century AD by King Juba II of Mauritania in honour of his doctor. Juba II had discovered a plant in the Atlas mountains (probably *Euphorbia resinifera* or *Euphorbia echinus*) whose latex had a particularly burning effect, and his doctor, Euphorbos, experimented with it as a treatment for syphilis. Ancient authors also refer to numerous other properties of euphorbia latex. To treat caries, for example, a drop of the latex of *Euphorbia characias* was applied to the hole in the tooth, having previously taken the precaution of protecting the gums with wax – otherwise there was a danger that all the patient's teeth might fall out following this treatment. Pliny cites a radical way of treating snake bites: regardless of which bit of the body has been bitten, an incision should be made in the top of the patient's skull and the latex poured into it until a cure is achieved. To combat phlegm, he suggests a spoonful of the seeds of *Euphorbia pithyusa* applied as a suppository – I don't recommend that you try this!

For a milder remedy an amazing euphorbia honey is still used in southern

Euphorbia echinus in the Atlas mountains. Because of the medicinal uses of their latex, King Juba II of Mauritania gave euphorbias the name of his doctor, Euphorbos.

Morocco (it is produced from *Euphorbia regis-jubae* – King Juba's euphorbia – which grows on the Atlantic coast near Cap Rihr). You can buy this honey at stalls on the road between Essaouira and Agadir from sellers who swear that it will cure every kind of cold, bronchitis or chest pain. Clara and I tried it last year: the first sensation was delicious, like lavender honey. Then suddenly our mouths were on fire and we felt a real burning of the throat that slowly descended to the lungs: no two ways about it, this was certainly euphorbia honey!

Euphorbia ceratocarpa

ORIGIN SICILY
HEIGHT 60 TO 80 CM, SOMETIMES MORE
SPREAD 80 CM TO 1 M
POSITION SUN OR SEMI-SHADE
HARDINESS −10 TO −12 °C
DROUGHT RESISTANCE CODE 4

An evergreen perennial with long green leaves furrowed by a broad pale vein. The dense foliage forms an elegant dome, while the stems take on an interesting red colour at their base as they become woody. The inflorescences are very branched, brilliant yellow, and open from May to July. The flowers are followed by small seed capsules covered in long horn-shaped protuberances (the name *ceratocarpa* comes from the Greek *keras*, 'horn', and *karpos*, 'fruit'). As with all euphorbias, these capsules explode with a sharp sound when they are ripe, projecting their numerous seeds over an area of several metres around the plant. *Euphorbia ceratocarpa* tolerates alkaline conditions well. It is not fussy about soil type and is a robust and generous perennial that is easy to grow.

Propagation is by seed in autumn or by softwood cuttings in spring.

Euphorbia characias subsp. characias

ORIGIN WESTERN MEDITERRANEAN BASIN
HEIGHT 80 CM
SPREAD 60 TO 80 CM
POSITION SUN
HARDINESS −12 TO −15 °C
DROUGHT RESISTANCE CODE 5

A multi-stemmed perennial that forms a lovely rounded clump. The long, evergreen, blue-grey leaves are turned downwards, forming a tight 'skirt' around the stems. In February a large cylindrical inflorescence appears: at first its tip unfurls like a crozier, then from March to June it opens fully. What look like individual acid-green flowers are technically cyathia, each decorated with dark glands, usually reddish-brown but sometimes violet-coloured or black (see box opposite). *Euphorbia characias* self-seeds very easily in the garden.

For months at a time, *Euphorbia ceratocarpa* forms a very decorative luminous mass.

It can be used as a pioneer plant to colonize slopes or wild areas on the edges of the garden, in combination with, for example, *Centranthus ruber* and *Dorycnium hirsutum*. It tolerates alkaline conditions well and prefers poor, stony, well-drained soils. The plant is long-lived, but each individual stem lives for only two years: it grows the first year, flowers the following spring, then dries out completely after flowering. Stems that have flowered can be cut to the base in autumn to keep the plant looking decorative in winter – but you need to wear gloves for this task to protect your hands from the latex.

Propagation is by seed in autumn.

• *Euphorbia characias* subsp. *wulfenii* has vigorous foliage and a remarkably regular architectural form that is extremely decorative. When the croziers of the inflorescences unfurl at the end of winter they give off a delicious and striking smell of freshly ground coffee. The large inflorescences then form massive and spectacular columns with luminous colours: brilliant yellow nectar glands juxtaposed with acid-green cyathia. *Euphorbia characias* subsp. *wulfenii* is one of the most decorative plants in our garden at the end of winter – if we could only plant one species of euphorbia, it would be this one! **ORIGIN** EASTERN MEDITERRANEAN **HEIGHT** 1 M TO 1.5 M **SPREAD** 1.25 M

Euphorbia corallioides

ORIGIN SOUTHERN ITALY, SICILY
HEIGHT 30 CM
SPREAD 40 CM
POSITION SUN OR SEMI-SHADE
HARDINESS −15°C AND BELOW
DROUGHT RESISTANCE CODE 3

A perennial with green leaves that are semi-evergreen – the plant loses some of its leaves in autumn, thus displaying its amazing bright red stems throughout the winter (the name *corallioides* comes from the Latin *corallium*, 'coral'). The luminous yellow inflorescences appear from May to July. It is a short-lived plant (sometimes considered a biennial), but self-seeds easily and so there is no problem retaining it in the garden. *Euphorbia corallioides* tolerates alkaline conditions well. It is unfussy about soil type and does well even on heavy soils that are dry in summer and wet in winter.

Propagation is by seed in autumn.

Euphorbia cyparissias

ORIGIN EUROPE
HEIGHT 20 TO 30 CM
SPREAD 1 M OR MORE
POSITION SUN OR SEMI-SHADE

HARDINESS −15 °C AND BELOW
DROUGHT RESISTANCE CODE 3

A perennial with very fine leaves of a pretty light green. As the young shoots emerge from the ground in spring they resemble young cypress seedlings (the name *cyparissias* comes from the Greek *kyparissos*, 'cypress'). The foliage is completely deciduous in winter and the stock spreads by means of long rhizomes, forming an invasive groundcover. The abundant luminous yellow-green inflorescences cover the plant from March to June. *Euphorbia cyparissias* tolerates alkaline conditions well and is unfussy about soil type. It can be used as a groundcover to create great

Euphorbia corallioides is undemanding as regards soil type and is also very adaptable: it flowers just as well in sun as in semi-shade.

patches of light beneath a dark-leaved shrub. For instance, acid-yellow carpets of *Euphorbia cyparissias* form a wonderful contrast in March with dark-blue-flowered rosemaries, such as the varieties 'Corsican Blue', 'Ulysse' or 'Sappho'.

Propagation is by division in autumn or by soft-tip cuttings at the end of winter, using non-flowering shoots.

• *Euphorbia cyparissias* **'Clarice Howard'** forms a low-growing carpet, not exceeding 15 to 20 cm in height. It has violet-tinged young shoots that create an attractive contrast with the flowers.

• *Euphorbia cyparissias* **'Tall Boy'** is a form with taller foliage and strong rhizomes. It is

THE SEX LIFE OF THE EUPHORBIA, A TALE OF GLANDS AND LATEX

As it pollinates this euphorbia, a greedy ant carefully licks the green glands that are glistening with nectar.

Euphorbias have curious inflorescences. There's no point looking for petals because there aren't any. Instead of a corolla the plant has leaves and bracts that are brilliantly coloured in order to attract insects. If you take a close look at a *Euphorbia rigida* in flower you will see at the top of each pedicel a small bright yellow receptacle formed by the fusion of two bracts into a cupule or small cup, which contains the plant's flowering organs: botanists call this the cyathium (from the Greek word for the cup used to serve wine from the wine-jar). At the centre of the cyathium sits a single naked female flower: it has no sepals or petals, but consists simply of an ovary crowned by a tuft of stigmas that delicately collect pollen from the underside of pollinating insects. To promote genetic diversity and prevent self-pollinization, this female flower opens well before the male flowers that surround it in the cyathium. By the time the male flowers develop, the female flower is already lying on the edge of the cyathium, its fertilized ovary now a heavy pendent capsule which will later burst open to expel the ripened seeds far and wide. The male flowers are reduced to the simplest form possible: a crown of stamens with their small load of bright yellow pollen. To attract pollinators, the cyathium also contains four red glands, glistening with nectar – a true delicacy for insects. All parts of the inflorescence ooze drops of the toxic latex as soon as they are cut: in the finely balanced sexual arrangements of the euphorbia everything is deadly poison to the browsing herbivores that are the plant's enemies, but sweetly tender to its pollinating insects.

Detail of an inflorescence of *Euphorbia rigida*. The single female flower, already fertilized, has turned into a heavy pot-bellied capsule. Awaiting passing insects, the bright yellow stamens surround the red nectar glands.

happy on wild slopes, where it can be grown in association with other invasive plants such as *Achillea nobilis* or *Potentilla reptans*.

Euphorbia dendroides
Tree Euphorbia

ORIGIN MEDITERRANEAN BASIN
HEIGHT 1 TO 1.5 M, SOMETIMES MORE
SPREAD 1 TO 1.5 M
POSITION SUN
HARDINESS −6 TO −8°C
DROUGHT RESISTANCE CODE 5

A shrub with long, narrow, green leaves. The leaves are evergreen in winter but fall in summer – the plant enters a period of dormancy when the hot weather arrives in order to get through the summer without suffering from drought. It is ornamental in the garden in a reverse-season manner: in June, before falling, the foliage takes on amazing 'autumn colours' – yellow, orange or violet-hued – that are highly decorative. In October, by contrast, with the first rains of autumn, the plant is covered with new shoots of a pretty pale green, just like spring foliage. The yellow-green flowers appear in April. The plant forms a regular-shaped mass with many branches, resembling the crown of a miniature tree (the name *dendroides* comes from the Greek *dendron*, 'tree'). Its rounded silhouette is characteristic of many coastal landscapes of the Mediterranean, particularly on islands: in Sardinia, Crete or Cyprus, it can be seen perched on the summit of coastal cliffs or on rocky hillsides sloping steeply down to the sea. *Euphorbia dendroides* tolerates alkaline conditions well and is resistant to salt spray. It prefers poor and stony soils with perfect drainage.

Propagation is by seed in autumn.

Euphorbia mellifera
Honey Spurge

ORIGIN MADEIRA, CANARY ISLANDS
HEIGHT USUALLY 1.5 TO 2 M IN THE GARDEN (UP TO 15 M IN THE WILD!)
SPREAD ABOUT 2 M IN THE GARDEN
POSITION SUN OR SEMI-SHADE
HARDINESS −8 TO −10 °C
DROUGHT RESISTANCE CODE 3

This large euphorbia grows into a true tree in the Canary Islands but does not usually exceed the size of a shrub in gardens in the South of France. Its large, evergreen, green leaves are marked by a broad, whitish, central vein. The plant has a fine architectural shape and is very decorative. Its vigorous foliage forms a dense rounded mass, with long leaves tightly arranged at the tips of the stems. Its brownish-orange inflorescences open in May–June and give off a pleasant smell of honey. *Euphorbia mellifera* grows in acid, neutral or slightly alkaline conditions. It prefers a deep, friable, well-drained soil. It grows fairly well in our garden, but it is in Brittany that we have seen the finest specimens (in the garden of the Retraite at Quimper and in the exotic garden at Roscoff): the mildness of the Atlantic climate suits it perfectly.

Propagation is by seed in autumn or by softwood cuttings in spring.

Euphorbia myrsinites

ORIGIN SOUTHERN EUROPE, NORTH AFRICA, CENTRAL ASIA
HEIGHT 20 CM
SPREAD 40 TO 50 CM
POSITION SUN
HARDINESS −15 °C AND BELOW
DROUGHT RESISTANCE CODE 5

A perennial with fine, grey-blue, evergreen foliage that is fat and almost succulent. The leaves, oval and pointed, resemble the leaf form of the myrtle (the name *myrsinites* comes from *myrsine*, the Greek name for myrtle). They are attractively arranged in a tight spiral along the stems. The plant has an unusual and very decorative architecture, its prostrate stems spreading out from the centre like tentacles. The abundant inflorescences, which lie on the ground, are produced repeatedly from March to June; their grey-green cyathia are decorated with bright yellow nectar glands. The plant self-seeds easily in our garden. It is an excellent rock-garden plant which we like to grow with *Globularia alypum* or *Lithodora fruticosa* to create attractive combinations of yellows and blues in early spring. *Euphorbia myrsinites* tolerates alkaline conditions well and prefers poor, stony and perfectly drained soils.

Propagation is by seed in autumn.

Euphorbia rigida

ORIGIN MEDITERRANEAN BASIN, ASIA MINOR
HEIGHT 50 CM
SPREAD 60 CM
POSITION SUN
HARDINESS −15 °C AND BELOW
DROUGHT RESISTANCE CODE 5

A perennial with pointed, evergreen, silvery-blue leaves. Like *Euphorbia myrsinites*, its leaves are attractively arranged in spirals along the stems – but here the stems have a stiff and upright growth habit. The first time we saw this euphorbia was in the Taurus mountains on the path to Mount Olympus (the Turkish Olympus) above Chimera: it was November and it was cold, and *Euphorbia rigida* had already taken on its beautiful winter colour. Since then we have been planting it everywhere in our garden, for it's a plant that attracts attention in every season. In summer the metallic grey of its leaves begins to be tinged

Maintenance is much reduced in an unwatered garden: perennials and shrubs cover the soil, limiting the germination of weeds. Here, an acid yellow carpet of *Euphorbia cyparissias* glows in the foreground.

Euphorbia myrsinites self-seeds very freely among rocks and in old walls.

In order to resist drought, *Euphorbia dendroides* lives its seasons in reverse — at the end of spring it takes on rich 'autumn colours' which brighten the starkness of limestone cliffs.

with pale pink. In autumn and winter the leaves take on amazing violet-red hues: the colder it gets, the stronger the colour. From January the inflorescences begin to appear in umbels at the tips of the stems, their colour a magnificent luminous yellow – this is one of the most attractive perennials in the garden in late winter. As the season advances the inflorescences change and become even more beautiful. The female flowers turn into heavy, pendent chocolate-coloured capsules, the bracts of the cyathium become an acid yellow-green, while the nectar glands turn a flamboyant red, visible from a distance and as much a delight for the gardener's eyes as they are for the pollinators. *Euphorbia rigida* tolerates alkaline conditions well; it prefers a poor, well-drained soil.

Propagation is by seed in autumn.

Euphorbia spinosa

ORIGIN MEDITERRANEAN BASIN
HEIGHT 30 CM
SPREAD 50 TO 60 CM
POSITION SUN
HARDINESS −12 TO −15 °C
DROUGHT RESISTANCE CODE 4

An evergreen sub-shrub with tightly packed, small, dark green leaves. Its numerous intricate branches form a low, dense cushion, perfectly regular in shape and very decorative in the rock garden. The small yellow-green inflorescences are produced in great abundance and cover the entire plant in May–June. After flowering, the flower stems of the inflorescences harden and give the plant a slightly thorny appearance. *Euphorbia spinosa* tolerates alkaline conditions well, and prefers a poor,

stony and perfectly drained soil. It looks good grown in association with other plants that form dense cushions, for instance *Rhodanthemum hosmariense* or *Scabiosa hymnetia*.

Propagation is by seed in autumn or by softwood cuttings in early spring, just before the lengthening of the stems that marks the beginning of flowering.

Among the numerous other euphorbia species that exist, here are some that do particularly well in our garden:

• *Euphorbia acanthothamnos* has small, pale green leaves, evergreen in winter. In spring the plant is covered in tiny yellow-green inflorescences. In summer it loses all its leaves, turning into a curious cushion of interwoven prickly spines (the name *acanthothamnos* comes from the Greek *akantha*, 'thorn', and *thamnos*, 'bush'). It is a plant for rock gardens and requires soil that is perfectly drained, otherwise it does not survive long: in our garden it unfortunately died a few years ago after a winter that was

too wet for its liking. We are planning to grow it again from seed, this time in a better-drained position. **ORIGIN** GREECE, TURKEY **HARDINESS** −8 TO −10 °C **DROUGHT RESISTANCE CODE** 5

• *Euphorbia amygdaloides*, the Wood Spurge, has long, green, evergreen leaves (the name *amygdaloides* means 'almond-like'). The thick stems have a fine red colour and the large, pale green, cylindrical inflorescences appear in April–May. This euphorbia does best in shade or semi-shade, beneath trees. **ORIGIN** EUROPE, NORTH AFRICA, TURKEY, CAUCASUS **HARDINESS** −15 °C AND BELOW **DROUGHT RESISTANCE CODE** 2

• *Euphorbia* × *martinii* is a natural hybrid between *Euphorbia characias* and *Euphorbia amygdaloides*. It has evergreen, grey-green leaves that contrast well with the clear red stems. The cylindrical inflorescences appear from March to June. The luminous yellow-green cyathia are ornamented with red nectar glands and are very decorative. The plant enjoys semi-shade. **HARDINESS** −12 TO −15 °C **DROUGHT RESISTANCE CODE** 3

RIGHT *Euphorbia spinosa* forms a perfectly regular cushion, decorative throughout the year.

BELOW LEFT With the first cold weather of winter, the silvery leaves of *Euphorbia rigida* take on violet tints.

BELOW RIGHT *Euphorbia amygdaloides* is happy at the margins of woodland. In the Taurus mountains it grows in stony clearings, surrounded by Judas trees, styrax and cedars.

Solidly anchored in the rock, *Euphorbia acanthothamnos* perches on clifftops in southern Crete, overlooking the Libyan Sea.

• ***Euphorbia × nicaensis*** has beautiful thick evergreen leaves that are blue-grey in colour, and more or less upright stems. The luminous yellow-green inflorescences appear from May to July. **ORIGIN** FROM SOUTHERN EUROPE TO CENTRAL ASIA **HARDINESS** −15 °C AND BELOW **DROUGHT RESISTANCE CODE** 5

• ***Euphorbia paralias*** has narrow, evergreen, blue-green leaves that are densely arranged along the length of the elegant, flexible stems. The green inflorescences appear at the stem tips from June to August. In nature this euphorbia is rarely seen outside sandy coastal zones (*paralios* means 'coastal' in Greek), but in the garden the plant can be acclimatized in a rock garden provided the soil is poor and has perfect drainage. **ORIGIN** COASTS OF EUROPE AND NORTH AFRICA **HARDINESS** −12 TO −15 °C **DROUGHT RESISTANCE CODE** 5

• ***Euphorbia pithyusa*** has pretty silvery-blue evergreen leaves tightly arranged on the stems. The inflorescences appear from May to August and have green cyathia furnished with orange nectar glands. **ORIGIN** MEDITERRANEAN BASIN, ON ROCKS OR SAND NEAR THE COAST **HARDINESS** −10 TO −12 °C **DROUGHT RESISTANCE CODE** 5

Ferula communis
(Apiaceae) Giant Fennel

ORIGIN MEDITERRANEAN BASIN
HEIGHT OF FOLIAGE 60 CM
HEIGHT IN FLOWER 2 TO 3 M

SPREAD 60 TO 80 CM
POSITION SUN
HARDINESS −10 TO −12 °C
DROUGHT RESISTANCE CODE 5

A perennial with foliage finely divided into long linear leaflets, giving it a light and

South of Essaouira, in Morocco, *Euphorbia paralias* colonizes the sand and coastal rocks.

ABOVE Before its spectacular flower spikes appear, the young shoots of *Ferula communis* grow rapidly in spring.

RIGHT A planting of grasses in the Barcelona Botanic Garden: *Leymus arenarius* at the top, *Festuca valesiaca* var. *glaucantha* on the right and *Festuca glauca* 'Elijah Blue' in the foreground.

BELOW *Festuca valesiaca* var. *glaucantha* and *Stipa tenuissima*. The foliage of grasses is perfect for softening the geometrical lines of a paved path.

Festuca valesiaca var. glaucantha
(Poaceae)

ORIGIN EUROPE
HEIGHT OF FOLIAGE 25 CM
HEIGHT IN FLOWER 50 CM
SPREAD 20 CM
POSITION SUN
HARDINESS −15 °C AND BELOW
DROUGHT RESISTANCE CODE 4

A grass that forms a tuft of evergreen, linear, blue-grey leaves. The numerous blue-grey spikelets appear in April–May; they take on a handsome golden colour as they mature, and remain on the plant all summer. *Festuca valesiaca* var. *glaucantha* tolerates alkaline conditions well; it likes friable, fairly deep, well-drained soils. It is an attractive grass for rock gardens and edging, and can also be combined with other silver plants such as *Stachys cretica* or *Artemisia caerulescens* subsp. *gallica*.

Propagation is by division in winter (propagation by seed produces plants with varying colours, more or less greenish or blueish).

• *Festuca glauca* 'Elijah Blue' forms a compact tuft of remarkably silvery-blue leaves surmounted by highly decorative silver spikelets. **ORIGIN** EUROPE **HARDINESS** −15 °C AND BELOW **DROUGHT RESISTANCE CODE** 2

Ficus pumila
(Moraceae) Creeping Fig

ORIGIN EAST ASIA
HEIGHT AND SPREAD 5 M
POSITION SUN OR SHADE
HARDINESS −8 TO −10 °C
DROUGHT RESISTANCE CODE 3

A climbing plant with evergreen leaves that are a pretty light green. The stems attach themselves firmly to their supporting

highly decorative appearance. The leaves appear with the first autumn rains and are evergreen throughout the winter. The floral spike emerges directly from the ground and grows rapidly in the spring to a height of 2 to 3 metres. In May–June large hemispherical umbels are produced, containing hundreds of small bright yellow flowers. In early summer the foliage dries out completely and the plant enters a dormant period, surviving the summer drought thanks to the reserves of water held in its tuberous rhizomes. All that remains to mark the plant's location is the tall dried out flower stem, which has an amazing lightness and strength. Schoolmasters once used this dried stem to chastise pupils who misbehaved (the name *Ferula* comes from the Latin *ferire*,

'to hit'). The hollow stem contains a fibrous lining which has the property of burning slowly without damaging the surrounding bark. In antiquity the stem was thus used to transport fire from one place to another.

Ferula communis tolerates alkaline conditions well and likes poor, stony, well-drained soils. It is sometimes said to behave like an annual if the seeds are left to ripen on the plant, but in our garden it is a faithful perennial, as robust as it is spectacular. We like to have it emerging from among dark-leaved shrubs, such as myrtles, phillyreas or pistacias, so that its giant flowering stem gives a wild touch to areas of the garden that are otherwise a little austere.

structures by aerial roots and secrete a transparent latex which hardens like cement as it dries. After a few years this plant makes an amazing green tapestry, clinging closely to its supports. When adult, the plant has a different kind of leaf at the tips of the stems, shrubby in appearance and large, shiny and tough. At this point it produces light green fig-like fruits (it is in fact a distant cousin of the fig tree), the seeds of which are sometimes eaten in Asia. *Ficus pumila* tolerates alkaline conditions well. It is happy in friable, fairly deep soils. This is a plant which is easy to grow and very useful for covering shady walls, since it does well in even the darkest corners.

Propagation is by softwood cuttings in spring.

Fremontodendron 'California Glory'
(Sterculiaceae) Flannel Bush

ORIGIN OF PARENTS CALIFORNIA
HEIGHT 3 TO 4 M
SPREAD 2 TO 3 M
POSITION SUN
HARDINESS −10 TO −12 °C (IN COLDER ZONES IT IS OFTEN GROWN TRAINED UP A BUILDING SO THAT IT CAN BENEFIT FROM THE HEAT GIVEN OFF BY THE WALL)
DROUGHT RESISTANCE CODE 4

Fremontodendron 'California Glory' is a hybrid of *Fremontodendron californicum* and *Fremontodendron mexicanum*. The young branches of this shrub are covered in hairs which can cause skin irritation when touched. The evergreen leaves, lobed like small fig leaves, are a matt green on their upper surfaces but furred with a golden-grey down on their undersides. In April–May the shrub is clothed in magnificent flowers that are a striking bright yellow. The flowers have an attractive shiny look, the result of the nectar that gently seeps from their centres. This nectar reflects the light and acts as a signal for the bees which pollinate *Fremontodendron* in its natural habitat: they can distinguish the shiniest flowers from a distance and are thus able to make straight for those that have the most nectar. *Fremontodendron* 'California Glory' tolerates alkaline conditions well; it prefers poor, stony, perfectly drained soils. Beware: it dies very quickly if the soil is damp in summer. As with ceanothuses, once it is established it should never be watered. During its first summer it should be given deep watering at intervals that are spaced so that the soil dries out completely between each watering. Like many plants linked to the fire ecology of the chaparral, it is a shrub with a relatively short lifespan, about ten to twelve years – but we forgive it for this because its flowering is absolutely spectacular.

Propagate by semi-ripe cuttings in autumn. Propagation is difficult and the rooting rate is usually poor.

Gaura lindheimeri
(Onagraceae)

ORIGIN TEXAS, MEXICO
HEIGHT IN FLOWER 1 M
SPREAD 60 TO 80 CM
POSITION SUN OR SEMI-SHADE
HARDINESS −12 TO −15 °C
DROUGHT RESISTANCE CODE 4

A perennial with deciduous leaves, though it sometimes retains an evergreen basal rosette in mild climates. The long green leaves are irregularly marked with red blotches. Its flowering is exceptionally generous: from May to September the plant bears innumerable pure white flowers that turn very slightly pink as they fade. With its long, light, branching stems, it seems unbothered by wind or drought and maintains its elegant, proud appearance throughout the summer (the name *Gaura* is from the Greek *gauros*, 'proud', 'splendid'). *Gaura lindheimeri* tolerates alkaline conditions well and is unfussy about soil type. It self-seeds profusely: in our garden we allow it to fill gaps in plantings of shrubs or perennials, which it then brightens with its cheerful flower spikes. Together with *Perovskia*, *Epilobum* or *Verbena bonariensis* it is one of the unbeatable perennials for summer colour in the dry garden.

Propagation is by seed in autumn or spring or by softwood cuttings in early spring.

Gazania rigens
(Asteraceae)

ORIGIN SOUTH AFRICA
HEIGHT 20 CM

SPREAD 40 TO 50 CM
POSITION SUN
HARDINESS −4 TO −6 °C
DROUGHT RESISTANCE CODE 2.5

A perennial with long, downy evergreen leaves. In winter the leaves are grey-green, but in the heat of summer they become a very attractive silvery-white. The spreading stems root wherever they touch the soil and the plant thus makes a handsome groundcover in the form of a dense cushion. The beautiful luminous flowers – bright yellow or orange according to the variety – open from April to June, complementing

There's no way of cheating with *Fremontodendron* 'California Glory': if you water it during the hot summer period it will die within a few weeks.

With its graceful and abundant flowering, *Gaura lindheimeri* is unbeatable for providing summer colour in a dry garden.

the light-coloured leaves in a very pleasing way. There may be a light repeat flowering in autumn, which will then continue until the first frosts. *Gazania rigens* tolerates alkaline conditions well. It is unfussy about soil type, but withstands cold better in dry, well-drained soil.

Propagation is by softwood cuttings in autumn or spring.

Genista aetnensis
(Fabaceae) Mount Etna Broom

ORIGIN SARDINIA, SICILY
HEIGHT 4 M OR MORE
SPREAD 2 M OR MORE
POSITION SUN
HARDINESS −10 TO −12 °C
DROUGHT RESISTANCE CODE 5

An elegant large shrub with a pliable, slightly weeping, growth habit. The long branches are almost bare of leaves, and photosynthesis is instead carried out by the chlorophyll contained in the green stems. In June the plant is covered in small yellow flowers that have a sweet scent of honey. *Genista aetnensis* tolerates alkaline conditions well. It is unfussy about soil type and is a robust shrub that is easy to grow. In the mountains of Sardinia we have seen it growing in dry watercourses, its yellow mingling with the fine blue spikes of *Vitex agnus-castus*, a combination we have copied in our own garden.

Propagation is by seed in autumn after hot water treatment: pour boiling water over the seeds then leave them to swell overnight.

• **Genista hispanica** is a sub-shrub that forms a spiny and very dense cushion. In April–May the plant disappears beneath a mass of bright yellow flowers. **ORIGIN** SOUTHWEST EUROPE **HARDINESS** −12 TO −15 °C **DROUGHT RESISTANCE CODE** 4

The flowers of *Gazania rigens* open in the sun and close in the evening.

Near the Namaqualand Desert, gazanias light up the rocky slopes on the west coast of South Africa. The sea fog that comes in over the coast every night allows a varied flora to survive in spite of the very low precipitation.

Geranium sanguineum
(Geraniaceae) Bloody Cranesbill

ORIGIN EUROPE, TURKEY
HEIGHT 20 CM
SPREAD 40 CM OR MORE
POSITION SUN OR SEMI-SHADE
HARDINESS −15 °C AND BELOW
DROUGHT RESISTANCE CODE 4

A perennial with evergreen or semi-evergreen cut leaves that take on a more or less pronounced red colour in winter. It is a fairly slow-growing plant and increases in spread by means of its rhizomes; in time it forms a good groundcover, getting thicker year by year. The pretty bright magenta flowers are produced in succession from April to July, and a lighter flowering may be repeated in autumn. The seedpods of *Geranium* have a characteristic long beak, resembling the beak of a crane (the name *Geranium* comes from the Greek *geranos*, 'crane'). *Geranium sanguineum* tolerates alkaline conditions well. In the wild it usually grows in stony soil, but in the garden it is unfussy about soil type – it is even happy in very clayey soils. As it can cope well with competition from tree roots, it is often planted under trees, where it makes an excellent groundcover. It self-seeds easily, often into the midst of other carpeting perennials such as *Thymus ciliatus* or *Phyla nodiflora*. We like to allow it to colonize freely in the areas where we try out lawn alternatives, to which it adds a cheerful note with its pretty spring flowers.

Propagation is by root cuttings in winter.

• *Geranium sanguineum* '**Album**' has pure white flowers. We use it to brighten shady areas of the garden.

• *Geranium sanguineum* var. *lancastriense* has pretty pale pink flowers, finely marked with mauve-pink lines.

• *Geranium macrorrhizum* makes a very good groundcover thanks to its long rhizomes (*macrorrhizum* comes from the Greek *makros*, 'long', and *rhiza*, 'root'). *Geranium macrorrhizum* does better in shade, in a friable, fairly deep soil. When crushed, its downy leaves give off a remarkable scent, sharp and strong, and reminiscent of rhubarb. The mauve-pink flowers are produced in succession from April to June. **ORIGIN** SOUTHERN EUROPE **HARDINESS** −15 °C AND BELOW **DROUGHT RESISTANCE CODE** 3

Globularia alypum
(Globulariaceae)

ORIGIN MEDITERRANEAN BASIN
HEIGHT 50 CM
SPREAD 40 CM
POSITION SUN
HARDINESS −12 TO −15 °C
DROUGHT RESISTANCE CODE 6

A small shrub with small, blue-green, thick and leathery evergreen leaves. Every year this plant's flowering takes one by surprise – in the middle of winter, indifferent to the bad weather, the large globular buds open into curious flattened heads of a

The flowers of *Geranium sanguineum* var. *lancastriense* glow in the evening light.

magnificent soft and luminous blue. Flowering begins in January, sometimes even in December, and continues until April. *Globularia alypum* tolerates alkaline conditions well. It requires poor, stony soil with perfect drainage. It is an extremely tough plant which can be seen proudly anchored among the stones of the garrigue in the South of France, but which we have also found in the Anti-Atlas growing in arid landscapes among *Argania* and cactiform euphorbias. In our garden we like to associate *Globularia alypum* with *Euphorbia rigida* as their blue and yellow flowers marry perfectly with one another in the winter light.

Propagation is by softwood cuttings in May, taken from the tender new shoots that appear just after flowering.

Geranium sanguineum, Erigeron karvinskianus and *Nepeta x faassenii* 'Six Hills Giant' mingle to make a pretty spring scene.

Globularia alypum is one of the first shrubs to flower in the garrigue at the end of winter.

The tightly packed heads of *Globularia vulgare* stand out above stepping stones.

A native of the Mongolian steppes, *Goniolimon speciosum* withstands cold as well as drought. Its light flowers open throughout the summer.

• *Globularia vulgare* is a perennial with spatulate leaves that forms a clump spreading over the ground. Its pretty sky-blue flowerheads on graceful stems open in March–April. **ORIGIN** SOUTH OF FRANCE, IBERIAN PENINSULA **HARDINESS** −15 °C AND BELOW **DROUGHT RESISTANCE CODE** 5

Goniolimon speciosum
(Plumbaginaceae)

ORIGIN STEPPES OF MONGOLIA AND SIBERIA
HEIGHT OF FOLIAGE 15 CM
HEIGHT IN FLOWER 40 CM
SPREAD 30 CM
POSITION SUN
HARDINESS −15 °C AND BELOW
DROUGHT RESISTANCE CODE 5

Sometimes classified as a *Limonium*, *Goniolimon speciosum* is a perennial with thick, green, evergreen leaves that may take on red hues in periods of severe drought. The plant forms a low clump which slowly spreads like a tight cushion. It is anchored by an underground central caudex, a sort of swollen base of the rootstock. This caudex acts as a reservoir of water and nutrients and enables the plant to survive the very harsh conditions in the saline steppes that are its natural habitat. From June to August it is covered in light and very decorative inflorescences (*speciosum* means 'beautiful' or 'eye-catching' in Latin). The flowers open in panicles that branch in a curious zigzag manner and are a pretty shade of blue-mauve that seems to soften the harsh light of full summer. The dry flower spikes can be kept for a long time as they retain their colour. *Goniolimon* tolerates alkaline

conditions well. It is unfussy about soil type and withstands salt spray and saline soils. In our garden it self-seeds freely, often at the edges of paths with other perennials such as *Asphodelus fistulosus* or *Scabiosa ucranica*.

Propagation is by seed in autumn.

Helianthemum apenninum
(Cistaceae)

ORIGIN MEDITERRANEAN BASIN
HEIGHT 20 TO 30 CM

SPREAD 30 CM
POSITION SUN
HARDINESS −12 TO −15 °C
DROUGHT RESISTANCE CODE 5

A sub-shrub with narrow, downy, silver-grey, evergreen leaves. In April–May the plant is covered in small, pure white flowers, as light as crumpled silk. As with all members of the Cistaceae family, the flowers last for just a day: the petals fall quickly in the afternoon, but dozens of swollen buds are already preparing to burst

Who ever said that there's no colour in dry gardens? With scant regard to good taste, a gaudy helianthemum has seeded itself beneath a *Salvia greggii* 'Furman's Red'.

into flower on the following day. *Helianthemum apenninum* tolerates alkaline conditions well. It prefers soils that are stony and that have perfect drainage. In our garden we like to reproduce a natural plant association seen in the garrigue at the foot of the Larzac plateau in the Hérault region, by growing *Helianthemum apenninum* in combination with *Teucrium aureum* and *Phlomis lychnitis*: in May the white and pale yellow flowers mix softly with the different shades of grey foliage.

Propagation is by seed in autumn or by softwood cuttings in spring.

• *Helianthemum* 'Wisley Primrose' is one of many frequently grown hybrids of *Helianthemum apenninum* and *Helianthemum nummularium*. It makes a pretty groundcover and produces its pastel yellow flowers generously. In the dry garden hybrid helianthemums do not live very long (usually not more than five or eight years). Among the many cultivars to be found in plant catalogues, we should mention 'Rhodanthe Carneum', with flowers of a gentle salmon pink, and 'Fire Dragon', with bright red-orange flowers.
HARDINESS −15 °C AND BELOW **DROUGHT RESISTANCE CODE** 2.5

Helianthus maximiliani
(Asteraceae)

ORIGIN CENTRAL AND SOUTHERN UNITED STATES
HEIGHT 1.5 TO 2 M
SPREAD 1 M OR MORE
POSITION SUN
HARDINESS −15 °C AND BELOW
DROUGHT RESISTANCE CODE 4

A perennial with long, deciduous, green leaves. The plant spreads by means of its fleshy rhizomes. It is a cousin of the Jerusalem artichoke (*Helianthus tuberosus*) and its roots are equally edible: they were traditionally eaten by the Sioux. In summer the stems grow rapidly taller and in September–October produce a multitude of brilliant yellow flowers. These flowers all turn towards the sun (the name *Helianthus* comes from the Greek *hēlios*, 'sun', and *anthos*, 'flower') as the parts of the stem in

The golden yellow flowers of *Helichrysum italicum* give off a strong scent of curry and honey. On the right, the first buds of *Epilobium canum* 'Western Hills' are barely showing their colour, while behind, *Perovskia* 'Blue Spire' is already in full flower.

shade grow faster than the parts exposed to the sun. *Helianthus maximiliani* tolerates alkaline conditions well. It is unfussy about soil type and is a robust plant that is easy to grow. In our garden we combine it with other late-flowering plants – *Caryopteris incana*, *Epilobium canum* 'Catalina' and *Ceratostigma griffithii* – to create a medley that livens up the garden in autumn.

Propagation is by division in winter or by softwood cuttings in spring.

• *Helianthus salicifolius* has long and very narrow arching foliage of a fine light green colour. The golden yellow flowers are borne in September–October at the tips of the long stems, which are sometimes so pliable that they bend under the weight of the flowers. ORIGIN NORTH AMERICA **HARDINESS** −15 °C AND BELOW

Helichrysum italicum
(Asteraceae) Curry Plant

ORIGIN MEDITERRANEAN BASIN
HEIGHT 50 CM
SPREAD 60 CM

POSITION SUN
HARDINESS −15 °C AND BELOW
DROUGHT RESISTANCE CODE 4

A sub-shrub with narrow, silver-grey evergreen leaves. The leaves give off a powerful spicy scent like curry and linseed oil. In June–July the plant is covered in golden yellow flowers (the name *Helichrysum* comes from the Greek *hēlios*, 'sun', and *chrysos*, 'gold'), which fill the hot air with a delicious scent of curry and honey. As with most everlasting flowers, the faded inflorescences remain on the plant, their golden bracts staying decorative for a long time after flowering. *Helichrysum italicum* tolerates alkaline conditions well. It likes light soils that are stony or sandy and perfectly drained, otherwise it is short-lived.

Propagation is by softwood cuttings in autumn or spring.

• *Helichrysum microphyllum* 'Lefka Ori' forms a miniature cushion, very decorative in a rock garden. The tiny golden-grey leaves are tightly packed along the stems

At the base of *Stachys taurica*, *Helianthemum* 'Wisley Primrose' is covered in pale yellow flowers in spring.

The branching inflorescences of *Helianthus maximiliani* stand out against the deep blue of the autumn sky.

The flowering stems of *Helichrysum orientale* form a pliable mass around the plant.

In the garden *Helichrysum orientale* is only happy in poor stony soils; in the wild it is a plant found in fissures in high cliffs.

like scales. They give off a powerful warm and spicy scent of curry. The flowers, grouped in golden yellow heads, open at the beginning of summer on short stalks. This cultivar from the White Mountains (or Lefka Ori) of Crete has been selected for its resistance to cold. In our garden it is the only *Helichrysum* that is really easy to grow and that ages well. **HARDINESS** −15 °C AND BELOW **DROUGHT RESISTANCE CODE** 5

• *Helichrysum stoechas* is as common on coastal dunes as it is in the inland garrigue. It always grows in very well-drained places, often among dolomitic rocks, as for example in the Mourèze corrie in the Hérault region of France. With its compact size it is a good plant for rock gardens. Its leaves give off a strong scent of curry. It does not adapt to cultivation in the garden unless the drainage is absolutely perfect. **ORIGIN** IBERIAN PENINSULA, FRANCE (MEDITERRANEAN AND ATLANTIC LITTORAL) **HARDINESS** −12 TO −15 °C **DROUGHT RESISTANCE CODE** 5

Helichrysum orientale

ORIGIN GREEK ISLANDS
HEIGHT OF FOLIAGE 30 CM
HEIGHT IN FLOWER 60 TO 80 CM
SPREAD 60 TO 80 CM
POSITION SUN
HARDINESS −10 TO −12 °C
DROUGHT RESISTANCE CODE 4

A sub-shrub with spatulate evergreen leaves that are silvery on the upper surface and cottony and white on the undersides. It develops into a rounded cushion, very regular in shape, making it an excellent structural plant for large rock gardens. In May the scaly buds, pale yellow with silver highlights, appear as flattened heads at the tips of the fine cottony stems. The flowers open in June and take on a handsome deep golden yellow colour. *Helichrysum orientale* tolerates alkaline conditions well.

In the wild *Helichrysum orientale* grows in fissures in high cliffs. It may be seen near the town of Sitia in eastern Crete, perched almost at the summit of the spectacular cliffs that descend vertically to the sea: if you follow the narrow goat track to reach this colony, close to 300 metres above the sea, you had better not suffer from vertigo! In the garden *Helichrysum orientale* requires soil with perfect drainage, otherwise it is short-lived. A clipping in early autumn helps maintain a good dense cushion shape.

Propagation is by softwood cuttings in autumn or spring.

Helleborus argutiflorus
(Ranunculaceae) Corsican Hellebore

ORIGIN CORSICA, SARDINIA
HEIGHT 60 CM
SPREAD 60 TO 80 CM
POSITION SHADE OR SEMI-SHADE
HARDINESS −12 TO −15 °C
DROUGHT RESISTANCE CODE 3

A perennial with tough, matt green, evergreen leaves divided into three toothed leaflets. The cup-shaped flowers open from January to March: they are an amazing luminous pistachio green in colour and nod gracefully downwards. *Helleborus argutiflorus* tolerates alkaline conditions well. It prefers fairly deep friable soils and is an excellent plant for lighting up shady areas, such as under trees, where it does well in spite of competition from the tree roots.

Propagation is by fresh seed immediately after harvesting (usually the end of April), directly into the open ground. The seeds germinate during the following winter after they have been through a period of cold weather.

Hertia cheirifolia
(Asteraceae)

ORIGIN NORTH AFRICA
HEIGHT 20 CM
SPREAD 50 CM OR MORE

A tiny cushion among an expanse of stone. *Helichrysum microphyllum* 'Lefka Ori' does well high in the mountains of Crete. The twisted shapes of centuries-old cypress trees dominate the screes.

Helichrysum stoechas among rocks at Saint-Guilhem-le-Désert, not far from Montpellier. This attractive plant is only for very well-drained rock gardens.

The luminous flowers of *Helleborus argutiflorus* open throughout the winter.

With its spreading or cascading foliage, *Hertia cheirifolia* makes an excellent groundcover.

POSITION SUN
HARDINESS −12 TO −15 °C
DROUGHT RESISTANCE CODE 4

A sub-shrub with thick, blue-grey, evergreen leaves. The plant forms a dense groundcover with spreading stems that root wherever they are in contact with the soil. It is a plant of unusual appearance due to the extremely regular arrangement of its leaves, all of which are oriented vertically along the length of the prostrate stems. The bright yellow daisy-like flowers are not abundant and appear in March–April, or sometimes even in February. *Hertia cheirifolia* tolerates alkaline conditions well and likes light, well-drained soils. It is a good groundcover for slopes and can also be grown cascading over stone walls. In periods of extreme drought the plant loses some of its leaves, enabling it to limit water loss but making it less ornamental at the end of summer.

Propagate by softwood cuttings in early spring.

Hesperaloe parviflora
(Agavaceae)

ORIGIN TEXAS, NORTHERN MEXICO
HEIGHT OF FOLIAGE 40 TO 60 CM, SOMETIMES MORE
HEIGHT IN FLOWER 1.2 M
SPREAD 50 CM OR MORE
POSITION SUN
HARDINESS −12 TO −15 °C
DROUGHT RESISTANCE CODE 6

A shrub with evergreen leaves arranged in dense rosettes. The plant spreads gradually, in time forming a thick groundcover. In Arizona and New Mexico it is often planted in large masses as groundcover in gardens where xeriscaping techniques are practised, in other words where lawns are replaced by extremely drought-resistant plants. The edges of the stiff, linear, gutter-shaped leaves fray into twisted fibres. From June to August the tall flowering spikes rise from the plant and then branch, their arching tips forming a contrast with the stiffness of the leaves. The small, tubular, salmon-pink flowers, rich in nectar, hang elegantly along the length of the flowering spikes. *Hesperaloe parviflora* tolerates alkaline conditions well; it prefers light, well-drained soils. Its remarkable architectural silhouette and its ability to flower in the middle of the summer are unique: it seems perfectly impervious even to the most intense heat and drought.

Propagation is by seed in autumn.

Hyparrhenia hirta
(Poaceae)

ORIGIN MEDITERRANEAN BASIN
HEIGHT 60 TO 80 CM

Hesperaloe parviflora in the Huntington Botanical Gardens, California.

SPREAD 50 CM OR MORE
POSITION SUN
HARDINESS −12 TO −15 °C
DROUGHT RESISTANCE CODE 5

A grass with narrow and flexible blue-green leaves that turn golden in winter. The plant forms an upright clump which spreads gradually from the base. Its very attractive flowering lasts for months, beginning in May–June and continuing more or less for the whole summer; it is then repeated for a long period in autumn and sometimes even into winter. The inflorescences consist of velvety and silky spikelets, grouped in pairs and surrounded by a sheath-like bract: they look just like an insect about to fly away. *Hyparrhenia hirta* tolerates alkaline conditions well and is unfussy about soil type. It self-seeds easily, especially along

Hyparrhenia hirta is a robust grass capable of establishing itself in the most difficult parts of the garden.

The flowers of *Hypericum balearicum*, with their protruding stamens, seem to have been set down on top of the curly foliage. Dotted with resin-producing glands, the leaves give off a strong balsamic scent when crushed.

In spite of its short lifespan, *Iberis gibraltarica* is much sought after by plantsmen. It needs a very well-drained site that is not too dry.

The bright yellow flowers of *Hypericum empetrifolium* are followed by red seedpods that remain decorative throughout the summer.

paths and in ground that has recently been disturbed. It is a robust and adaptable grass, useful for furnishing the most difficult spots in the garden.

Propagation is by seed in autumn or by division in winter.

Hypericum balearicum
(Clusiaceae) Balearic St John's Wort

ORIGIN BALEARIC ISLANDS
HEIGHT 50 CM, SOMETIMES MORE
SPREAD 60 CM
POSITION SUN OR SEMI-SHADE
HARDINESS −12 TO −15 °C
DROUGHT RESISTANCE CODE 5

A shrub with small, tough, dark green, evergreen leaves with wavy edges. The foliage forms a dense and regular ball as if it had been clipped as topiary. A brief observation with a magnifying glass will allow you to see distinctly the resin-producing glands dotted over the underside of the leaves. When crushed, the leaves give off a balsamic scent of cypress, with an underlying note of citrus, reminiscent of the fruit of *Maclura pomifera*. The bright yellow flowers open in June–July, the shiny texture of their petals contrasting well with the dark foliage. *Hypericum balearicum* tolerates alkaline conditions well. In the wild it grows in rocky, well-drained ground; however, it is an undemanding plant in the garden which adapts well to many conditions, even tolerating very clayey soils.

Propagate by semi-ripe cuttings in autumn.

Hypericum empetrifolium

ORIGIN GREECE, PARTICULARLY THE ISLANDS AND CRETE
HEIGHT 50 CM
SPREAD 60 TO 80 CM
POSITION SUN
HARDINESS −10 TO −12 °C
DROUGHT RESISTANCE CODE 5

A sub-shrub with small, linear, evergreen leaves which have their edges rolled over. The fine foliage can resemble that of a heather (*Hypericum* comes from the Greek,

hyperikos derived from *hypo*, 'sub', in other words 'almost', and *ereikē*, 'heather'). When crushed, the leaves give off a sharp and flowery scent, reminiscent of roses and citrus leaves. In May the plant disappears beneath a mass of small bright yellow flowers, grouped together at the tips of the stems. The plant is subsequently covered in small reddish-brown seedpods that are very decorative throughout the whole summer. *Hypericum empetrifolium* tolerates alkaline conditions well and requires a stony soil with perfect drainage. It is a very common plant in Crete where it grows on stony slopes together with *Satureja thymbra*, *Cistus creticus* and *Salvia pomifera*, making a lovely natural picture along the roadsides.

Propagation is by seed in autumn.

• *Hypericum aegypticum* forms a compact cushion of small grey-blue leaves. The flowers are scattered over the foliage like small soft yellow stars from April to July. **ORIGIN** MEDITERRANEAN BASIN **HARDINESS** −12 TO −15 °C **DROUGHT RESISTANCE CODE** 5

• *Hypericum olympicum* is a suckering perennial that forms a good small groundcover for rock gardens or for edging. The bright yellow flowers appear in June to July. **ORIGIN** GREECE, BALKANS, TURKEY **HARDINESS** −15 °C AND BELOW **DROUGHT RESISTANCE CODE** 3

Iberis semperflorens
(Brassicaceae)

ORIGIN SICILY
HEIGHT 30 CM
SPREAD 50 CM
POSITION SUN
HARDINESS −10 TO −12 °C
DROUGHT RESISTANCE CODE 3

Not to be confused with the classic Candytuft (*Iberis sempervirens*), *Iberis*

A close-up of *Iberis gibraltarica*. In order to take this photo, I had to scramble up the screes right next to the military zone at the foot of the cliffs of Gibraltar. A few seconds later the first police car arrived below – you don't play around with Her Majesty!

LEFT At the end of winter *Iris lutescens* lights up the garrigue with its multicoloured flowers.

ABOVE There is nothing easier than propagating *Iris germanica* in late summer, and its thick knotted rhizomes are perfect for combating erosion on steep slopes.

BELOW The large flowers of *Iris lutescens* seem disproportionate to their tiny leaves, which valiantly emerge between the stones.

semperflorens is a little-known plant. It is a sub-shrub with evergreen dark green leaves, thick and almost succulent. The dense corymbs of brilliant white flowers contrast well with the foliage. But it is the length of its flowering period that makes *Iberis semperflorens* truly remarkable. Flowering continues from November to April with a heedless abundance, the plant seemingly totally impervious to cold, rain or wind (*semperflorens* comes from the Latin, *semper*, 'always', and *florens*, 'in flower'). It is quite simply the best winter-flowering plant in our garden. *Iberis semperflorens* tolerates alkaline conditions well. It prefers light and well-drained soils and is a very useful plant for edging or in a rock garden. It can also be grown in containers to decorate patios and terraces for months on end.

Propagation is by seed in autumn or by semi-ripe cuttings in early autumn.

• *Iberis gibraltarica* forms little spreading cushions in the screes below the cliffs of Gibraltar. In April to May the plant is covered in large flowers, in which pale pink and white are subtly mingled. It is a somewhat capricious plant: it needs a site that is well drained and yet not too dry. In spite of its short lifespan, this is a plant much sought after by plantsmen for its unrivalled charm. **ORIGIN** GIBRALTAR, MOROCCO (RIF) **HARDINESS** −10 TO −12 °C **DROUGHT RESISTANCE CODE** 2.5

Iris unguicularis
(Iridaceae) Algerian Iris

ORIGIN GREECE, TURKEY, SYRIA, ALGERIA
HEIGHT 30 CM
SPREAD 50 CM OR MORE
POSITION SUN OR SEMI-SHADE
HARDINESS −12 TO −15 °C
DROUGHT RESISTANCE CODE 5

A perennial with narrow, tough, upright green leaves that are evergreen. The plant spreads slowly by means of its thick rhizomes. The delicate blue-mauve flowers are lightly scented and are held barely clear of the foliage when they appear in winter, from December to March. *Iris unguicularis* tolerates alkaline conditions well; it likes light, well-drained soils. It self-seeds freely in stony areas of the garden, for example at the edges of gravel paths where it may naturally form a very pretty edging.

Propagation is by division in early autumn.

• *Iris unguicularis* 'Alba' has creamy-white flowers with a yellow band on the sepals.

• *Iris lutescens* is the delightful dwarf iris that flourishes in stony garrigues. The large flowers seem out of proportion with the short, thick, ground-hugging foliage. Depending on the variety, the flowers may

be white, yellow, pale blue, dark blue or mauve. Every year in March we await the flowering of this iris in the garrigue near our nursery, where large colonies of it grow in the midst of orchids and wild tulips. **ORIGIN** SOUTH OF FRANCE, SPAIN, ITALY **HARDINESS** −12 TO −15 °C **DROUGHT RESISTANCE CODE** 5

• *Iris germanica*, the bearded iris, is available in numerous different colours. In Greek mythology, Iris, the messenger of the gods, was believed to travel between heaven and earth on the rainbow. In old gardens it was the blue-mauve variety that was used most (as well as the white-flowered Florentine iris), often to colonize the driest slopes. Its thick, knotted rhizomes form a strong mesh which acts as an excellent protection against erosion. **ORIGIN** UNCERTAIN (PROBABLY A HYBRID OF SEVERAL EUROPEAN SPECIES) **HARDINESS** −15 °C AND BELOW **DROUGHT RESISTANCE CODE** 5

There are numerous other botanical species of *Iris* that are perfectly adapted to dry gardens. Jean-Louis Latil has a large collection of them in his specialist nursery Lewisia (see appendix Useful Addresses).

Jasminum humile var. *revolutum*
(Oleaceae) Jasmine

ORIGIN KASHMIR
HEIGHT 2 M
SPREAD 1.5 M
POSITION SUN
HARDINESS −12 TO −15 °C
DROUGHT RESISTANCE CODE 3.5

A shrub with evergreen green leaves that are divided into thick, slightly leathery leaflets. The branching vegetation forms an upright bush, dense from the base. The clusters of pleasantly scented yellow flowers appear in succession from April to June. *Jasminum humile* var. *revolutum* tolerates alkaline conditions well and is unfussy about soil type. Although little used in gardens, it is a robust shrub that would be good planted, for example, in a flowering hedge.

Propagate by semi-ripe cuttings in autumn.

• *Jasminum grandiflorum* has a bushy, slightly spindly habit. It is tender and should be planted in a sheltered spot such as in the angle of a south- or west-facing wall; it is also easily cultivated in a pot. On summer nights its white flowers have an extraordinarily sweet and insistent scent, like a whiff of nostalgia for the lanes of Seville or Athens. **ORIGIN** ACCORDING TO SOME EXPERTS IT IS A FORM OF JASMINUM OFFICINALE (ORIGINATING IN ASIA) **HARDINESS** −4 TO −6 °C **DROUGHT RESISTANCE CODE** 3

• *Jasminum mesnyi* has long, pliable, arching branches, often seen cascading over the walls of old properties in the South of France. Its yellow, semi-double flowers, larger than those of *Jasminum nudiflorum*, are produced in succession from February to May. **ORIGIN** CHINA **HARDINESS** −10 TO −12 °C **DROUGHT RESISTANCE CODE** 2.5

A bench in the Los Angeles County Arboretum. The flowers of *Jasminum grandiflorum* give off an extraordinarily sweet and insistent scent.

Juniperus horizontalis 'Blue Chips' forms a vigorous carpeting groundcover, just thick enough to prevent the germination of weeds. Its foliage takes on fine mauvish-grey hues in winter.

• *Jasminum nudiflorum*, Winter Jasmine, is covered in bright yellow flowers in mid-winter, when its rambling branches have lost their leaves. It can be trained to grow over a support, for example through deciduous shrubs, but is much more interesting either cascading over a wall or used as a groundcover on slopes. It is equally happy in sun or shade. Its flowering branches last well in water and make cheerful flower arrangements for Christmas. **ORIGIN** CHINA **HARDINESS** −15 °C AND BELOW **DROUGHT RESISTANCE CODE** 3

Juniperus phoenicea
(Cupressaceae) Juniper

ORIGIN MEDITERRANEAN BASIN
HEIGHT 2 TO 3 M, SOMETIMES A LOT MORE IN OLD SPECIMENS
SPREAD 1.5 M OR MORE
POSITION SUN
HARDINESS −15 °C AND BELOW
DROUGHT RESISTANCE CODE 5

A shrub or small tree with dark green, aromatic, evergreen leaves. To reduce the surface from which evaporation takes place, the leaves are reduced to tiny overlapping scales along the length of the fine, branching stems. The compact vegetation develops naturally into a ball or broad spindle shape, as if the plant had been clipped regularly. The discreet flowers are followed by numerous small cones, fleshy and shiny (botanists call them galbules); these are green during their first year, then turn a reddish-chestnut colour as they ripen during their second year. *Juniperus phoenicea* tolerates alkaline conditions well. It lives naturally in rocky or sandy soil, but in our experience adapts easily to garden

conditions whatever the soil type, even clay. It can withstand salt spray perfectly.

Propagation is by fresh seed in autumn. To overcome seed dormancy, a long cold period is needed: in cold areas the seed can be sown outdoors in September and germination will take place from March onwards. Otherwise the seeds must be stratified by soaking them for 48 hours and then keeping them in the refrigerator for 5 or 6 months in a bag of damp vermiculite, at a temperature of about 4 °C. They should then be sown in spring. The seeds can be scarified with sulphuric acid to increase the germination rate, which is usually poor. Propagation by heel cuttings in early autumn is also possible.

• *Juniperus horizontalis* 'Blue Chips' spreads into a vigorous carpet about 15 centimetres high and almost 2 metres wide. Its blue-grey foliage takes on an amazing violet hue in winter. It is an excellent groundcover for a large rock garden or for slopes. **ORIGIN** NORTH AMERICA **HARDINESS** −15 °C AND BELOW **DROUGHT RESISTANCE CODE** 4

• *Juniperus oxycedrus* has narrow, pointed blue-grey leaves (*oxycedrus* comes from the Greek *oxy*, 'pointed', 'sharp'). The upper surface of the leaves is marked by two fine white bands. The hard, fine-grained and very scented wood is used for lathe-work and sculpture; it is reputed never to rot. Distillation of the wood yields a strong-smelling essential oil used as an antiseptic and parasiticide. *Juniperus oxycedrus* looks good emerging from masses of grey-leaved plants, or in a mixed, free-growing hedge. Centuries-old specimens can sometimes be seen which have acquired the form of small

ABOVE To limit water loss, the leaves of *Juniperus oxycedrus* are reduced to simple needles.

RIGHT The tall spikes of *Kniphofia sarmentosa* reach towards the winter sky. It is one of the rare plants to flower in our garden in January.

FAR RIGHT In spite of the heat, the orange spikes of *Kniphofia* 'Géant' open every year in July.

trees. **ORIGIN** MEDITERRANEAN BASIN **HARDINESS** −15 °C AND BELOW **DROUGHT RESISTANCE CODE** 5

Kniphofia sarmentosa
(Asphodelaceae) Red Hot Poker

ORIGIN SOUTH AFRICA, ALONG THE BANKS OF DRY WATERCOURSES IN THE WEST KAROO
HEIGHT OF FOLIAGE 40 CM
HEIGHT IN FLOWER 80 CM
POSITION SUN
HARDINESS −10 TO −12 °C
DROUGHT RESISTANCE CODE 3

A perennial with narrow, blueish-green, evergreen leaves that form an upright clump. The stock spreads gradually by means of its fleshy rhizomes, which store water and nutrients, thus allowing the plant to get through the dry period. In January–February long, handsome, spindle-shaped orange inflorescences open at the tips of the tall stems. The closely packed tubular flowers open from the bottom upwards; the buds are coral red and the flowers salmon-orange fading to pale yellow. *Kniphofia sarmentosa* tolerates alkaline conditions well; it likes well-drained stony soils. It is one of the most spectacular winter-flowering perennials: its cheerful flower spikes light up the garden when the weather is dreary. In times of extreme drought the foliage partially dries out in summer, making the plant less ornamental.

Propagation is by seed in autumn.

• *Kniphofia* 'Géant' is a hybrid of uncertain origin which forms a powerful clump of dark green leaves. The large, brilliant orange spikes, perched on pliable stems, proudly dominate perennial beds in July.
HARDINESS −12 TO −15 °C **DROUGHT RESISTANCE CODE** 3

Lavandula
(Lamiaceae) Lavender

There are a great many different lavenders, although they are often sold commercially without much precision as to their names. Nevertheless, when choosing a lavender it is worth spending a few minutes to make sure that it is suitable for your conditions. For the different species and varieties have very different requirements as regards their tolerance of alkalinity, for example, or their resistance to cold. They all, however, have one important thing in common: in the wild they always live in habitats that are poor, stony, dry and very well drained. In the garden they detest summer watering, which causes them to become diseased or die. Lavenders are particularly prone to fungal diseases (affecting the foliage or the collar of the plant) that develop when moisture and heat are present together. To grow lavenders well, it is essential to imitate their natural conditions: in winter they require perfect drainage and, above all, in summer they should never be watered.

Lavenders often grow too fast in the garden. In the wild they grow more slowly in poor soil and harsh conditions, never become leggy and are longer-lived. To ensure a longer life for your lavenders, they should be clipped every autumn, beginning when they are young plants. They will thus remain more compact and branching and will in time form magnificent dense cushions. And when you plant them, refrain from giving them any fertilizer or potting compost: what they like are a few generous spadefuls of sand and gravel!

To avoid the 'roundabout effect' – in other words that eternal square of lavenders as depressing as the centuries-old olive

tree that tends to go with them – I would suggest planting as many different lavenders as possible. By scattering them throughout the garden among perennials and shrubs you can discover some interesting combinations: *Lavandula* × *intermedia* 'Alba' emerging from a purple carpet of *Teucrium ackermanii*, for instance, or *Lavandula lanata* blending into the softness of *Sideritis cypria*, or the bright blue of *Lavandula angustifolia* acting as a counterpoint to the brilliant yellow of *Oenothera macrocarpa*. In our garden we grow more than a hundred different species and varieties of lavender, a true feast of colour to celebrate the beginning of summer. Here is a small selection of those which seem to me most beautiful and easiest to cultivate.

Lavandula angustifolia

ORIGIN MEDITERRANEAN BASIN, MOUNTAINS, GENERALLY AT AN ALTITUDE OF BETWEEN 500 AND 1,500 M
HEIGHT OF FOLIAGE 20 TO 30 CM
HEIGHT IN FLOWER 40 TO 60 CM
POSITION SUN
HARDINESS −15 °C AND BELOW
DROUGHT RESISTANCE CODE 3

A shrub with aromatic grey-green foliage that is deciduous or semi-evergreen. The edges of the leaves are folded over to reduce the surface from which evaporation takes place, making them appear linear (*angustifolia* comes from the Latin *angustus*, 'narrow'). The size of the plant varies according to the particular clone, but it develops into a dense and compact ball: this is one of the smaller-growing lavenders. In June the short flower spikes open on a hedgehog-like multitude of stems, transforming the plant for a few weeks into a magnificent ball of blue-mauve flowers.

In the dry garden, the great diversity of lavenders can be used to create vast flowering scenes in early summer.

Each flower is surrounded by a calyx of a more or less dark colour, affecting our perception of the flower colour when we look at it from a distance. The flowers are traditionally distilled to produce the finest essence of lavender, used in perfumes or aromatherapy. *Lavandula angustifolia* tolerates alkaline conditions well. Forget the hackneyed postcard pictures – to see a few plants of *Lavandula angustifolia* caught in the silver tresses of *Stipa pennata* among linums, astragalus and euphorbias is to discover one of the finest sights of the hillsides of the South of France.

Propagate by seed in autumn to obtain genetically variable populations. Cultivars, by contrast, should be propagated by stem section cuttings taken from ripe wood in autumn.

• *Lavandula angustifolia* 'Alba' has pure white flowers – a ball of light that makes a magnificent contrast in darker plantings.

• *Lavandula angustifolia* 'Folgate' has pretty violet-blue flowers. This is a slow-growing plant that develops into a small, very compact ball, like a dwarf lavender.

• *Lavandula angustifolia* 'Hidcote Blue' has magnificent, intense violet-blue flowers whose calyces have an even darker velvety colour. This cultivar is very prone to die if it doesn't have the best drainage. We have had better success with it in our garden since we began to plant it in a sloping border mulched with a thick layer of pure gravel.

• *Lavandula angustifolia* 'Hidcote Pink' has delicate pale pink flowers, very original.

To ensure good drainage, these cultivars of *Lavandula angustifolia* have been planted in a raised border. *Lavandula angustifolia* 'Alba' is set among the cultivars 'Hidcote Blue' (in the background) and 'Lumière des Alpes' (in the foreground).

• *Lavandula angustifolia* 'Lumière des Alpes', selected by Catherine Coutoulenc, has inflorescences that seem bicoloured. The pale mauve flowers are set off by velvety calyces of a fine dark violet.

• *Lavandula angustifolia* 'Munstead' has luminous blue-mauve flowers and forms a vigorous and regular ball shape. It is easy to grow and long-lived in our garden.

• *Lavandula angustifolia* 'Twickel Purple' has long spikes of a soft purple-mauve and is a very floriferous cultivar.

Lavandula dentata

ORIGIN IBERIAN PENINSULA, MOROCCO
HEIGHT OF FOLIAGE 60 TO 80 CM, SOMETIMES MORE
SPREAD 60 TO 80 CM, SOMETIMES MORE
POSITION SUN

HARDINESS −6 TO −8 °C
DROUGHT RESISTANCE CODE 6

In France this plant is called 'English lavender' while in England, just to be fair, it is known as 'French lavender': it is of course neither French nor English but grows wild in Spain and Morocco.

Lavandula angustifolia on the Sainte-Baume massif in Provence. Lavenders like poor soil with perfect drainage.

The dark flowers of *Lavandula angustifolia* 'Hidcote Blue' contrast well with the pale yellow of *Teucrium flavum*.

The dark foliage of *Frankenia laevis* sets off the pale pink of *Lavandula angustifolia* 'Hidcote Pink'.

Lavandula angustifolia 'Twickel Purple' in full flower at the beginning of June. The buds of the later flowering *Lavandula* × *intermedia* 'Julien' are just beginning to colour.

Lavandula dentata and *Lavatera maritima* colonize a rocky hillside near Valencia in Spain.

Lavandula dentata is a shrub with highly aromatic evergreen leaves. The edges of the green leaves are finely cut into countless tiny and easily visible teeth (*dentata* comes from the Latin, *dens*, 'tooth'). The plant has a noticeable seasonal variation in its leaves: its winter and spring leaves are large to ensure photosynthesis during the plant's growth period, while its summer leaves are markedly smaller and are held vertically, tightly packed along the stems, in order to reduce their exposure to solar radiation in periods of drought. In mild climates the plant flowers unceasingly and remarkably generously from October to July, with a rest period only during the driest months of summer. In colder climates the main flowering period is in spring, followed by a repeat flowering in autumn. The sturdy spikes are composed of small, pale blue flowers topped by decorative purple-mauve floral bracts. The plant develops into a large rounded mass and its exceptional flowering makes it worth planting in a sheltered spot in the garden, for example beneath a wall with a good orientation. *Lavandula dentata* tolerates alkaline conditions well and withstands salt spray. We have noticed that it withstands cold a lot better in parts of the garden where the soil remains really dry in winter. By contrast, in heavy soils which hold moisture in winter, it can easily suffer frost damage even when the temperature does not fall very low.

Propagation is by softwood cuttings in autumn.

• *Lavandula dentata* 'Ploughman's Blue' has large floral bracts, noticeably darker: seen from a distance, the spike looks a very attractive dark purple-blue.

• *Lavandula dentata* 'Imi n'Ifri' is a pretty pink-flowered form which we collected in Morocco. It grows near the natural bridge of Imi n'Ifri in a landscape dominated by the massive shapes of *Euphorbia resinifera*, the magnificent cactiform euphorbia of the Atlas mountains.

• *Lavandula dentata* var. *candicans* has grey downy foliage that marries perfectly with the soft mauve colour of the flowers. This is the most common variety in southern Morocco, where it grows as well on the coast as it does in the mountains, up to 2,000 metres. We are trying out clones from different altitudes, in the hope of being able to select ones that are more resistant to cold.

Lavandula lanata

ORIGIN SPAIN
HEIGHT OF FOLIAGE 20 TO 30 CM
HEIGHT IN FLOWER 60 CM
SPREAD 40 TO 50 CM
POSITION SUN
HARDINESS −10 TO −12 °C (PERHAPS MORE IN VERY DRY SOIL)
DROUGHT RESISTANCE CODE 5

A shrub with silvery aromatic evergreen foliage that becomes almost white in summer. The leaves are soft to the touch and are covered in a thick down which

BELOW *Lavandula dentata* 'Ploughman's Blue', growing here with *Achillea coarctata*. has beautiful purple-blue spikes dominated by large floral bracts.

RIGHT Pink *Convolvulus althaeoides* twines around *Lavandula dentata*.

Lavandula dentata 'Imi n'Ifri' to the north of djebel M'Goun in Morocco, with the regular architecture of *Euphorbia resinifera* in the background.

under a magnifying glass resembles the fleece of a sheep. The plant develops naturally into a large spreading cushion without needing to be clipped. In July to August the dark purple spikes open on long, supple, elegant branching stems. This species can be seen growing in Andalucia, in the mountains south of Granada, where its foliage contrasts with the spiny cushions of *Erinacea anthyllis*, the striking blue-flowered broom.

Lavandula lanata tolerates alkaline conditions well. It is sometimes difficult to keep in gardens because it is only happy in poor stony soils with perfect drainage. Our first attempts weren't very successful since we planted it in soil that was too heavy. Yet because of the beauty of its foliage it is one of our favourite lavenders. We then took the trouble to plant it in raised borders, adding a lot of sand and gravel at planting, and we now manage to keep it without problem. We like to combine it with other silver plants such as *Stachys cretica, Convolvulus cneorum* or *Helichrysum orientale* to create attractive mixtures of soft and silky foliage.

Propagation is by seed in autumn. The young seedlings are very susceptible to rot and must be kept in a well-ventilated place.

Lavandula latifolia
Aspic Lavender

ORIGIN WESTERN MEDITERRANEAN BASIN, IN PLAINS AND FOOTHILLS TO AN ALTITUDE OF 700 M
HEIGHT OF FOLIAGE 20 TO 30 CM
HEIGHT IN FLOWER 60 CM
SPREAD 40 TO 50 CM
POSITION SUN
HARDINESS −12 TO −15 °C
DROUGHT RESISTANCE CODE 4

A shrub with highly aromatic evergreen foliage (it has a very pleasant strong smell of camphor), grey-green in spring and becoming silver in summer. The fairly broad leaves have a spatulate shape (*latifolia* comes from the Latin, *latus*, 'broad'). The plant develops into a low clump, from which emerge long, branching and slightly drooping stems carrying pale mauvey-blue spikes. Apparently impervious to drought and heat, the plant flowers repeatedly throughout the entire summer, never dramatic but always pretty, resembling a delicate mauvey-blue mist. *Lavandula*

latifolia tolerates alkaline conditions well. It is often found in the garrigues of the South of France in very stony soil, frequently clinging to fissures in the limestone rocks, into which its long roots manage to penetrate to seek the small amount of moisture available deep down.

Propagation is by seed in autumn.

Lavandula × chaytorae 'Richard Gray'

HEIGHT OF FOLIAGE 20 TO 30 CM
HEIGHT IN FLOWER 40 TO 50 CM
SPREAD 40 TO 50 CM
POSITION SUN
HARDINESS −12 TO −15 °C
DROUGHT RESISTANCE CODE 4

Lavandula × chaytorae 'Richard Gray' is a hybrid of *Lavandula lanata* and *Lavandula angustifolia*. Inheriting the good qualities of both its parents, it has attractive narrow, silver, evergreen leaves and develops into a dense, compact, rounded cushion. In June–July the plant is covered in spikes borne on short stems that form a tight mass. The magnificent deep purple flowers make an interesting contrast with the silver foliage: it is one of the most beautiful lavenders in our garden. *Lavandula × chaytorae* 'Richard Gray' tolerates alkaline conditions well. If planted in light, well-drained soil it is robust and very easy to grow. It ages well since it has less of a tendency to become leggy than *Lavandula angustifolia* and *Lavandula × intermedia*.

Propagation is by section cuttings taken from ripe wood in autumn.

In the Alpujarras mountains of Andalucia, the apparent starkness of the landscape is deceptive. *Lavandula lanata*, with its magnificent velvety foliage, is one of the many species that contribute to the richness of the matorral.

Lavandula latifolia is happy in cracks between limestone slabs. Its long roots explore the rock to find pockets of humidity deep down.

Compact and floriferous, Lavandula x *chaytorae* 'Richard Gray' is one of the best lavenders in our garden. A few undisciplined suckering shoots of *Dicliptera erecta* are growing through the lavender.

Unusual and spectacular, Lavandula x *intermedia* 'Alba' deserves to be planted more often.

• *Lavandula* × *chaytorae* 'Sawyers' has a more spreading habit and forms a good groundcover: it is one of the lowest-growing lavenders in our collection.

• *Lavandula* × *chaytorae* 'Silver Frost' has remarkable woolly foliage that is almost white and particularly luminous. The plant is vigorous and forms a large rounded mass.

Lavandula × ginginsii 'Goodwin Creek Grey'

HEIGHT OF FOLIAGE 30 CM
HEIGHT IN FLOWER 60 TO 80 CM, SOMETIMES MORE
SPREAD 60 CM
POSITION SUN
HARDINESS −6 TO −8 °C (TO −10 °C AND BELOW IN VERY DRY SOIL)
DROUGHT RESISTANCE CODE 5

A hybrid of *Lavandula dentata* and *Lavandula lanata*, this lavender has aromatic, woolly, grey, evergreen foliage. The leaves seem to hesitate between the characteristics of the two parents: they are sometimes irregularly cut into large teeth and sometimes almost entire. The seasonal dimorphism of the leaves is quite pronounced: in winter and spring broad grey-green leaves ensure photosynthesis, while in summer they are replaced by narrow silvery leaves. The plant spreads vigorously, forming a cushion that can be used as groundcover. From April to September, large spikes open on tall, pliable stems, the dark purple of the flowers set off by the downy grey of the calyces. *Lavandula* × *ginginsii* 'Goodwin Creek Grey' tolerates alkaline conditions well. It is an outstanding plant with abundant, very ornamental flowering. It has only one requirement: even more than most lavenders, it needs poor, stony soil with perfect drainage, as dry as possible, if it is to get through the winter.

Propagation is by softwood cuttings in autumn.

Lavandula × intermedia

HEIGHT OF FOLIAGE 40 TO 80 CM, DEPENDING ON THE CULTIVAR
HEIGHT IN FLOWER 80 CM TO 1.2 M, SOMETIMES MORE
SPREAD 60 CM TO 1 M, DEPENDING ON THE CULTIVAR
POSITION SUN
HARDINESS −15 °C AND BELOW
DROUGHT RESISTANCE CODE 4

Lavandula × *intermedia* is a hybrid of *Lavandula angustifolia* and *Lavandula latifolia*. These two species frequently interbreed naturally in the mid-mountain zone where they grow wild together. *Lavandula* × *intermedia* has grey-green evergreen foliage that is extremely aromatic. (The name *Lavandula* comes from the Latin *lavo*, 'to wash', referring to the tradition of putting a few drops of lavender essence in the bath for its calming and antiseptic properties, and of placing dried bunches of lavender among linen, not only for its fragrance, but also for its effectiveness as an insecticide.) The size of both the leaves and the whole plant varies widely depending on the cultivar, often indicating the dominance of one or the other of the parent species. Its remarkably abundant flowering turns the plant into a regular ball, bristling with flowers like a hedgehog, which has become an almost legendary symbol of Provence.

There are dozens of cultivars of *Lavandula* × *intermedia*. The monograph by Tim Upson and Susyn Andrews, *The Genus Lavandula*, provides detailed information on the history of these cultivars, as well as on the confusion, frequently encountered in commercial horticulture, surrounding their names and synonyms (see Further Reading). All cultivars of *Lavandula* × *intermedia* tolerate alkaline conditions well and need dry soil with perfect drainage.

• *Lavandula* × *intermedia* 'Alba' has long spikes of pure white flowers surrounded by fine green calyces. This vigorous and floriferous cultivar is one of the best in our collection. Our oldest specimen has a spread of almost 1.5 metres.

• *Lavandula* × *intermedia* 'Dutch' has fine spikes of light mauve flowers borne on long stems. The flowering is slightly disappointing since it is never very abundant. It does, however, last for several months, from June to September: this is the only cultivar of *Lavandula* × *intermedia* that flowers all summer in our garden. But the plant's main attraction is its foliage, which is a handsome, dense, silvery grey. It forms a massive ball that is very decorative in winter and spring.

• *Lavandula* × *intermedia* 'Grosso' is a hybrid with a compact habit and narrow grey-green leaves, showing that *Lavandula angustifolia* is its dominant parent. Its early flowers are a luminous purple enhanced by darker purple calyces. Flowering is remarkably profuse: covered in its violet spikes, this plant perfectly evokes the idea of lavender that everyone seems to be searching for.

• *Lavandula* × *intermedia* 'Hidcote Giant' is distinguished by its plump spikes borne on long, strong stems. The purple flowers are surrounded by purple-grey calyces. It is a large-leaved cultivar, with particularly vigorous foliage. We have planted it on top of a small mound, where it proudly dominates our lavender garden.

• *Lavandula* × *intermedia* 'Julien' has long purple spikes surrounded by purple-grey calyces. It is a cultivar that is useful for its late flowering: in our garden it is just beginning to flower in July when most other lavenders are already fading.

• *Lavandula* × *intermedia* 'Super' is an elegant cultivar with pretty light mauve flowers. These have a very delicate scent, similar to that of *Lavandula angustifolia*.

Leucophyllum frutescens
(Scrophulariaceae) Barometer Bush

ORIGIN CHIHUAHUA DESERT, TEXAS AND MEXICO
HEIGHT 1.5 M
SPREAD 1 M OR MORE
POSITION SUN
HARDINESS −10 TO −12 °C
DROUGHT RESISTANCE CODE 6

Lavandula × intermedia 'Grosso' is a popular lavender that deserves its success. The early flowers, arranged in a regular spiky ball, are a beautiful luminous purple.

An evergreen or semi-evergreen shrub with downy, silver-grey leaves which have whitish undersides (the name *Leucophyllum* comes from the Greek *leukos*, 'white', and *phyllon*, 'leaf'). Its flowering is timed to follow the desert plant cycle: intense and brief, it is triggered by the first rain after a long period of drought.

In our garden it generally flowers at the end of September or the beginning of October. The flowers are covered in downy hairs and appear in each leaf axil of that year's growth. In the soft autumn light they transform the plant into an incredible ball of pale pink. For a few weeks it is exceptionally beautiful, without any doubt the most spectacular plant in our garden in October.

Leucophyllum frutescens tolerates alkaline conditions well. It likes light, very well-drained soils; it has poor resistance to cold if the soil remains damp in winter. It has a tendency to become leggy with age: the tips of the stems may be shortened annually in late autumn in order to maintain a more compact habit.

Propagation is by softwood cuttings in spring.

• *Leucophyllum frutescens* 'Green Cloud' has grey-green leaves that contrast well with its beautiful pinkish-purple flowers.

• *Leucophyllum langmaniae* has grey-green leaves and a naturally dense and compact habit. Its bright pink flowers scattered among the foliage are produced in succession in September–October, with a profusion that varies from year to year. The more intense the summer drought, the more abundant its autumn flowering. **ORIGIN** MEXICO, CHIHUAHUA DESERT **HARDINESS** −10 TO −12 °C **DROUGHT RESISTANCE CODE** 6

Lavandula × intermedia 'Hidcote Giant' is distinguished by its plump spikes borne on very long stems.

Lavandula × intermedia 'Super' is an easily grown cultivar with delicate spikes of a pretty pale mauve flowers.

Spotted and hairy, the mysterious throats of the flowers of *Leucophyllum frutescens* 'Green Cloud' await the visit of a pollinator.

Leymus arenarius
(Poaceae)

ORIGIN COASTAL DUNES OF EUROPE
HEIGHT OF FOLIAGE 50 CM
HEIGHT IN FLOWER 80 CM
SPREAD 2 M OR MORE
POSITION SUN
HARDINESS −15 °C AND BELOW
DROUGHT RESISTANCE CODE 5

A grass with large, flat, fraying leaves of an amazing silvery blue colour, turning yellow in winter. The plant spreads vigorously by means of its rhizomes and can form an extensive groundcover with a tendency to be invasive. Long, silvery blue flower spikes appear in June, which become a fine golden colour as they ripen by the end of summer. *Leymus arenarius* tolerates alkaline conditions well. It prefers friable, sandy soils (*arenarius* comes from the Latin *arena* or *harena*, 'sand'). It also adapts to compact, clayey soils, but in this case will spread less. It can be used to colonize slopes or wild areas of the garden along with other invasive perennials such as *Potentilla reptans* or *Achillea nobilis*.

Propagation is by division in winter.

Lithodora fruticosa
(Boraginaceae)

ORIGIN SPAIN, SOUTH OF FRANCE
HEIGHT 40 CM
SPREAD 40 CM
POSITION SUN
HARDINESS −12 TO −15 °C
DROUGHT RESISTANCE CODE 5

A sub-shrub with linear, green, evergreen leaves whose edges are folded under to reduce the surface area from which evapotranspiration takes place. The leaves bristle with stiff hairs and are curiously rough to the touch. The small flowers open in April–May. They are an extraordinarily intense blue at first, then gently turn a fine purple colour as they fade. *Lithodora fruticosa* tolerates alkaline conditions well. It requires poor, perfectly drained soil, otherwise it is short-lived. In fact it is happiest among stones (the name *Lithodora*

comes from the Greek *lithos*, 'stone', and *dōron*, 'gift' – the plant is like a present from the garrigue). In order to grow it in our garden we have planted it in a raised border consisting almost entirely of sand and gravel, and have combined it with other plants that like very freely draining soils – *Helichrysum stoechas*, *Teucrium cossonii* and *Globularia alypum*.

Propagation is by softwood cuttings taken from new growth just after flowering in late spring.

Lobelia laxiflora var. *angustifolia*
(Campanulaceae)

ORIGIN SOUTHWESTERN UNITED STATES, MEXICO
HEIGHT 50 CM OR MORE
SPREAD 80 CM OR MORE
POSITION SUN OR SHADE
HARDINESS THE VEGETATION IS BURNT BY THE COLD FROM THE FIRST FROSTS, BUT THE STOCK CAN WITHSTAND −8 TO −10 °C
DROUGHT RESISTANCE CODE 2.5

A perennial with long, narrow leaves that are a pretty light green. The plant is evergreen in mild climates, but is generally deciduous in the South of France. In our garden it is entirely demolished by the cold each winter, but sprouts again from the stock extremely well in spring, suckering vigorously to form a dense groundcover. The bright orange tubular flowers, with a handsome yellow throat, are produced in succession from May to July, and sometimes throughout the whole summer if conditions are not too dry. In the wild the flowers are pollinated by hummingbirds, which come to drink the nectar contained at the bottom of the corolla (and also by large bees which cut through the base of the flower with their mandibles in order to reach the nectar). In Arizona *Lobelia laxiflora* var. *angustifolia* grows beneath oaks and poplars (*Quercus arizonica* and *Populus fremonti*), which inhabit the bottoms of the canyons. In the garden it is a useful perennial for shady areas which often lack colour. *Lobelia laxiflora* var. *angustifolia* tolerates alkaline conditions well. It is unfussy about soil type and is a tough, cheerful perennial which does equally well in the open ground or in a pot.

Propagation is by softwood cuttings in early autumn before the first frosts. We take cuttings only on grey, damp days because in dry weather they wilt rapidly, even when kept in the humidity of a propagation case.

Lonicera etrusca
(Caprifoliaceae) Etruscan Honeysuckle

ORIGIN SOUTHERN EUROPE
HEIGHT 2 M OR MORE
SPREAD 1.5 TO 2 M
POSITION SUN OR SHADE

HARDINESS −15 °C AND BELOW
DROUGHT RESISTANCE CODE 4

A deciduous shrub with light green, slightly leathery leaves. The young shoots are a fine purplish-red colour and are twining, enabling the plant to climb through other shrubs in the garrigue. In May–June the clusters of fragrant flowers appear at the tips of the stems. The elegant flowers consist of a long pink tube, opening at the end into two orange-yellow lips from which the graceful bunch of stamens protrudes. *Lonicera etrusca* tolerates alkaline conditions well and it is unfussy about soil type. It is an easily grown shrub that can be used as part of a mixed, free-growing hedge, which it sets off with its pretty springtime flowering.

Propagation is by softwood cuttings in spring.

Lonicera japonica 'Halliana'
Japanese Honeysuckle

ORIGIN EAST ASIA
HEIGHT AND SPREAD 10 M OR MORE
POSITION SUN OR SEMI-SHADE
HARDINESS −15 °C AND BELOW
DROUGHT RESISTANCE CODE 3.5

A climber with green, evergreen or semi-evergreen leaves. The twining young shoots coil easily round supports, allowing the plant to climb or to spread sideways very rapidly. The flowers open white before turning yellowish, and are grouped in pairs in the leaf axils of the current year's growth. Flowering is profuse in May–June and is then repeated more sparsely until September. The flowers are deliciously scented and in still weather can perfume an entire section of the garden. *Lonicera japonica* 'Halliana' tolerates alkaline conditions well and prefers friable, fairly deep soils. It is an excellent climber for

Lonicera etrusca colonizes old stone walls that bear witness to earlier cultivation, buried beneath the garrigue.

covering a pergola, and can also be used to cover wire fences, to cascade from the top of walls or to cover large slopes.

Propagation is by softwood cuttings in autumn or spring.

• *Lonicera japonica* '**Chinensis**' has purple young shoots. The flowers are white and light red at first, then mature into a warm mixture of orange-pink and gentle yellow.

• *Lonicera fragrantissima* is a deciduous or sometimes semi-evergreen shrub. In mid-winter the highly scented creamy-white flowers open along the length of the previous year's stems. **ORIGIN** CHINA **HARDINESS** −15 °C AND BELOW **DROUGHT RESISTANCE CODE** 2.5

• *Lonicera implexa*, the Balearic honeysuckle, grows wild in garrigues, where its twining stems form an interweaving mass among kermes oaks and lentisks (*implexa* means 'interwoven' in Latin). It is easy to recognize by its thick, slightly glaucous evergreen leaves which are curiously soldered together in pairs, the red stem apparently piercing through the middle. The red and yellow flowers appear in May–June at the tips of the new shoots. **ORIGIN** MEDITERRANEAN BASIN **HARDINESS** −12 TO −15 °C **DROUGHT RESISTANCE CODE** 4.5

• *Lonicera syringantha* is a small, very branching, deciduous shrub. Its highly fragrant spring flowers are as discreet as they are charming. They have both the colour and the scent of lilac (the name *syringantha* comes from *Syringa*, lilac). **ORIGIN** CHINA, TIBET **HARDINESS** −15 °C AND BELOW **DROUGHT RESISTANCE CODE** 2.5

• *Lonicera tatarica* '**Arnold Red**' is a deciduous shrub whose upright branches are fairly fast-growing. In March–April its beautiful light red flowers mingle with the tender green of the new leaves. It is a good shrub for a free-growing hedge. **ORIGIN** RUSSIA, CENTRAL ASIA **HARDINESS** −15 °C AND BELOW **DROUGHT RESISTANCE CODE** 3

Lygeum spartum
(Poaceae)

ORIGIN MOROCCO, SPAIN, SOUTHERN ITALY, CRETE
HEIGHT 60 CM
SPREAD 60 TO 80 CM
POSITION SUN
HARDINESS −15 °C AND BELOW
DROUGHT RESISTANCE CODE 6

A grass with long, narrow, leathery leaves that remain green throughout the year. They resemble the leaves of rushes, being rolled into a tight gutter shape, thus protecting the stomata on the inner side in order to limit evapotranspiration, allowing the plant to survive in arid conditions. The pliable, tough leaves have traditionally been used in the manufacture of ropes and cords and are used in Morocco to make mats or baskets, along with other grasses such as *Ampelodesmos mauritanicus* and *Stipa tenacissima* (the name *spartum* comes from the Greek *sparté*, 'rope', referring to the use made of the leaves). The rhizomatous stock develops slowly into a crown shape, like a nest. The very decorative flowers appear in

In the empty period of winter the subtle perfume of *Lonicera fragrantissima* scents the icy air.

June–July. They have a curious shape – the silvery spike, clad in a lengthy horizontal bract and covered in long silky hairs, terminates in two delicate glumes, resembling the dishevelled head of a bird. *Lygeum spartum* tolerates alkaline conditions well and withstands salt spray. It is unfussy about soil type and is a tough and decorative plant, one of the few grasses to remain green throughout the year.

Propagation is by seed in autumn or by division in winter.

Macfadyena unguis-cati
(Bignoniaceae) Cat's Claw Vine

ORIGIN SOUTH AMERICA, FROM MEXICO TO ARGENTINA
HEIGHT AND SPREAD 15 M OR MORE
POSITION SUN OR SEMI-SHADE
HARDINESS THE FOLIAGE IS KILLED BY THE COLD AT −4 TO −6 °C, BUT THE PLANT WILL SPROUT AGAIN FROM THE STOCK AFTER EVEN LOWER TEMPERATURES
DROUGHT RESISTANCE CODE 4

A rapidly growing climber with delicate, pliable stems. The foliage is normally evergreen but may be deciduous in cold weather, the plant having a good ability to sprout again from the stock in spring. The leaves are divided into two tough, dark green leaflets and are furnished with a long tendril that ends in three little hooks, enabling the plant to cling firmly to all kinds of support. If you put your finger beneath a tendril you will be surprised to find these little hooks digging into your skin, just like a cat's claws (*unguis-cati* means 'cat's claw' in Latin). The tendrils can become tuberous roots, allowing the plant to spread like an immense groundcover. From April to June the pretty bright yellow flowers open into wide-mouthed trumpets. In a favourable position the plant can be extremely vigorous, to the point of being almost invasive. An absolutely spectacular specimen can be seen in Barcelona, covering a monumental wall on the Avinguda del

Deliciously scented, the flowers of *Lonicera japonica* 'Chinensis' open in May–June, with a repeat flush in September.

Parallel, on the left before the port. *Macfadyena unguis-cati* tolerates alkaline conditions well and withstands salt spray. It prefers friable, well-drained soils that are fairly deep.

Propagation is by seed in autumn or by softwood cuttings in autumn or spring.

Malephora crocea
(Aizoaceae)

ORIGIN SOUTH AFRICA
HEIGHT 20 CM
SPREAD 50 CM OR MORE
POSITION SUN
HARDINESS −8 TO −10 °C
DROUGHT RESISTANCE CODE 4

A sub-shrub with cylindrical, succulent, evergreen leaves. The leaves and young stems are grey-green and covered in a delicate bloom that gives them a glaucous look. The plant spreads over the ground, its prostrate stems rooting wherever they come into contact with the soil. Flowering is repeated from April to October, interrupted by a summer rest period only when conditions are extremely dry. The flowers, with ray-like petals of a fine coppery colour,

open in the sun and close in the evening. *Malephora crocea* tolerates alkaline conditions well and withstands salt spray; it likes light, well-drained soils.

In California *Malephora crocea* has long been planted as a fire-retardant groundcover along the roadsides, as its water-filled stems slow the advance of the flames. Mixed with other South African succulent plants, it forms an amazing multicoloured landscape along the famous Highway 1, which follows the Pacific coast from San Francisco to Los Angeles, and has become invasive on the rocky shore. In gardens around the Mediterranean it is a good groundcover for rock gardens. It can also be planted on green roofs where it survives in a very shallow substrate with an occasional watering. In coastal gardens it is advisable to take care that this plant does not escape into the wild.

Propagation is by softwood cuttings in spring or autumn.

• *Malephora crocea* var. *purpureocrocea* has purple-red buds that open into orange flowers.

• *Malephora lutea*, with yellow flowers, is remarkable for its excellent ability to withstand heat. It is used as a groundcover in xeriscaping – the arid-zone gardening often practised in Tucson and Phoenix, Arizona. In our experience it is one of the rare plants (along with *Drosanthemum hispidum*) that is able to survive without watering on green roofs in the climatic conditions of the South of France. In periods of severe hydric deficit *Malephora lutea* may lose a large part of its leaves, making it less ornamental until the autumn rains arrive once more. **ORIGIN** SOUTH AFRICA **HARDINESS** −8 TO −10 °C **DROUGHT RESISTANCE CODE** 6

Marrubium incanum
(Lamiaceae) Horehound

ORIGIN SOUTHERN EUROPE
HEIGHT 40 TO 60 CM
SPREAD 60 CM
POSITION SUN
HARDINESS −12 TO −15 °C
DROUGHT RESISTANCE CODE 4

A shrub with silky grey, evergreen leaves, the undersides of which are covered in long tangled white hairs (*incanum* comes from

Lygeum spartum is exceptionally drought-resistant. Its decorative inflorescences, which resemble a dishevelled bird's head, open in early summer.

The water stored in the succulent leaves of *Malephora crocea* var. *purpureocrocea* enables the plant to withstand long periods of drought.

The undersides of the leaves of *Marrubium incanum* are covered in long tangled hairs to limit water loss.

the Latin *canus*, 'white-haired'). The plant spreads into a broad rounded mass, and it is worth cutting it back annually in winter in order to prevent the foliage from becoming sparse at the base. The small white flowers appear in June–July grouped in dense spires, with each successive 'storey' tightly packed around the stem in the manner characteristic of many plants of the Lamiaceae family. *Marrubium incanum* tolerates alkaline conditions well and likes light, well-drained soils. In our garden we combine it in plantings with *Ballota acetabulosa*, *Salvia leucophylla* 'Figueroa' and *Buddleja marrubiifolia* to create a soft silvery screen that sets off brightly-coloured perennials.

Propagation is by seed in autumn.

Medicago arborea
(Fabaceae) Medick, Moon Trefoil

ORIGIN MEDITERRANEAN BASIN
HEIGHT 1 TO 2 M
SPREAD 1 M
POSITION SUN
HARDINESS −10 TO −12 °C
DROUGHT RESISTANCE CODE 4

A branching, bushy shrub with white, silky stems. The leaves are evergreen in winter, but almost entirely deciduous in summer to limit evapotranspiration during the dry period. The flowering period is early, extending from January to April, and sometimes even beginning in December or November if the winter is mild. The flowers are a luminous and warm orangey-yellow, and are grouped in tightly packed heads in the leaf axils. They are followed by the curious seedpods of the lucernes – flat and curled into a spiral. *Medicago arborea* tolerates alkaline conditions well and withstands salt spray. It is happy in stony, well-drained soil. In the wild it does well on coastal rocks and cliffs, often in very poor soil. Like many leguminous plants, *Medicago arborea* has the ability to fix

nitrogen from the atmosphere and make it available in the soil: it is a pioneer species on degraded soils, facilitating the subsequent arrival of a richer flora. When you plant it, take a good look at the roots: you will often see dense clusters of small balls the size of pinheads arranged along the roots – these are the nitrogen-fixing nodules.

Propagation is by seed in autumn after hot water treatment: pour boiling water over the seeds then leave them to swell overnight. Softwood cuttings may also be taken in autumn, removing the flower buds with your fingernails.

Melianthus major
(Melianthaceae) Honey Bush

ORIGIN SOUTH AFRICA
HEIGHT AND SPREAD 2 TO 3 M
POSITION SUN
HARDINESS THE VEGETATIVE PARTS OF THE PLANT ARE ENTIRELY DESTROYED AT −4 TO −6 °C, BUT WHEN THE PLANT IS WELL ESTABLISHED IT WILL SPROUT AGAIN FROM THE ROOTSTOCK AFTER TEMPERATURES OF ABOUT −8 °C
DROUGHT RESISTANCE CODE 3

A sub-shrub with large, blue-green, evergreen leaves divided into large leaflets with toothed margins. The plant can form an imposing clump with a striking architectural silhouette. From May to July large, reddish-brown flowering spikes emerge from the foliage. The flowers attract bees (the name *Melianthus* comes from the Greek *meli*, 'honey', and *anthos*, 'flower'). If the foliage sometimes seems damp or sticky, don't worry, it's not a disease – it is

The cheerful flowers of *Medicago arborea* decorate the garden during the long winter months.

simply because the flowers are so full of nectar that it is overflowing and dripping gently on to the leaves. *Melianthus major* tolerates alkaline conditions well. It likes friable, fairly deep, well-drained soils. Once established, the plant withstands cold relatively well since it is able to put out new shoots from the rootstock when the vegetative parts have been completely destroyed by frost. However, when the plant is young its rootstock can easily freeze. To help it get through its first winter we protect it in our garden by covering it with an upturned bucket weighted down by a large stone, not very attractive to look at, but effective for gaining a few degrees in temperature on the soil surface.

Propagation is by seed in autumn or by cuttings from the young shoots emerging from the ground in spring.

Micromeria fruticosa
(Lamiaceae)

ORIGIN TURKEY, LEBANON, ISRAEL
HEIGHT 40 CM
SPREAD 30 TO 40 CM
POSITION SUN
HARDINESS −6 TO −8 °C (THE PLANT WITHSTANDS COLD BETTER IN VERY DRY SOIL)
DROUGHT RESISTANCE CODE 5

A shrub with small, grey-green, evergreen leaves that become almost white in summer. The plant seems impervious to drought: from July to October it is covered in a mass of small white flowers arranged on loose spikes. When crushed, the stems and leaves give off an extraordinary scent of mint with a hint of oregano: this is one of the most aromatic plants in our garden. In the eastern Mediterranean Basin it is known for its many medicinal properties, in particular as an antiseptic for skin infections or as a stimulant of appetite (it makes a delicious seasoning in summer salads). In the wild the plant gives off volatile compounds that inhibit the germination of competing species. Research is currently under way in Israel on the potential use of essential oil of *Micromeria fruticosa* as an anti-germinating herbicide for crops cultivated on a large scale. *Micromeria fruticosa* tolerates alkaline conditions well and likes light, well-drained soils. It self-seeds freely in stony areas, such as the margins of gravel paths, where it may form a natural edging. Indeed, it is because it self-seeds that we have been able to keep it in our garden – otherwise it would rapidly have disappeared as a result of frost.

Propagation is by seed in autumn or by softwood cuttings in autumn or spring.

Miscanthus sinensis 'Yaku-jima'
(Poaceae)

ORIGIN JAPAN
HEIGHT 1 M
SPREAD 1 M
POSITION SUN OR SEMI-SHADE
HARDINESS −15 °C AND BELOW
DROUGHT RESISTANCE CODE 3

Miscanthus species are among the grasses most widely used in the garden – but if they are to give generously of their foliage and flowers they really do need water. However, among the various cultivars that we have tested *Miscanthus sinensis* 'Yaku-jima' has a place apart. No doubt because of its small size (it is a dwarf variety originating on the Japanese island of Yaku-shima), the ratio between evapotranspiration from the leaves and absorption of water by the roots is a lot better: its resistance to drought is perfectly respectable. It forms a dense tuft of green leaves marked with a central white mid-rib, which become golden in winter. The rhizomatous rootstock spreads slowly, so that with time the plant becomes as wide as it is high, with an arching, fountain-like habit. In September it is covered in numerous feathery panicles, composed of graceful spikes borne on delicate pedicels (the name *Miscanthus* comes from the Greek *mischos*, 'stalk' or 'pedicel', and *anthos*, 'flower'). These panicles are barely taller than the foliage and are coppery-red when they first open. They remain on the plant for a long time and turn a fine silvery colour in winter. *Miscanthus sinensis* 'Yaku-jima' tolerates alkaline conditions well; it prefers friable, fairly deep soils.

Propagation is by division in winter.

Melianthus major in the Botanic Garden of Kirstenbosch, South Africa. Table Mountain, which dominates Cape Town, is accessible directly from the Botanic Garden, providing an interesting transition between cultivated and wild plants.

Myrsine africana
(Myrsinaceae) Cape Myrtle

ORIGIN WIDE DISTRIBUTION IN CHINA, THE HIMALAYAS
AND SOUTH AFRICA
HEIGHT 1 M AND MORE
SPREAD 1 M
POSITION SUN OR SEMI-SHADE
HARDINESS −10 TO −12°C
DROUGHT RESISTANCE CODE 4

A shrub with small, thick, leathery evergreen leaves that are dark green and glossy, calling to mind the leaves of *Myrtus communis* subsp. *tarentina* (*Myrsine* is the Greek name for myrtle). The foliage is naturally very dense and the plant, which is slow-growing, forms a thick mass. *Myrsine africana* tolerates alkaline conditions well and withstands salt spray; it is unfussy about soil type. Its fine glossy foliage and its adaptability make it a valuable shrub for difficult places, for example in semi-shade under old trees, where it can be grown together with other plants with decorative foliage such as *Nandina domestica* and *Choisya ternata*.

Propagation is by seed in autumn or by softwood cuttings in spring.

Myrtus communis
(Myrtaceae) Myrtle

ORIGIN MEDITERRANEAN BASIN
HEIGHT 2 TO 3 M
SPREAD 1 M OR MORE
POSITION SUN OR SHADE
HARDINESS −10 TO −12 °C (TENDER YOUNG AUTUMN
SHOOTS ARE REGULARLY SCORCHED BY THE COLD AT −6
TO −8 °C)
DROUGHT RESISTANCE CODE 4

An upright, bushy shrub with brilliant dark green evergreen leaves that are remarkably aromatic, with a scent both pungent and fruity. The myrtle is one of the plants that give the maquis of Corsica its characteristic and powerfully evocative scent. All I have to do is crush a few myrtle leaves and the memories come flooding back: wonderful botanical hikes in search of the wild orchids of Corsica, an omelette flavoured with *bruccio* and mint eaten at a mountain inn…

The myrtle has a dense and branching habit. It flowers in full summer, from July to September, which always seems surprising in a plant so well adapted to drought. The pretty white flowers with a broad boss of protruding stamens appear in the leaf axils of the new growth. In autumn they are followed by plentiful dark blue-black (or sometimes white) berries, used in cooking or to flavour liqueurs. In the past, the leaves and flowers were distilled to produce 'angel water', considered to possess the property of restoring to the elderly something of their youth. A symbol of peace to the Jews, of love to the Greeks, and

Sculpted by the salt spray, *Myrtus communis* and *Olea europaea* var. *sylvestris* form draperies of vegetation on the coast near Piana in Corsica.

associated with death in the Maghreb countries, the myrtle has long enjoyed an outstanding reputation as a medicinal plant; it was also used ornamentally in Roman and Andalusian gardens. It deserves a place in the modern mediterranean garden, too, since it is a robust plant and easy to grow. Its ability to tolerate alkaline conditions depends on the ecotype: the myrtles of Corsica, for example, will only grow in acid soil, while myrtles growing naturally on the La Clape mountain in the Aude region of France have a good tolerance of alkalinity. The myrtle prefers friable, well-drained soils. It can withstand direct salt spray.

Propagation is by fresh seed in late autumn or by softwood cuttings from new growth in autumn or spring.

We are studying many myrtles in our garden in order to compare their behaviour and their tolerance of alkalinity. Here are a few that can be used in gardens in the South of France, as they are perfectly tolerant of alkaline conditions.

• *Myrtus communis* 'Alhambra' is a vigorous form with white berries, very decorative in autumn. There is a magnificent specimen in the corner of the courtyard of the palace of Charles V in Granada. The leaves have a delicious and very fruity scent, with strong tones of raspberry.

• *Myrtus communis* 'Baetica' is a cultivar with broad leaves that appear tightly packed along the stems, with very little space between them. Originating in Baetica (the

name of the Roman province corresponding to Andalucia), it is a plant which the Moors took with them when they were expelled from Granada as a token of their hopes to recreate a small part of their lost paradise, and it is still to be seen growing in some palaces in Fès (according to Jamal Bellakhdar's excellent book *Le Maghreb à travers ses plantes*, see Further Reading). It is slow-growing – the one in our garden is 80 cm tall after ten years. Its scent is sharp and strong, reminiscent of bay leaves.

• *Myrtus communis* 'Flore Pleno' is a vigorous and floriferous cultivar with large leaves. The curious, many-petalled flowers are visible from a distance. The scent of the foliage is sweet and fruity. Its rapid growth makes this a good plant for a free-growing hedge.

• *Myrtus communis* 'La Clape' is a vigorous cultivar with large purple berries which we collected on the La Clape mountain near Narbonne, where it grows spontaneously in alkaline soil (in the dense shade of Aleppo pines). Its scent is sharp and strong, almost like a lentisk.

• *Myrtus communis* subsp. *tarentina* has small leaves closely packed along the stems. The naturally dense and compact foliage lends itself well to clipping: this subspecies is often used for topiary or low hedges, as in the famous Court of the Myrtles of the Alhambra in Granada. Its balanced scent, at the same time sharp and fruity, is most agreeable. This subspecies may bear black or white berries, depending on the form.

Nandina domestica
(Berberidaceae) Heavenly Bamboo

ORIGIN INDIA, CHINA, JAPAN
HEIGHT 1 TO 1.5 M, SOMETIMES MORE
SPREAD 1 M
POSITION SUN OR SHADE
HARDINESS −12 TO −15 °C
DROUGHT RESISTANCE CODE 4

A shrub with evergreen or semi-evergreen leaves divided into numerous green leaflets which take on attractive red or bronze hues in winter. The plant has an interesting habit, its stiff stems contrasting with the light foliage. In July–August it produces numerous small white flowers in conical panicles, followed by clusters of brilliant red berries, which are highly decorative and last through autumn and winter. It is a handsome plant throughout the year: in spring for the red colour of its new shoots, in summer for its abundant white flowers, and from autumn onwards for its bright red berries among the foliage that takes on its colours with the cold weather, making the plant a cheerful sight in the winter light. *Nandina domestica* tolerates alkaline conditions well. It prefers friable, deep, well-drained soils.

Propagation is by fresh seed at the end of winter.

Nepeta x faassenii 'Six Hills Giant'
(Lamiaceae) Cat Mint

HEIGHT IN FLOWER 60 CM
SPREAD 60 CM
POSITION SUN
HARDINESS −15 °C AND BELOW
DROUGHT RESISTANCE CODE 3.5

A hybrid of *Nepeta nepetella* and *Nepeta racemosa*, *Nepeta* × *faassenii* 'Six Hills Giant' is a perennial with deciduous or semi-deciduous grey leaves. These are highly aromatic and when crushed give off a curious scent that resembles a mixture of buckwheat pancake, mint and the grease of an animal's coat! In spring the plant forms a handsome velvety cushion and in May–June is covered in a profusion of long, supple spikes of tender blue-mauve flowers. If it is clipped after flowering, it will again form a cushion of dense foliage during the summer and will flower abundantly afresh in autumn. *Nepeta* × *faassenii* 'Six Hills Giant' tolerates alkaline conditions well. It requires a light, well-drained soil: although it withstands cold, the plant may die in winter if the soil is too heavy since the stock rots easily in cold, wet conditions. Apart from this, it is a robust, easily grown perennial. The softness of its foliage and the beauty and generosity of its flowers make it an unbeatable plant for the dry garden.

Propagation is by cuttings in spring.

• *Nepeta* × *faassenii* '**Dropmore**' has flowers of a fine, pronounced violet-blue.

• *Nepeta cataria* has green leaves and branching spikes of pinkish-white flowers in June–July. The leaves, stems and flowers are all aromatic: when crushed, they give off a strong smell reminiscent of mint and lemon verbena. Cats love it, breathing in the scent and lying or rolling on or around the plant, hence its common name catnip. It has long been believed to have the property of repelling mice, but doubtless this is simply because it attracts cats. **ORIGIN** EUROPE, ASIA **HARDINESS** −15°C AND BELOW **DROUGHT RESISTANCE CODE** 2.5

• *Nepeta racemosa*, often called *Nepeta mussinii* by nurserymen, has small grey aromatic leaves. The compact spikes of light blue flowers open in May. *Nepeta racemosa* self-seeds freely in the garden. **ORIGIN** CAUCASUS, TURKEY, IRAN **HARDINESS** −15 °C AND BELOW **DROUGHT RESISTANCE CODE** 4

• *Nepeta racemosa* '**Snow Flake**' has pure white flowers.

• *Nepeta tuberosa* has pretty grey-green leaves, thick and silky. The plant spreads by means of tuberous rhizomes, which give it a good resistance to drought. The flowers and bracts are covered in silky hairs, so that the plant has a striking appearance silhouetted against the light when the sun is low in the evening or early morning. **ORIGIN** SOUTHERN PORTUGAL, SPAIN **HARDINESS** −12 TO −15 °C **DROUGHT RESISTANCE CODE** 5

Nerium
(Apocynaceae) Oleander

The name *Nerium* comes from the ancient Greek name for the oleander, *nērion*. This is said to derive from Nereus, a sea divinity in Greek mythology; the Nereids, his fifty daughters, represent the waves of the sea. F. Pagen states that the ancient Greeks had sacred groves of oleander in honour of the Nereids, who were considered as infallible guides (see Further Reading). According to another theory, *Nerium* comes from the Greek *nēros*, originally meaning 'fresh', and later 'moist', referring to the plant's natural habitat: the oleander grows wild in the watercourses, usually dry in summer, that furrow the land around the Mediterranean.

Although it is a plant that grows by rivers and streams, the oleander has a surprising ability to withstand drought.

In May–June *Nepeta* x *faassenii* 'Six Hills Giant' is covered in long, supple spikes of blue-mauve flowers. On the right the yellow inflorescences of *Phlomis grandiflora* stand erect, while at the back the downy mass of *Ballota pseudodictamnus* softens the scene.

The silky spikes of *Nepeta tuberosa* seem to shine when seen against the light.

In Crete it is frequently seen growing on the sides of gorges, along with other phrygana plants, often far from the watercourse: its particularly long roots are able to draw water from great depth. Its thick and leathery leaves concentrate their stomata on the undersides, at the bottom of cavities fringed with hairs. These 'stomatic crypts' enable the plant to limit water loss even in extremely hot weather. In the Negev Desert in Israel, as well as in the Hamada south of the Anti-Atlas mountains in Morocco, the oleander is one of the rare plants that manages to survive the burning desert heat, growing with *Retama* and *Acacia* along ravines in areas where it rarely rains.

In periods of major water stress, the oleander has the ability to regulate its total leaf surface: to reduce evapotranspiration, it loses part of its foliage, starting with the oldest leaves and moving progressively up the stems. The plant then enters a state of partial dormancy, waiting for better times. In the wild, the flowering period is usually different from the one we are familiar with in our gardens. In dry conditions, the wild oleander flowers from April to June, before

the great heat sets in. It is only if it has access to water that it flowers generously and continuously throughout the summer.

The oleander tolerates alkaline conditions well and is unfussy about soil type. However, it does not like having its foliage regularly wetted. For example, when it is planted in the middle of a lawn that is watered by sprinklers, it is prone to diseases such as bacteriosis or *Aescochyta* that spread when the foliage is damp. In the wild the oleander is a tough plant, relatively unsusceptible to diseases and pests. In gardens it is often excessive watering or fertilizing that makes it prone to aphids, red spider mites and scale insect. Aphid infestation never lasts long, but red spider mites and scale insects can seriously weaken the plant. In cases of severe infestation, the simplest remedy is to encourage new growth by cutting the plant back severely (to 10 or 20 centimetres from the ground), for the oleander has an excellent ability to sprout from the base, producing new growth that is perfectly healthy. It is better not to prune the oleander annually: pruning may markedly reduce the following year's

The oleander has a remarkable ability to adapt to the harshest conditions. In southern Morocco, in the heat of the Hamada Desert, oleanders and *Acacia* survive in ravines that are dry for most of the year.

Oleanders next to the Libyan Sea. The name *Nerium* is said to derive from Nereus, a sea divinity in Greek mythology. Sometimes growing right on the shore, the oleander can withstand salt spray and even salt water infiltration of the soil.

flowering, since flowers are produced only on stems that have reached a certain length.

Beware, all parts of the plant are poisonous if ingested. In India several cases of suicide by oleander poisoning have been reported: seven leaves are said to be enough to kill a man. Luckily, the milky sap has an unpleasant, horribly bitter taste, making one want to rinse out one's mouth immediately. Most accidents happen when a leaf of oleander is confused with a bay leaf in the kitchen, or when its long stems are used as skewers for kebabs.

The history of the oleander as an ornamental plant goes back a long way. *Trompe-l'oeil* oleanders were painted on the walls of peristyles in Pompeii to make the small walled gardens seem larger. In China, the cultivation of oleanders was for a long time a favourite pastime of men of letters, who found a subtle evocation of grace and beauty in their flowers. The oleander was one of the most widely used shrubs in Arab gardens of the 12th century, together with roses, myrtle and pomegranates. In the time of Louis XIV, the orangery at Versailles housed more than a thousand oleanders grown in containers.

The numerous cultivars currently available from nurseries are usually hybrids of *Nerium oleander* subsp. *oleander* (unscented or barely scented), which grows wild around the Mediterranean, and *Nerium oleander* subsp. *indicum* (strongly scented), which grows wild from Iran to China. Their colours range from white to pink, salmon pink, yellow and red, with single, double or triple flowers, and they may be scented or unscented. Of the more

The cultivation of the oleander goes back to antiquity. The ancient Greeks had sacred groves of oleanders in honour of the Nereids, who were considered to be infallible guides.

than 150 cultivars that we grow, here are a few of those that I would choose if I had to limit myself to ten or so.

Nerium 'Louis Pouget'

HEIGHT 3 M OR MORE
SPREAD 2 M OR MORE
POSITION SUN
HARDINESS (OF THE CULTIVAR 'LOUIS POUGET') FIRST DAMAGE TO THE FOLIAGE AT ABOUT −8 °C, BUT THE PLANT CAN SPROUT AGAIN FROM THE BASE AFTER MUCH LOWER TEMPERATURES
DROUGHT RESISTANCE CODE 4

A shrub with long, dark green, evergreen, leaves. The plant sprouts vigorously from the base and forms a strong shrub. The flowers, a luminous pale pink with a double row of petals, are grouped in heavy and slightly drooping clusters. They are very scented in hot weather, with a honey and almond fragrance. In our unwatered garden flowering starts at the beginning of May and the flowers are produced in abundant succession until mid-July, after which they continue to appear sporadically and less profusely until the end of August or the beginning of September. 'Louis Pouget' is a cultivar selected in 1898 by the Sahut nursery at Montpellier, which had a remarkable collection of oleanders. We have planted a specimen near our terrace so that we can enjoy its delicious scent on long summer evenings.

Propagation is by stem section cuttings of the current year's growth in autumn. It is also easy to propagate from a branch placed in a bottle of water.

• *Nerium* 'Alsace' has elegant, single, white or barely pink flowers preceded by delicate pink buds. 'Alsace' is an old French cultivar that has probably had many different names over the course of the centuries. Outstanding specimens, more than a hundred years old, can be seen growing in imposing containers in the Jardin du Luxembourg in Paris. The orangery of this garden is equipped with a strong pulley which is used to lift the oleanders out of their containers every year. Generations of

Not all the numerous oleander cultivars have the same ability to withstand cold, and so it is important to choose them carefully, according to the climatic zone where they will be planted. The most resistant to cold is a pretty single-flowered cultivar named 'Villa Romaine'.

gardeners have sawed away part of the rootball and replaced the old roots with new potting compost, thus helping these oleanders to live for an extraordinarily long time. **HARDINESS** FIRST DAMAGE TO THE FOLIAGE AT ABOUT –6 °C

• *Nerium* 'Album Maximum' is the most vigorous oleander in our collection. In favourable conditions it can reach a height of 5 or 6 metres in ten years, and the spectacular leaves can measure more than 30 centimetres in length. The single flowers are a very gentle white, with ivory highlights. 'Album Maximum' is an old cultivar, described in Italy in 1880; it has become rare in gardens and seems to have fallen into oblivion, but deserves to be reinstated. **HARDINESS** FIRST DAMAGE TO THE FOLIAGE AT ABOUT –8 °C

• *Nerium* 'Angiolo Pucci' has single flowers of an amazing colour: the creamy yellow petals, just tinged with pink, surround a beautiful luminous orange throat. 'Angiolo Pucci' is a compact cultivar, reaching just 1 to 1.5 metres in height in ten years. For a low-growing bed of shrubs, it can be planted together with other cultivars that have a compact habit, such as 'Papa Gambetta', with flamboyant orange-red flowers, or 'Caro', with flowers of a light, slightly peachy pink. **HARDINESS** FIRST DAMAGE TO THE FOLIAGE AT ABOUT –6 °C

• *Nerium* 'Commandant Barthélemy' has double, scented flowers of an intense fuchsia-pink veering to red, preceded by large, globular, dark red buds. It is a robust, moderately floriferous cultivar which adapts easily to a variety of conditions: it is able to flower well in semi-shade, for example. 'Commandant Barthélemy' is an old cultivar, selected in the 19th century by the Sahut nurseries at Montpellier. **HARDINESS** FIRST DAMAGE TO THE FOLIAGE AT ABOUT –8 °C

• *Nerium* 'Grandiflorum' is one of the rare single-flowered cultivars that is scented. The large, raspberry-pink petals surround a whitish, cottony centre. **HARDINESS** FIRST DAMAGE TO THE FOLIAGE AT ABOUT –8 °C

• *Nerium* 'Mrs Roeding' has short and narrow leaves that are almost linear. The pretty, scented, triple flowers are a rich salmon-pink mixed with yellow, with a touch of cream. The plant has an unusual growth habit: instead of having upright branches like most oleanders, 'Mrs Roeding' has pliable branches, with the strong side branches spreading over the ground. Wider than it is tall (1 metre in height and 2 metres

in spread after about ten years), the plant can be used as groundcover for large slopes. 'Mrs Roeding' is widely grown in the United States: for kilometre after kilometre the freeways in California are bordered by this plant. It was selected in 1905 by Francher Creek Nurseries, an American nursery, from among seedlings grown from seed from Japan. **HARDINESS** FIRST DAMAGE TO THE FOLIAGE AT ABOUT –6 °C

• *Nerium* 'Tito Poggi' is a very floriferous cultivar with single flowers. The petals are a gentle and luminous salmon-pink, and the throat is yellow with bright pink stripes. 'Tito Poggi' is one of a series of interesting cultivars selected during the 1950s by the Gambetta nurseries in Italy, which also includes 'Marie Gambetta', a beautiful intense yellow oleander sought after by plantsmen. **HARDINESS** FIRST DAMAGE TO FOLIAGE AT ABOUT –6 °C

• *Nerium* 'Villa Romaine' has single flowers whose pale pink, propeller-shaped petals surround a bright pink throat. 'Villa Romaine' is the first cultivar we selected for our investigation into the cold-hardiness of oleanders. It has survived prolonged low temperatures of about –12 to –15 °C in North Germany, grown by one of our collaborators in our research, without showing visible damage to the foliage. Among the other cultivars selected as being very hardy we can mention 'Cavalaire', with pretty, scented, bright pink, triple flowers, and 'Atlas', with single pink flowers (collected high in the Atlas mountains).

Oenothera macrocarpa
(Onagraceae) Ozark Sundrops, Evening Primrose

ORIGIN CENTRAL AND SOUTHERN UNITED STATES
HEIGHT 20 CM
SPREAD 40 TO 50 CM
POSITION SUN
HARDINESS –15 °C AND BELOW
DROUGHT RESISTANCE CODE 5

A perennial with deciduous, light green leaves with clearly visible white veins, which contrast well with the red stems. In June–July the large, cup-shaped, bright lemon-yellow flowers open in succession, taking on a fine orange-red colour before withering half-way through the day. The new flowers open in the evening and give off a sweetish scent to attract the nocturnal sphinx moth that pollinates them. At the end of summer the plant produces large seedpods, curiously winged (*macrocarpa* comes from the Greek, *makros*, 'long', and *karpos*, 'fruit'). *Oenothera macrocarpa* tolerates alkaline conditions well. It prefers light, well-drained soils. It is an easily grown perennial which we like to mix into borders of *Lavandula angustifolia*, *Perovskia* 'Blue Spire' and *Nepeta racemosa*, to set off their blue and mauve colours with a touch of yellow.

Propagation is by seed in autumn.

• *Oenothera drummondii* has grey-green, velvety leaves that are evergreen. Its bright yellow flowers appear in succession throughout the summer, even when the weather is very dry. The plant has a relatively short lifespan, but self-seeds

Nerium 'Album Maximum' is a giant among oleanders: in favourable conditions it may attain a height of 5 or 6 metres in ten years.

The bright yellow flowers of *Oenothera macrocarpa* open in the evening, giving off a sweet scent to attract nocturnal pollinators.

freely in poor soil with perfect drainage. **ORIGIN** TEXAS, NEW MEXICO **HARDINESS** −10 TO −12 °C **DROUGHT RESISTANCE CODE** 6

Olea europaea 'Cipressino'
(Oleaceae) Pyramidal Olive

HEIGHT 4 TO 5 M OR MORE
SPREAD 2 TO 3 M OR MORE
POSITION SUN
HARDINESS −10 TO −12 °C
DROUGHT RESISTANCE CODE 5

For time out of mind the olive tree has been an integral part of the Mediterranean landscape, although its exact origins remain uncertain. *Olea europaea* 'Cipressino' is a cultivar with a pyramidal habit and very dense foliage, its upright branches being very fast-growing. Its long, evergreen leaves are grey-green on the upper surface but reveal their silvery undersides as soon as the mistral or tramontane begins to blow. The pyramidal olive tolerates alkaline conditions well and is unfussy about soil type. Although it does produce black olives, it is mainly used as a vigorous shrub for windbreaks, mixed in tall, free-growing hedges with holm oak, arbutus, bay tree, the Montpellier maple or the Judas tree. When these species mature and become bare at the base, a shorter hedge can be planted in front of them, consisting of shrubs which tolerate both shade and root competition, for example lentisk, phillyrea, myrtle or laurustinus.

Propagation is by softwood cuttings in spring.

• *Olea europaea* var. *sylvestris*, or oleaster, is the wild olive of the garrigue. It is recognizable from its small leathery leaves, dark green above and silvery on the undersides, and its short, stiff branches which form a tangled mass. It is not used much in gardens, yet has numerous qualities, including its remarkable tolerance of clipping: in Corsica it can be seen growing right beside the sea, sculpted by the salt spray into amazing sheets of vegetation. In Crete it is the goats that transform it into

futuristic-looking topiary. **PRESUMED ORIGIN** MEDITERRANEAN BASIN **HARDINESS** −12 TO −15 °C **DROUGHT RESISTANCE CODE** 6

• *Olea europaea* subsp. *africana* has handsome dark green foliage. We like to use it to create a contrast with grey-leaved shrubs such as *Teucrium fruticans* or *Phlomis grandiflora*. **ORIGIN** SOUTH AFRICA **HARDINESS** −8 TO −10°C **DROUGHT RESISTANCE CODE** 5

There are also of course numerous varieties of olive for fruit production which can be planted in the dry garden. They are often given drip irrigation aimed at increasing their yield, but they are perfectly adapted to drought – the magnificent hilly landscape between Granada and Córdoba bears witness to this, as does the ancient 'sea of olives' that spreads beneath the archaeological site of Delphi. A word of advice: plant your olives young – you'll be surprised how fast they grow. Olives are capable of forming fine, productive trees in a dozen years. So rather than buying a centuries-old olive tree, fresh off the lorry from Spain, which is of uncertain hardiness and irremediably betrays a hastily planned garden, ask a specialist nurseryman about local varieties that are well adapted to the climate of your area. You will, for example, receive excellent advice at the nursery of Michel and Béné Bachès, where apart from old local varieties of olive you will also find the most extensive collection of citruses imaginable (see appendix Useful Addresses).

Origanum syriacum
(Lamiaceae) Oregano

ORIGIN SYRIA, LEBANON, ISRAEL
HEIGHT 60 TO 80 CM
SPREAD 50 CM
POSITION SUN OR SEMI-SHADE
HARDINESS −12 TO −15 °C
DROUGHT RESISTANCE CODE 5

A sub-shrub with velvety, grey-green, evergreen leaves that are very aromatic. The strong stems form an upright, slightly stiff, bush. A multitude of small white flowers, arranged in branching panicles on the tips of the stems, appear in June–July. *Origanum syriacum* tolerates alkaline conditions well and likes poor, light, well-drained soils. It is one of the ingredients of a spice mixture widely used in the Middle East, *za'atar*, which consists of the flowers

As far as the eye can see, olive trees harmonize with the rolling hills between Granada and Córdoba in Andalucia.

Perfectly adapted to drought, the olive tree has become a symbol of the Mediterranean landscape.

and leaves of this oregano roasted with sesame and salt, to which are sometimes added savory (*Satureja thymbra*), thyme (*Thymus capitatus*) and the ground berries of *Rhus coraria*. Mixed with olive oil and served on hot pitta bread, *za'atar* forms a delicious breakfast in Lebanon. In our garden we harvest the flowers, which have a strong spicy taste, to decorate and flavour summer salads.

Propagation is by seed in autumn or by softwood cuttings in spring.

• *Origanum dictamnus* (Dittany) has been used since antiquity for its medicinal properties as an antiseptic and bacteriocide. It is a small, very decorative plant for rock gardens, but is only happy in soil that is very well drained. In summer its silvery leaves, covered in a thick coat of woolly hairs, serve as a backdrop for its curious pendent inflorescences, in which small pink flowers emerge from magnificent purple bracts. **ORIGIN** THE MOUNTAINS OF CRETE **HARDINESS** −10 TO −12 °C **DROUGHT RESISTANCE CODE** 4

• *Origanum dubium* is a rare jewel, little known in gardens. Its grey, silky leaves have an extraordinarily penetrating scent, warm and spicy, and at the same time subtly powdery, like a very soft perfume. The spikes of minute white flowers appear in June–July. **ORIGIN** CYPRUS, TURKEY **HARDINESS** −8 TO −10 °C **DROUGHT RESISTANCE CODE** 5

• *Origanum laevigatum* has a rhizomatous stock which spreads to make a groundcover. Its blue-green leaves contrast well with its reddish stems. The numerous, small, mauvey-pink flowers open in airy panicles and continue in generous succession throughout the whole summer. In our garden we grow it in association with *Teucrium divaricatum* and *Lavandula* × *chaytorae* 'Richard Gray' to create a small summer scene of mauve and violet hues. **ORIGIN** CYPRUS, TURKEY **HARDINESS** −12 TO −15 °C **DROUGHT RESISTANCE CODE** 4

• *Origanum majorana* (Marjoram) is famed for its delicately aromatic foliage, whose scent is noticeably milder than that of the other oreganos. The spikes of white flowers open in June–July. **ORIGIN** SOUTHERN EUROPE, TURKEY **HARDINESS** −10 TO −12 °C **DROUGHT RESISTANCE CODE** 4

• *Origanum microphyllum* forms a cushion of tiny grey leaves. In June–July the loose inflorescences are covered in small, violet-coloured flowers with silver bracts, forming a light mist over the plant. In Crete, on the mountain path that leads from the Omalos plateau to the Kallergi refuge, *Origanum microphyllum* clings to the rocks, along with *Helichrysum microphyllum* and *Teucrium microphyllum* – a good illustration of a common strategy for resisting drought, whereby plants reduce the size of their leaves in order to limit evapotranspiration (*microphyllum* comes from the Greek *mikros*, 'small', and *phyllon*, 'leaf'). **ORIGIN** THE MOUNTAINS OF CRETE **HARDINESS** −12 TO −15 °C **DROUGHT RESISTANCE CODE** 5

• *Origanum onites* has pretty pure white flowers arranged in dense flat clusters. It is a species whose luminous flowering brightens

Beneath the softness of its silver hairs, *Origanum dictamnus* hides an essential oil with a strong and piquant taste that has been used since antiquity as an antiseptic and bacteriocide.

the slopes of dry mountains in spring in the whole of southern Greece and Crete (the name *Origanum* comes from the Greek *oros*, 'mountain', and *ganos*, 'brightness', or 'gladness'). The highly aromatic foliage has a scent that is strong, but not spicy. It is the finely chopped leaves of *Origanum onites* that flavour the large chunks of feta in the delicious salads served in all the mountain villages of Greece. **ORIGIN** BALKANS, GREECE **HARDINESS** −12 TO −15 °C **DROUGHT RESISTANCE CODE** 5

• *Origanum vulgare* subsp. *hirtum* is sometimes called *Origanum heracleoticum*. Its foliage is markedly more aromatic than that of the common oregano, *Origanum vulgare*. Thanks to its rhizomatous stock the plant makes a good groundcover. The tiny white flowers appear in June–July. **ORIGIN** GREECE, TURKEY **HARDINESS** −15 °C AND BELOW **DROUGHT RESISTANCE CODE** 3

Parthenocissus tricuspidata 'Robusta'
(Vitaceae) Boston Ivy

ORIGIN CHINA, JAPAN
HEIGHT AND SPREAD 15 M OR MORE
POSITION SUN OR SHADE
HARDINESS −15 °C AND BELOW
DROUGHT RESISTANCE CODE 4

A climber with broad, deciduous, brilliant green leaves that have three, pointed lobes (*tricuspidata* comes from the Latin, *tri*, 'three' and *cuspis*, 'point'). The stems are furnished with fine tendrils which end in adhesive discs, enabling the plant to cling on to all kinds of support, even the smoothest. The flowers, which are barely visible, are followed by clusters of small dark berries that are the delight of birds in

The flowering clumps of *Origanum onites* brighten the mountains of Greece.

late summer. In autumn the foliage takes on magnificent flamboyant colours – red, orange or purplish. *Parthenocissus tricuspidata* 'Robusta' tolerates alkaline conditions well; it prefers friable and fairly deep soils. It is an extremely vigorous climber which can cover entire buildings and has an interesting function in regulating their temperature. In summer the dense foliage gives protection from the sun, while in winter the bare stems leave the walls open to its rays to act as a storage heater. The plant should occasionally be pruned when it reaches the top of the building, since it has a tendency to spread on to the roof and infiltrate between the roof tiles.

Propagation is by hardwood cuttings in winter.

• *Parthenocissus quinquefolia*, Virginia Creeper, has leaves divided into five leaflets. It needs a rough surface to cling to because its tendrils are not adhesive. The long, fast-growing stems enable it to cover large pergolas. **ORIGIN** EASTERN UNITED STATES **HARDINESS** −15 °C AND BELOW **DROUGHT RESISTANCE CODE** 4

Pelargonium × fragrans
(Geraniaceae)

ORIGIN SOUTH AFRICA
HEIGHT 40 TO 60 CM
SPREAD 40 TO 60 CM

BELOW *Parthenocissus tricuspidata* has an interesting function as a thermal regulator for buildings on which it grows: the foliage provides cooling shade in summer, while in winter the bare stems leave the façade open to the sun to act as a storage heater.

BOTTOM The rapidly growing stems of *Parthenocissus quinquefolia* enable it to cover large pergolas.

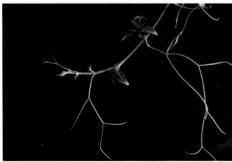

POSITION SUN
HARDINESS −4 TO −6 °C
DROUGHT RESISTANCE CODE 4

Pelargonium × fragrans is a natural hybrid of *Pelargonium exstipulatum* and *Pelargonium odoratissimum* which grows in the high plateaus of the Karoo in South Africa. It is a compact shrub with small, evergreen, grey leaves that have a velvety look. When crushed, the foliage gives off a rich spicy scent, like a mixture of nutmeg and pine. In South Africa the leaves are used in cooking to add a special seasoning to cakes or stewed apples, and sometimes to flavour coffee. The delicate umbels of white flowers appear from May to October, and almost throughout the year in mild climates. *Pelargonium × fragrans* tolerates alkaline conditions well and prefers light, well-drained soils. Its ability to withstand cold is markedly better if the soil remains really dry in winter. It grows well in containers: we've had a good specimen decorating our terrace for years, slightly sheltered against a wall.

Propagation is by softwood cuttings in autumn or spring.

Perovskia abrotanoides
(Lamiaceae) Russian Sage

ORIGIN DRY MOUNTAINS OF IRAN AND TURKMENISTAN
HEIGHT IN FLOWER 1 M
SPREAD 60 TO 80 CM
POSITION SUN
HARDINESS −15 °C AND BELOW
DROUGHT RESISTANCE CODE 4

A sub-shrub with highly aromatic, deciduous, grey-green leaves. The leaves are finely cut (they resemble the fine foliage of

Artemisia abrotanum, hence the name *abrotanoides*). An essential oil with medicinal properties is extracted from the leaves. In Iran the crushed roots of *Perovskia abrotanoides* were traditionally used in poultices to treat diseases such as the cutaneous form of leishmaniosis (a parasitic disease). The tall stems, covered in a fine white down, set off the attractive flowers. In June–July the branching stems open into a multitude of small bright blue flowers, forming a very decorative light mass. The flowers are surrounded by velvety purple calyces, which remain on the flowering spikes for a long time after the flowers have fallen, extending the ornamental appearance of the plant through the summer. *Perovskia abrotanoides* tolerates alkaline conditions well and withstands salt spray. It prefers light, well-drained soils. It can be cut right down at the end of summer to encourage vigorous and floriferous new growth.

Propagate by seed in autumn or by softwood cuttings in spring.

• *Perovskia atriplicifolia* 'Longin' has leaves that are entire and slightly toothed. The blue flowering spikes are markedly larger than those of *Perovskia abrotanoides*. **ORIGIN** DRY MOUNTAINS OF AFGHANISTAN **HARDINESS** −15 °C AND BELOW **DROUGHT RESISTANCE CODE** 4

• *Perovskia* 'Blue Spire', probably a hybrid of *Perovskia abrotanoides* and *Perovskia atriplicifolia*, has more vigorous vegetation than its parents. The leaves are very aromatic. When crushed, they at first give off a sharply animal smell, reminiscent of a

Perovskia 'Blue Spire' flowers from June to September, when most plants are dormant. The light colour of the flowers brings a touch of freshness to the summer garden.

It wasn't gardeners who invented the art of topiary. By grazing on *Phillyrea angustifolia* near the Omalos plateau in Crete, goats patiently transform it into a futurist sculpture.

billy-goat (this is the 'head scent' of perfume makers, strong and volatile, but not lasting). If one continues to breathe in the scent, after a moment a new, decidedly minty scent is dominant (this is the 'heart scent'). Then, much later, when the head and heart scents have dissipated, a light but persistent scent is perceptible, sweet and sugary, reminiscent of lychees (this is the 'base scent'). In the dry garden it is worth pausing to analyse the scents of many aromatic plants, allowing them the time to express their exceptional scent palettes, which are one of the charms of the summer garden. *Perovskia* 'Blue Spire' flowers from June to September with an absolutely outstanding generosity. In our garden we like to create great splashes of summer colour by mixing *Perovskia* 'Blue Spire' with *Gaura lindheimeri*, *Epilobium canum* 'Western Hills', *Oenothera drummondii* and *Salvia darcyi*. **HARDINESS** −15 °C AND BELOW **DROUGHT RESISTANCE CODE** 4

Phillyrea angustifolia
(Oleaceae) Mock Privet

ORIGIN MEDITERRANEAN BASIN
HEIGHT 2 TO 3 M
SPREAD 2 M
POSITION SUN OR SHADE
HARDINESS −12 TO −15 °C
DROUGHT RESISTANCE CODE 5

A shrub with dark green, evergreen leaves and bronze-tinted young shoots in spring. The size and shape of the leaves may vary, but they are usually fairly narrow. Being both thick and leathery, they represent almost a model of sclerophyllous leaves, with their upper surface glossy to limit

evaporation during the summer period. The inconspicuous greenish-white, scented, flowers appear from March to May. They are followed by numerous black berries that ripen in autumn and provide a feast for birds. *Phillyrea angustifolia* tolerates alkaline conditions well and is unfussy about soil type: in the garrigue it thrives among stones, but it is equally happy in the most clayey part of our garden, where the soil is heavy and asphyxiating. It is a good shrub for free-growing hedges. Thanks to its ability to tolerate shade and root competition, it can also be used to create a shrubbery beneath pines or oaks, together with *Pistacia lentiscus*, *Rhamnus alaternus* and *Viburnum tinus*. It withstands salt spray very well. It has an excellent tolerance of regular pruning and can be used to create original topiary shapes.

Propagation is by fresh seed in autumn or by softwood cuttings in spring (rooting may take a long time).

• *Phillyrea latifolia* has fairly large oval leaves, often with toothed margins. Old specimens can form magnificent small trees of a very regular shape. In the Jardin des Plantes at Montpellier, a venerable *Phillyrea latifolia* is said to be the oldest in France, reputedly dating from the 16th or 17th century. For centuries it has served as a post-box for lovers, who hide their love-letters in the crevices in its extraordinary knotted trunk, thus providing amusing reading for the gardeners who come here from time to time to tidy up. **ORIGIN** MEDITERRANEAN BASIN **HARDINESS** −12 TO −15 °C **DROUGHT RESISTANCE CODE** 5

Phlomis (Lamiaceae)

Phlomis is not a fashionable genus, and although there is a remarkable diversity of *Phlomis* species, they have always been little-used in gardens. Most gardeners only know *Phlomis fruticosa* and don't even suspect that there are more than forty other species growing wild around the Mediterranean, with flowers that are white, pink, mauve, yellow or dark orangey-yellow. The flora of Turkey alone includes some twenty-four species, ranging from a small carpeting perennial to a shrub almost 3 metres tall. They are robust and adaptable plants that are easy to grow and, unlike a great many other mediterranean plants, they are long-lived. Thanks to their interesting strategies for resisting drought they are particularly well suited to the dry garden. We have gradually developed a great enthusiasm for this genus and have amassed a large collection of species and natural hybrids in our garden. Here is a small selection of those which seem easiest to grow.

Phlomis bourgaei

ORIGIN SOUTHWEST TURKEY (ON STONY HILLSIDES AND IN WOODLAND CONSISTING OF OAK OR PINE)
HEIGHT 1 M
SPREAD 80 CM
POSITION SUN OR SEMI-SHADE
HARDINESS −12 TO −15 °C
DROUGHT RESISTANCE CODE 5

An evergreen shrub with long, pointed leaves whose edges are curiously twisted. The foliage has a marked seasonal dimorphism. In winter and spring, the broad green leaves are spread horizontally to catch the rays of the sun, ensuring photosynthesis during the plant's growing season. After the yellow flowers have appeared in May, these large leaves fall as the heat sets in. The plant then produces new leaves, noticeably smaller and packed together along the stems to reduce the area of leaf surface exposed to the sun. These new leaves are covered in a thick coat of golden-brown hairs, effectively reducing evapotranspiration. *Phlomis bourgaei* tolerates alkaline conditions well and is unfussy about soil type. It is a remarkable shrub in the dry garden in summer: the drier the weather, the more beautiful it becomes.

Propagation is by softwood cuttings in autumn. Phlomis *species are easy to propagate by seed in autumn, but we prefer to take cuttings as they hybridize very easily, as much in the garden as in the wild.*

Phlomis chrysophylla

ORIGIN LEBANON, SYRIA, JORDAN
HEIGHT 80 CM
SPREAD 1 M
POSITION SUN
HARDINESS −10 TO −12 °C
DROUGHT RESISTANCE CODE 6

An evergreen shrub with oval or rounded leaves. In winter and spring the leaves are a pretty light green, while in summer they take on a surprising golden colour that is very decorative (*chrysophylla* comes from the Greek *chrysos*, 'gold', and *phyllon*, 'leaf'). The plant develops naturally into a fat, rounded cushion, with inflorescences barely taller than the foliage. This *Phlomis* does not need to be clipped in autumn, which is a great advantage – most species are unpleasant to prune because their leaves and stems release tiny hairs that are irritating to the skin and mucous membranes. The bicoloured flowers have a yellow hood and a white lower lip. *Phlomis chrysophylla* tolerates alkaline conditions well and is unfussy about soil type. We like to set off the unusual colour of its summer foliage by combining it with blue-flowered plants such

as *Perovskia* 'Blue Spire', *Lavandula* × *intermedia* 'Julien', *Caryopteris incana* or *Ceratostigma plumbaginoides*.

Propagation is by softwood cuttings in autumn.

Phlomis fruticosa
Jerusalem Sage

ORIGIN EASTERN MEDITERRANEAN BASIN
HEIGHT 1 TO 1.5 M
SPREAD 1.5 TO 2 M
POSITION SUN
HARDINESS −12 TO −15 °C
DROUGHT RESISTANCE CODE 5

A shrub with evergreen, grey-green leaves which have a whitish underside. The dense and branching vegetation forms a large rounded mass (*fruticosa* in Latin means 'bushy'). In May the extremely abundant flowering turns the plant into a ball of bright yellow flowers. As with most *Phlomis* species, the flowers are verticillate, i.e. they are grouped in whorls along the stems. *Phlomis fruticosa* tolerates alkaline conditions well and withstands salt spray. It is unfussy about soil type. It is a robust and long-lived shrub: some specimens in gardens are almost fifty years old. A regular pruning each autumn helps the plant to maintain a regular habit and remain bushy at the base. You can prune it in rainy weather to avoid being annoyed by the tiny hairs detaching themselves from the foliage.

Propagation is by softwood cuttings in autumn.

Phlomis grandiflora

ORIGIN TURKEY
HEIGHT OF FOLIAGE 1.5 TO 2 M
HEIGHT IN FLOWER 2.5 M OR MORE
SPREAD 1.5 TO 2 M
POSITION SUN OR SEMI-SHADE
HARDINESS −12 TO −15 °C
DROUGHT RESISTANCE CODE 5

An evergreen shrub with a pronounced seasonal dimorphism of its foliage. In winter and spring the grey-green leaves are surprisingly large – they can be more than

The fresh green of *Euphorbia acanthothamnos* sets off the generous flowering of *Phlomis fruticosa*.

15 centimetres long. In May the plump verticillate inflorescences, borne on long stems, stand well clear of the foliage. In summer the new leaves are very short and folded over to make a tight gutter. These summer leaves are silvery-grey with noticeably white, cottony undersides. *Phlomis grandiflora* tolerates alkaline conditions well and is unfussy about soil type. It is a common shrub in the mountains of southwest Turkey, where large populations can be found at an altitude of about 1,000 metres, growing at the foot of

To reduce water loss by evapotranspiration, the summer leaves of these three *Phlomis* species are covered in a thick coat of golden hairs. This is a strategy of drought resistance which accentuates the plants' ornamental quality: the drier the garden, the more beautiful the plant becomes! From left to right *Phlomis bourgaei*, *Phlomis chrysophylla*, *Phlomis lycia*.

the Cedars of Lebanon (*Cedrus libani* subsp. *stenocoma*) that form magnificent forests in the Taurus mountains. It is a large-growing *Phlomis* that can be used in medium-sized hedges, where its light foliage makes an interesting contrast with, for example, *Cistus* × *cyprius*, *Pistacia lentiscus* or *Myrtus communis* subsp. *tarentina*.

Propagation is by softwood cuttings in autumn.

Phlomis lanata

ORIGIN CRETE, LEBANON, SYRIA
HEIGHT 60 TO 80 CM
SPREAD 60 TO 80 CM
POSITION SUN
HARDINESS −10 TO −12 °C
DROUGHT RESISTANCE CODE 5

A shrub with small, evergreen, green leaves whose undersides are a cottony silver-grey. The plant develops into a compact cushion without the need for clipping. The yellow flowers appear in May on short stems, barely taller than the foliage. In summer the stems are covered in dense hairs and take on a striking golden-brown colour that contrasts well with the foliage. *Phlomis lanata* tolerates alkaline conditions well and is unfussy about soil type. We like to copy in our garden a natural association that we saw in southwest Crete, where *Phlomis lanata* was growing in the midst of *Ballota pseudodictamnus*, *Sarcopoterium spinosum* and *Thymus capitatus*, in an

The massive form of *Phlomis grandiflora* beneath *Cedrus libani* subsp. *stenocoma* near the Kuruovabeli Pass in the Taurus mountains.

In May *Phlomis grandiflora* is covered in long inflorescences of yellow flowers.

amazing landscape that consisted only of cushion-shaped plants, perfectly adapted to drought.

Propagation is by softwood cuttings in autumn.

Phlomis lychnitis

ORIGIN SOUTH OF FRANCE, SPAIN, PORTUGAL
HEIGHT OF FOLIAGE 15 CM
HEIGHT IN FLOWER 40 TO 50 CM
SPREAD 30 TO 40 CM
POSITION SUN
HARDINESS −12 TO −15 °C
DROUGHT RESISTANCE CODE 5

A sub-shrub with pretty evergreen leaves that are long and very narrow. They are grey-green above and covered in a fine silvery down on the undersides. The prostrate stems radiate from the stock and the plant forms a very decorative small groundcover for rock gardens or edging. In May the remarkably abundant yellow flowers are borne on short upright stems. *Phlomis lychnitis* tolerates alkaline conditions well and prefers poor, well-drained soils. Its rolled up leaves were traditionally used to make wicks for oil lamps (the name *Phlomis* derives from the Greek *phlox*, 'flame' – and, since botanists

like everything to be crystal clear, *lychnitis* comes from the Greek *lychnos*, 'lamp'). If you don't possess any oil lamps, you might be interested in another use of *Phlomis lychnitis*: in the popular medicine of southern Spain it is reputed to have soothing properties when applied directly to haemorrhoids.

Propagation is by seed in autumn: this species does not lend itself well to cuttings and does not hybridize with most other Phlomis *species. The young plants are prone to rotting, so they should be kept in a well-ventilated place and watered as little as possible.*

Phlomis purpurea

ORIGIN SPAIN, PORTUGAL
HEIGHT 1 TO 1.2 M
SPREAD 1 M OR MORE
POSITION SUN
HARDINESS −10 TO −12 °C
DROUGHT RESISTANCE CODE 5

A shrub with evergreen, grey leaves. The plant develops into a dense, rounded mass, spreading little by little by means of suckers from its roots. The flowers open in May–June and are a very soft mauvey-pink, which blends perfectly with the grey foliage. In times of intense drought the foliage may become deciduous in summer, making the plant less ornamental until the first autumn rains arrive. *Phlomis purpurea* tolerates alkaline conditions well and is unfussy about soil type, though we have found that

Phlomis lanata has an excellent ability to withstand salt spray. In the garden its foliage forms a compact cushion that is ornamental throughout the year.

The sweetness of spring flowering: this border along the edge of a path is composed of *Phlomis purpurea, Lavandula dentata* var. *candicans, Myrtus communis* subsp. *tarentina* and *Stipa barbata*.

its ability to withstand cold is much better if it is grown in poor, stony soil with very good drainage. The tender tips of new autumn shoots easily suffer from frost damage in a hard winter, in which case it is worth giving the plant a light clipping to tidy it up in early spring. *Phlomis purpurea* withstands salt spray well.

Propagation is by softwood cuttings in autumn.

• *Phlomis purpurea* 'Alba' is a form with pure white flowers: one of the most beautiful phlomises in our garden.

• *Phlomis purpurea* subsp. *almeriensis* has bicoloured flowers, with a violet hood above a white lower lip. In our collection, it stands out for its fine silvery foliage which becomes almost white in summer. To create points of interest in the summer, when few plants are flowering, we like to grow it in association with other plants whose foliage becomes attractive in very dry conditions, such as *Centaurea pulcherrima, Salvia leucophylla* or *Ballota acetabulosa*. **ORIGIN CABO DE GATA AND THE ALMERÍA REGION OF SPAIN**

(THIS IS THE DRIEST PART OF SPAIN) **HARDINESS** −8 TO −10 °C **DROUGHT RESISTANCE CODE** 6

Phlomis samia

ORIGIN GREECE, TURKEY, THE FORMER YUGOSLAVIA, GENERALLY BENEATH OAKS OR PINES
HEIGHT OF FOLIAGE 20 TO 30 CM
HEIGHT IN FLOWER 1 M
SPREAD 60 TO 80 CM
POSITION SUN OR SHADE
HARDINESS −12 TO −15 °C
DROUGHT RESISTANCE CODE 3.5

A perennial with large, semi-evergreen, green leaves that are a velvety grey on the undersides. The plant spreads slowly by means of its rhizomes and in time forms a broad groundcover. The leaves, arranged in regular rosettes, are shaped exactly like the ace of spades. In June–July, tall, sticky inflorescences emerge from the heart of the rosettes. Even more than the curious greenish-brown colour of the flowers, it is the striking form of the inflorescence which is eye-catching. All along the stem, each layer of flowers is positioned on an amazing crown of extremely decorative and delicate spiny bracts. We have seen *Phlomis samia*

The pure white flowers of *Phlomis purpurea* 'Alba' rise up behind *Cistus* × *purpureus* f. *holorhodeos*.

Sheltered beneath a downy hood, the stamens of *Phlomis purpureus* subsp. *almeriensis* wait patiently for bees.

The pale pink flowers of *Phlomis bovei* subsp. *maroccana* are grouped along the stems in regular whorls.

growing in woodland in the Taurus mountains together with *Acanthus spinosus,* another plant with inflorescences equipped with decorative spiny bracts. As far as wild boars are concerned the resemblance doesn't stop there: they turn over stones in order to find the fleshy rhizomes of both plants, leaving the ground under the trees churned up like a battlefield.

Propagation is by seed in autumn.

• *Phlomis bovei* **subsp.** *maroccana* is a vigorous perennial with a woody base. The exceptionally large flowers are pollinated by impressive black carpenter bees: the pretty pale pink lower lip of the flower spreads

Phlomis samia is late-flowering. The striking silhouette of its inflorescences stands out in early summer.

wide to give them a good landing place. It is surmounted by a large white hood which the bees push up, receiving as they do so a generous shower of pollen. **ORIGIN** MOROCCO (THE ATLAS MOUNTAINS NORTH OF DJEBEL M'GOUN) **HARDINESS** −10 TO −12 °C **DROUGHT RESISTANCE CODE** 4

• *Phlomis chimerae* has small leaves, grey on the upper surface and whitish or slightly golden on the undersides. In summer, to reduce the surface exposed to the sun, the leaves fold in the middle so that they resemble a narrow gutter. The plant makes a handsome round cushion, covered in bright yellow flowers in May. Chimera is a curious site in southwest Turkey where flames spring straight out of the black rocks as escaping methane gas ignites spontaneously when it comes into contact with the air. In antiquity, sailors set their course by these flames, which at night can be seen from the

sea. *Phlomis chimerae* grows all around Chimera, in a low garrigue in which *Euphorbia rigida* and *Cistus creticus* var. *tauricus* are also mixed. **ORIGIN** SOUTHWEST TURKEY **HARDINESS** −10 TO −12 °C **DROUGHT RESISTANCE CODE** 5

• *Phlomis cretica* is a compact shrub with thick and woolly leaves. In the mountains of Crete this species displays a great variability: it may have grey-green or silvery or golden leaves, depending on the particular clone. Velvety, dark orange buds open into yellow flowers. **ORIGIN** CRETE **HARDINESS** −12 TO −15 °C **DROUGHT RESISTANCE CODE** 5

• *Phlomis herba-venti* is a perennial with green leaves that fall after the plant has finished flowering. It then enters into a dormant state in order to get through the summer and avoid suffering from the

At Chimera in Turkey flames leap from the black rocks, the result of methane seepages that ignite spontaneously on contact with the air. All around the site of Chimera a handsome dwarf *Phlomis* grows in compact cushions – *Phlomis chimerae*, which acclimatizes easily in the garden.

Phlomis cretica in its natural habitat, on slopes above the Samaria Gorge in Crete. This *Phlomis* can be recognized by its woolly foliage and fine dark yellow flowers, preceded by orange buds.

Phlomis herba-venti colonizes roadside slopes in the South of France.

In spite of their good resistance to drought, *Phlomis* species are not yet properly appreciated in mediterranean gardens. Paradoxically, it is in England that they are most widely used. This long border in the Cambridge Botanical Garden is composed of *Phlomis russeliana*, *Stipa gigantea* and *Nepeta* × *faassenii* 'Six Hills Giant'.

As they emerge from the dark green foliage, the bright yellow flowers of *Phlomis viscosa* contrast with the purple-brown stems.

drought. On a very windy day the dry vegetation may be completely snapped off and blown around at the mercy of the wind (hence the name *herba-venti*), which ensures that the seeds are dispersed far and wide. This species, common on slopes beside roads in the South of France, can be found high in the Provençal Alps, where its balls of mauve-pink flowers are visible among magnificent fields of *Stipa pennata*. **ORIGIN** MEDITERRANEAN BASIN **HARDINESS** −12 TO −15 °C **DROUGHT RESISTANCE CODE** 4

• *Phlomis italica* has long leaves that are grey-green above and covered in a thick fleece of silver hairs on the undersides. Once the spring leaves have fallen, the new summer leaves grow tightly packed vertically around the tips of the stems. Now only the undersides of the leaves are visible, giving the plant a woolly and very decorative appearance. In April–May the pretty pink flowers melt into the soft foliage. **ORIGIN** BALEARIC ISLANDS **HARDINESS** −8 TO −10 °C **DROUGHT RESISTANCE CODE** 5

• *Phlomis leucophracta* has triangular leaves, green on the upper surface and covered with a golden felt on the undersides. The edges of the leaves, irregularly cut and wavy, have an amazing silver or gold margin (*leucophracta* comes from the Greek *leukos*, 'white', and *phraxis*, 'a barricade', referring to the leaf margins). The bicoloured flowers, with a yellow lower lip surmounted by an orange-brown hood, open in May–June. **ORIGIN** TURKEY **HARDINESS** −12 TO −15 °C **DROUGHT RESISTANCE CODE** 5

• *Phlomis lycia* is easily recognized by its acid yellow-green leaves. Its summer leaves are eye-catching: packed vertically up the orange stems, they are a remarkably intense yellow. The plant is transformed in summer into a golden ball, very ornamental during the dry period. It is one of the most handsome shrubs in our garden in summer. **ORIGIN** LYCIA (A COASTAL REGION IN SOUTHWEST

TURKEY) **HARDINESS** −10 TO −12 °C **DROUGHT RESISTANCE CODE** 5

• *Phlomis russeliana* is a perennial with large cordate (heart-shaped) green leaves that are semi-evergreen. The plant spreads by means of rhizomes and makes a good groundcover. It prefers friable, fairly deep soils. *Phlomis russeliana* is happy in semi-shade: in the wild it grows in light woodland of pines and oaks. The tall inflorescences rise in May from the centre of the rosettes. The flowers have a soft colour, with a lemon-yellow lower lip and a cream hood. **ORIGIN** TURKEY **HARDINESS** −15 °C AND BELOW **DROUGHT RESISTANCE CODE** 3

• *Phlomis viscosa* is distinguished by its dark green leaves. The plant forms a massive ball, very decorative in May when the bright yellow flowers contrast with the curious mauve-brown, almost black, stems. **ORIGIN** PALESTINE, LEBANON, SYRIA, TURKEY **HARDINESS** −10 TO −12 °C **DROUGHT RESISTANCE CODE** 4

To learn more about *Phlomis*, see Jim Mann Taylor's book, *Phlomis, the Neglected Genus* (see Further Reading).

Photinia serratifolia
(Rosaceae)

ORIGIN CHINA, JAPAN
HEIGHT 6 TO 8 M, SOMETIMES UP TO 10 M OR MORE
SPREAD 4 M AND MORE
POSITION SUN OR SHADE
HARDINESS −12 TO −15 °C
DROUGHT RESISTANCE CODE 3

A small tree with handsome, dark green, evergreen foliage. The glossy leathery leaves are toothed with small, regular, pointed indentations (*Photinia* comes from the Greek, *phōteinos*, 'shining with light', and *serratifolia* from the Latin *serrula*, 'a small saw'). At the end of winter the large and very decorative red buds start to swell slowly among the bronze-coloured new leaves. The panicles of white flowers appear in March–April and have a penetrating and slightly insipid scent which some people find rather disagreeable. *Photinia serratifolia* tolerates alkaline conditions well; it prefers friable, fairly deep soils. In gardens it is usually planted as part of a large free-growing hedge, but it can easily be trained as a small tree by removing the lower branches. When cut, the wood gives off a strong smell of bitter almond. In traditional Chinese medicine a decoction of the wood is famed for its stimulating and aphrodisiac properties.

Propagation is by ripewood cuttings in autumn.

The white flowers of *Photinia serratifolia* are preceded by large red buds that slowly swell at the end of winter.

Phyla nodiflora
(Verbenaceae) Lippia

ORIGIN A WIDE DISTRIBUTION IN THE EASTERN
MEDITERRANEAN AND ASIA MINOR, AS WELL AS IN MANY
REGIONS WITH A SUBTROPICAL CLIMATE
HEIGHT 1–10 CM DEPENDING ON THE MOISTURE AND
SHADE AVAILABLE
SPREAD 1 M OR MORE
POSITION SUN OR SEMI-SHADE
HARDINESS –10 TO –12 °C
DROUGHT RESISTANCE CODE 3

A perennial with small, deciduous leaves
that may be evergreen in areas with a mild
climate. The stems root at the nodes
wherever they touch the soil. The plant
grows rapidly and has a tendency to
colonize all available space, branching in
every direction and forming an attractive
groundcover that is flat and dense. The
small, pinkish-white flowers, rich in nectar
and very profuse, appear in May–June.
They can continue in succession until
September if the summer is not too dry.
In cases of severe drought, the foliage may
dry out partially in summer, but the plant
rapidly becomes green again with the first
rains. *Phyla nodiflora* tolerates alkaline
conditions well and withstands salt spray;
it is unfussy about soil type. It can endure
being walked on a fair amount and makes
an excellent lawn alternative for small areas.
We like to plant it with other carpeting
species that have a complementary growth
cycle. It can, for instance, be combined
with *Achillea crithmifolia*, which enters
into partial dormancy when *Phyla nodiflora*
is in full growth. Then in winter *Achillea
crithmifolia* is dominant, while *Phyla* loses
its leaves and becomes less attractive.

*Propagation is by division at the end of winter
or by softwood cuttings in spring.*

Pistacia lentiscus
(Anacardiaceae) Lentisk, Mastic Tree

ORIGIN MEDITERRANEAN BASIN
HEIGHT 1 TO 3 M
SPREAD 2 TO 5 M
POSITION SUN OR SHADE
HARDINESS –12 TO –15 °C
DROUGHT RESISTANCE CODE 6

A shrub or small tree with dark green,
evergreen leaves that are divided into thick
and leathery leaflets and have a strong smell
of resin. In summer the young leaves are a
tender light green, while in winter they take
on amazing bronze or mauve tints. The
plant develops into a rounded and very
branching mass, often wider than it is tall.
The lentisk is used for its amber-coloured
resin which oozes out like blond teardrops
when the trunk is cut into. This resin makes
gum mastic, the disinfectant and antiseptic
properties of which have been famed since
antiquity for purifying the breath and
caring for the teeth. The most sought after
mastic has always come from the Aegean
islands, and especially from Chios. *Pistacia
lentiscus* tolerates alkaline conditions well.
It is unfussy about soil type, even tolerating
heavy and asphyxiating soils. Found all
round the Mediterranean, it is capable of
adapting to the harshest conditions: it
withstands direct salt spray, can cope with
the poorest of soils and does equally well
under the blazing sun and in the dense
shade of pine or oak forests. In the dry
garden it is one of the best shrubs for
providing a permanent backbone in
plantings or for use in free-growing hedges.
It tolerates pruning perfectly and is long-
lived, often attaining a venerable age.

Propagation is by fresh seed in winter.

• *Pistacia atlantica* is a tree with a majestic
habit, capable of surviving in the arid
regions of the Maghreb. Some sacred trees
in Morocco, the remnants of forests now
lost, have a striking stature, with trunks of

Phyla nodiflora is one of the best lawn alternatives for a dry garden. Its height depends on the amount it is walked on.

Pistacia lentiscus is well able to withstand both salt spray and drought, thanks to the glossy cuticle that covers its leaves. By the sea it hugs the ground, forming magnificent patches several metres wide.

The winter shoots of Pistacia lentiscus are a pretty bronze colour.

imposing dimensions. Since it is slow-growing, it is usually treated as a large shrub in the garden. **ORIGIN** NORTH AFRICA, ASIA **HARDINESS** −12 TO −15 °C **DROUGHT RESISTANCE CODE** 6

• *Pistacia terebinthus*, the Turpentine Tree, has deciduous matt green leaves with a strong smell of resin. The new shoots are red and very decorative in spring, while in autumn the foliage takes on fine shades of yellow and orange. It can be planted in a free-growing hedge, in association with *Cercis siliquastrum*, *Cotinus coggygria* 'Grace' and *Acer monspessulanum*, for flamboyant autumn colours. **ORIGIN** MEDITERRANEAN BASIN **HARDINESS** −15 °C AND BELOW **DROUGHT RESISTANCE CODE** 6

• *Pistacia vera* is the pistachio tree that produces the edible nuts. Like all pistacias, it is dioecious, in other words both a male and a female plant are needed to obtain fruit. Fruit-bearing cultivars are propagated by grafting on to the stock of *Pistacia terebinthus* (or sometimes *Pistacia lentiscus* or *Pistacia atlantica*). Shield bud or 'chip' grafts are made in late spring or early summer. Grafting is easier on host plants that are growing outside in the ground: it is thus better to start by planting *Pistacia terebinthus* in the garden so that later on you can try to find grafting slips of *Pistacia vera*. **PROBABLE ORIGIN** SYRIA, IRAN, AFGHANISTAN **HARDINESS** −15 °C AND BELOW **DROUGHT RESISTANCE CODE** 6

Pittosporum truncatum
(Pittosporaceae)

ORIGIN CHINA
HEIGHT 2 TO 3 M, SOMETIMES MORE
SPREAD 2 TO 3 M
POSITION SUN OR SHADE
HARDINESS −12 TO −15 °C
DROUGHT RESISTANCE CODE 3

A large and sometimes tree-like shrub with leathery evergreen leaves that are a glossy dark green with light green undersides. The leaves often have their tips bent downwards, hence the species name which refers to the truncated appearance of the foliage. The plant develops into a massive bush, naturally dense and branching. The pale yellow flowers, pleasantly scented, appear in April–May arranged in umbels in the leaf axils. In autumn they are followed by capsules that open to reveal reddish-orange seeds coated in a sticky resin-like substance (*Pittosporum* comes from the Greek *pitta*, 'resin' and *sporos*, 'seed'). *Pittosporum truncatum* tolerates alkaline conditions well and is unfussy about soil type. It withstands being pruned, even severely. It can be grown in a container, as topiary, or as a low clipped hedge like myrtle or box. We like it in free-growing hedges, where its scent perfumes a whole area of the garden in spring.

Propagation is by cuttings in winter.

• *Pittosporum phillyroides* is an elegant shrub with supple branches and an airy, slightly weeping, habit. The leathery leaves are so long and narrow that they are almost linear. In spring the small flowers open into delicate, scented little bells. The decorative fruits consist of bright yellow capsules that gape wide to offer their scarlet seeds to the birds. **ORIGIN** AUSTRALIA **HARDINESS** −6 TO −8 °C **DROUGHT RESISTANCE CODE** 5

• *Pittosporum tobira* has thick, leathery, dark green leaves with a rounded tip. In May the creamy-white flowers have a delicious scent, reminiscent of orange blossom: in the evening in still weather they can perfume an entire area of the garden. Aged specimens can sometimes be seen in old parks, with short trunks and

In autumn the warm hues of Pistacia terebinthus light up the stands of oak and pine.

hemispherical crowns that call to mind large mushrooms. *Pittosporum tobira* is often planted by the sea, where its foliage withstands direct salt spray perfectly. **ORIGIN** CHINA, JAPAN **HARDINESS** −12 TO −15 °C **DROUGHT RESISTANCE CODE** 3

Potentilla verna
(Rosaceae)

ORIGIN SOUTHERN EUROPE
HEIGHT 10 CM
SPREAD 40 TO 50 CM
POSITION SUN
HARDINESS −15 °C AND BELOW
DROUGHT RESISTANCE CODE 3

A perennial with evergreen leaves divided into five leaflets with toothed margins. The stems root wherever they touch the soil and

alternative for small areas that are rarely walked on. If drought persists, the plant loses part of its foliage and becomes temporarily less ornamental until it greens up again with the first rains of autumn.

Propagation is by division in winter or by softwood cuttings in autumn or spring.

Punica granatum
(Lythraceae) Pomegranate

ORIGIN SOUTHEAST EUROPE TO THE HIMALAYAS
HEIGHT 4 M OR MORE
SPREAD 3 M OR MORE
POSITION SUN
HARDINESS −12 TO −15 °C
DROUGHT RESISTANCE CODE 5

The pomegranate has been cultivated since remotest antiquity. It appears in ancient Egyptian reliefs, and Homer mentions it in the *Odyssey* growing in the luxuriant gardens of King Alcinoos, father of the beautiful Nausicaa whom Odysseus met on the beach where he had fallen asleep naked. The pomegranate thrived in the hanging gardens of Babylon, one of the Seven Wonders of the World. The Romans discovered the pomegranate in Carthage and called it *malum punicum*, or 'Carthaginian apple'. It was introduced into

Potentilla verna forms a regular carpet around stepping stones. In intense drought the foliage may dry out in summer, becoming green again with the first autumn rains.

the plant makes a pretty, flat groundcover. In March–April it disappears beneath a carpet of yellow flowers – a charming springtime scene (*verna* means belonging to spring in Latin). *Potentilla verna* tolerates alkaline conditions well and prefers light, well-drained soils. It is a robust and easily grown perennial, lending itself to many uses in the garden: as a small groundcover in rock gardens or between stepping stones, as a carpet through which spring-flowering bulbs emerge, or even as a striking lawn

With its swelling fruits full of fleshy seeds, the pomegranate has long been associated with procreation and fertility. The cultivar 'Fruits Violets' has skin as glossy as leather.

Spain by the Moors, who planted it with roses and myrtle in the gardens of the Alhambra – the town of Granada owes its name to the pomegranate.

With its fruits swelling with fleshy seeds (*granatum* means full of grain or seed), the pomegranate tree was for a long time associated with procreation and fertility. According to Greek mythology, it was Aphrodite, the goddess of love, who planted the first pomegranate in Cyprus. For the Greeks it was a symbol of birth and life, but also of the cycle of the seasons. Persephone, goddess of springtime and sowing, was condemned to live for six months every year in the underworld: by succumbing to the temptation to eat a few pomegranate seeds in the garden of the realm of the dead, she found herself married against her will to Hades, the king of the dead.

Punica granatum is a deciduous, branching shrub or small tree, forming a tangled, often slightly spiny, mass of branches. It is decorative for a very long period. Its young shoots are an amazing bronze colour that seems almost translucent in the spring light. The bright orange-red flowers are abundant in June–July and are then produced more sporadically throughout the whole summer. The crumpled petals emerge from a thick calyx whose waxy texture already evokes the skin of the future fruit. In autumn the heavy fruits take on gold, pink, red or mauve hues as they ripen, depending on the variety. When ripe they split open, revealing to the greedy eye a profusion of seeds, pale pink or red depending on the variety, surrounded by a pulp that may be more or less sweet or acid. The leaves now become a beautiful luminous yellow before winter arrives and the plant enters into a well-deserved period of dormancy. *Punica granatum* tolerates alkaline conditions well and is unfussy about soil type. Although it withstands drought remarkably well, its flowering and fruiting are more copious if its roots can find some coolness and moisture deep in the ground.

Propagation is by winter hardwood cuttings or softwood cuttings in spring.

The Roman author Pliny the Elder already listed nine pomegranate cultivars. There are now a great many, each country having its own local selections. Here are some cultivars that are especially beautiful in our garden.

• *Punica granatum* 'Antalaya' is a cultivar we brought back from Turkey a few years ago. It seems to have become naturalized in hedges and copses throughout the Antalya region. Its fruit have a shining dark red skin and magnificent dark mauve seeds, too acid to be eaten but used for making juice. Itinerant street sellers push their way through the lanes of Istanbul with their barrows piled with pyramids of this magnificent pomegranate. For the modest sum of a million Turkish liras (then) you could buy delicious beakers of freshly squeezed juice, purple-black, as tart and refreshing as grapefruit juice. In the country, the juice of this pomegranate is boiled for a long time in heavy pots on a wood fire until it is reduced to a thick syrup, served as a condiment with salads.

• *Punica granatum* 'Fruits Violets' has very dense vegetation and spiny branches. Its early flowering is followed in July by a profusion of non-edible fruits. These fruits have a smooth and glossy skin whose amazing intense purple colour contrasts with the single, luminous orange-red flowers that continue to be produced in succession throughout the summer. In autumn the branches are heavy with fruit,

The heavy flowers of *Punica granatum* 'Legrelliae' appear in succession throughout the summer.

which remains decorative for a long time, even after the leaves have fallen.

• *Punica granatum* 'Legrelliae' has double flowers, heavy with petals bicoloured orange and cream. It is a vigorous plant with an upright habit and branches without spines.

• *Punica granatum* 'Luteum Plenum' has large double flowers of a soft pale yellow. In our garden we like to plant it with *Vitex agnus-castus* 'Latifolia' which flowers at the same time, with its long spikes of deep blue flowers.

• *Punica granatum* 'Maxima Rubra' has big double flowers that are bright orange-red. Like the other double-flowered forms, it does not bear fruit.

• *Punica granatum* 'Mollar de Elche' is an excellent productive cultivar, grown on a large scale in southern Spain. It has single bright orange flowers. The pale yellow fruits

The seeds of *Punica granatum* 'Antalaya' yield a dark purple, almost black, juice when squeezed, as acid and refreshing as grapefruit juice.

Punica granatum 'Mollar de Elche' produces delicious pomegranates with sweet and juicy pulp surrounding soft seeds.

are marbled with pink or red when they are ripe. The pulp is sweet and juicy and the seeds tender. Another delicious cultivar that we grow in our garden is 'Fina Tendral', with lighter-skinned fruit, which only bears well in the hottest of summers.

• *Punica granatum* 'Nana Gracillissima' is a dwarf cultivar, not exceeding 40 centimetres in height. It is often grown in containers to ornament patios and terraces. Throughout the summer the plant is covered in small, bright red, tubular flowers. These are followed in autumn by decorative, miniature, non-edible fruits which remain on the plant for a long time.

Quercus coccifera
(Fagaceae) Kermes Oak

ORIGIN MEDITERRANEAN BASIN
HEIGHT 2 TO 3 M (SOMETIMES UP TO 10 M IN OLDER SPECIMENS)
SPREAD 3 M OR MORE
POSITION SUN OR SEMI-SHADE
HARDINESS −12 TO −15 °C
DROUGHT RESISTANCE CODE 5

A shrub or small tree with leathery, evergreen leaves that are a glossy dark green and have spiny edges. In the spring the catkins give the plant a pretty golden appearance. The kermes oak is host to an insect which breeds in galls that have long been harvested for the production of a bright red dye (*coccifera* comes from the Greek *kokkos*, 'grain' or 'berry', referring to these galls, and from the Latin *fero*, 'to bear'). In the South of France the kermes oak is a low-growing bush, its spiny and impenetrable vegetation covering areas of garrigue that have suffered the onslaught of fire too frequently. Its stock has the ability to sucker vigorously when the above-ground parts of the plant are destroyed by fire or by repeated cutting. However, when given the chance to achieve its natural growth habit, the kermes oak becomes a small tree with a thick trunk and a very decorative, perfectly regular crown. Magnificent specimens can be seen in the mountains of southwest Crete. Like enormous mushrooms, their centuries-old silhouettes dot the rocky expanses inhabited by sheep: over-grazing protects them from fire and allows these kermes oaks to attain a remarkable size. *Quercus coccifera* tolerates alkaline conditions well. It is very adaptable and thrives even in the most compact rocky soils. In the garden it can be used as a contrast plant, its dark foliage setting off grey or silver plants such as *Ballota pseudodictamnus*, *Artemisia arborescens* or *Teucrium fruticans*.

Propagation is by seed in autumn.

Tangled bushes of *Quercus coccifera* form impenetrable masses in garrigue that experiences frequent fires. However, when it gets the chance to grow to its full size, the kermes oak develops into a small tree with a perfectly regular crown like a large mushroom.

• *Quercus ilex*, the holm oak, is a tree, although in the garrigue it often grows in a shrub-like manner with multiple trunks. Coppiced for centuries, it was used as firewood or to make good-quality charcoal. The leaves are variable and may resemble those of holly (because of the similarity of their leaves, *ilex* is the name of this species of oak and *Ilex* is the name of the holly genus). The leaves are evergreen, dark green and leathery. Their upper surface is glossy to limit evaporation, while the stomata are concentrated on the undersides, which have fine soft hairs to minimize transpiration, typical of the interesting adaptation of sclerophyllous plants to drought in the mediterranean climate. Indeed, the distribution of the holm oak is considered by some authors to be more representative an indicator of the limits of mediterranean climate zones than that of the olive. The holm oak tolerates pruning well. It can be combined with the bay tree or the pyramidal olive to make tall, free-growing hedges. Patient gardeners may also plant it as a shade tree. **ORIGIN** MEDITERRANEAN BASIN **HARDINESS** −12 TO −15 °C **DROUGHT RESISTANCE CODE** 5

Retama raetam
(Fabaceae)

ORIGIN NORTH AFRICA, THE MIDDLE EAST
HEIGHT 2 TO 3 M
SPREAD 2 M
POSITION SUN
HARDINESS −8 TO −10 °C
DROUGHT RESISTANCE CODE 6

A shrub with supple stems that are grey-green with a silvery sheen. The few narrow leaves appear briefly in the rainy season; they then fall rapidly and photosynthesis is carried out by the young branches. The plant is exceptionally drought-resistant, enabling it to survive in desert conditions. The stomata on young branches are deeply sunk in 'stomatic crypts', a sort of cavity fringed with hairs, to limit water loss. The very extensive root system allows the plant to absorb small quantities of water from a vast area. The roots produce an excellent charcoal, renowned for millennia: the exceptional heat it gives off in braziers is mentioned in the Old Testament. At the end of winter the plant is covered in delicate, scented flowers with pure white petals and shiny purple calyces. *Retama raetam* tolerates alkaline conditions well. It is unfussy about soil type: in the wild it grows in sandy or rocky soil, but in our garden it seems perfectly happy in an area where the soil is clayey and compact. Able to survive in extreme conditions, it is a light and graceful shrub. To enjoy its charm you will need to have a little patience: during its first years it is slow-growing.

Propagation is by seed in autumn after hot water treatment: pour boiling water on the seeds and leave them to swell overnight. The germination rate is irregular and usually rather poor. It can be improved by scarifying the seeds by milling them before pouring the boiling water over them, to attack their hard and impermeable protective coating.

• *Retama monosperma* bears a mass of white, highly scented flowers in spring.

A light and graceful shrub, *Retama raetam* flowers in mid-winter.

The delicate silky stems have a supple and slightly weeping habit. Grown for the cut-flower market, *Retama monosperma* transforms the beautiful terraced landscape near the Italian border between Menton and Genoa into cascades of white; commercial horticulture is a tradition here. **ORIGIN** SPAIN, PORTUGAL, MOROCCO **HARDINESS** −6 TO −8 °C **DROUGHT RESISTANCE CODE** 6

• *Retama sphaerocarpa* is distinguished by the profusion of its elegant flowers, golden yellow with a lemon-yellow calyx, hence its pretty name in Spanish, *lluvia de oro*. The young branches look silky and form a dense and pliable mass, grey with a silvery sheen. This species was grown in Spain for its wood, which has a high calorific value and was used to fuel bread ovens. **ORIGIN** IBERIAN PENINSULA, NORTH AFRICA **HARDINESS** −8 TO −10 °C **DROUGHT RESISTANCE CODE** 6

Rhamnus alaternus
(Rhamnaceae) Buckthorn

ORIGIN MEDITERRANEAN BASIN
HEIGHT 4 TO 5 M
SPREAD 2 M OR MORE
POSITION SUN
HARDINESS −10 TO −12 °C
DROUGHT RESISTANCE CODE 4

An evergreen shrub with shiny, dark green, leathery leaves, that are lighter coloured underneath. The well-branched vegetation, with a slightly stiff habit, is fairly fast-growing. Small and inconspicuous yellowish flowers open in April–May, followed by small red fruits which become black as they ripen and are a delight to birds in autumn. *Rhamnus alaternus* tolerates alkaline conditions well and withstands salt spray. It prefers stony, well-drained soils. It can cope with competition from tree roots and can be used, together with *Phillyrea*, lentisk and laurustinus, to form the shrubby structure of a woodland garden under oaks or pines.

Propagation is by fresh seed in autumn or by softwood cuttings in spring.

Rhodanthemum hosmariense
(Asteraceae)

ORIGIN MOROCCO (ATLAS MOUNTAINS)
HEIGHT 20 CM
SPREAD 40 TO 50 CM
POSITION SUN
HARDINESS −10 TO −12 °C
DROUGHT RESISTANCE CODE 4

A sub-shrub with beautiful silky and finely cut evergreen leaves that are a silver colour. The plant develops into a compact and perfectly regular cushion. The flower buds appear from January and are very decorative – surrounded by scaly bracts they contrast well with the light foliage. The white daisy flowers open on short flowering spikes in March–April. *Rhodanthemum hosmariense* tolerates alkaline conditions well. It prefers light, well-drained soils and is an excellent rock plant, easy to grow and long-lived.

Propagation is by softwood cuttings in autumn.

• *Rhodanthemum catananche* forms a small cushion of grey-green leaves, with notched tips. The small daisy flowers are an unusual

RIGHT *Rhodanthemum catananche* produces a mass of delicate-coloured spring flowers, here contrasting with a dark carpet of *Thymus serpyllum* 'Lemon Curd' on the left, and the silver foliage of *Tanacetum densum* subsp. *amanii* behind.

BELOW *Rhodanthemum hosmariense* is a magnificent rock plant that is easy to grow.

colour, coppery yellow mixed with salmon pink and cream. **ORIGIN** MOROCCO **HARDINESS** −10 TO −12 °C **DROUGHT RESISTANCE CODE** 3

Rhus lancea
(Anacardiaceae) Sumach

ORIGIN SOUTH AFRICA
HEIGHT 5 M OR MORE
SPREAD 4 TO 5 M
POSITION SUN OR SEMI-SHADE
HARDINESS −8 TO −10 °C
DROUGHT RESISTANCE CODE 6

A shrub or small tree with evergreen foliage of a fine dark green. The leaves are divided into three tapering lobes, giving a light appearance to the dense mass of the foliage. The plant grows fast, thanks to its vigorous young branches which are supple and tough – they were traditionally used by the San people of South Africa to make bows. The greenish-yellow flowers are inconspicuous. The plant is dioecious: only females bear the clusters of small yellowish-red fruits so much appreciated by birds. *Rhus lancea* tolerates alkaline conditions well and is unfussy about soil type. Its rapid growth

Near Windhoek, in the plateaux of central Namibia, *Rhus lancea* makes a small tree that provides welcome shade. The golden tufts of *Hyparrhenia hirta* give colour to the surrounding hills.

and fine foliage make it an excellent plant for large, free-growing hedges. It can also be planted as a single specimen tree, useful for its dense shade.

Propagation is by fresh seed. If the seeds are not fresh, they should be treated to break their dormancy: scarify them by soaking them for half an hour in sulphuric acid, then stratify them by keeping them for three to four months in the refrigerator at a temperature of about 4 °C. The plant can also be propagated by softwood cuttings in spring (irregular rooting), or by air layering carried out in autumn.

Romneya coulteri
(Papaveraceae) California Tree Poppy

ORIGIN CALIFORNIA
HEIGHT 1.5 M OR MORE
SPREAD INDEFINITE
POSITION SUN
HARDINESS −10 TO −12 °C
DROUGHT RESISTANCE CODE 6

A woody-based perennial with deciduous or semi-deciduous vegetation, depending on how cold the winter is. The blueish-grey leaves have irregularly cut margins. The vigorous stock spreads by means of powerful rhizomes, which have a tendency to become invasive. In some California gardens we have seen *Romneya* specimens covering an area of more than 25 square metres! The spectacular flowering takes place in May–June and may recur more or less throughout the summer. The scented flowers,

resembling enormous poppies, open on tall branching stems that sway in the slightest breeze. The white petals, with a curiously crumpled texture, surround a large cluster of golden yellow stamens. Decorative seedpods follow the flowers: arranged in dry bunches, they remain on the plant for a long time and look like delicate cages for miniature birds. *Romneya coulteri* tolerates alkaline conditions well; it requires friable, deep soil with perfect drainage. A generous addition of sand and pebbles at planting gets the plant off to a good start. It is often said that you should put in three plants to ensure that one becomes established: the rootlets are fragile and do not like being disturbed. *Romneya* dislikes water and well-intentioned gardeners often kill it by excessive irrigation. The vegetation can be cut down short at the end of winter to regenerate the plant and to encourage vigorous new growth.

Propagation is difficult and so Romneya coulteri *is still relatively rarely grown. Cuttings can be taken in autumn from the deep horizontal rhizomes, but their rooting is slow and capricious.*
Propagation by seed is also possible, provided that its dormancy is broken by smoke treatment,

Perched on long stems, the enormous flowers of *Romneya coulteri* sway gently in the wind.

for the plant is linked to the fire ecology of the chaparral where it is not the heat but the chemical action of the smoke that triggers germination. The seeds can be soaked with 'smoke discs' sold by the Kirstenbosch Botanic Garden. Another solution is to sow seed in a substrate that has been impregnated with smoke. To 'smoke' the substrate, you can put it in a mason's sieve placed on a tripod over a fire smothered with branches – I use armfuls of Pistacia lentiscus, Laurus nobilis, Myrtus communis *and* Cistus ladanifer. *The germination rate is good, but pricking out the seedlings afterwards is an extremely delicate operation. The propagation of* Romneya coulteri *requires a serious effort, but what a pleasure when your first plants appear!*

Rosa banksiae 'Lutescens'
(Rosaceae) Banksia Rose

ORIGIN CHINA
HEIGHT AND SPREAD 10 M OR MORE
POSITION SUN
HARDINESS −15 °C AND BELOW
DROUGHT RESISTANCE CODE 4

A vigorous climbing shrub with light, evergreen or semi-evergreen foliage. The leaves are divided into five shiny dark green leaflets. The smooth branches are completely free of thorns. In March the plant is covered in buds arranged in small, tight clusters along the length of the previous year's growth. They open in April into an extraordinary mass of small, single flowers, butter-yellow and highly scented. The flowering season is short but outstanding: three weeks of pure bliss. In early May the flowers fade in the space of just a few days, covering the ground in a rain of tender yellow petals. Growth begins soon after flowering. The young branches shoot in June and become progressively longer, like giant asparaguses. They grow fast and by the middle of the summer are 4 to 5 metres long. Gracefully arched and pendent, they give this rose the spectacular form of a monumental fountain. Throughout winter the branches bear clusters of small reddish-brown fruits about the size of peas, much sought after by birds. *Rosa banksiae* 'Lutescens' tolerates alkaline conditions well and is unfussy about soil type. It is particularly happy when it can grow into trees, where it gives full rein to all the conquering vigour of its extraordinary vegetation. There are references to old Banksia roses that have climbed more than 15 metres into trees and bear hundreds of thousands of flowers each spring. This form with single yellow flowers is rarely grown and it should be much more widely distributed in mediterranean gardens. It is our favourite rose: we have chosen it to cover the large pergola abutting on to the south side of our house. In a few years its long pliable branches have covered it, providing perfect shade for the terrace.

Propagation is by softwood cuttings in summer. Young tips root most easily, but stem section cuttings can also be taken, though with a less regular success rate.

• *Rosa banksiae* 'Alba Plena' is covered in scented, very double white flowers like little pompoms. The branches are thornless. It flowers in May.

• *Rosa banksiae* 'Lutea' has double yellow flowers, very pretty but with little scent. This form is reputed to be the most vigorous of all Banksia roses.

• *Rosa banksiae* var. *normalis* has very fragrant single white flowers, with a scent of violets. It is the only form whose branches bear stout thorns.

Rosa brunonii
Himalayan Musk Rose

ORIGIN AFGHANISTAN, NEPAL
HEIGHT AND SPREAD 10 M OR MORE
POSITION SUN OR SEMI-SHADE
HARDINESS −12 TO −15 °C
DROUGHT RESISTANCE CODE 2.5

A twining shrub with light green, slightly matt, semi-evergreen leaves divided into drooping leaflets. The strong branches are armed with curving thorns. The single flowers, with a musk-like scent, are grouped in lax clusters and open in May–June. Their ivory-coloured, slightly separated petals surround a bunch of lovely golden yellow stamens. *Rosa brunonii* tolerates alkaline conditions well. It is a rose that is unfussy about soil type. Very beautiful specimens can be seen in old gardens on the Côte d'Azur, especially in the Hanbury Gardens, where the cultivar 'La Mortola' was selected for its great vigour.

Propagation is by softwood cuttings in summer.

Rosa chinensis 'Sanguinea'
China Rose, Bengal Rose

ORIGIN CHINA
HEIGHT AND SPREAD 3 TO 4 M
POSITION SUN OR SEMI-SHADE
HARDINESS −12 TO −15 °C
DROUGHT RESISTANCE CODE 3

A shrub with fine, dark green, shiny, evergreen leaves. The stems are variably thorny. The young red shoots only just precede the appearance of the flower buds, the successive flowerings being in rhythm with the plant's growth cycle throughout the whole year. The single flowers are composed of beautiful, velvety dark red petals surrounding a bunch of golden yellow stamens. They first open in April to May. A few flowers then continue to appear in summer, in spite of the heat, and after the first autumn rains a generous new flush of flowers opens. In winter there is a third magnificent flowering season: it is often at Christmas that the specimen in our garden

Rosa chinensis 'Sanguinea' flowers several times a year. In our garden it often has the greatest number of flowers at Christmas.

produces the most flowers. The flowers are followed by large ovoid hips, initially green then turning red. *Rosa chinensis* 'Sanguinea' tolerates alkaline conditions well and prefers friable, fairly deep soils. It is easy to grow and is an excellent plant either as a single specimen or as part of a free-growing hedge.

Propagation is by ripewood section cuttings in autumn or in spring.

• *Rosa chinensis* 'Mutabilis' produces a remarkable profusion of flowers in April–May, preceded by pretty orange buds. The flowers are a light beige when they open, then turn orange, pink or red before fading, turning the plant into a multicoloured bouquet. Flowering may be repeated several times throughout the year, though more irregularly than *Rosa chinensis* 'Sanguinea'.

Rosa moschata
Musk Rose

PROBABLE ORIGIN ASIA OR NORTH AFRICA
HEIGHT AND SPREAD 3 M OR MORE
POSITION SUN OR SEMI-SHADE
HARDINESS −12 TO −15 °C
DROUGHT RESISTANCE CODE 3

A shrub with evergreen leaves divided into light green leaflets. The gracefully arched branches have a slightly twining habit and are furnished with sparse thorns. Flowering continues from July to November: in our

Rosa banksiae 'Lutescens' climbs into old trees and in April is covered in thousands of small, deliciously scented flowers.

The flowers of *Rosa chinensis* 'Mutabilis' are pale beige when they open and then progressively turn orange, pink or red, making the plant a bouquet of multicoloured blossoms.

The ivory-coloured flowers of *Rosa moschata* var. *nastarana* give off a heavy scent of musk, perfuming the garden in still weather.

Rosa primula has pretty pale yellow flowers, but it is the magnificent red thorns that make one stop to admire it.

garden this is the only rose that is in flower throughout the summer, in spite of the drought. The single flowers, grouped in long bunches at the tips of the stems, have pure white petals and a delicate scent of musk. The name *moschata* comes from the Latin *muscus*, 'musk', derived from the Sanskrit *muskā*, testicle – natural musk comes from a substance produced during the rutting season from a testicle-shaped gland in the abdomen of the male *Moschus moschiferus*, the musk-deer of Central Asia. *Rosa moschata* tolerates alkaline conditions well and is unfussy about soil type. Long cultivated for its medicinal virtues (the petals are an excellent laxative), it has become naturalized in many countries, from Spain to China.

Propagation is by softwood cuttings in early summer.

• *Rosa moschata* var. *nastarana* has a more compact, shrubby habit. The flowers, which have a heavy scent of musk, open in May, and there is a repeat flush in autumn. The beautiful ivory petals overlap one another, making the flower look semi-double. The name of this rose presents problems, since it may be a hybrid of *Rosa brunonii*. We love it, as it is the most scented rose in our garden. **ORIGIN** UNCERTAIN, PERHAPS PERSIA? **HARDINESS** –15 °C AND BELOW **DROUGHT RESISTANCE CODE** 3

• *Rosa laevigata* is a twining shrub, with beautiful glossy evergreen leaves. It is the rose with the most handsome foliage in our garden. The large single flowers open in May–June and are scented. Their rounded petals are creamy-white and surround a large bunch of golden yellow, protruding stamens. After pollination these stamens turn a dark colour, almost black, which sets off the very soft colour of the flower. **ORIGIN** CHINA **HARDINESS** –10 TO –12 °C **DROUGHT RESISTANCE CODE** 3

• *Rosa primula* is a small shrub with finely cut, aromatic leaves. In hot weather they

give off a surprisingly sharp smell, reminiscent of incense, which can be detected for several metres round the plant. The red-brown stems are equipped with magnificent red thorns, particularly decorative when seen against the light. The small, scented flowers, a very soft primrose yellow, open in April. **ORIGIN** FROM TURKESTAN TO NORTHERN CHINA **HARDINESS** –15 °C AND BELOW **DROUGHT RESISTANCE CODE** 3

• *Rosa sempervirens* has delicate twining branches that are flexible and vigorous, and evergreen leaves that are glossy and dark green. The small white flowers open in May–June and are scented. It is a vigorous and easily grown climbing rose which tolerates semi-shade well and is often used to clamber through trees. 'Félicité et Perpétue', bred from *Rosa sempervirens*, is a cultivar with beautiful double flowers that are scented and a very soft white, barely tinged with pink. A magnificent specimen can be seen cascading through trees at the Hanbury Gardens near Menton. **ORIGIN** SOUTHERN EUROPE, TURKEY, NORTH AFRICA **HARDINESS** –12 TO –15 °C **DROUGHT RESISTANCE CODE** 4

• *Rosa indica* 'Major', an old variety traditionally grown as stock for grafts, makes a good-looking evergreen bush in our garden. The pink, very double flowers are pleasantly scented. They open in April/May. **ORIGIN** PROBABLE HYBRID OF *Rosa multiflora* AND *Rosa chinensis* **HARDINESS** –15 °C AND BELOW **DROUGHT RESISTANCE CODE** 3

• *Rosa* × *dupontii* is a hybrid of *Rosa moschata* and *Rosa gallica*. It is a vigorous shrub with an arching, more or less spreading habit. It tolerates semi-shade well. The single or semi-double scented flowers open in May. Their beautiful creamy-white petals, just touched with pink, surround a large bunch of golden yellow stamens. The brilliant red hips remain decorative all winter long. **HARDINESS** –15 °C AND BELOW **DROUGHT RESISTANCE CODE** 3

Rosmarinus officinalis
(Lamiaceae) Rosemary

ORIGIN MEDITERRANEAN BASIN
HEIGHT FROM 40 CM TO 2 M, DEPENDING ON THE VARIETY
SPREAD FROM 1 M TO MORE THAN 3 M
POSITION SUN
HARDINESS –8 TO –15 °C, DEPENDING ON THE VARIETY
DROUGHT RESISTANCE CODE 5

A shrub with narrow, green, evergreen leaves, which have cottony and whitish undersides. To reduce the surface area from which evapotranspiration takes place, the edges of the leaves are folded over, making them appear linear. The very aromatic leaves and young shoots become sticky in hot weather. They give off a volatile essential oil with a characteristic resin smell, which protects the plant from being eaten by herbivores. In addition to its numerous flavouring and medicinal properties, rosemary was long considered to purify the air and provide protection from evil spirits: all round the Mediterranean it was used as an incense substitute. In Greek its common name is *dendrolivano*, or 'incense tree'.

Rosemary forms a dense bush, with either upright or prostrate stems, depending on the clone. Creeping rosemaries make excellent groundcovers since their branches root easily when they come in contact with the soil. Creeping forms often grow naturally near the sea, as for example at the wonderful rosemary site on Cape Pertusato, near Bonifacio, Corsica: to minimize the harmful effects of wind and salt spray, the plants have evolved genetically into remarkable carpeting forms. Although they also colonize the garrigues of the interior, rocky soils by the sea are the rosemary's preferred habitat. The name *Rosmarinus* comes from the Latin *ros,* 'dew', and *marinus,* 'of the sea', indicative of the plant's ability to withstand salt spray; according to another interpretation, however, the first part of the name comes from the Greek *rhous,* 'sumach', a generic name given to many shrubs.

Rosemaries tolerate alkaline conditions well. They like poor and stony soils, dry in summer and perfectly drained in winter. They absolutely should not be watered in summer: they are prone to infection by *Phytophthora,* a fungus affecting the collar of the plant that develops in hot, damp conditions. The better drained the soil, the better rosemaries will survive the winter: we have noted a great variation in the hardiness of rosemaries depending on the dampness of the soil. In gardens they are often grown in soil that is too rich, which makes them grow too fast, and they age badly, becoming bare at the base and leggy. To increase the lifespan of upright rosemaries, a small annual pruning will help them maintain a more compact, branching shape. Creeping rosemaries generally age better, since their stems layer themselves and regenerate the plant naturally, one of their major qualities.

In our garden, the flowers open at the beginning of autumn, and then again in early spring. The dates of flowering vary from year to year according to climatic conditions: if the weather is mild, rosemary can flower without interruption from September to March. Grouped in short clusters in the leaf axils, the flowers are very profuse. They are a delight to the bees that come to plunder them at a season when flowers are rare. The famous Narbonne honey, with its creamy texture and delicate flavour, is a rosemary honey – the Romans held it to be the best honey in the world. Flower colour in the wild is variable, each region often having a dominant colour. Near Narbonne, pale blue abounds in the garrigues of Corbières. Pure white is often seen round the creeks of Marseille, and a superb blueish-white at Cape Béar, near Collioure. In the Sierra de Cazorla in Spain a pretty pink rosemary grows, while the coasts of Sardinia are bathed in the luminous blue of a particularly delightful rosemary. The darkest coloured rosemaries are found in Corsica – an incomparable violet-blue.

We are fascinated by the diversity of rosemaries and grow a collection of more than fifty cultivars in our garden: they make a festival of blue in the empty period of winter. Here are some of those we love best.

Rosmarinus officinalis flowers throughout the autumn below Mont Sainte-Victoire in Provence.

• *Rosmarinus officinalis* 'Boule' has spreading and incredibly vigorous growth. The oldest specimen in our garden measures more than 4 metres across. In its first year it forms a spreading ball, like a plump, regular cushion. The branches then root as they touch the soil and the plant spreads rapidly, making a thick groundcover. It is in fact one of the best groundcovers in our garden. It can be planted on slopes, where it can grow unrestrained. If planted on top of a wall, it makes a magnificent cascade. The sky-blue flowers mingle with the dense, grey-green leaves that are tightly packed on the white, felted stems. **HARDINESS** −10 TO −12 °C

• *Rosmarinus officinalis* 'Corsican Blue' has a slightly shaggy habit. The branches begin by growing upright, then seem to hesitate and bend horizontally before hanging downwards or sometimes growing upright again. The adult plant forms a broad, spreading dome. The large flowers, a sumptuous violet-blue, are illuminated by a big white blotch. **HARDINESS** −8 TO −10 °C

• *Rosmarinus officinalis* 'Majorcan Pink' has a loose habit. The branches are fastigiate at first, but have a tendency to open outwards as the plant ages. The unusual pale pink flowers are abundant. **HARDINESS** −8 TO −10 °C

Rosmarinus officinalis 'Boule' is a cultivar with strong growth. The spreading or drooping branches root wherever they come in contact with the soil.

Rosemaries are very variable in the wild. There are forms with pale blue or dark blue flowers, or indeed with pink or pure white flowers.

• *Rosmarinus officinalis* 'Miss Jessop's Upright' is an English selection, renowned for its excellent ability to withstand cold. The plant has very narrow foliage on upright, straight branches. The flowers are pale blue. **HARDINESS** −12 TO −15 °C

• *Rosmarinus officinalis* 'Montagnette' is a carpeting variety that does not grow too big, and so is suitable for a rock garden. We have planted it beside a small flight of steps. The white flowers contrast with the green foliage. **HARDINESS** −8 TO −10 °C

• *Rosmarinus officinalis* 'Sappho' is the upright rosemary we like best. The flowers are a brilliant dark blue, reminiscent of some ceanothuses. Planted in association with *Coronilla glauca* 'Citrina', it makes a pretty spring scene in our garden. **HARDINESS** −10 TO −12 °C

• *Rosmarinus officinalis* 'Tuscan Blue' is an upright variety with strongly growing vegetation, often planted as a small hedge in Tuscany. In good conditions it can attain a height of 1.5 metres. The green leaves are markedly bigger than those of most rosemaries. The large flowers are a pretty sky-blue and the foliage is particularly aromatic: this variety is often used in the kitchen to flavour grilled meat. **HARDINESS** −10 TO −12 °C

Planted on top of a wall, *Rosmarinus officinalis* var. *repens* can make impressive cascades.

The flowers of *Rosmarinus officinalis* 'Sappho' are a magnificent brilliant dark blue when they open, gradually becoming lighter in colour as flowering progresses.

• *Rosmarinus officinalis* var. *repens* has light blue flowers. Its vigorous branches make an excellent carpeting groundcover. If planted on top of a wall, it can grow 2 or 3 metres downwards, like a vegetal wallpaper clinging to the wall. **HARDINESS** −10 TO −12 °C

Ruta graveolens
(Rutaceae) Rue

ORIGIN BALKANS
HEIGHT 60 TO 80 CM
SPREAD 60 CM
POSITION SUN
HARDINESS −12 TO −15 °C
DROUGHT RESISTANCE CODE 4

A sub-shrub with blue-green, evergreen leaves that are finely cut. A brief observation with a magnifying glass will enable you to see clearly the essential oil glands dotted on the undersides of the leaves. These glands give off a penetrating and extremely strong smell (*graveolens* comes from the Latin *gravis*, 'heavy', and *olens*, 'smelling'). Gardeners generally agree that the smell of rue is unpleasant, yet some people like it, and indeed in the past the leaves were used to flavour many kinds of food. As with many highly aromatic plants, rue was considered as a veritable panacea in folk medicine. Apart from its renowned abortive properties, it was ascribed a wide range of virtues. As well as being an antidote against snakebite, it also improved the vision, gave protection against spells and calmed those prone to frequent erotic dreams. In the garden it is a plant that possesses a discreet charm, with its acid yellow flowers with delicately fringed petals. It can be grown in combination with *Artemisia herba-alba*,

In spite of its aggressively strong smell, it is worth bending over rue to see its delicately fringed petals.

During the summer drought the foliage of *Salvia apiana* becomes remarkably luminous.

Thymus mastichina or *Santolina insulare* – plants whose strong smells make an unusual attraction in the garden. *Ruta graveolens* tolerates alkaline conditions well; it prefers poor, stony, perfectly drained soils.

Propagation is by seed in autumn.

Salvia
(Lamiaceae) Sage

With more than 900 species distributed around the world, the sages comprise a genus as fascinating as it is complex. Depending on their geographic place of origin, they have different requirements. In our experimental garden our first trials of sages were not very conclusive: a great many species rapidly died, either of cold or of drought. After a few years of discouragement, we started once more to investigate this genus. This time the results were a lot better: our choices were based on wiser criteria. Their generous scents, their diversity of foliage and the beauty of their flowers make sages exceptional plants in the dry garden. Here is a short list of those that are happiest in our own garden.

Salvia apiana
California White Sage

ORIGIN SOUTHERN CALIFORNIA
HEIGHT OF FOLIAGE 60 CM
HEIGHT IN FLOWER 1 TO 1.5 M
POSITION SUN
HARDINESS −8 TO −10 °C
DROUGHT RESISTANCE CODE 5

A sub-shrub with silvery-grey evergreen leaves. During the summer drought the foliage takes on a striking pure white colour. The leaves give off an intense, almost suffocating, scent. Some Native American tribes in California considered this plant to be sacred: branches of it were tied together in a sort of broad bundle, which was then burnt as a purificatory incense during ceremonies. From April to June the plant produces long spikes of white flowers, sometimes very slightly tinged with pink. The flowers are very rich in nectar, making

a strongly scented honey (*apiana* is from the Latin *apis*, 'bee'). *Salvia apiana* tolerates alkalinity if the soil is light and well-drained. In heavy soil it easily becomes chlorotic and is short-lived.

Propagation is by seed in autumn or by softwood cuttings in spring.

Salvia barrelieri

ORIGIN SOUTHERN SPAIN AND NORTH AFRICA
HEIGHT OF FOLIAGE 20 CM
HEIGHT IN FLOWER 1.5 M
SPREAD 60 CM
POSITION SUN OR SEMI-SHADE
HARDINESS −10 TO −12 C°
DROUGHT RESISTANCE CODE 4

A perennial with large, downy, grey-green leaves that have undulating margins and a crimped texture. The leaves are arranged in basal rosettes and are evergreen in winter. In spring strong branching inflorescences rise from the centre of the rosettes, bearing a profusion of large, bicoloured flowers in May–June. In order to be visible from a distance the lower lip, on which pollinating insects land, is white. The upper lip, curved like a sickle, is a beautiful tender violet-blue. The long pistil which extends from it gives the plant an elegant look: its purpose is to collect pollen from the backs of the pollinators, which are often fat carpenter bees. As in all sages, the stamens are articulated: as the insect penetrates the corolla, its head pushes against the bottom of the stamen which acts as a lever, setting off a clever balance mechanism that makes the stamens bend to powder the visitor's back with pollen.

Salvia barrelieri tolerates alkaline conditions well. It prefers friable, fairly deep, well-drained soils. The dry inflorescences can be removed after flowering to encourage the plant to make more rosettes of leaves. However, in our garden we prefer to leave them on the plant so that the shiny black seeds can sow themselves abundantly in nearby plantings.

Propagation is by seed in autumn.

Salvia canariensis
Canary Island Sage

ORIGIN CANARY ISLANDS
HEIGHT 1.5 TO 2 M
SPREAD 1 M
POSITION SUN
HARDINESS THE AERIAL PARTS FREEZE AT ABOUT −4 °C, BUT THE STOCK WILL PUT OUT NEW SHOOTS IN SPRING AFTER TEMPERATURES OF ABOUT −8 TO −10 °C
DROUGHT RESISTANCE CODE 3

A shrub with aromatic, light green, evergreen leaves. The triangular leaves have a saggitate base – that is shaped like an arrowhead. The stems, young shoots and the undersides of the leaves are covered in a thick felt of long white hairs. If you look at them through a magnifying glass you will see a multitude of shining droplets at the tips of the hairs. These are the essential oil glands which give the plant its acrid scent and protect it against herbivores. The large branching inflorescences appear from May to July. The violet-mauve flowers emerge from large reddish calyces, underpinned by long coloured bracts. Both calyces and bracts remain on the plant for a long time after flowering, making it decorative throughout the summer. *Salvia canariensis*

Salvia barrelieri is a vigorous perennial which self-seeds freely in light soils.

tolerates alkalinity if the soil is light and well-drained. In heavy soil it easily becomes chlorotic. It thrives in friable, fairly deep soils. In our garden the vegetation is destroyed by the cold almost every winter, but the plant has a good ability to put out new growth from the rootstock in spring. The new shoots grow fast and the plant faithfully flowers in summer, even if its aerial parts have suffered frost damage in winter.

Propagation is by softwood cuttings in early autumn.

• *Salvia canariensis* var. *candidissima* has silvery-white young shoots that are spectacular in spring. The magenta flowers contrast strikingly with the very light-coloured, almost white, foliage (*candidissima* comes from the Latin *candidus*, 'white', of which it is the superlative).

• *Salvia canariensis* 'Albiflora' has white flowers set off by beautiful acid-green calyces.

Salvia candelabrum

ORIGIN STONY HILLSIDES OF SOUTHERN SPAIN
HEIGHT OF FOLIAGE 30 TO 40 CM
HEIGHT IN FLOWER 1.2 TO 1.5 M
POSITION SUN
HARDINESS −10 TO −12 °C
DROUGHT RESISTANCE CODE 5

A sub-shrub with long, grey-green, evergreen leaves. The upper surface of the leaves is rough, while the underside is soft and silky, and they have a strong but pleasant scent, more refined that than of *Salvia officinalis*, the common sage. The plant forms a large spreading cushion, from which emerge the amazing flowering stems, very long and elegantly branched like a candelabrum. In May–June they are covered in magnificent blue-mauve flowers; their widely spreading lower lip, divided into velvety lobes, is reminiscent of the labellum of certain orchids. *Salvia candelabrum* tolerates alkaline conditions well. It requires poor, stony soil with perfect drainage, otherwise it is short-lived. To ensure its survival in the clayey soil of our garden, we added a generous amount of sand and gravel when we planted it. It is well worth this small amount of effort: without doubt it is the most beautiful sage one can grow in a dry garden.

Propagation is by seed in autumn.

Salvia chamaedryoides

ORIGIN MEXICO, TEXAS
HEIGHT 40 TO 60 CM
SPREAD 60 CM
POSITION SUN
HARDINESS −10 TO −12 °C
DROUGHT RESISTANCE CODE 5

A shrub with small, silver-grey, evergreen leaves. When crushed, the foliage gives off a subtle scent, at the same time soft and acid, rather like that of pears or mandarins. The plant forms a compact, rounded bush and its intensely blue flowers on graceful spikes contrast well with the silver foliage. In the wild, *Salvia chamaedryoides* flowers in summer: it comes from the high Chihuahua plateaux, a semi-desert region where the irregular rains fall mostly in summer, triggering the flowering. By contrast, in our garden flowering occurs in two distinct waves separated by a rest period caused by drought: a May–June flowering is followed by a second generous flowering in September–October. *Salvia chamaedryoides* tolerates alkaline conditions well; it prefers light, well-drained soils. Clipping the plant to about a third of its height in late winter encourages it to produce vigorous new growth, which will flower freely.

Propagation is by seed in autumn or by softwood cuttings in spring.

Salvia chamelaeagna

ORIGIN SOUTH AFRICA, FROM THE CAPE TO THE KAROO AND NAMAQUALAND
HEIGHT 80 CM OR MORE
SPREAD 60 CM
POSITION SUN
HARDINESS −8 TO −10 °C
DROUGHT RESISTANCE CODE 6

A shrub with evergreen leaves of a pretty light green. When crushed, the foliage gives off a strong smell of wet wool and wool grease. The vegetation forms a dense bush (the name *chamelaeagna*, hard to spell, comes from the Greek *chamai*, 'close to the ground', and *elaia*, 'olive', describing the compact and tufty habit of this plant). In full summer, when most plants have already been resting for some time, this salvia flowers, apparently impervious to heat and drought. Enveloped in large mauve calyces, the bicoloured flowers have a deep blue upper lip and a pale lower lip with a yellow mark in the centre. All parts of the inflorescence are covered in thick glandular hairs which give off an essential oil with numerous medicinal properties. Bunches of the flowering stems are sold in the markets of South Africa and these are used to make a decoction for colds and bronchitis. *Salvia chamelaeagna* tolerates alkaline conditions well. It is unfussy about soil type, but we have noticed that it resists cold markedly better in light, well-drained soil. It withstands salt spray perfectly.

Propagation is by softwood cuttings in early autumn.

The mauve flowers of *Salvia canariensis* emerge from large reddish calyces which remain on the plant for a long time after flowering has finished.

The young shoots of *Salvia canariensis* 'Candidissima' are covered with thick white hairs. By forming a microclimate over the surface of the leaves, these hairs limit water loss by evapotranspiration and help the plant withstand drought.

In this springtime scene *Salvia chamaedryoides* is on the left, along with (moving clockwise) *Phlomis lycia*, *Helichrysum orientale*, *Santolina viridis* and *Artemisia lanata*, with *Thymus ciliatus* in the middle.

Salvia clevelandii
Jim Sage

ORIGIN SOUTHERN CALIFORNIA
HEIGHT 60 CM OR MORE
SPREAD 60 TO 80 CM
POSITION SUN
HARDINESS −8 TO −10 °C
DROUGHT RESISTANCE CODE 5

A shrub with narrow, grey-green, evergreen leaves which give off a sharp and powerful scent of camphor, with a surprisingly fruity note reminiscent of pineapple – *Salvia clevelandii* is one of the plants most prized by lovers of aromatic plants. In the chaparral it is said that you can smell the plant before seeing it. In hot weather its foliage can perfume an entire area of the garden. The vegetation forms a large cushion, covered in pliable, more or less spreading inflorescences in May–June. The tubular flowers are a magnificent brilliant dark blue and are verticillate, i.e. arranged in regular whorls up the stem. After flowering, the whorls remain for several months, making the withered inflorescences ornamental. In times of extreme drought the plant loses some of its leaves and enters

into a rest period until autumn. *Salvia clevelandii* tolerates alkaline conditions well; it requires a light soil with perfect drainage. In heavy soils it is capricious and short-lived. It is prone to *Phytophthora*, a fungus affecting the collar of the plant that develops in hot and humid conditions: it is important to respect the plant's summer resting period and absolutely avoid watering it in summer. We like to combine this sage with other plants with very aromatic foliage, such as *Cistus ladanifer* var. *sulcatus* or *Tagetes lemonii*, so that their mingled scents create an amazing olfactory experience in the summer heat.

Propagation is by softwood cuttings in spring.

• *Salvia* 'Allen Chickering' is a hybrid of *Salvia clevelandii*, probably from a cross with *Salvia leucophylla*. The plant has a vigorous, upright habit. The handsome silver foliage sets off the violet-blue flowers that are produced abundantly in May–June. **HARDINESS** −8 **TO** −10 °C **DROUGHT RESISTANCE CODE** 5 (LIKE *Salvia clevelandii*, THE PLANT MAY LOSE SOME OF ITS LEAVES IN SUMMER)

Salvia fruticosa

ORIGIN EASTERN MEDITERRANEAN BASIN
HEIGHT 80 CM OR MORE
SPREAD 1 M
POSITION SUN
HARDINESS −8 TO −10 °C
DROUGHT RESISTANCE CODE 4

A shrub with evergreen, grey-green leaves that have a soft and silky texture. The long leaves have two characteristic small lobes at

To acclimatize *Salvia clevelandii* in the garden it is essential to respect its period of summer dormancy and to avoid giving it any water in summer.

LEFT *Salvia* 'Allen Chickering', *Tagetes lemonii* and *Stipa gigantea* in a garden open to the surrounding landscape.

ABOVE A dry garden in June, with *Salvia greggii* 'Variegata' in full bloom between *Perovskia* 'Blue Spire' and *Helichrysum italicum*.

BELOW The foliage of *Salvia fruticosa* gives off a strong smell of camphor. It can be used in the kitchen instead of common sage. In the background *Cistus × purpureus* is in full bloom.

their base, giving rise to the former name of this species, *Salvia trilobata*. The foliage gives off a strong scent of camphor when crushed. This sage is often used in cooking instead of *Salvia officinalis* and has been renowned since antiquity for its numerous medicinal properties. In Greece the leaves are used to make a tisane, called *faskomilo* (the general name for sage in modern Greek), sweetened with honey because of its strong taste. The plant develops into a dense bush, strongly branching from the base (the name *fruticosa* comes from the Latin *frutex*, 'a bush'). In March–April it is a veritable mass of soft and luminous mauve-pink flowers, arranged on dense spikes that seem to submerge the whole plant. *Salvia fruticosa* tolerates alkaline conditions well. It requires poor, stony soil with perfect drainage, without which it dies easily. In our garden we like to combine it with *Cistus albidus* and *Scabiosa cretica* to create a harmony of pastel tones in the spring light.

Propagation is by seed in autumn or by softwood cuttings in early spring.

Salvia greggii
Autumn Sage

ORIGIN TEXAS, MEXICO ON THE CHIHUAHUA DESERT PLATEAUX
HEIGHT 40 TO 50 CM
SPREAD 40 TO 50 CM
POSITION SUN
HARDINESS −10 TO −12 °C
DROUGHT RESISTANCE CODE 4

A shrub with small and very narrow dark green, evergreen leaves. In the heat the leaves become sticky, giving off an essential oil with a pleasant smell, fresh and sharp. In times of extreme drought the plant may lose some of its leaves, with fresh leaf buds

appearing as soon as the first autumn rains fall. The small bright red flowers open in May–June, and there is an even more generous flowering from November onwards (which is why in the United States this plant is called 'autumn sage'). *Salvia greggii* tolerates alkaline conditions well. It requires soil that is light and well-drained, otherwise it is short-lived. To maintain a compact shape, it can be cut back to about a third of its height every year at the end of winter.

Propagation is by softwood cuttings in spring.

• *Salvia greggii* 'Alba' has pure white flowers.

• *Salvia greggii* 'Furman's Red' flowers with remarkable abundance. The plant is covered in sumptuous dark red velvety flowers.

• *Salvia greggii* 'Variegata' has leaves variegated with cream. The flowers have a particularly luminous colour.

Salvia interrupta

ORIGIN MOROCCO
HEIGHT OF FOLIAGE 20 CM
HEIGHT IN FLOWER 60 CM
SPREAD 50 CM
POSITION SUN
HARDINESS −10 TO −12 °C
DROUGHT RESISTANCE CODE 4

A sub-shrub with lightly aromatic evergreen leaves divided into five leaflets. The leaves are grey-green on their upper surface and covered in white felt on the undersides. The vegetation forms a loose cushion which spreads slowly over the years as the lower branches may root where they are in contact with the soil. The flowers open in

May–June and there is often a repeat flowering in September–October. The flowers are arranged on the stems in widely spaced whorls, giving the flowering spike a discontinuous look (hence the name *interrupta*). They are a fine deep violet-blue colour and the broad lower lip is marked by two white bands which guide pollinating insects to the nectaries, like a lit-up runway. *Salvia interrupta* tolerates alkaline conditions well. It requires a light and well-drained soil, without which it is short-lived. In times of extreme drought the plant loses some of its leaves in summer, making it temporarily less ornamental.

Propagation is by seed in autumn or by softwood cuttings in spring.

Salvia lavandulifolia subsp. blancoana

ORIGIN SOUTHERN EUROPE, NORTH AFRICA
HEIGHT OF FOLIAGE 20 CM
HEIGHT IN FLOWER 40 TO 50 CM
SPREAD 60 TO 80 CM
POSITION SUN
HARDINESS −12 TO −15 °C
DROUGHT RESISTANCE CODE 4

An evergreen sub-shrub with narrow, aromatic, grey-green leaves. The leaves give off a strong smell of camphor, with an underlying penetrating and slightly insipid scent reminiscent of the black soap found in every souk in North Africa. The vegetation initially develops into a compact cushion, then gradually spreads, its lower branches rooting wherever they come into contact with the soil. In time the plant forms an excellent groundcover, very decorative as edging or in rock gardens. In April–May it is covered in dense spikes of bright blue flowers. *Salvia lavandulifolia* tolerates alkaline conditions well and prefers light, well-drained soils.

It has the same culinary and medicinal properties as the common sage, *Salvia officinalis*. Indeed, in mountainous regions of the South of France hybrids of these two species often occur where *Salvia officinalis* has become naturalized after escaping from gardens, making their identification in the wild rather tricky. In the dry garden,

however, these species are recognizable by their behaviour: the lavender-leaved sage is a robust and thriving plant which is long-lived, whereas the common sage is often very capricious in mediterranean conditions. Of the two, it is therefore the lavender-leaved sage that we prefer to use in our garden.

Propagation is by seed in autumn or by softwood cuttings in spring.

• **Salvia lavandulifolia** subsp. *vellerea* has silvery leaves which give off an extraordinary strong and fresh scent, reminiscent of lavender and eucalyptus. Fairly slow-growing, this plant has a good ground-covering habit and may in time spread significantly. In the Sierra Huétor, near Granada in southern Spain, magnificent specimens can be seen forming bushes 40 centimetres high and almost 2 metres wide. The tender blue flowers, borne on graceful spikes, open in May–June.
HARDINESS −10 TO −12 °C **DROUGHT RESISTANCE CODE** 5

Salvia leucophylla
Chaparral Sage, San Luis Purple Sage

ORIGIN SOUTHERN CALIFORNIA
HEIGHT 1.5 TO 2 M
SPREAD 1 TO 1.5 M
POSITION SUN
HARDINESS −8 TO −10 C
DROUGHT RESISTANCE CODE 5

A shrub with aromatic evergreen leaves, which in hot weather give off a curious thick smell like a mixture of bitumen and mint. To resist drought, the plant produces two distinct kinds of leaf. In winter and spring the grey-green leaves are held horizontally to catch the rays of the sun and ensure photosynthesis during the growing season. In early summer these leaves fall and are replaced by new ones. The summer leaves are narrow and packed tightly together to reduce the exposed surface area; they are covered in a fine silver down and in drought take on a magnificent white colour (*leucophylla* comes from the Greek, *leukos*, 'white' and *phyllon*, 'leaf'). In April–May

the flowers open, their very soft mauve-pink colour in perfect harmony with the light colour of the foliage. The large spires, as regular as honeycombs, last long after flowering is over, giving the plant an ornamental appearance all summer long. *Salvia leucophylla* tolerates alkaline conditions well and prefers light, well-drained soils.

Propagation is by seed in autumn or by softwood cuttings in spring.

• **Salvia leucophylla** 'Figueroa' keeps its silver, almost white, leaves throughout the year. In our garden we like to use it as a contrast plant, combining it with dark-foliaged plants such as *Cistus* × *purpureus*, *Myrtus communis* subsp. *tarentina* or *Choisya* 'Aztec Pearl'. The plant has a compact habit, not exceeding 1 m in height.

• **Salvia** 'Bee's Bliss' is a hybrid of *Salvia leucophylla*, probably from a cross with a Californian sage with a carpeting habit, *Salvia sonomensis*. *Salvia* 'Bee's Bliss' forms a remarkable, fast-growing groundcover. We were introduced to this sage by Betsy Clebsch, who grows a huge collection of sages in her California garden: it was planted in large masses, making a perfect groundcover for the large slopes around the garden. The handsome silver-grey leaves are very aromatic. The plant grows horizontally, with successive layers of long, supple branches that hug the ground. In spring the tender mauve flowers are borne on pliable, gracefully spreading inflorescences.
HARDINESS −6 TO −8 °C **DROUGHT RESISTANCE CODE** 4

Salvia interrupta requires well-drained soil, otherwise it is short-lived.

Salvia lavandulifolia subsp. *blancoana* can be used as a very decorative groundcover for rock gardens or as edging.

The foliage of *Salvia leucophylla* 'Figueroa' maintains its beautiful silver colour throughout the year.

Salvia microphylla

ORIGIN MOUNTAINS OF MEXICO
HEIGHT 80 CM TO 1 M
SPREAD 80 CM TO 1 M
POSITION SUN OR SEMI-SHADE
HARDINESS −8 TO −10 °C
DROUGHT RESISTANCE CODE 3

An evergreen shrub with green leaves with finely crenellated margins. In the garden the leaves are usually fairly large, but in the plant's natural habitat they are extremely small (the name *microphylla* comes from the Greek *mikros*, 'small', and *phyllon*, 'leaf'). When crushed, the leaves give off a sweet fruity scent. In Mexico they are used to make a pleasant-tasting tea – the plant is known there as *myrto de los montes*, 'mountain myrtle'. There are two distinct waves of flowering, separated by a summer rest period. The first flowering takes place from May to the beginning of July; a second generous flowering follows from September to November, sometimes even continuing into the winter in mild climates. The small flowers are brightly coloured – pink veering towards crimson. *Salvia microphylla* tolerates alkaline conditions well. It is unfussy about soil type, but we have noticed that it is hardier if the soil has perfect drainage. It is a robust plant and easy to grow. The older branches can be cut short each year at the end of winter to encourage vigorous and floriferous new growth.

Propagation is by softwood cuttings in autumn or spring.

• *Salvia microphylla* 'Royal Bumble' is a particularly floriferous cultivar with magnificent velvety dark red flowers.

Salvia 'Bee's Bliss' forms a good groundcover, its long supple branches growing closely over the surface of the soil.

• *Salvia* 'Christine Yeo' is a hybrid of *Salvia microphylla* and *Salvia chamaedryoides*. Blending the colours of its two parents, it has beautiful mauve flowers. **HARDINESS** −10 TO −12 °C **DROUGHT RESISTANCE CODE** 3.5

Salvia palaestina

ORIGIN SYRIA, IRAQ, IRAN, LEBANON, ISRAEL
HEIGHT OF FOLIAGE 20 CM
HEIGHT IN FLOWER 60 TO 80 CM
POSITION SUN
HARDINESS −12 TO −15 °C
DROUGHT RESISTANCE CODE 5

A rhizomatous perennial with large, grey-green leaves arranged in evergreen basal rosettes. The leaves and inflorescences are covered in a thick felt of glandular hairs. In hot weather these give off a pleasant smell of musk and passion fruit. The remarkably abundant flowers open in May–June. They are arranged in tight whorls along the strong stems, which have a very branching habit, making an impressive hemispherical mass above the plant. The beautiful pale lilac flowers are supported by large purplish-mauve bracts. *Salvia palaestina* tolerates alkaline conditions well and prefers light, well-drained soils.

Propagation is by soft tip cuttings in autumn or by seed in autumn. Unfortunately the plant does not produce seed in our garden – in its native habitat it is pollinated by a specific insect.

Salvia pomifera

ORIGIN EASTERN MEDITERRANEAN BASIN
HEIGHT 80 CM TO 1 M
SPREAD 80 CM
POSITION SUN
HARDINESS −8 TO −10 °C (IN WELL-DRAINED SOIL)
DROUGHT RESISTANCE CODE 5

A shrub with evergreen grey leaves that sometimes have gold highlights. The tapering, lance-shaped leaves have irregularly undulating margins. When crushed, they give off a strong smell of camphor, similar to that of *Salvia officinalis* but more intense. In Greece, incidentally, this sage has traditionally been used for the same culinary or medicinal purposes as *Salvia officinalis*, but in smaller quantities. In its natural habitat the young branches bear curious, slightly transparent galls that look like little apples (*pomifera* comes from

The bright red flowers of Salvia microphylla mingle with the silky shoots of Dorycnium hirsutum.

the Latin *pomum*, 'apple', and *ferre*, 'to bear'). These pungent and juicy galls are eaten as a great delicacy by children throughout the eastern Mediterranean. The large, blue-mauve flowers open in May. They contrast with the reddish-purple bracts, which remain on the plant for a long time after flowering, becoming more and more voluminous and decorative. *Salvia pomifera* tolerates alkaline conditions well. It requires poor, stony soil with perfect drainage since it is not very able to withstand winter wet.

Propagation is by seed in autumn or by softwood cuttings in autumn or spring.

Salvia sclarea
Clary

ORIGIN SOUTHERN EUROPE, NORTH AFRICA, ASIA
HEIGHT IN FLOWER 1 TO 1.2 M
SPREAD 60 TO 80 CM
POSITION SUN
HARDINESS −10 TO −12 °C
DROUGHT RESISTANCE CODE 4

A perennial or biennial with large crimped leaves and velvety young shoots. The leaves are arranged in large rosettes which are evergreen in winter. The foliage gives off a sharp, fresh and penetrating smell reminiscent of musk and grapefruit. In spring the strong branching inflorescences rise from the rosette and gradually unfurl their spectacular croziers. The bicoloured flowers, with a pale blue upper lip and a white lower lip, open in May–June, set off by large mauvey-pink bracts that are extremely decorative. All parts of the inflorescence are glandular and aromatic. Famed since antiquity for its numerous medicinal properties, clary is now cultivated for an essence used in the making of perfume. In Haute Provence, escapee clary plants can sometimes be spotted showing off their monumental inflorescences in the midst of fields of lavender, creating a lovely scene which has inspired us to copy it in our garden. *Salvia sclarea* tolerates alkaline conditions well and prefers light, well-drained soils. If the plant is allowed to set seed it may die after flowering. However, we can forgive it for this since it self-seeds so easily, filling any gaps in the border. Alternatively, the inflorescences can be

The large, decorative bracts of *Salvia sclarea* last for a long time after flowering.

removed just as they begin to dry out, which will keep the plant as a perennial and also prevent it from self-seeding everywhere.

Propagation is by seed in autumn.

Salvia × jamensis

ORIGIN A NATURAL HYBRID OFTEN SEEN IN THE MOUNTAINS OF MEXICO
HEIGHT 60 TO 80 CM
SPREAD 80 CM OR MORE
POSITION SUN
HARDINESS −15 °C AND BELOW
DROUGHT RESISTANCE CODE 3

A natural hybrid of *Salvia greggii* and *Salvia microphylla*, *Salvia × jamensis* is a shrub with narrow, dark green, evergreen leaves. In the heat the young shoots become sticky, releasing an essential oil with a strong, acid scent. The vigorous vegetation forms a regular mass, often wider than it is tall. The small velvety crimson flowers harmonize well with the dark foliage. They open first in May–June, then the plant has a second flowering from September to November, often even more generous. *Salvia × jamensis* tolerates alkaline conditions well and is

The inflorescences of *Salvia palaestina* are covered in glandular hairs, and in hot weather give off an agreeable scent of musk and passion fruit.

The spectacular flowering spikes of *Salvia sclarea* can light up an entire border.

unfussy about soil type. It is a robust plant that is easy to grow. It can be combined with *Rosmarinus officinalis* 'Boule', *Ceanothus griseus* var. *horizontalis* 'Yankee Point' and *Cistus × pulverulentus* to colonize large borders or slopes which you want to cover quickly.

Propagation is by softwood cuttings in spring.

• *Salvia africana-lutea* is a shrub with handsome and very aromatic grey-green foliage. In a mild climate it can flower continuously from spring until autumn. The large flowers are bright yellow when they open, quickly turning orange-brown. They are surrounded by large, rust-coloured calyces, shaped like an inverted bell, which remain on the plant long after flowering is finished and give it a striking appearance. *Salvia africana-lutea* can be seen growing in the fynbos near the Cape of Good Hope, together with *Myrsine africana* and *Lessertia frutescens* in a landscape sculpted by the violent winds. It withstands salt spray perfectly. **ORIGIN** SOUTH AFRICA **HARDINESS** −4 TO −6 °C **DROUGHT RESISTANCE CODE** 5

• *Salvia argentea* is a perennial or biennial with a rosette of crimped evergreen leaves. Entirely covered in long white hairs, the silvery leaves have a remarkable and very decorative texture. The white flowers, borne on solid branching inflorescences, open in May–June. To be on the safe side, the plant should be pruned after flowering to make sure it remains perennial – otherwise it may die, having devoted all its energy to producing seeds. **ORIGIN** SOUTHERN EUROPE, NORTH AFRICA **HARDINESS** −15 °C AND BELOW **DROUGHT RESISTANCE CODE** 4

• *Salvia darcyi* is a rhizomatous perennial with very aromatic grey-green foliage. The vegetation is completely deciduous, often causing anxiety in novice gardeners since the plant looks utterly dead in winter. Nevertheless, faithfully every year, numerous shoots emerge from the soil in spring as soon as the ground is warm. The stems grow rapidly and flower in early summer. The tubular flowers are full of nectar and are the delight of hummingbirds in their natural habitat, while their bright coral red colour is the delight of gardeners. **ORIGIN** MEXICO, IN THE MOUNTAINS **HARDINESS** −10 TO −12 °C **DROUGHT RESISTANCE CODE** 4

• *Salvia dominica* is a shrub with grey leaves covered in glandular hairs which release an essential oil with a smell so intense and acrid that it is almost suffocating. Francis Hallé, whose colourful courses thrilled a whole generation of young botanists at Montpellier, considered the

RIGHT Pollinated by hummingbirds in its natural habitat, *Salvia darcyi* has tubular flowers full of nectar.

BELOW *Salvia argentea* shelters from the heat beneath a thick mantle of white hairs.

smell of *Salvia dominica* to be like the armpit of a boxer after a difficult fight. The branching spikes of white flowers open from April to June. **ORIGIN** SYRIA, LEBANON, ISRAEL **HARDINESS** −10 TO −12 °C **DROUGHT RESISTANCE CODE** 5

• *Salvia indica* has beautiful undulating leaves covered in silky hairs, among which are thousands of essential oil glands. It is a perennial or biennial with a basal rosette that is evergreen in winter but entirely deciduous after the spring flowering. The sumptuous violet-blue flowers, with an upper lip gracefully curved in a sickle shape, are arranged in widely spaced spires on velvety stems. **ORIGIN** EASTERN MEDITERRANEAN BASIN, MIDDLE EAST **HARDINESS** −8 TO −10 °C **DROUGHT RESISTANCE CODE** 5

• *Salvia mellifera* is a shrub with handsome dark green, aromatic foliage (in California it is known as 'black sage' because of its very dark foliage). We like to use it as a contrast plant among plants with silver foliage, such as *Salvia leucophylla*, *Ballota acetabulosa* or *Artemisia arborescens*. The small white flowers on discreet spikes open in April–May, attracting hordes of bees (hence the name *mellifera*). **ORIGIN** CALIFORNIA, IN THE COASTAL CHAPARRAL **HARDINESS** −6 TO −8 °C **DROUGHT RESISTANCE CODE** 4

• *Salvia officinalis*, the common sage, is a medicinal plant renowned since antiquity for its countless virtues. In the Middle Ages so many properties were attributed to it that it was held to be a plant of salvation (the name *Salvia* comes from the Latin *salvare*, 'to save'). It was for a long time used to treat

gynaecological problems and was known as the 'fertility plant'. Unfortunately, in the dry garden the common sage is capricious and not very reliable. In our garden the numerous cultivars with green, purple or variegated leaves are distinguished by the rapidity with which they die. Only *Salvia officinalis* 'Berggarten', with particularly broad leaves, just about manages to survive for us. I often advise lovers of aromatic plants to replace common sage with the leaves of lavender, which has similar culinary and medicinal properties, but which is a lot easier to grow. **ORIGIN** BALKANS **HARDINESS** −15 °C AND BELOW **DROUGHT RESISTANCE CODE** 2

• *Salvia staminea* is a perennial with green leaves arranged in ground-hugging rosettes. The tall, branching spikes bear a multitude of beautiful white flowers, sometimes tinged with pink, in May–June. The upper lip of the flower is prolonged by a gracefully arched stigma, like a long thread (*staminea* comes from the Latin *stamineus*, 'equipped with a thread'). The plant self-seeds prolifically in poor, stony soil. It can be used as a colonizing plant, along with *Euphorbia characias* and *Centranthus ruber*, to fill wild areas in the garden. **ORIGIN** MOUNTAINOUS REGIONS OF TURKEY, ARMENIA AND IRAN **HARDINESS** −15 °C AND BELOW **DROUGHT RESISTANCE CODE** 4

To learn more about sages, I recommend Betsy Clebsch's very well-documented book *The New Book of Salvias* (see Further Reading).

Santolina chamaecyparissus
(Asteraceae) Cotton Lavender

ORIGIN SOUTH OF FRANCE, SPAIN
HEIGHT 20 TO 40 CM, SOMETIMES MORE
SPREAD 40 TO 80 CM, SOMETIMES MORE
POSITION SUN
HARDINESS −12 TO −15 °C
DROUGHT RESISTANCE CODE 5

A shrub with narrow, silver-grey, evergreen leaves that are finely cut. When crushed, the foliage gives off a penetrating smell like a mixture of olive oil and turpentine. It has vermifuge and insecticidal properties and has traditionally been used, like lavender, to keep wardrobes moth-free. The plant develops into a dense cushion, its height varying widely depending on the soil and growing conditions. The vegetation gradually spreads to form a large groundcover, thanks to the fact that its side branches root easily wherever they are in contact with the soil. The rounded heads of golden-yellow flowers open in June. As they fade they emit a sweetish and not very pleasant smell. The plant can be clipped immediately after flowering, which both removes the fading flowers and keeps the plant compact. *Santolina chamaecyparissus* tolerates alkaline conditions well. In gardens it is often grown in soil that is too rich, which makes it soft and sad-looking. Poor, stony, hot soils with perfect drainage are what it likes. In its natural habitat it can be seen clinging to cracks in the rocks, for instance on the crest of the Sainte-Baume massif in Provence where it forms striking miniature cushions. Beware, all santolinas are prone to *Phytophthora*, a fungus affecting the collar of the plant which develops in hot moist conditions: you must above all avoid watering them in summer.

Propagation is by semi-ripe cuttings in autumn.

• *Santolina benthamiana* has grey-green foliage. Gardeners who don't particularly like the usual yellow colour of santolina flowers will be delighted by this species, which has flowers of a subtle ivory-tinged white. **ORIGIN** SPAIN **HARDINESS** −12 TO −15 °C **DROUGHT RESISTANCE CODE** 4

In the garden santolinas are often grown in conditions that are too rich for them. Stony ground and perfect drainage are what they like best. Here, *Santolina chamaecyparissus* grows on the crest of the Sainte-Baume massif in Provence.

Not all santolinas have bright yellow flowers – the different species cover a range of colours from white, ivory, sulphur yellow to golden yellow. From left to right: *Santolina benthamiana*, *Santolina lindavica* and *Santolina viridis* 'Primrose Gem'.

• *Santolina insulare*, very similar to *Santolina chamaecyparissus*, is distinguished by its aggressive smell, like a whiff of ether, hot metal and industrial solvent. You should sniff it rather tentatively, for it's a fairly violent experience. This plant is found in the limestone mountains of western Sardinia, where it colonizes the stony expanses wandered over by sheep, goats, wild pigs (and occasionally botanists): there's nothing like a nauseating smell to keep aggressors away. Naturally very compact, this plant is exceptionally robust. **ORIGIN** SARDINIA **HARDINESS** −10 TO −12 °C **DROUGHT RESISTANCE CODE** 5

• *Santolina lindavica* has grey-green foliage with a delicate scent and flowers of a soft primrose yellow. The plant forms a regular ball shape and is particularly long-lived: it is our favourite santolina. We like to use it as a contrast plant, to set off the shades of blue in our large lavender garden. Of uncertain origin, this plant may be a hybrid of *Santolina chamaecyparissus* and *Santolina benthamiana*. **HARDINESS** −12 TO −15 °C **DROUGHT RESISTANCE CODE** 5

• *Santolina neapolitana* 'Edward Bowles' has leaves that are cut into long lacy feathers. The flowers of this santolina are a pretty luminous lemon-yellow colour. **ORIGIN** ITALY **HARDINESS** −10 TO −12 °C **DROUGHT RESISTANCE CODE** 4

• *Santolina rosmarinifolia* 'Caerulea' is very different from other santolinas. It has linear, untoothed leaves of an amazing silvery-blue colour that contrasts well with the golden yellow flowers. **ORIGIN** SPAIN **HARDINESS** −10 TO −12 °C **DROUGHT RESISTANCE CODE** 4

• *Santolina viridis* 'Primrose Gem' has finely toothed dark green leaves. When crushed they give off a rich, pleasant scent of olives, eucalyptus and bergamot-flavoured sweets. The flowers are a soft colour, hesitating between pastel yellow and ivory. The plant has dense vegetation that lends itself well to clipping as topiary, so it can be turned into a perfect ball. **ORIGIN** SPAIN **HARDINESS** −12 TO −15 °C **DROUGHT RESISTANCE CODE** 4

Sarcopoterium spinosum
(Rosaceae) Spiny Burnet

ORIGIN EASTERN MEDITERRANEAN BASIN
HEIGHT 40 TO 50 CM, SOMETIMES UP TO 1 M OR MORE
SPREAD 60 TO 80 CM, SOMETIMES A LOT MORE
POSITION SUN
HARDINESS −12 TO −15 °C
DROUGHT RESISTANCE CODE 6

A shrub with small, dark green, finely cut leaves that are evergreen in winter. The stems end in branching spines, forming a very dense and impenetrable mass. In extreme drought the plant may lose all its leaves in summer, revealing its amazing skeleton of interlocking thorns. It is very common around Jerusalem and is said to have been used for Christ's crown of thorns. The plant develops very variably, depending on the conditions to which it is subject. In the wild, where it faces extremely harsh conditions, it often forms very tight balls, characteristic of the degraded garrigues of the eastern Mediterranean Basin. In gardens, by contrast, it may grow to a considerable size, becoming a monstrous mass which looks as if it wants to devour all the other plants around it.

In spite of their thorny appearance the branches are fairly pliable. Following a traditional Bedouin custom, the Israeli army sometimes uses it as an emergency mattress, since the fine thorns do not pierce through the thickness of a good blanket. Minute red flowers appear in spring, followed by clusters of small brown fruits. *Sarcopoterium spinosum* tolerates alkaline conditions well and withstands salt spray perfectly. It prefers poor, stony, well-drained soils. In our garden we like to use its spiny structure to create a contrast with the soft texture of *Ballota acetabulosa*, *Cistus albidus* or *Phlomis purpurea*.

Propagation is by seed in autumn or by softwood cuttings in spring.

Satureja thymbra
(Lamiaceae) Savory

ORIGIN EASTERN MEDITERRANEAN BASIN
HEIGHT 50 TO 60 CM
SPREAD 60 TO 80 CM
POSITION SUN
HARDINESS −8 TO −10 °C
DROUGHT RESISTANCE CODE 5

A shrub with small, dark green, evergreen leaves that are thick and leathery. If you look at them under a magnifying glass you will clearly see the countless essential oil glands that are dotted over their undersides. The leaves give off a strong hot and piquant smell, reminiscent of oregano. The different species of savory are very useful in the kitchen for flavouring sauces and grilled meat. They also have numerous medicinal properties, one of which is especially famous. In ancient Greece savory was renowned for its aphrodisiac qualities, while in Egypt it was an ingredient of all love philtres. And the Marquis de Sade would give his conquests a sweet made of powdered savory and honey to arouse them before bedtime. In the Middle Ages savory was considered to be a plant of the devil because of the diabolical sexual appetite it awoke in decent people (*Satureja* comes from the Greek *satyros*, 'satyr').

The plant forms a perfectly regular large cushion. From April to June it is covered in pretty pinkish-mauve flowers grouped on short verticillate spikes. *Satureja thymbra*

In the garden *Sarcopoterium spinosum* can grow to a considerable size, burying neighbouring plants under its monumental vegetation.

he spiny shape of *Sarcopoterium spinosum* characterizes coastal landscapes in the eastern Mediterranean.

tolerates alkaline conditions well; it prefers poor, stony, well-drained soils. It is an easily grown, long-lived and very decorative plant.

Propagation is by seed in autumn or by softwood cuttings in spring.

• *Satureja montana,* Winter Savory, has a slightly peppery scent, milder than that of *Satureja thymbra.* The numerous white flowers appear from May to July and sometimes continue until September if the summer is not too dry. They are very rich in nectar and produce a delicious, rare honey, even more delicate than lavender honey. **ORIGIN** SOUTHERN EUROPE **HARDINESS** −15 °C AND BELOW **DROUGHT RESISTANCE CODE** 3.5

Scabiosa cretica
(Dipsacaceae)

ORIGIN MEDITERRANEAN BASIN (BUT NOT CRETE)
HEIGHT 60 CM
SPREAD 60 TO 80 CM
POSITION SUN
HARDINESS −10 TO −12 °C
DROUGHT RESISTANCE CODE 5

Sometimes classified as belonging to the genus *Lomelosia, Scabiosa cretica* is a shrub with velvety, ash-green, evergreen leaves. The plant naturally forms a regular ball shape. The remarkably abundant flowers appear in succession from March to July. A soft lavender blue, they harmonize perfectly with the silky foliage. They are followed by large spherical seed heads that are ornamental throughout the whole summer. These seed heads have a papery texture and

rattle in the wind like the dry heads of *Catananche.* In times of extreme drought the plant becomes dormant and loses part of its foliage, so that it is temporarily less ornamental until the first rains of autumn. *Scabiosa cretica* tolerates alkaline conditions well and withstands salt spray. In the wild it lives in cracks in seaside cliffs, but in gardens it is very adaptable and seems unfussy about soil type.

Propagation is by seed in autumn or by softwood cuttings in early spring.

• *Scabiosa ucranica* is a perennial with light foliage, covered in small, creamy-white flowers from May to September. The plant self-seeds prolifically, producing a 'lawn' of seedlings that fill any gaps in the border. We like to combine it with other colonizing perennials, such as *Erodium trifolium, Goniolimon speciosum* or *Asphodelus fistulosus,* to fill neglected parts of the garden rapidly. **ORIGIN** EASTERN MEDITERRANEAN BASIN **HARDINESS** −12 TO −15 °C **DROUGHT RESISTANCE CODE** 4

Sedum sediforme
(Crassulaceae) Stonecrop

ORIGIN MEDITERRANEAN BASIN
HEIGHT OF FOLIAGE 10 TO 15 CM
HEIGHT IN FLOWER 20 TO 30 CM
POSITION SUN
HARDINESS −15 °C AND BELOW
DROUGHT RESISTANCE CODE 5

A perennial with fleshy evergreen leaves that are cylindrical and pointed. The leaves,

arranged in tight spirals along the length of the stems, are grey-green with blue highlights, but may take on reddish tints in winter. The stems root on contact with the soil and the plant forms a small, very decorative groundcover. In the wild it likes stony ground and stone walls, where it can live almost without any soil. In June upright stems bear panicles of pretty pale yellow flowers which seem to soften the harsh light of early summer. *Sedum sediforme* tolerates alkaline conditions well; it prefers poor, stony soils with perfect drainage. It is one of the most robust sedums, capable of surviving in very difficult conditions, for example on green roofs with a very thin layer of substrate.

Propagation is by stem section cuttings in autumn, winter or spring. You can also pull the plant to pieces and simply place leaves and bits of stem on to a light substrate, where they will root after a few weeks.

• *Sedum album* likes shallow stony soils, where it forms a carpet of small, shiny, fleshy leaves. Green in spring, these turn red to a greater or lesser degree in summer in periods of intense drought. The plant is covered in white flowers in late spring. **ORIGIN** EUROPE, ASIA MINOR, NORTH AFRICA **HARDINESS** −15 °C AND BELOW **DROUGHT RESISTANCE CODE** 4

• *Sedum album* 'Coral Carpet' takes on a spectacular red colour throughout the winter.

Beneath its innocent flowers, *Satureja thymbra* conceals a fiery temperament (*Satureja* comes from the Greek *satyros,* 'a satyr').

Grouped in large heads, the flowers of *Scabiosa cretica* appear in succession from March to July, followed by ornamental spherical seedheads.

• *Sedum ochroleucum* has leaves arranged in narrow spirals along the length of the stems. The green foliage takes on very decorative hues in winter, from metallic grey to mauve. The tender yellow flowers appear in early summer. **ORIGIN** SOUTHERN EUROPE, ASIA MINOR **HARDINESS** −15 °C AND BELOW **DROUGHT RESISTANCE CODE** 4

• *Sedum palmeri* forms a clump of light green leaves, marked with red in winter. It is an easily cultivated plant that is often grown in pots on balconies, where it needs minimal maintenance. It is appreciated for its abundant golden yellow spring flowering. In gardens it is happy on drystone walls, in which it can anchor its deep roots. **ORIGIN** MEXICO **HARDINESS** −10 TO −12 °C **DROUGHT RESISTANCE CODE** 4

There are numerous other species of *Sedum* of interest for the dry garden. Patrick Nicolas grows a huge collection of them in his specialist nursery (see Useful Addresses).

Sempervivum tectorum
(Crassulaceae) House Leek

ORIGIN MOUNTAINS OF SOUTHERN EUROPE
HEIGHT OF FOLIAGE 5 TO 10 CM
HEIGHT IN FLOWER 15 TO 20 CM
SPREAD 30 CM OR MORE
POSITION SUN
HARDINESS −15 °C AND BELOW
DROUGHT RESISTANCE CODE 3

A perennial that forms a rosette of thick and leathery succulent leaves, packed together like an artichoke. The green leaves end in a

Sedum sediforme seems to survive almost without soil in rubble walls that surround formerly cultivated areas now overrun by the garrigue.

Sedum album is a carpeting plant that likes poor, well-drained soil.

Sedum palmeri is a plant that is easy to grow either in the ground or in a pot.

dark point and often take on a red colour when the plant is growing in tough conditions. The plant spreads by stolons and in a few years forms a dense mass of juxtaposed rosettes. In early summer the inflorescences rise up bearing clusters of pretty pink star-shaped flowers. The main rosette dies after flowering and is quickly replaced by many side rosettes. The plant is renowned for its numerous medicinal virtues. The sap of the leaves applied directly to corns on the feet is, it would seem, very effective. The plant is happy in cracks between rocks or in the joints of stone walls. It has a remarkable ability to survive in a very small amount of soil (*Sempervivum* comes from the Latin *semper*, 'always', and *vivus*, 'alive'). In mountain regions it was traditionally planted on the roofs of houses, where it was believed to give protection from lightning (*tectorum* comes from the Latin *tectum*, 'roof'). It is an excellent plant for growing in a pot on the terrace, where it requires little care and tolerates irregular watering. It prefers light, well-drained soils.

Propagation is by division of the rosettes in autumn or winter.

Senecio cineraria
(Asteraceae)

ORIGIN WESTERN MEDITERRANEAN BASIN
HEIGHT 60 CM
SPREAD 60 TO 80 CM
POSITION SUN
HARDINESS −12 TO −15 °C
DROUGHT RESISTANCE CODE 5

A sub-shrub with evergreen leaves divided into irregular lobes. The upper surface of the leaves is covered in a light, ash-grey felt (*cineraria* comes from the Latin *cinis*, genitive *cineris*, 'ash'). The inflorescences, young branches and the undersides of the leaves are covered in an even thicker white felt, enabling the plant to minimize evapotranspiration effectively. The golden yellow flowers open in May–June and are grouped in numerous heads on the branching flowering stems. The seeds are easily dispersed by the wind, thanks to their large plume of white silk (*Senecio* is from the Latin *senex*, 'old man', alluding to the strands which crown the seeds like white hair). *Senecio cineraria* tolerates alkaline conditions well. It prefers light, well-drained soils: stagnant winter wet can cause its stock to rot. Its excellent ability to withstand salt spray means that is often planted as a first-line plant close to the sea.

Propagation is by seed in autumn or by softwood cuttings in spring.

• *Senecio vira-vira* has beautiful, finely cut leaves of a remarkable and very luminous, silver-white. The very soft creamy-yellow colour of the flowers blends harmoniously into the light foliage. *Senecio vira-vira* is a good plant for inclusion in large beds of other silver-leaved plants, for instance *Centaurea pulcherrima*, *Buddleja marrubiifolia* and *Helichrysum orientale*. **ORIGIN** ARGENTINA **HARDINESS** −8 TO −10 °C **DROUGHT RESISTANCE CODE** 3

There is nothing easier than propagating *Sempervivum tectorum*: its delicate aerial roots are already waiting around the base of each rosette.

ABOVE *Senecio cineraria* is often grown in seaside gardens because of its excellent ability to withstand salt spray.

RIGHT The heavy bunches of flowers on *Sesbania punicea* are produced in succession throughout the summer, provided that the developing seedpods are regularly removed.

Sesbania punicea
(Fabaceae)

ORIGIN SOUTH AMERICA, FROM BRAZIL
TO ARGENTINA
HEIGHT 2 M
SPREAD 1 M
POSITION SUN
HARDINESS –6 TO –8 °C
DROUGHT RESISTANCE CODE 4

A shrub with elegant green leaves that are deciduous and divided into many leaflets. giving the plant an airy look. The bright orange-red flowers, grouped in heavy hanging clusters, appear in June–July and are followed by numerous winged seedpods. If these seedpods are removed while still green, flowering will continue uninterrupted from June to September, making *Sesbania* one of the most spectacular plants in the dry garden in summer.

The plant self-seeds easily and flowers in its first year. We always leave a few seedlings to grow on to ensure that we have a replacement for the plant, since its lifespan is short – about five to eight years. *Sesbania punicea* tolerates alkaline conditions well; it prefers friable, fairly deep soils. We like to combine it with *Caesalpinia gilliesii*, *Campsis grandiflora* and *Kniphofia* 'Géant' in a large planting with hot colours which celebrate the arrival of summer.

Propagation is by seed in autumn after hot-water treatment: pour boiling water on to the seeds and leave them to swell overnight.

Spartium junceum
(Fabaceae) Broom

ORIGIN SOUTHERN SPAIN, NORTH AFRICA,
WESTERN ASIA

HEIGHT 2 TO 3 M
SPREAD 1 TO 2 M
POSITION SUN
HARDINESS –12 TO –15 °C
DROUGHT RESISTANCE CODE 5

An upright shrub with tapering, cylindrical, rush-like branches. To reduce evapotranspiration, the few small leaves fall before the onset of the heat: it is the green stems that carry out photosynthesis for almost all the year. Artisans have long extracted from these stems their pliable and very strong fibres by retting, in order to make ropes (the name *Spartium* comes from the Greek *spartē*, 'rope'). In the Roman period the fibres were also used to make sails, while in the South of France they were woven into tough clothing. The clusters of flowers appear in May–June on the tips of the stems, transforming the shrub into a spectacular ball of yellow. The flowers are pleasantly scented – in still weather they can perfume an entire section of the garden. *Spartium junceum* tolerates alkaline conditions well and is unfussy about soil type. Its lifespan is relatively short, but it self-seeds freely, especially in poor, stony parts of the garden.

Propagation is by seed in autumn after hot-water treatment: pour boiling water on to the seeds and leave them overnight to swell.

Sphaeralcea ambigua
(Malvaceae)

ORIGIN SEMI-DESERT ZONES OF THE SOUTHWESTERN
UNITED STATES
HEIGHT 1 TO 1.25 M
SPREAD 1 M OR MORE
POSITION SUN
HARDINESS –10 TO –12 °C
DROUGHT RESISTANCE CODE 6

The scented flowers of *Spartium junceum* perfume the garden in late spring.

A sub-shrub with evergreen grey leaves with crenellated margins, sometimes irregularly lobed. The plant spreads slowly by means of its rhizomatous stock, in time forming a large, light and rounded mass (*Sphaeralcea* comes from the Greek *sphaira*, 'globe', and *Alcea*, the name of various plants of the Malvaceae family). The flowers, grouped in each leaf axil, are shaped like small open cups and are a delicate translucent salmon pink veined with bright orange. The plant flowers throughout its growing season, usually from April to July and again from September to November, but in mild climates sometimes throughout the year. *Sphaeralcea ambigua* tolerates alkaline conditions well; it prefers light, well-drained soils. It can be cut back hard at the end of winter to encourage vigorous and very floriferous new growth.

Propagation is by seed in autumn or by softwood cuttings in autumn or spring.

Stachys cretica
(Lamiaceae)

ORIGIN MEDITERRANEAN BASIN
HEIGHT OF FOLIAGE 15 CM
HEIGHT IN FLOWER 40 TO 50 CM
POSITION SUN
HARDINESS −12 TO −15 °C
DROUGHT RESISTANCE CODE 4

A perennial with basal rosettes of evergreen leaves. The leaves are grey-green, with a delicately embossed texture, and are covered in long silky hairs that give them a soft and velvety appearance. The small, pinkish-mauve flowers open in May–June. They are not very visible amongst the silky mass of spires – it is really the graceful spikes that are of visual interest (*stachys* means an ear of corn in Greek). *Stachys cretica* tolerates alkaline conditions well. It prefers light, well-drained soils, as the stock easily rots if there is excess winter wet. The faded inflorescences can be cut back at the end of summer to encourage the growth of new leaves, which form a very decorative velvety carpet in autumn.

Propagation is by seed in autumn.

A native of the semi-desert regions of the southwest United States, *Sphaeralcea ambigua* is extremely drought resistant.

• *Stachys byzantina* is famed for its elongated leaves covered in long silky hairs which have given it its common name, 'Lamb's Ears'. The plant does best in friable, deep and well-drained soil, where it forms an extensive groundcover thanks to its rhizomes. The small mauveish flowers are held on large woolly spikes, which can be cut back at the end of flowering to prevent the plant from becoming bare at the base. **ORIGIN** FROM THE CAUCASUS TO IRAN **HARDINESS** −15 °C AND BELOW **DROUGHT RESISTANCE CODE** 3

Stipa calamagrostis
(Poaceae) Feather Grass

ORIGIN MOUNTAINS OF CENTRAL AND SOUTHERN EUROPE
HEIGHT OF FOLIAGE 50 CM
HEIGHT IN FLOWER 70 CM
SPREAD 60 TO 80 CM, SOMETIMES MORE
POSITION SUN
HARDINESS −15 °C AND BELOW
DROUGHT RESISTANCE CODE 4

Sometimes classed in the *Achnaterum* genus, *Stipa calamagrostis* is a grass with dense and pliant foliage. The tightly packed stems develop from short rhizomes that enable the stock to spread gradually until it forms a strong clump (*calamagrostis* comes from the Greek, *kalamos*, 'reed', and the Latin *agrōstis*, 'grass'). The long green leaves turn straw-yellow in winter. In spring they open wide to catch the sun and ensure photosynthesis during the growing season. Conversely, in summer they roll up in a gutter shape, protecting the stomata on their undersides in order to reduce water loss. In June–July the luminous silver-green

Stachys cretica in the White Mountains of Crete.

inflorescences open into long plumed spindles, whose weight gives the plant a magnificent fountain-like habit. As they fade, the flowerheads take on a fine, warm golden colour and remain on the plant until the first autumn frosts, making it ornamental for many months. *Stipa calamagrostis* tolerates alkaline conditions well; it prefers light, well-drained soils.

Thanks to its long summer flowering, it is one of the most interesting grasses for a dry garden. We like to place it in the

The cottony spikes of *Stachys byzantina* rise among the faded flowerheads of *Allium christophii*.

ABOVE In spite of drought, *Stipa calamagrostis* flowers throughout the summer.

ABOVE RIGHT *Stipa capillata*, a mass of softness, is one of the easiest grasses to cultivate in the dry garden.

RIGHT The 'angel's hair' of *Stipa barbata* bows down in wave after wave under the blustery tramontane wind.

foreground in front of *Pistacia lentiscus*, *Myrtus communis* subsp. *tarentina* or *Cistus* × *ledon*, their dark foliage setting off the lightness of its fine silvery inflorescences.

Propagation is by seed in autumn.

• *Stipa barbata* compensates for its rather meagre clump of leaves by a flowering that is sumptuously extravagant. In June its long 'angel's hair' opens in stunning volutes that come alive in the slightest breeze, creating a most striking sight in the low evening sunlight. ORIGIN STEPPES OF SOUTHERN EUROPE, NORTH AFRICA AND ASIA MINOR HARDINESS −12 TO −15 °C DROUGHT RESISTANCE CODE 5

• *Stipa capillata* is an easily grown grass that deserves to be more widely planted in dry gardens. In June–July delicate silver inflorescences appear which have a tousled silhouette and take on a fine golden colour as they mature. ORIGIN SOUTHERN EUROPE, ASIA MINOR HARDINESS −15 °C DROUGHT RESISTANCE CODE 5

• *Stipa gigantea* (Golden Oats) is a robust and extremely decorative plant. In May–June the light inflorescences at the tips of the strong, upright stems dominate the compact mass of the foliage. The faded inflorescences remain on the plant for months, maintaining its elegance

through summer and autumn. ORIGIN SPAIN, PORTUGAL, MOROCCO HARDINESS −12 TO −15 °C DROUGHT RESISTANCE CODE 5

• *Stipa pennata* covers vast expanses of the high plateaux of the South of France with its 'angel's hair', growing among *Teucrium aureum*, *Lavandula angustifolia* and *Euphorbia cyparissias*. Although markedly more compact than *Stipa barbata*, *Stipa pennata* has the same delicacy and lightness, as well as the same 'hair', which moves in the mistral or tramontane to create moments of great beauty. ORIGIN MOUNTAINOUS REGIONS OF SOUTHERN EUROPE AND ASIA MINOR HARDINESS −15 °C AND BELOW DROUGHT RESISTANCE CODE 5

• *Stipa tenacissima* is appreciated by the sheep and dromedaries that cross the steppe-like plateaux of Morocco, where

the plant, known as 'alfa', is very common. Its long leaves are supple and very strong and arc used for making ropes, baskets and house mats, as well as the mats used in oil presses. Alfa fibres are also woven together with goat's hair for the tents used by nomads. The plant is covered in long inflorescences in spring and early summer, giving it a handsome silhouette, tall and slim. ORIGIN SPAIN, MOROCCO HARDINESS −12 TO −15 °C DROUGHT RESISTANCE CODE 6

• *Stipa tenuissima* has arching linear leaves growing in the shape of a fountain. In early summer the fine, silver inflorescences are followed by seeds packed together in a mass that is rough to the touch like unspun fibres (*Stipa* is the Latin for 'tow' – the coarse fibres of plants prepared for spinning). The plant self-seeds prolifically and can become invasive. It is advisable to take care that it does not escape into the wild. **ORIGIN** TEXAS, NEW MEXICO, MEXICO **HARDINESS** −12 TO −15 °C **DROUGHT RESISTANCE CODE** 5

Tagetes lemonii
(Asteraceae) Mountain Marigold

ORIGIN ARIZONA, NEW MEXICO, MEXICO
HEIGHT 1 M OR MORE
SPREAD 1 M OR MORE
POSITION SUN OR SEMI-SHADE
HARDINESS THE VEGETATION IS DESTROYED AT ABOUT −4 °C, BUT THE STOCK SURVIVES TO −8 TO −10 °C
DROUGHT RESISTANCE CODE 4

A sub-shrub with green leaves finely cut into toothed leaflets. In a mild climate the vegetation is evergreen, but in our garden it is cut down by the cold every winter. However, in spring the plant easily sends out fresh growth from the stock, the new shoots piercing directly through the ground (*Tagetes* comes from *Tages*, the name of an Etruscan divinity who was supposed to have emerged from freshly worked soil). The leaves give off a strong and pungent smell, fresh and acid, like a mixture of parsley, mandarins and mint tea. They are traditionally used in Mexico to make a delicious tisane. In our garden the first flowers open as soon as the nights become

Stipa tenuissima self-seeds prolifically in the most difficult parts of the garden.

cooler at the end of summer. They then continue in succession throughout the whole of the autumn, and sometimes right through until spring if the plant doesn't

suffer from frost in the winter. The single, bright yellow-orange daisy flowers are grouped in large corymbs at the tips of the stems. *Tagetes lemonii* tolerates alkaline

Stipa tenacissima and *Chamaerops humilis* at Cabo de Gata, the driest area in Spain.

conditions well; it prefers friable, fairly deep, well-drained soils. We like to grow it in combination with *Caryopteris incana*, *Ceratostigma griffithii* and *Salvia chamaedryoides* to create a lovely autumn scene of yellow and blue.

Propagation is by softwood cuttings in spring.

Tanacetum densum subsp. amanii
(Asteraceae)

ORIGIN ANATOLIA
HEIGHT 15 CM
SPREAD 30 TO 40 CM
POSITION SUN
HARDINESS −15 °C AND BELOW
DROUGHT RESISTANCE CODE 4

A sub-shrub with evergreen silver leaves that become almost white in summer. The plant forms a thick carpet, spreading gradually by means of its stems which root wherever they come in contact with the soil. In time it makes an excellent groundcover. The leaves are finely cut like delicate lace and are covered in a cottony down that reflects the light. When crushed, they release a sweet-smelling essential oil, reminiscent of powdered milk and linseed oil. The yellow flowers, grouped in rounded heads on short, branching inflorescences, appear in late spring and remain on the plant for a long time (the name *Tanacetum* is thought to derive from the Greek word *athanatos*, 'immortal', referring to the inflorescences, which can be dried like those of everlasting flowers). The plant does not flower abundantly, but its beauty lies first and foremost in its extraordinary foliage. *Tanacetum densum* subsp. *amanii* tolerates alkaline conditions well. It requires a light soil with perfect drainage since it dislikes stagnant damp in winter. In extreme drought, some of the foliage at the base of the stems may dry out, making the plant temporarily less ornamental until the first autumn rains arrive.

Propagation is by softwood cuttings in autumn or spring.

• *Tanacetum cinerariifolium* has light, blue-green leaves divided into pointed segments. The white flowers open from April to June,

covering the plant in pretty, simple daisies. Pyrethrum, a well-known natural insecticide, is produced from the leaves. Its active compounds, pyrethrins, attack the nervous system of insects and inhibit female mosquitoes by preventing them from biting. **ORIGIN** DALMATIA **HARDINESS** −15 °C AND BELOW **DROUGHT RESISTANCE CODE** 3

Teucrium cossonii
(Lamiaceae)

ORIGIN BALEARIC ISLANDS
HEIGHT 20 CM
SPREAD 50 CM
POSITION SUN
HARDINESS −8 TO −10 °C
DROUGHT RESISTANCE CODE 4

A shrub with linear, evergreen leaves covered in a silky silver felt. In order to reduce water loss, the edges of the leaves are folded under, protecting the stomata on the undersides. When crushed, the leaves give off a delicate scent of peppery sausage. The plant develops into a soft cushion. Its violet-purple flowers form a magnificent contrast with the silver foliage; they open in May–June and have a sweet scent of honey. *Teucrium cossonii* tolerates alkaline conditions well. It requires a poor, stony, perfectly drained soil, otherwise it is short-

lived. An ideal position for it is on top of a drystone wall, with plenty of sand and gravel added at planting. It is well worth this effort for it is an exceptionally beautiful rock plant.

Propagation is by softwood cuttings in autumn or spring.

Teucrium flavum

ORIGIN MEDITERRANEAN BASIN
HEIGHT 40 TO 50 CM
SPREAD 50 TO 60 CM
POSITION SUN OR SEMI-SHADE
HARDINESS −12 TO −15 °C
DROUGHT RESISTANCE CODE 3.5

A shrub with crenellated evergreen leaves that are dark green on their upper surface and a lighter colour on their velvety undersides. They give off a curious medicinal scent when crushed. The plant forms a small rounded bush and in May–June is covered in pale yellow flowers arranged on dense spikes that contrast with the red stems and the dark foliage. The faded flowerheads release a rain of little shiny black seeds which self-sow very freely in the garden. *Teucrium flavum* tolerates alkaline conditions well and is unfussy about soil type. It can be clipped lightly in autumn to emphasize its natural rounded form or to turn it into a small piece of dark topiary. We like to use it as a colonizing plant in uncultivated parts of our garden, together with *Euphorbia characias*, *Dorycnium hirsutum* and *Asphodelus fistulosus*.

Propagation is by seed in autumn or by softwood cuttings in spring.

Teucrium fruticans
Tree Germander

ORIGIN SOUTHERN SPAIN, SOUTHERN PORTUGAL, MOROCCO
HEIGHT 1.5 TO 2 M
SPREAD 1.5 TO 2 M
POSITION SUN
HARDINESS −10 TO −12 °C
DROUGHT RESISTANCE CODE 4

A bushy shrub with small evergreen leaves that are grey on their upper surfaces and white and cottony on their undersides. The plant forms a tangled mass of narrow, white, woody branches (*fruticans* means 'woody' or 'shrubby'). The pale blue flowers, delicately veined with violet, open from February to June. Not very visible from a distance, they blend in soft harmony with the grey leaves. *Teucrium fruticans* tolerates alkaline conditions well and is unfussy about soil type. Being naturally branching, it lends

itself extremely well to clipping. In severe drought *Teucrium fruticans* has the ability to become dormant: it loses a large proportion of its leaves, revealing the decorative skeleton of its white branches. It can survive like this for months, with a slower rate of photosynthesis, waiting for better times.

Propagation is by softwood cuttings in autumn.

• *Teucrium fruticans* **'Azureum'** has compact vegetation and beautiful deep blue flowers. Like the cultivars that follow, it is more sensitive to cold, the tips of the stems beginning to suffer frost damage at temperatures of −6 to −8 °C.

• *Teucrium fruticans* **'Casablanca'** has pure white flowers.

The white silhouette of *Teucrium fruticans* sets off the foliage of *Bupleurum fruticosum* (on the left) and *Coronilla glauca* (on the right).

The Dadès Gorge in southern Morocco: to withstand drought, woody teucriums have the ability to lose all their leaves in summer, thus exposing their white skeleton of tangled branches.

• ***Teucrium fruticans*** '**Gibraltar**' is fast-growing and has large green leaves, very different from those of the other cultivars: in spring the young leaves look almost like the leaves of *Rhamnus alaternus*. The flowers are a lovely pastel colour, white washed with blue.

• ***Teucrium fruticans*** '**Ouarzazate**' has splendid flowers of a deep violet-blue which goes well with the very silver foliage.

Teucrium marum
Cat Thyme

ORIGIN ISLANDS OF THE WESTERN MEDITERRANEAN BASIN
HEIGHT 30 CM
SPREAD 40 CM
POSITION SUN
HARDINESS −10 TO −12 °C
DROUGHT RESISTANCE CODE 5

A shrub with small triangular evergreen leaves that are silver-grey and borne on highly visible white stems. When crushed, the leaves give off a pungent scent: a certain amount of care should be taken when smelling this plant since the first whiff can be fairly aggressive, like plunging one's head into a jar of ether and mustard. If you have cats, you will need to protect young plants until they are well established with pea sticks or a piece of wire netting, for this plant triggers off a sort of frenzy in cats – they roll and roll on it so much that they may even uproot a young plant. *Teucrium marum* develops into a thick cushion, very

The brilliant and velvety flowers of *Teucrium fruticans* 'Ouarzazate' are a beautiful, intense violet-blue.

decorative in a rock garden or as edging. In early summer it is covered in a mass of small mauve-pink flowers, all facing in the same direction along the length of the stems. *Teucrium marum* tolerates alkaline conditions well and withstands salt spray. It prefers light, well-drained soils and is an easily grown and long-lived plant. We like to combine it with *Thymus ciliatus*, *Stachys cretica* and *Teucrium ackermanii* to create a pretty mixture of pink flowers and grey foliage.

Propagation is by cuttings in autumn.

Teucrium × lucidrys

HEIGHT 30 CM
SPREAD 50 CM OR MORE
POSITION SUN OR SHADE
HARDINESS −15 °C AND BELOW
DROUGHT RESISTANCE CODE 4

A hybrid of *Teucrium chamaedrys* and *Teucrium lucidum*, *Teucrium × lucidrys* is a sub-shrub that has small, evergreen leaves that are glossy dark green, with crenellated margins. The plant spreads slowly by means of its rhizomatous stock and in time forms an excellent groundcover: the vegetation is thick enough to suppress weeds effectively. The pink flowers, arranged in spikes, open in May–June. *Teucrium × lucidrys* tolerates alkaline conditions well and adapts easily to all types of soil. It is an easily grown and long-lived plant. It can be combined with *Centaurea bella*, *Origanum laevigatum* and

Salvia lavandulifolia subsp. *blancoana* to form a striking and low-maintenance groundcover.

Propagation is by division at the end of winter or by softwood cuttings in autumn or spring.

• ***Teucrium ackermanii*** forms a handsome carpet of ash-grey linear leaves, covered in late spring with purple flowers that have a sweet scent of honey. **ORIGIN** MEDITERRANEAN BASIN **HARDINESS** −10 TO −12 °C **DROUGHT RESISTANCE CODE** 4

• ***Teucrium aureum*** has small, silver silver leaves, crenellated and silky. It forms a low carpeting groundcover whose stems root wherever they touch the soil. It is covered in spring with very decorative acid-greenish-yellow flowers. **ORIGIN** SOUTH OF FRANCE, SPAIN **HARDINESS** −12 TO −15 °C **DROUGHT RESISTANCE CODE** 5

• ***Teucrium chamaedrys*** forms a groundcover with small deciduous leaves. It spreads by means of its rhizomes. The bright pink flowers open in early summer. **ORIGIN** SOUTHERN EUROPE **HARDINESS** −15 °C AND BELOW **DROUGHT RESISTANCE CODE** 4

• ***Teucrium creticum*** is an upright shrub with linear leaves – it is called the 'rosemary-leaved teucrium'. The soft pink flowers open on long flowering spikes in early summer. **ORIGIN** EASTERN MEDITERRANEAN BASIN **HARDINESS** −4 TO −6 °C **DROUGHT RESISTANCE CODE** 5

• ***Teucrium hircanicum*** is a perennial with velvety grey-green leaves arranged in numerous basal rosettes which may become deciduous in summer. The name *hircanicum* (from the Latin *hircus*, 'billy-goat') might be taken to suggest that the plant must have a heavy male odour, but when the foliage is crushed it merely gives off a subtle animal scent, like a sheepfold barely perceptible in the distance. The

The white flowers of *Teucrium fruticans* 'Casablanca' open in mid-winter.

The silver foliage of *Teucrium marum* is covered in a multitude of mauve-pink spikes in early summer. When crushed, the leaves give off a surprisingly pungent smell.

The masses of flowers on *Teucrium ackermanii* completely hide the foliage in May.

flowers, arranged in magnificent purple-red spikes, open in early summer. **ORIGIN** CAUCASUS, IRAN **HARDINESS** −15 °C AND BELOW (BUT IT DISLIKES WINTER WET) **DROUGHT RESISTANCE CODE** 3

• *Teucrium laciniatum* is a perennial with deciduous or semi-evergreen green leaves, finely cut into narrow segments. The stock spreads gradually, thanks to its rhizomes. In May–June large white flowers, finely striped with violet, appear on the tips of the stems. **ORIGIN** TEXAS **HARDINESS** −10 TO −12 °C **DROUGHT RESISTANCE CODE** 4

• *Teucrium lusitanicum* has young shoots, stems and inflorescences that are covered in golden hairs, the foliage becoming increasingly markedly coloured just before flowering. The creamy-white flowers open in late spring. **ORIGIN** SOUTHERN SPAIN, PORTUGAL **HARDINESS** −8 TO −10 °C **DROUGHT RESISTANCE CODE** 5

• *Teucrium luteum* forms a small, well-rounded cushion. In late spring the tender yellow flowers are preceded by acid-greenish-yellow buds. It is an easily grown plant, perfect for a rock garden. **ORIGIN** SOUTHERN SPAIN **HARDINESS** −10 TO −12 °C **DROUGHT RESISTANCE CODE** 5

• *Teucrium subspinosum* is a miniature plant for a small rock garden. To reduce evapotranspiration its leaves are tiny and the plant develops slowly into a convex and extremely tight, slightly thorny cushion. The tiny pale pink flowers open in early

Native to the mountains of southern Spain, *Teucrium luteum* forms a small round cushion.

The leaves of *Teucrium laciniatum* are finely cut into linear segments. Its delicate flowers open in May–June.

summer. **ORIGIN** BALEARIC ISLANDS **HARDINESS** −10 TO −12 °C **DROUGHT RESISTANCE CODE** 5

Thymus
(Lamiaceae) Thyme

The thymes form a vast group of aromatic shrubs. A brief observation under a magnifying glass will clearly reveal the numerous essential oil glands dotted over the leaves. Thymes are useful both in the kitchen and for their medicinal virtues: their antiseptic, deodorizing and disinfectant properties have been known since antiquity. The Romans burned thyme in their houses to purify the air, the Greeks used it to perfume temples, and the Egyptians used it in their mummification process. The nomenclature of thymes is complex and remains a matter of huge debate to botanists. Thymes behave very differently, depending on the conditions in their natural habitat – some have an excellent resistance to drought, while others, native to humid mountains, struggle to survive in an unwatered garden. Among the many species of thyme that we have tested, here are the ones that are happiest in our garden.

Thymus capitatus

ORIGIN MEDITERRANEAN BASIN
HEIGHT 40 TO 50 CM
SPREAD 40 TO 50 CM
POSITION SUN
HARDINESS −10 TO −12 °C
DROUGHT RESISTANCE CODE 5

A shrub with white stems and small green evergreen leaves that are narrow and leathery. When crushed, the foliage gives off a strong warm and pungent smell, rather like that of *Satureja thymbra* – the ancient Greeks used the name *thymon* for various different aromatic plants with a similar scent, including thyme, savory and oregano. The leaves are used in cooking for their spicy flavour, and thyme is one of the ingredients of *za'atar*, the basic spice mixture used throughout the eastern Mediterranean. The plant forms a stiff, very branching ball shape. In spite of the heat, its pinkish-mauve flowers open in June–July and sometimes continue until September if the summer is not too dry. They are grouped in tight heads on the tips of the stems (*capitatus* means 'large-headed'). The flowers attract a multitude of bees, happy to find nectar during the summer period: in the mountains of Crete a thick honey is made from this thyme, dark and delicious. In conditions of intense drought the plant may lose almost all its leaves at the end of summer, leaving its tangled white stems visible. *Thymus capitatus* tolerates alkaline conditions well and prefers poor, stony, well-drained soils. It withstands salt spray perfectly. We like to grow it in combination with *Ballota pseudodictamnus* and *Sarcopoterium spinosum* in a bed consisting of low-growing ball-shaped plants that remind us of the coastal landscapes of Crete and Cyprus.

Propagation is by soft-tip cuttings in autumn.

Thymus ciliatus

ORIGIN NORTH AFRICA
HEIGHT 5 CM
SPREAD 50 CM OR MORE
POSITION SUN
HARDINESS −12 TO −15 °C
DROUGHT RESISTANCE CODE 2.5

A sub-shrub with small grey-green evergreen leaves that are slightly aromatic. The leaves are covered in numerous stiff hairs that look like little eyelashes (*ciliatus* means 'equipped with eyelashes'). The creeping stems root wherever they are in contact with the soil and after a few years the plant makes a good, flat groundcover. In the cold of winter it may take on interesting grey-mauve tints. The tender pink flowers, grouped in downy heads, cover the plant entirely in May, giving it a soft, springy look. *Thymus ciliatus* tolerates alkaline conditions well and prefers friable, deep, well-drained soils. In conditions of prolonged drought, the foliage turns red and then partially falls, making the plant temporarily less ornamental. *Thymus ciliatus* may be used as a lawn alternative for small areas that are not much walked on. Combined with *Phyla nodiflora*, *Achillea crithmifolia* and *Potentilla verna* it makes a natural-looking carpet that requires little maintenance.

Propagation is by softwood cuttings in autumn or spring.

Thymus mastichina

ORIGIN SPAIN, PORTUGAL
HEIGHT 30 TO 40 CM
SPREAD 30 CM
POSITION SUN
HARDINESS −10 TO −12 °C
DROUGHT RESISTANCE CODE 5

A shrub with small silver-grey evergreen leaves. When crushed, the foliage gives off a penetrating scent, reminiscent of liquorice, eucalyptus and turpentine. Of all the thymes, this is the one most reputed for its antiseptic and disinfectant properties. An essential oil is extracted from its flowering tips which is used to treat infections of the respiratory tract, colds and sinusitis. The plant develops into a small, upright bush with an open habit. In May to June the tips of the stems are covered in spherical inflorescences with a feathery look, the small white flowers lost among the hairs of the ball-shaped calyces. *Thymus mastichina* tolerates alkaline conditions well; it prefers poor, stony soils with perfect drainage. It is an unusual and decorative plant, one of the gems of the aromatic garden.

Propagation is by softwood cuttings in autumn.

Thymus ciliatus forms a vigorous groundcover. Its velvety foliage is covered in pale pink flowers in May.

An essential oil is extracted from the flowering heads of *Thymus mastichina* – it has a penetrating scent and is used to treat colds, sinusitis and bronchitis.

Thymus vulgaris is happy in the fissured rocks of the garrigue, together with euphorbias and sedums.

Thymus vulgaris
Common Thyme

ORIGIN WESTERN MEDITERRANEAN BASIN
HEIGHT 25 CM
SPREAD 30 CM OR MORE
POSITION SUN
HARDINESS −15 °C AND BELOW
DROUGHT RESISTANCE CODE 4

A shrub with evergreen, grey-green leaves with a characteristic scent that evokes the rocky expanses of the garrigues of the South of France. To limit water loss, the edges of the narrow leaves are folded under, with the stomata hidden among the fine down that covers the undersides. Common thyme develops into a compact ball, spreading gradually as it ages. The flowers, tender pink or sometimes white or bright pink depending on the variety, open in April–May. Thyme that is to be dried for culinary use is usually picked in May, since it is at the end of the flowering period that the plant is richest in essential oil, the composition of which varies according to the clone. *Thymus vulgaris* tolerates alkaline conditions well and adapts easily to all soil types. In extreme drought the foliage may dry out and become a sad brown: bunches of minute leaves then appear in the axils of the dry leaves, making the most of the shade they offer to maintain photosynthesis at a slower rate.

Propagation is by cuttings in autumn or spring.

• ***Thymus herba-barona*** forms a shaggy carpet with delicate woody stems which infiltrate themselves between pebbles. Its foliage gives off a warm, spicy scent, decidedly reminiscent of cumin. **ORIGIN** MOUNTAINS OF CORSICA AND SARDINIA **HARDINESS** −12 TO −15 °C **DROUGHT RESISTANCE CODE** 2

• ***Thymus leucotrichus*** forms a dense cushion. Its grey-green leaves become silver in summer, sheltering from the heat beneath a fine velvet of white hairs (*leucotrichus* comes from the Greek, *leukos*, 'white' and *trichos*, 'hair'). When crushed, they give off a subtle scent of pine resin. In April–May the plant is covered in highly decorative flowers of an intense pinkish-mauve. **ORIGIN** MOUNTAINS OF GREECE **HARDINESS** −12 TO −15 °C **DROUGHT RESISTANCE CODE** 4

• ***Thymus polytrichus*** forms a very low-growing, flat carpet, its stems rooting wherever they come in contact with the soil. In April–May the pink flowers contrast well with the handsome dark green foliage. When crushed, the leaves give off a powerful scent reminiscent of juniper and bergamot. **ORIGIN** MOUNTAINS OF SOUTHERN EUROPE **HARDINESS** −15 °C AND BELOW **DROUGHT RESISTANCE CODE** 2

• ***Thymus serpyllum*** 'Lemon Curd' is a cultivar of *Thymus serpyllum* with remarkably vigorous and carpeting vegetation (*serpyllum* comes from the Latin *serpere*, to 'creep' or 'crawl'). It forms a thick mattress whose foliage gives off a delicious lemony scent when crushed. In our garden it grows best between stepping stones: in summer its roots benefit from the moisture which remains for a longer time beneath the stones. **ORIGIN** EUROPE **HARDINESS** −15 °C AND BELOW **DROUGHT RESISTANCE CODE** 2

When crushed, the velvety leaves of *Thymus leucotrichus* give off a subtle scent of pine resin.

Trachelospermum jasminoides
(Apocynaceae) Star Jasmine

ORIGIN CHINA
HEIGHT AND SPREAD 8 M OR MORE
POSITION SUN OR SHADE
HARDINESS −12 TO −15 °C
DROUGHT RESISTANCE CODE 3

A climber with glossy and dark green evergreen leaves that are thick and leathery. The new shoots in spring are a pretty bronze colour. Although slow-growing in its early years, the plant can become very vigorous once established. To give it a good start it should be attached to a support, after which its twining branches put out aerial roots, enabling the plant to cling to walls like ivy. The clusters of small white flowers, with petals arranged in a pretty propeller-like form, appear in the leaf axils in June–July. They have a heavy perfume, sweet and heady, which can scent an entire corner of the garden. *Trachelospermum jasminoides* tolerates alkaline conditions provided the ground is not too wet in winter: in asphyxiating soils it very rapidly shows symptoms of chlorosis. It prefers friable, deep soils with perfect drainage. It can also be used as a groundcover, for example in the shade of deciduous trees, where it will ultimately cover a large area.

Propagation is by softwood cuttings in autumn or spring.

Tulbaghia violacea
(Alliaceae) Society Garlic

ORIGIN SOUTH AFRICA
HEIGHT OF FOLIAGE 20 TO 30 CM
HEIGHT IN FLOWER 60 CM OR MORE
POSITION SUN
HARDINESS −10 TO −12 °C
DROUGHT RESISTANCE CODE 5

A fleshy-rooted perennial that forms a slowly spreading clump by means of its rhizomes. The thick, light green leaves, shaped like narrow ribbons, are evergreen. Perched on the long stems, elegant umbels of mauve-pink flowers give off a strong smell of garlic. In our garden the plant flowers from April to June and then again from September to November – in mild climates the flowers may appear in succession throughout the year. They are edible and can be used to decorate salads or cold dishes, to which they add a slightly piquant flavour like chives and wild asparagus. *Tulbaghia violacea* tolerates alkaline conditions well; it prefers light, well-drained soils. We like to plant it so that it emerges from carpeting plants such as *Artemisia lanata* or *Tanacetum densum* subsp. *amanii*, their silver foliage setting off the elegant umbels of the *Tulbaghia*.

The elegant upright shape of *Tulbaghia violacea* is decorative in a gravel garden. In mild climates its flowers may appear in succession almost throughout the entire year.

Propagation is by division at the end of winter or by fresh seed in autumn. When they begin to swell before germination the seeds give off a strong smell of garlic, pervading our propagation greenhouse each year.

Verbena bonariensis
(Verbenaceae)

ORIGIN SOUTH AMERICA, FROM BRAZIL TO ARGENTINA
HEIGHT OF FOLIAGE 20 TO 30 CM
HEIGHT IN FLOWER 1.2 M OR MORE
POSITION SUN
HARDINESS −8 TO −10 °C
DROUGHT RESISTANCE CODE 2.5

A perennial with long, green, tooth-edged leaves. Depending on how cold the winter is, the basal leaves of the plant may remain evergreen or may become deciduous. In late spring the vigorous and rough-textured square stems shoot upwards. They bear numerous panicles of mauve flowers, light and delicate, which for months on end attract a host of butterflies. Flowering continues from May to October, though often with a rest period in mid-summer if the drought is intense. *Verbena bonariensis* tolerates alkaline conditions well; it prefers friable, deep, well-drained soils. The plant has a short lifespan, but the small brown dust-like seeds self-sow very easily, thus ensuring that old plants are replaced. We like to let it drift freely through the garden, adding a touch of freshness and lightness to perennial borders. *Verbena bonariensis* can sometimes become invasive, especially in hot and humid climates: care should be taken that it does not escape into the wild.

Propagation is by seed in autumn or by soft-tip cuttings in spring.

• *Verbena venosa* forms a deciduous groundcover which spreads vigorously by means of its rhizomes. The purple flowers are very abundant and open from May to July. The cultivar 'Lilacina' has beautiful pale lilac flowers, both delicate and luminous. **ORIGIN** SOUTHERN BRAZIL, ARGENTINA **HARDINESS** −10 TO −12 °C **DROUGHT RESISTANCE CODE** 3

Like a light curtain that gives depth to the garden, the flowers of *Verbena bonariensis* open in early summer.

Viburnum tinus
(Caprifoliaceae) Laurustinus

ORIGIN MEDITERRANEAN BASIN
HEIGHT 2 M OR MORE
SPREAD 1.5 M
POSITION SUN OR SHADE
HARDINESS −12 TO −15 °C
DROUGHT RESISTANCE CODE 3

An evergreen shrub with leaves that are dark green above and lighter on their undersides. The new spring shoots are tender green and downy, giving a soft look to the plant. The white flowers, grouped in flattened cymes, are produced in succession from January to March, sometimes even beginning in November if the winter is mild. They are followed by bunches of small blue fruits that become black as they ripen. Birds love them and help disperse the seeds: the plant self-sows easily under trees, where birds tend to deposit them.

Viburnum tinus tolerates alkaline conditions well and is unfussy about soil type. It is an excellent plant for woodland areas, where it thrives in spite of shade and competition from tree roots. It is a robust and easily-grown shrub, always welcome in the garden since its long winter flowering period makes it irreplaceable. There is a small downside to all its good qualities: when the foliage dries after autumn rain it gives off a powerful smell of urine, as surprising as it is unpleasant, but luckily not lasting long.

Propagation is by ripewood cuttings in autumn or winter.

• *Viburnum tinus* 'Villa Noailles' is a cultivar with a compact habit. The white flowers are preceded by very decorative bright pink buds.

BELOW The white flowers of *Viburnum tinus* 'Villa Noailles' are preceded by bright pink buds.

Vinca major
(Apocynaceae) Periwinkle

ORIGIN WESTERN MEDITERRANEAN BASIN
HEIGHT 30 CM
SPREAD UNLIMITED!
POSITION SUN OR SEMI-SHADE
HARDINESS −15 °C AND BELOW
DROUGHT RESISTANCE CODE 2.5

A sub-shrub with leathery green, evergreen leaves and long flexible stems (*Vinca* is said to come from the Latin *vinco*, 'to conquer', referring to the way the plant's foliage triumphs over winter – or, according to another interpretation, from *vincio*, 'to bind', referring to the pliability of its stems). Wherever they are come into contact with the soil, the stems put out strong roots, enabling the plant to spread vigorously and continuously. In time the stems form a thick, tangled mat which may cover vast areas. The beautiful violet-blue flowers, with petals arranged in the shape of a propeller, open from February to April. *Vinca major* tolerates alkaline conditions well and is unfussy about soil type. It can cope with root competition from old trees and is one of the best groundcovers for colonizing woodland in old parks, where it becomes naturalized, often together with acanthus. It can also be used to cover slopes, where it combats erosion effectively.

Propagation is by softwood cuttings in autumn.

• *Vinca minor*, the lesser periwinkle, forms a small, dense groundcover. It is less invasive than *Vinca major* and very ornamental, and so is more suitable for medium-sized

gardens. The blue flowers appear very early in winter. The cultivar 'La Grave' has flowers of a beautiful deep violet-blue.

ORIGIN EUROPE, SOUTHERN RUSSIA, CAUCASUS
HARDINESS −15 °C AND BELOW **DROUGHT RESISTANCE CODE** 3

Vitex agnus-castus 'Latifolia'
(Verbenaceae) Chaste Tree, Monk's Pepper

ORIGIN MEDITERRANEAN BASIN, ASIA MINOR
HEIGHT 4 TO 5 M, SOMETIMES MORE
SPREAD 2 TO 3 M, SOMETIMES MORE
POSITION SUN
HARDINESS −12 TO −15 °C
DROUGHT RESISTANCE CODE 4

A shrub with aromatic deciduous leaves divided into tapering lobes. The rapidly growing stems have a remarkable strength and flexibility. In Greece they have long been used to make strong ties (like the name *Vitis*, the vine, *Vitex* comes from the Latin *viere*, to 'tie' or 'plait'). Odysseus is supposed to have used the supple branches of *Vitex* to bind his companions beneath the bellies of sheep in order to escape from the cave of the Cyclops Polyphemus. In June–July the plant is covered in spectacular spikes of beautiful deep blue flowers. They are followed by very fragrant berries that can be used as a spice instead of pepper. These berries, renowned for their anaphrodisiac properties, have been used since antiquity to suppress sexual urges. In the Middle Ages *Vitex* was planted near monasteries so that monks and nuns could regularly eat the berries to help them combat the torments of the flesh (hence the name *agnus-castus*, repeating the message in two languages: *agnus* comes from the Greek

From February onwards the propellor-shaped flowers of *Vinca minor* 'La Grave' decorate shady borders.

Vitex agnus-castus 'Latifolia' is a fast-growing woody shrub. It is one of the most beautiful shrubs in our garden in early summer, when it is covered in long spikes of blue flowers.

agnos, 'pure', while *castus* means 'chaste' in Latin). *Vitex agnus-castus* tolerates alkaline conditions well. It is unfussy about soil type and withstands not only salt spray but also salt-water infiltration. In the wild it often grows in association with the oleander in dry watercourses: its deep roots are able to find whatever small amount of moisture is available.

Propagation is by hardwood cuttings in winter.

• *Vitex agnus-castus* 'Alba' is a fine form with pure white flowers.

• *Vitex negundo* var. *cannabifolia* is covered in pale blue spikes in early summer. Its cut leaves and rounded habit could be mistaken for cannabis. If you have a bad-tempered neighbour who spies on you, plant this *Vitex* against his hedge and give it a lot of attention and ritual tip-pinchings, just to see how long it will take him to call the police. **ORIGIN** NORTHERN CHINA, MONGOLIA **HARDINESS** −15 °C AND BELOW **DROUGHT RESISTANCE CODE** 2.5

Yucca rostrata
(Agavaceae)

ORIGIN TEXAS, NEW MEXICO
HEIGHT 4 TO 5 M
SPREAD 1 TO 1.5 M
POSITION SUN
HARDINESS −12 TO −15 °C
DROUGHT RESISTANCE CODE 6

A shrub with a thick trunk bearing a large, spherical crown of linear, grey-blue leaves. This arrangement is both very decorative

and an effective strategy for drought resistance as it enables the surface area carrying out photosynthesis to be increased, while at the same time evapotranspiration is reduced. As the position of the sun moves during the course of the day, only a small proportion of the leaves are directly exposed to its rays. In old specimens the dry leaves form a tight skirt up the length of the trunk, which helps to limit water loss in the desert conditions of the plant's natural habitat. The leaves end in a sharp,

The arrangement of the leaves of *Yucca rostrata* reduces the area exposed to evapotranspiration: as the sun moves during the course of the day, only a small proportion of the leaves are exposed in turn to its rays.

potentially dangerous, point. In May–June the single inflorescence develops into a monumental panicle, a giant beak emerging from the spherical head of the plant (*rostrata* means 'beaked' in Latin). It consists of a central axis from which radiate numerous secondary flower spikes bearing thousands of large white downward-pointing bell-shaped flowers. The petals are fleshy with a waxy texture reminiscent of an artichoke. They are edible, with a light, smooth taste, and can be included in salads. Native Americans traditionally used the yucca in many ways. The leaf fibres were used to make sandals, mats and baskets, while the saponine extracted from its roots and leaves was used to soothe joint inflammations, rather like a low dose of cortisone. *Yucca rostrata* tolerates alkaline conditions well; it prefers light soils with perfect drainage. Although it is said to be slow-growing, in our garden it is the *Yucca* species that has grown fastest, having developed after a few years into a magnificent plant with a spectacular silhouette.

Propagation is by seed in autumn.

• *Yucca brevifolia* forms a small, slow-growing tree with a branching shape. It is known as the Joshua Tree: the Mormon pioneers who crossed the desolate stretches of the Mojave Desert saw its upright branches as the arms of Joshua beckoning them. In the garden it will only survive in soils with the very best drainage, winter wet often proving fatal to it. **ORIGIN** DESERTS OF CALIFORNIA, ARIZONA AND UTAH **HARDINESS** −8 TO −10 °C **DROUGHT RESISTANCE CODE** 6

The flowers of *Yucca rostrata* have thick, fleshy petals that can be eaten in a salad.

Yucca gloriosa at Strybing Arboretum in San Francisco, with a roup of *Puya caerulea* on the left.

traditionally used like soap (in the United States the common name for *Yucca elata* is Soap Tree). In early summer the narrow flower spikes thrust upwards, well clear of the foliage. **ORIGIN** TEXAS, ARIZONA, NEW MEXICO. **HARDINESS** −12 TO −15 °C **DROUGHT RESISTANCE CODE** 6

• *Yucca gloriosa* has narrow gutter-shaped green leaves arranged in rosettes on top of the branches. The large branching spikes of white flowers emerge from the bunches of leaves in early summer. **ORIGIN** SOUTHEASTERN UNITED STATES **HARDINESS** −15 °C AND BELOW **DROUGHT RESISTANCE CODE** 5

• *Yucca torreyi* has young leaves that are shaped like curious twisted gutters prostrate on the ground. The mature leaves form stiff rosettes, their centres well festooned with fibres, that rise slowly on a thick trunk. The short thick spikes of cream-coloured flowers open in early summer. **ORIGIN** TEXAS, NEW MEXICO **HARDINESS** −12 TO −15 °C **DROUGHT RESISTANCE CODE** 6

• *Yucca elata* forms a crown of very fine leaves whose silver margins fray into a fringe of numerous twisted fibres. When the roots are pounded in water they produce foam,

Yucca torreyi and *Nepeta* x *faassenii* 'Dropmore'. The mulch between the plants limits the germination of weeds, while at the same time conserving moisture in the soil.

FURTHER READING

Bailey, L. H. & E. Z., *Hortus Third: A Concise Dictionary of Plants Cultivated in the United States and Canada* (Macmillan, 1979).

Bakker, E., *An Island Called California: An Ecological Introduction to its Natural Communities* (University of California Press, 1984).

Baumann, H., *Greek Wild Flowers and Plant Lore in Ancient Greece* (The Herbert Press, 1986).

Bellakhdar, J., *Le Maghreb à travers ses plantes* (editions Le Fennec, 2003).

Blondel, J. & Aronson, J., *Biology and Wildlife of the Mediterranean Region* (Oxford University Press, 1999).

Bornstein, C., Fross, D. & O'Brien, B., *California Native Plants for the Garden* (Cachuma Press, 2005).

Brenzel, K., *Western Garden Book* (Sunset Publishing Corporation, 1998).

Bygrave, P. (ed. Robert G. Page), *Cistus, A Guide to the Collection at Chelsea Physic Garden* (NCCPG, 2001).

Cavanagh, L., *Mediterranean Garden Plants* (Bapica Publicaciones SC, 2005).

Chatto, B., *The Dry Garden*, (J.M. Dent, 1978; Sagapress, 1996).

Chatto, B., *Beth Chatto's Gravel Garden: Drought-Resistant Planting Through the Year* (Frances Lincoln, 2000).

Clebsch, B., *The New Book of Salvias* (Timber Press, 2003).

Cuche, P., *Jardins du Midi* (Edisud, 1997).

Cuche, P., *Plantes du Midi* (2 vols) (Edisud, 1999).

Dallman, P. R., *Plant Life in the World's Mediterranean Climates* (Oxford University Press; University of California Press, 1998).

Darke, R., *The Colour Encyclopedia of Ornamental Grasses* (Weidenfeld & Nicolson/Timber Press, 1999).

Darke, R., *The Encyclopedia of Grasses for Livable Landscapes* (Timber Press, 2007).

Demoly. J.-P., 'Notes taxonomiques, chorologiques et nouveautés nomenclaturales pour le genre *Cistus L.* élargi, incluant *Halimium* (Dunal) Spach (Cistaceae)', in *Acta botanica gallica*, 153 (3) (2006), 309–23.

Drénou, C., *Les Racines, face cachée des arbres* (Institut pour le développement forestier, 2006).

Duffield, M. R. & Jones, W. D., *Plants for Dry Climates* (HP Books, 1992).

Eggenberg, R. & M. H., *The Handbook on Oleanders* (Tropical Plants Specialists, 1996).

Elliot, R., *Australian Plants for Mediterranean Climate Gardens* (Rosenberg, 2003).

Emberger, L., Gaussen, H., Kassas, M., & de Philippis, A., *Carte bioclimatique de la region méditerranéenne* (UNESCO, 1962).

Fielding, J. & Turland, N. J. (ed. B. Mathew), *Flowers of Crete* (The Royal Botanic Gardens, Kew, 2004).

Fross, D. & Wilken, D., *Ceanothus* (Timber Press, 2006).

Gildemeister, H., *Gardening the Mediterranean Way. Practical Solutions for Summer-Dry Climates* (Thames & Hudson/Harry N. Abrams, 2004).

Gildemeister, H., *Mediterranean Gardening, A Waterwise Approach* (University of California Press, 2002).

Harlow, N., *Plants and Landscapes for Summer-dry Climates of the San Francisco Bay Region* (East Bay Municipal Utility District, 2004).

Huxley, A. & Taylor, W., *Flowers of Greece and the Aegean* (Hogarth Press, 1989).

Jeppe, B., *Spring and Winter Flowering Bulbs of the Cape* (Oxford University Press, 1989).

Jones, L., *Gardens in Provence* (Flammarion, 1992).

Larner, J., *Gardening With a Wild Heart: Restoring California's Native Landscapes at Home* (University of California Press, 1999).
Latymer, H., *The Mediterranean Gardener* (Frances Lincoln, 2001).

Le Houérou, H. N., *The Isoclimatic Mediterranean Biomes: Bioclimatology, Diversity and Phytogeography* (2 vols) (Le Houérou, 2005).

Lieutaghi, P., *Petite ethnobotanique méditerranéenne* (Actes Sud, 2006).

Manning, J., Goldblatt, P. & Snijman, D., *The Color Encyclopedia of Cape Bulbs* (Timber Press, 2002).

Marchant, N. & others, *Flora of the Perth Region* (Western Australian Herbarium, 1987).

North, C., *A Botanical Tour Round the Mediterranean* (Arm Crown Ltd, 1997).

Nottle, T., *Plants for Mediterranean Climate Gardens* (Rosenberg, 2004).

Ornduff, R., *Introduction to California Plant Life* (University of California Press, 2003).

Pagen, F. J. J., *Oleanders,* Nerium *L. and the Oleander Cultivars* (Agricultural University Wageningen Papers, 1987).

Payne, G., *Garden Plants for Mediterranean Gardens* (The Crowood Press, 2006).

Perry, B., *Landscape Plants for Western Regions* (Land Design Publishing, 1992).

Phillips, R. & Foy, N., *Herbs* (Pan, 1990); *The Random House Book of Herbs* (Random House, 1990).

Phillips, R. & Rix, M., *Shrubs* (Macmillan, 1989); *The Random House Book of Shrubs* (Random House, 1989).

Phillips, R. & Rix, M., *Perennials* (Pan, 1991); *The Random House Book of Perennials* (Random House, 1991) (2 vols).

Polunin, O., *Flowers of Greece and the Balkans* (Oxford University Press, 1980).

Polunin, O. & Smythies, B. E., *Flowers of South-West Europe* (Oxford University Press, 1973).

Royal Horticultural Society, *Drought-Resistant Gardening* (RHS Practical Guides, 1999).

Schmidt, M., *Growing California Native Plants* (University of California Press, 1980).

Smith, M. N., *Native Treasures, Gardening with the Plants of California* (University of California Press, 2006).

Smithen, J., *Sun-Drenched Gardens: The Mediterranean Style* (Harry N. Abrams, 2002).

Snape, D., T*he Australian Garden. Designing with Australian Plants* (Garden Art Press, 2003).

Snoeijer, W., *Agapanthus, a Revision of the Genus* (Timber Press, 2004).

Sutton, J., *The Gardener's Guide to Growing Salvias* (David & Charles/Timber Press, 1999).

Taylor, J., *Phlomis, the Neglected Genus* (National Council for the Conservation and Preservation of Gardens, 1998).

Taylor, J., *Plants for Dry Gardens: Beating the Drought* (Frances Lincoln, 1999).

Thompson, J., *Plant Evolution in the Mediterranean* (Oxford University Press, 2005).

Turner, R., *Euphorbias* (B.T. Batsford/Timber Press, 1995).

Tyrwhitt, M. J., *Making a Garden on a Greek Hillside* (Denise Harvey, 1998).

Upson, T. & Andrews, S., *The Genus Lavandula*, The Royal Botanic Gardens, Kew, 2004.

Van Wyk, B.-E. & Smith, G., *Aloes of South Africa*, Briza Publications, 2003.

Waters, G. & Harlow, N. (eds), *The Pacific Horticulture Book of Western Gardening* (David Godine, 1990).

Welsh, P., *Southern California Gardening* (Chronicle Books, 1998).

Wilson, M., *RHS New Gardening* (Mitchell Beazley, 2007).

JOURNALS

Pacific Horticulture
a quarterly journal published by Pacific Horticultural Foundation, P.O. Box 680, Berkeley, California, 94701.

The Mediterranean Garden
a quarterly journal published by the Mediterranean Garden Society, P.O. Box 14, Peania 199002, Greece.
www.mediterraneangardensociety.org

SOCIETIES

California Horticultural Society, San Francisco County Fair Building, 9th Avenue at Lincoln Way, San Francisco, CA 94122, USA
www.calhortsociety.org

The Royal Horticultural Society, 80 Vincent Square, London, SW1P 2PE
www.rhs.org.uk
includes advice on drought-resistant gardening and drought-resisting plants:
www.rhs.org.uk/advice/profiles1105/drought.asp
www.rhs.org.uk/advice/profiles0406/drought_resistant.asp

The Wildflower Society of Western Australia Inc., PO Box 519, Floreat, WA, Australia.
members.ozemail.com.au/~wildflowers/dynamic.php

BOTANICAL GARDENS

Kings Park and Botanic Garden, Perth, Western Australia
www.bgpa.wa.gov.au/

Kirstenbosch National Botanical Garden, Rhodes Drive, Newlands, Private Bag X7, Claremont, RSA
www.sanbi.org

The Royal Botanic Gardens, Kew, Richmond, Surrey, TW9 3AB
www.kew.org

including a section on dry gardening:
www.kew.org/medsummer/mediterranean/gardening.htm

The Royal Botanic Gardens, Melbourne, Birdwood Avenue, South Yarra, Victoria, 3141, Australia,
www.rbg.vic.gov.au

San Francisco Botanical Garden at Strybing Arboretum, 9th Avenue at Lincoln Way, San Francisco, CA 94122, USA
www.sfbotanicalgarden.org

USEFUL ADDRESSES

EUROPE

UNITED KINGDOM

Architectural Plants, Cooks Farm, Nuthurst, Horsham, West Sussex, RH13 6LH
www.architecturalplants.com
Specialist in striking, evergreen, 'architectural' plants, many from mediterranean-climate regions.

Aromafolia, Barbers Farm, Leys Lane, Old Buckenham, Norfolk, NR17 1NT
myweb.tiscali.co.uk/aromafolia/index.html
Plants with aromatic foliage, including Salvia.

Avon Bulbs Ltd, Burnt House Farm, Mid Lambrook, South Petherton, Somerset, TA13 5HE
www.avonbulbs.co.uk
Large bulb list, including some for the dry garden.

Special Plants, Greenways Lane, Cold Ashton, Chippenham, Wilts, SN14 8LA
www.specialplants.net
Unusual plants from all over the world.

The Beth Chatto Gardens, Elmstead Market, Colchester, Essex, CO7 7DB
www.bethchatto.co.uk
Many rare and unusual plants, from a gardener with experience in dry gardening.

The Place for Plants, East Bergholt, Suffolk, CO7 6UP
www.placeforplants.co.uk
Long list of plants, including those for the dry garden.

Trevena Cross Nurseries, Breage, Helston, Cornwall, TR13 9PS
www.trevenacross.co.uk
South African, Australian, New Zealand and South American plants, as well as succulents.

FRANCE

Bulb'Argence, Lauw de Jager, Mas d'Argence, 30300 Fourques
www.bulbargence.com/fr
Bulbs native to mediterranean climate regions.

Cultures méditerranéennes, Monique and Pierre Cuche, Devantville, 83830 Claviers
A collection of plants native to mediterranean climate regions.

Ets. Railhet, Chantal and Thierry Railhet, 19, chemin du Pradel, 31790 Saint-Jory
www.ets-railhet.fr
Plants from Africa, Australia and Zealand, a collection of Proteaceae and Myrtaceae.

Iris de Thau, Elisabeth Segui, route de Villeveyrac, 34140 Mèze
Iris germanica *cultivars.*

Jardin de Rochevieille, Dominique Permingeat and Jean-François Giraud, La Moutte, 07220 Viviers
jaroche.club.fr
A collection of buddlejas, plants from Chile.

Lewisia, Jean-Louis Latil, Le Maupas, 05300 Lazer
Plants from North America, species irises.

Pépinière Bachès, Bénédicte and Michel Bachès, Mas Bachès, 66500 Eus
Citrus fruits and olives.

Pépinière Baud, Geneviève and Pierre Baud, Le Palis, 84110 Vaison-la-Romaine
www.fig-baud.com
Fig trees, pomegranates, jujube trees.

Pépinière Cavatore, Gérard Cavatore, 488, chemin de Bénat, 83230 Bormes-les-Mimosas
www.fdconcept.com/cavatore/sommaire.htm
A collection of acacias.

Pépinière de la Vallée de l'Huveaune, Robert Pélissier, CD2, route de Gémenos, 13400 Aubagne
Ornamental plants and fruit trees adapted to conditions in Provence.

Pépinière de l'Armalette, Isabelle and Benoît Beauvallet, chemin de la Piscine, 83690 Sillans-la-Cascade
Plants for cold and dry climates.

Pépinière de Vaugines, Gérard Weiner, chemin du Mont-Senis, 84160 Vaugines
Plants for cold and dry climates.

Pépinière du Grand Plantier, Béatrice and Bruno Tisserand, 1107, route d'Uzès, 30500 Saint-Ambroix
www.pepinieredugrandplantier.com
Aromatic and medicinal plants.

Pépinière du Mas de Quinty, Marion and Bertrand Ferraud, 30440 Roquedur
Ceanothuses, eucalyptuses.

Pépinière Filippi, Clara and Olivier Filippi, RN 113, 34140 Mèze
www.jardin-sec.com
Plants for dry gardens.

Pépinière Issa, Brigitte and Jo Issa, 67, avenue de Grenache, 34270 Valflaunès
pagesperso-orange.fr/pepiniere.issa
South African plants.

Pépinière La Soldanelle, Sylvie and Christian Mistre, CD 1, quartier Mauresque, 83170 Rougiers
la-soldanelle.info
Lime-tolerant perennials.

Pépinière Les Senteurs du Quercy, Mélie Portal and Frédéric Prévot, Mas de Fraysse, 46230 Escamps
www.iris-fleurs.fr
Includes a collection of salvias.

Pépinière Patrick Nicolas, Patrick Nicolas, 8, sentier du Clos-Madame, 92190 Meudon
www.patricknicolas.fr
A collection of sedums and sempervivums.

GREECE & CYPRUS

Chrysanthi Parayiou, 6-8 Asklipiou/Socratous Street, 151 27 Melissia, Attica
Small nursery specializing in Greek native plants.

'O Dendros', PO Box 20800, Nicosia 1663
Plants for mediterranean-climate gardening.

ITALY

Le essenze di Lea, loc. Martinoni 6 - 55010 Spianate, Lucca
www.leessenzedilea.com
A unique Salvia collection.

Vivai Fattoria La Parrina, La Parrina, 58010 Albinia di Orbetello, Grosseto
www.vivaiparrina.it
Plants for mediterranean-climate gardening.

Vivaio Il giardino vivace, via Scatena 1, 55066 S.Margherita, Lucca
Plants for mediterranean-climate gardening.

Vivai Stefano Capitanio, C/da Conghia 298, Monopoli, Bari
www.vivaicapitanio.it
Plants for mediterranean-climate gardening.

PORTUGAL

Viveiro dos Rosmaninhos, Rua da Devesa s/n, Belazaima do Chão, Águeda, 3750 - 362 Belazaima do Chão
www.viveirodosrosmaninhos.com
Plants for mediterranean-climate gardening, Portugese native plants.

SPAIN

Arverd, C/Jesús Vilar, 7, 12510 Sant Rafel del Riu, Castelló
www.arverd.info/
Mediterranean and subtropical plants.

Horticultor Isart, Ctra. Vallvidrera, s/n, Apt. Correus 92, 08960 Sant Just Desvern, Barcelona
Plants for mediterranean-climate gardening.

Vivers Bioriza, Ctra. Borgonyà-Orriols, Km 1,9, 17844 Cornellà del Terri, Girona
www.bioriza.com
Iberian peninsula native plants.

Vivers Sala Graupera, Carretera NII, Km 650,800, Apt. Correus 88, 08392 Sant Andreu de Llavaneres, Barcelona
www.salagraupera.com
Plants for mediterranean-climate gardening.

Vivers Santa Maria, Camí del Raiguer, 77, 07320 Santa Maria del Camí, Mallorca
www.viverssantamaria.com
Plants for mediterranean-climate gardening.

UNITED STATES OF AMERICA

Buena Creek Gardens, 418 Buena Creek Road, San Marcos, CA 92069
www.buenacreekgardens.com
Drought-tolerant plants for mediterranean-climate gardening.

California Flora, 2990 Somers Street, Fulton, CA 95439
www.calfloranursery.com
California native plants, grasses, and perennials for mediterranean climates.

Mostly Natives Nursery, 27235 Highway One, Tomales, CA 94971
www.mostlynatives.com
Drought-tolerant plants, especially coastal California native plants.

Native Sons Wholesale Nursery, 379 West El Campo Road, Arroyo Grande, CA 93420
nativeson.com
Drought-tolerant plants for mediterranean-climate regions (wholesale only).

Sierra Azul Nursery, 2660 East Lake Avenue, Watsonville, CA 95076
www.sierraazul.com
Perennials and drought-tolerant plants for California's mediterranean climate.

Suncrest, 400 Casserly Road, Watsonville, CA 95076
www.suncrestnurseries.com
California native plants and plants from the world's mediterranean-climate regions (wholesale only).

The Dry Garden, 6556 Shattuck Avenue, Oakland, CA 94609
Unusual cacti, succulents, grasses, and plants for mediterranean-climate regions.

Theodore Payne Foundation, 10459 Tuxford Street, La Tuna Canyon, CA 91352
www.theodorepayne.org
California native plants and seeds.

Tree of Life Nursery, 33201 Ortega Highway, San Juan Capistrano 92693
www.treeoflifenursery.com
California native plants.

Walter Anderson Nursery, 3642 Enterprise Street, San Diego, CA 92110
www.walterandersen.com
Founded in 1928, specialist in unusual perennials, palms, cacti, cycads and vines.

Yerba Buena Nursery, 19500 Skyline Boulevard, Woodside, CA 94062
www.yerbabuenanursery.com
One of California's oldest native plant nurseries.

REST OF THE WORLD

AUSTRALIA

Lambley Nursery, 'Burnside', Lesters Road, Ascot, Victoria 3364
www.lambley.com.au

ISRAEL

Mashtelat Nataf -Nataf, D. N. Harey Yehuda, 90804
www.nataf-plants.com
Plants for mediterranean-climate gardening (wholesale only), Israeli native plants.

Shtiley-har, P.O.B. 38 Kiryat Anavim, 90833
Plants for mediterranean-climate gardening.

SEED SUPPLIERS

Alplains, 32315 Pine Crest Court, PO Box 489, Kiowa, CO 80117-0489, USA
www.alplains.com

B & T World Seeds, Paguignan, 34210 Aigues-Vives, France
www.b-and-t-world-seeds.com

Chiltern Seeds, Bortree Stile, Ulverston, Cumbria, LA12 7PB, UK
www.edirectory.co.uk/chilternseeds

Kirstenbosch Seed Catalogue, The Seedroom, Kirstenbosch National Botanical Garden, Privat Bag X7, Claremont 7735, South Africa

J. L. Hudson, Seedsman, Box 337, La Honda, CA 94020
www.jlhudsonseeds.net

Köhres, Postfach 1217, D-64387 Erzhausen, Germany.
www.koehres-kaktus.de

Larner Seeds, P.O. Box 407, Bolinas, CA 94924, USA.
larnerseeds.com

Nindethana Seed Service Pty Ltd, PO Box 2121, Albany, Western Australia 6331, Australia
members.iinet.net.au/~nindseed/index.html

Renee's Garden, 6116 Highway 9, Felton, CA 95018, USA
www.reneesgarden.com

Sandeman Seeds, 7, route de Burosse, 64350 Lalongue, France
www.sandemanseeds.com

Seed Hunt, PO Box 96, Freedom, CA 09019-0096, USA
seedhunt.com

Silverhill Seeds, PO Box 53108, Kenilworth, 7745 Cape Town, South Africa
www.silverhillseeds.co.za

TABLE OF HARDINESS ZONES

°F	Zone	°C
below −50	1	below −45
−50 to −40	2	−45 to −40
−40 to −30	3	−40 to −34
−30 to −20	4	−34 to −29
−20 to −10	5	−29 to −23
−10 to 0	6	−23 to −17
0 to 10	7	−17 to −12
10 to 20	8	−12 to −7
20 to 30	9	−7 to −1
30 to 40	10	−1 to 5

INDEX OF PLANT NAMES

Common names of plants are cross-referred to the botanical names.

Page numbers in **bold** indicate pages where the plant is described in detail.

Pages numbers in *italic* indicate where a plant is mentioned in a caption.

Caesalpinia gilliesii **89**, *89*, 184

Calamintha nepeta 33, **89**

Calamint, Lesser, see *Calamintha nepeta*

California Fuchsia, see *Epilobium canum*

California Poppy, see *Eschscholzia californica*

California Tree Poppy, see *Romneya coulteri*

Californian Lilac, see *Ceanothus* 'Concha'

Callistemon acuminatus 89, **90**

Callistemon rigidus **89–90**

Callistemon salignus **90**, 90

Callistemon viminalis 'Little John' **90**

Callistemon 'Violaceus' **90**

Calystegia soldanella 44

Campsis grandiflora **90**, 90, 184

Campsis radicans **90**

Campsis radicans 'Flava' **90**

Campsis × tagliabuana 'Madame Galen' **90**

Canary Island Sage, see *Salvia canariensis*

Caper, see *Capparis spinosa*

Capparis spinosa 10, 57, **90–91**

Capparis spinosa 'Inermis' **91**

Caryopteris incana 74, **91**, 91, 127, 154, 188

Caryopteris mongholica **91**

Caryopteris × clandonensis 'Kew Blue' **91**

Catananche caerulea **91**, 182

Cat Mint, see *Nepeta*

Cat Thyme, see *Teucrium marum*

Cat's Claw Vine, see *Macfadyena unguis-cati*

Ceanothus 'Concha' **91–92**

Ceanothus griseus var. *horizontalis* 'Yankee Point'
    84, 91, **92**, 178

Ceanothus 'Ray Hartman' **91**

Ceanothus 'Skylark' **91**

Centaurea bella **92**, 92, 190

Centaurea pulcherrima 26, 84, 87, **92**, 183

Centaurea ragusina 92, **92**

Centranthus angustifolius 80, **93**, 93

Centranthus angustifolius 'Mauve' **92**

Centranthus ruber 92, **93**, 111, 116, 179

Century Plant, see *Agave americana*

Cerastium candidissimum 93, **94**

Cerastium tomentosum **93–94**

Ceratostigma griffithii 74, **94**, 127, 188

Ceratostigma plumbaginoides 91, 93, **94**, 110, 154

Ceratostigma wilmottianum **94**

Cercis siliquastrum **94**, 150, 161

Cestrum parqui 15

Chamaemelum nobile 'Flore Pleno' **94**

Chamaerops humilis 187

Chamaerops humilis var. *cerifera* 43

Chamomile, see *Chamaemelum nobile*

Chapparal Sage, see *Salvia leucophylla*

Chaste Tree, see *Vitex agnus-castus*

China Rose, see *Rosa chinensis* 'Sanguinea'

Chocolate Vine, see *Akebia quinata*

Choisya 'Aztec Pearl' *94*, **95**, 106, 175

Choisya ternata 71, **94**, 145

Cistus albidus 27, 46, 51, *95*, 95, **96**, *96*, 100, 102,
    111, 174, 180s

Cistus atriplicifolius *96*, **96**

Cistus clusii 43

Cistus creticus 27, **96–98**, *97*, 100, 102, 103, 130,
    157

Cistus creticus 'Bali' 96

Cistus creticus f. *albus* **98**

Cistus crispus 51, 102

Cistus ladanifer f. *maculatus* 51, 95, **98**, 99, 100,
    100, 102, 104, 166

Cistus ladanifer var. *sulcatus* 95, **98**, 100, 173

Cistus ladanifer var. *sulcatus* f. *bicolor* **98**

Cistus laurifolius 95, 95, **98**, 98, 100, *100*

Cistus laurifolius subsp. *atlanticus* 98

Cistus parviflorus 46, 101, 103

Cistus populifolius 46, 99, 101

Cistus salviifolius 51, 52, 71, 95, *95*, **98–99**, 100,
    101, 104

Cistus salviifolius 'Bonifacio' **99**

Cistus × aguilari **99**, *99*

Cistus × aguilari 'Maculatus' **99**, *100*

Cistus × argenteus 'Blushing Peggy Sammons' *98*,
    100

Cistus × argenteus 'Peggy Sammons' **100**

Cistus × cyprius **100**, *100*, 155

Cistus × cyprius nvar. *ellipticus* 'Elma' **100**

Cistus × florentinus **100**, *101*

Cistus × florentinus 'Tramontane' **100**, 106

Cistus × hybridus **101**, *101*

Cistus × ledon 186

Cistus × pauranthus **101**

Cistus × pauranthus 'Natacha' **101**, *101*

Cistus × pulverulentus 51, **102**, *102*, 178

Cistus × pulverulentus Gp *Delilei* **102**

Cistus × purpureus **102**, *102*, 175

Cistus × purpureus 'Alan Fradd' **103**

Cistus × purpureus f. *holorhodeos* **103**, *156*

Cistus × ralletii **103**, *103*

Cistus × skanbergii **103**, *103*

Cistus × verguinii 'Paul Pècherat' **104**, *104*

Clary, see *Salvia sclarea*

Clematis armandii **104**, *104*

Clematis cirrhosa **104**, *105*

Clematis flammula **105**

Coleonema album **105**, *105*

Coleonema pulchrum **105**

Colutea arborescens **105–06**, *106*

Convolvulus althaeoides 136

Convolvulus cneorum **106**, *106*, 137

Convolvulus sabatius **106**

Copiapoa columna-alba 14, 32

Coronilla emerus **106**

Coronilla glauca **106**, *107*, 111, *189*

Coronilla glauca 'Citrina' **106**, *107*, 170

Coronilla juncea **106–07**, *107*

Coronilla minima 57, **107**

Coronilla ramosissima **107**

Correa alba **108**

Corsican Hellebore, see *Helleborus argutiflorus*

Cotinus coggygria **108**, *108*

Cotinus coggygria 'Grace' **108**, *108*, 161

Cotinus coggygria 'Royal Purple' **108**

Cotton Lavender, see *Santolina chamaecyparissus*

Cranesbill, Bloody, see *Geranium sanguineum*

Cretan Cistus, see *Cistus creticus*

Crocus sativus **108**, *109*

Crossvine, see *Bignonia capreolata*

Cupid's Dart, see *Catananche caerulea*

Curry Plant, see *Helichrysum italicum*

Cynodon 'Santa Ana' 64

Cytisus battandieri 98, **108** 09

Dasylirion acrotrichum **109**, *109*

Dasylirion longissimum **109**, *109*

Delosperma cooperi **109–10**, *110*

Dianthus anatolicus **110**, *110*

Dianthus corsicus 69, **110**, *110*

Dianthus pyrenaicus 'Cap Béar' **110**

Dianthus pyreneus 29

Dicliptera suberecta 74, **111**, *111*, 138

Dittany, see *Origanum dictamnus*

Dittany, False, see *Ballota pseudodictamnus*

Dorycnium hirsutum 93, **111**, 116, *176*, 189

Dorycnium pentaphyllum **111**, *111*

Drosanthemum hispidum 19, **111**, *111*, 142

Ebenus cretica 11, 12, 57, **111–12**, *112*

Echinops ritro **112**, *112*

Echinopsis chilensis 15